Clinical Intervention
with Families

Clinical Intervention with Families

Mark A. Mattaini

NASW PRESS
National Association of Social Workers
Washington, DC

Josephine A. V. Allen, PhD, ACSW, *President*
Josephine Nieves, MSW, PhD, *Executive Director*

Paula L. Delo, *Executive Editor*
Steph Selice, *Senior Editor*
William Schroeder, *Staff Editor*
Doris Margolis, Editorial Associates, *Copy Editor*
Enid L. Zafran, Indexing Partners, *Indexer*
Chanté Lampton, *Acquisitions Associate*
Heather Peters, *Editorial Secretary*

Cover by Jane Weber, Weber Design, Alexandria, Virginia
Typeset by Maryland Composition, Glen Burnie, Maryland
Printed and bound by Victor Graphics, Inc., Baltimore, Maryland

© 1999 by NASW Press

Library of Congress Cataloging-in-Publication Data

Clinical intervention with families / Mark A. Mattaini.
    p.   cm.
Includes bibliographical references.
ISBN 0-87101-308-8 (alk. paper)
1. Family social work.   2. Family psychotherapy.   I. NASW Press.   II. Title.
HV697.M42   1999
362.82—dc21   99-20801
                                                            CIP

Printed in the United States of America

For Christine . . .
For My Family . . .
For All My Relations . . .

CONTENTS

Introduction   ix

SECTION 1:   General Principles and Strategies   1

CHAPTER 1   An Ecobehavioral Perspective on the Family   3
CHAPTER 2   The Practice Process with Families   24
CHAPTER 3   Interventive Strategies: Enhancing Environmental
             Exchanges   60
CHAPTER 4   Interventive Strategies: Modifying Exchanges
             within the Family   85
CHAPTER 5   Interventive Strategies: Enhancing
             Communication and Acceptance in Families   114

SECTION 2:   Strategies For Work With Particular Family
              Configurations and Issues   141

CHAPTER 6   Work with Couples   143
CHAPTER 7   Parenting   177
CHAPTER 8   Constructing Alternatives to Antisocial Behavior   211
CHAPTER 9   Intervening in Child Maltreatment   237
CHAPTER 10   Substance Abuse and Serious Mental Illness in
             Families   264
CONCLUSION   295
INDEX   299
ABOUT THE AUTHOR   315

Introduction

NASW Press introduces *Clinical Intervention with Families,* second in a set of best practice guidebooks, to offer practical assistance for practice as social work begins its second century. This newest volume, a companion to *Clinical Practice with Individuals,* extends our knowledge of improved professional process and outcomes, which are emerging at an unprecedented rate. It is often difficult, however, for the hard-pressed social worker to access current findings and remain current, despite the ethical obligation to do so.

These volumes on clinical intervention and practice must meet several criteria. First, they must incorporate the best and most current knowledge available. Second, they must have a strong focus on applied methodology and offer specific guidance for day-to-day practice in ordinary agency and private practice settings. Finally, they must take social work's historic commitment to social justice and diversity seriously. As a discipline, we now know much more than we apply. This set of best practice guidebooks is one way to further inform practice and to move toward healing and enhancement of the collective web in which we are all organically linked.

SECTION I

GENERAL PRINCIPLES AND STRATEGIES

CHAPTER ONE

An Ecobehavioral Perspective on the Family

"Happy families are all alike; every unhappy family is unhappy in its own way" (Tolstoy, *Anna Karenina*). Actually, not all "happy families" look alike, even though at a very abstract level they often share certain core dynamics. Families in trouble may indeed struggle in many different ways. The contemporary families seen by social workers face enormous challenges, often including a complex mix of personal troubles, environmental and relational stresses, and systematic oppression.

A good deal has been written about "the changing American family," and families are changing, in terms of structure, function, and economics. For example, nearly half of couples who marry eventually divorce, and two-thirds of those who divorce remarry. As a result, many children grow up in "blended families." Cross-cultural and interracial marriages are increasingly common; half of Native Americans who marry choose mates of other races, and the majority of Japanese American children born in this country are of mixed racial heritage. The numbers for other groups are smaller, but still quite substantial (Spickard, Fong, & Ewalt, 1995). While families were once primarily economic units, today, increasing emotional demands are placed on family members who are often far removed geographically and culturally from their extended families.

At the same time, economic hardships continue to increase for poorer families, with recent welfare changes expected to exacerbate those stresses (the Urban Institute projects a 20 percent increase in child poverty as a result of welfare reform). Twenty-one percent of American children were living in poverty in 1995, up from 14 percent in 1969 (Petit & Curtis, 1997). Nearly half of African American children are poor, as are two-thirds of children living with single, never-married mothers. Over the past two decades, concern over maintaining jobs and economic security also has grown among working and middle class families. Given these and related issues and shifts,

3

family-centered social work practice is neither simple, nor sufficient. Still, such practice can contribute to the well-being of individuals, their families, and the social web that connects them. This is the vision of this book.

For the purposes of this book, "families" are not defined structurally in terms of economics, legal arrangements, or biology. Families include persons in heterosexual or gay, married or cohabiting, single or multigenerational relationships. The material in this book can be applied to practice with any group of two or more people who view themselves as a family. The diversity of contemporary families involves more than structure and economics; cultural variations, often deeply rooted in ethnicity, race, and class, are central factors in practice with families. For example, returning to Tolstoy, one of the elements common to "happy" families is an adequate and stable rate of positive exchanges. However, what is valued as positive, what rate is "adequate" as compared with inadequate or excessive, and specifics of how such exchanges occur, vary enormously. In some cultures, failure to use severe physical discipline often is viewed as a lack of parental caring, while in others, such practices are judged as abusive. In some groups, children's participation in adult conversations is expected, in others, it is considered disrespectful. These challenges are explored in considerable detail in subsequent chapters.

Given such variations, how can the social worker comprehensively and coherently understand families? In an ecobehavioral model, all families have some elements in common. Over time (and often generations), every family develops a "family culture"—a set of interlocking practices that occur at relatively predictable times, or under predictable circumstances. Even apparently chaotic families are enveloped in a "culture of chaos" in which stress, for example, may produce escape, aggression, or desperate attempts at closeness. These family cultures, in turn, are related transactionally to environmental events and larger cultural entities to which the family and its members belong (schools, jobs, ethnic and religious groups, neighborhoods), each with its own patterns for managing relationships.

A major focus of this book is on work with the family as a microculture and as an organic component of larger sociocultural systems (neighborhoods, communities, and ethnic cultures). Connecting the family with new networks and in some cases helping family members to create such new cultural entities is often required to build supports for maintaining changes in the family. Aversive conditions, events and exchanges with the extra-family environment that may have a profound impact on individuals and the family as a whole are also crucial to examine. The effects of poverty and oppression, job stresses, school failure, neighborhood collapse, and other such experiences have an impact not only on each individual, but on the family as a culture.

Some family practices produce satisfaction, while others produce dissatisfaction; working with the family to change the mix is central to family-centered practice. Some issues that a family faces may originate in individual problems. For example, families where substance abuse or domestic violence occur are often deeply stressed and troubled. Under these circumstances, it is crucial not to "blame the victim" (too often, the woman) as sometimes happens when oversimplified constructs like "codependency" are used (Anderson, 1994). At the same time, family members can do certain things that may contribute to solving problems like substance abuse and violence (see chapters 4 and 10).

Thinking ecosystemically (Meyer, 1993, Mattaini & Meyer, 1998) is the only way to capture all of this at once. The ecobehavioral model of family practice presented in this volume is an ecosystemic approach that relies on state-of-the-art behavioral, cognitive-behavioral, and cultural-analytic research and theory that are well supported by research. The transactional ecomap (Mattaini, 1993, 1997a) is a useful tool for conceptualizing such complexity. Figure 1-1 is a simple transactional ecomap, demonstrating connections among family members, and between the family and external systems.

Figure 1-1

A simple transactional ecomap.

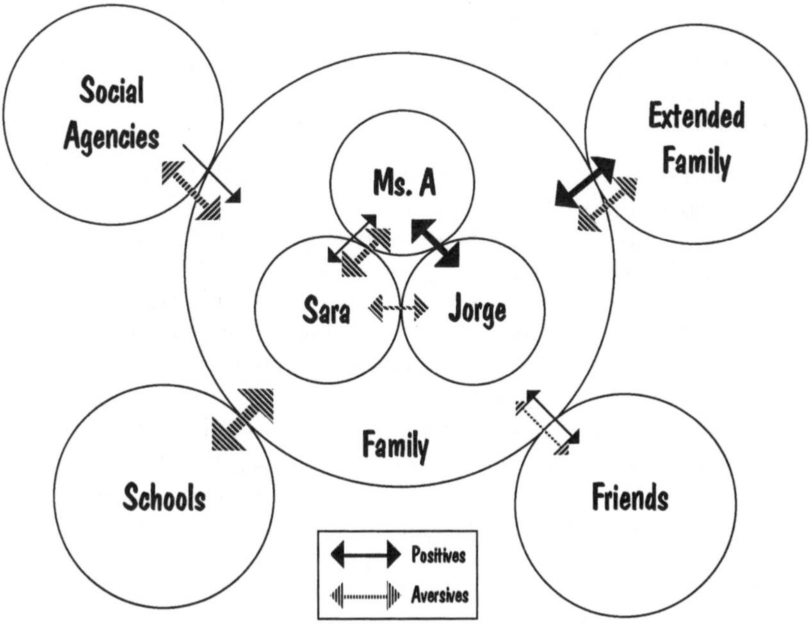

The arrows, which represent active exchanges (or, where they are miss-ing, deficits in such exchanges) are most important to observe and focus on in this figure. The active exchanges occurring at the boundaries where one system contacts another are crucial. Social work practice is primarily about verbs (for example, patterns of "recognizing," "hurting," "providing") rather than about nouns (reified constructs like "connections" or "stressors").

The material that follows provides an introduction to behavioral termi-nology and basic theoretical constructs used and elaborated on in subse-quent chapters, and includes some constructs clarified by research only in the past several years. The ways in which these basic elements interact to produce the ecobehavioral dynamics within families and between family and environment will then be summarized.

BASIC TERMS AND CONCEPTS

Behavior and Cultural Practices

The term *behavior* as used here covers a broad range of phenomena—not only actions observable to others but cognitive and emotional events as well. It is useful to categorize action in terms of four central behavioral modali-ties:

1. motor behavior (slapping someone, tensing muscles)
2. verbal behavior (praising someone, self-talk)
3. observational behavior (looking at or listening to someone, troubling memories)
4. visceral behavior (sweating, digestive upsets).

It should be noted that each of these modalities includes both public acts (those that others can see), and private events (Poppen, 1989). Some experiences involve several modalities; a person who feels "down" is experi-encing a visceral state, but often, cognitive (covert verbal), motor, and even observational dimensions are involved as well. Excesses and deficits in each modality can be relevant to the behavior of family members. For example, Figure 1-2 is a behavioral profile of an abusive mother once seen by the au-thor in family treatment (from Mattaini, 1997b).

Notice the wide range of behavioral excesses and deficits occurring in each modality, many of which had profound effects on the family function-ing, which were often in part themselves shaped by that functioning.

Family members' behavioral repertoires develop in part in response to events in the family, and in part in response to other experiences in each person's life history, in transaction with biological factors. In addition, over time, each family develops its own culture, shaping and maintaining *cultural*

Figure 1-2

Behavioral profile of one family member, the abusive mother of a teenage girl.

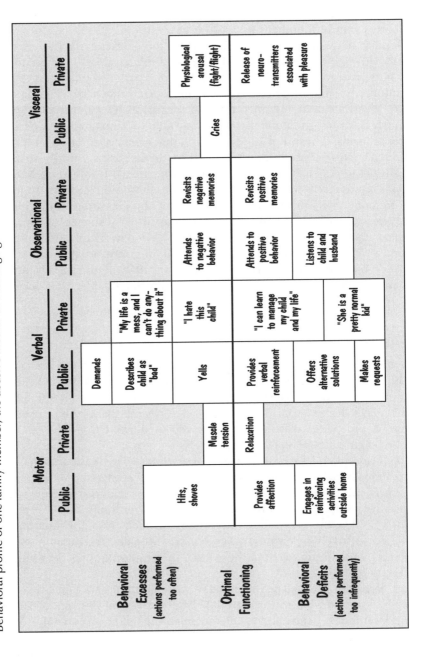

	Motor		Verbal		Observational		Visceral	
	Public	**Private**	**Public**	**Private**	**Public**	**Private**	**Public**	**Private**
Behavioral Excesses (actions performed too often)	Hits, shoves	Muscle tension	Demands / Describes child as "bad"	"My life is a mess, and I can't do anything about it"	Attends to negative behavior	Revisits negative memories		Physiological arousal (fight/flight)
			Yells	"I hate this child"			Cries	
Optimal Functioning	Provides affection	Relaxation	Provides verbal reinforcement	"I can learn to manage my child and my life"	Attends to positive behavior	Revisits positive memories		Release of neuro-transmitters associated with pleasure
Behavioral Deficits (actions performed too infrequently)	Engages in reinforcing activities outside home		Offers alternative solutions	"She is a pretty normal kid"	Listens to child and husband			
			Makes requests					

practices (usually called *family practices* in this book) that are transmitted among family members and often across generations (Glenn, 1991). Because of the family system's support for these practices, they tend to persist, with one of them, say "being loud and demanding," interlocking with others, say "giving in." Other cultural entities, from work groups to ethnic cultures, are also organized by such interlocking practices.

Family dynamics (family cultures) consist of such behavioral interlocks, in which different family members may take on similar roles over time or generations. These repeated patterns that constitute family culture are roughly equivalent to what Minuchin describes as "family structure" (Minuchin, 1974; Minuchin, Lee, & Simon, 1996). In his work, Minuchin does not aim only for behavior change (which would rapidly disappear if it were not consistent with family culture) but also for a more comprehensive "restructuring" of the family, a change in the interlocking cultural practices that organize the family. For example, in a coercive family either a parent or a child may initiate a conflict by making a nonnegotiable demand; the other may then refuse to comply (Patterson, 1976). Other family members may commonly try to placate those in conflict. Such stable, interlocking patterns constitute the family culture.

Consequences

Why do people keep doing what they do, and not do (or stop doing) other things? Why are family practices perpetuated? While multiple factors discussed below need to be considered for a complete view, consequences usually play a decisive role. Those actions that pay off, that produce results that are in some way satisfying, tend to be repeated, while those that do not, all else being equal, tend to be dropped.

Consequences that tend over time to produce increases in behavior are technically called *positive reinforcers*. Unexpected events can sometimes function as reinforcers. For example, children who seldom receive consistent positive attention may continue problem behavior in the face of events that look unpleasant, like yelling or spanking. In such cases, the attention associated with yelling may actually be a positive reinforcer, not a punisher (which by definition *decreases* behavior). Deprivation can result in surprising phenomena.

Behavior can also be increased in more aversive ways (a process technically, but somewhat confusingly, labeled *negative reinforcement*). Negative reinforcement is nearly always an issue in conflicted families. In this process, one or more family members do (or threaten to do) something unpleasant until another family member does what the first wants. Aggressive children, for example, often escalate until a parent withdraws a request, or have a tantrum until the parent gives them what they want. Patterson (1976, 1982) described children in such families as "victims and architects of a coercive system." Coercion of one kind or another is common in troubled families.

Coercive consequences can also be used to decrease behavior. This is the definition of *punishment.* An enormous body of research demonstrates that punishment can cause a variety of troubling side-effects (for example, aggression, depression, escape) and is also difficult to implement effectively (Sidman, 1989). While some mild aversives (like brief time-out with children, for example—see chapter 7) are useful under limited circumstances, reinforcement-based strategies in which desirable actions are reinforced, and undesirable ones aren't (*planned nonreinforcement* or *extinction*), are essential in the long run. (Refer to chapter 7, for example, for more effective alternatives to the commonly raised "What if the child runs into the street?" scenario.) Both negative reinforcement and punishment are *aversive* processes. *Aversive* is defined as any condition or event that one will escape or avoid, all else being equal.

Specific behaviors and practices that occur within families can be understood in these terms, but an ecobehavioral social worker is interested in a much bigger picture. The overall configuration of positives and aversives occurring within a family's life space constitutes the case. In the ecomap shown in Figure 1-3, not only are the specific positive and negative ex-

Figure 1-3

A transactional ecomap for a family experiencing a relatively high level of aversive exchanges with other persons and systems.

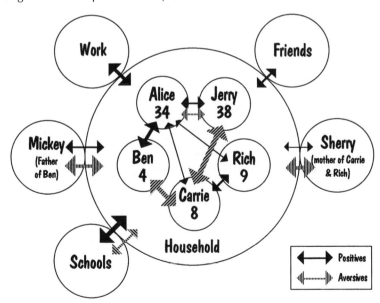

changes (and the behaviors and practices they support) important; so are the overall patterns.

The blended family shown in the figure experiences significant aversive exchanges internally as well as with the children's noncustodial parents. The overall preponderance of aversive exchanges presents a serious issue for the family.

At base, behavior—including family practices—is shaped and selected by such patterns of positive and negative events. Positives may reinforce either healthy (for example, cooperation) or troubling (for example, skipping school) behaviors, and aversives may support negative behaviors, punish positive ones, or produce problematic side-effects. Even these simple principles can produce very complicated patterns, as they transact and interlock in complex ways.

Understanding such configurations of consequences is crucial to understanding behavior; however, *antecedents* (conditions and events that occur before a behavior) are also important because of their connections with consequences.

Antecedents

One important class of antecedents is *occasions*. A behavior (including an instance of a generalized family practice like complaining) may pay off under certain contextual conditions and not under others. If one parent pays a great deal of attention to such complaining and another does not, the presence of the first is likely to become an occasion—a signal that reinforcement will follow—for complaining, for example.

Under some conditions, people are more motivated to take certain actions than they are under other conditions. For example, a teenager deprived of affection within her family system may be more likely to become involved in certain risky behaviors such as sexual promiscuity. Deprivation (of many kinds) is an important *motivating antecedent*. By the same token, satiation may decrease motivation. Technically, a motivating antecedent is any event or condition that increases (or decreases) sensitivity to particular consequences and evokes a behavior that produces those consequences. Another type of motivating antecedent is *reinforcer sampling,* in which exposure to a new positive experience, say time together without distractions for a parent and child, may potentiate that experience as a reinforcer in the future, for one or both of the people involved. Many motivating antecedents are verbal. If a family rule is "Children are to be seen and not heard," for example, an assertive statement from a preteen may be more aversive, and more likely to evoke a punitive response, than if the family verbal practices include, "Everyone should at least be heard."

Many of the most powerful exchanges that occur among people, within the family as well as with outsiders involved in transactions with the family, are verbal. As noted above, verbal behaviors can be motivating antecedents, but verbal actions often function as important consequences (both as reinforcers and punishers) as well. Other especially relevant classes of verbal antecedents within families include *rules* and *equivalence relations*. The term *rules* has been used in a variety of ways in family practice and family therapy. The word is sometimes used in a very broad sense to describe any regular pattern of interaction within the family; in this volume such patterns are referred to as family dynamics or interlocking family practices. The word *rule* is used here in a narrower, technical sense to refer to a verbal description of the way events and exchanges operate (in particular, the consequences that specific actions will likely have on specific kinds of occasions).

Such rules might include "You can never trust anyone outside the family [because they will take advantage of you]," or "If you talk back to Mother, you will be sorry." Notice that all the elements of such rules need not be articulated, but easily can be if the social worker inquires. Depressed individuals have often adopted the rule, "Nothing I can do can improve my terrible situation." As a result, the individual may feel very disempowered, a condition that may resonate throughout the family system. Expectations of each other (another form of rule), can be based on limited knowledge about developmental trajectories or overly romanticized notions of how easy intimate relationships should be, for example, and they often need to be examined and tested with families. The rules people have learned need not be accurate. Helping family members to reexamine inaccurate rules is often a valuable intervention, and is the core of cognitive therapy.

Equivalence relations, an important area of emerging research, is an additional class of verbal acts that can powerfully influence family members and family cultures. Examples of equivalence relations include the verbal connections that people learn among words and things, for example

$$\{me \approx failure \approx worthless\}$$

(The "$\approx$" symbol should be read as "is equivalent to." The curly brackets show the connections of equivalence relations with mathematical set theory. The central notion of equivalence classes is that members of the class may in some way be substitutable and function in similar ways.) Through a social shaping process, the word "me" can come to evoke the other members of the relation—and the others, like "failure" can also come to evoke "me." Such relations are of critical clinical importance in understanding, for example, how *death* can come to be equated with *peace* for some suicidal persons (Hayes, 1992). No one has ever personally tested that equivalence, but verbal relations can be very powerful. Note that while members of an equivalence relation may evoke each other or similar responses, they are not necessarily the same in all ways. A horse and the word "horse," for example, are members of an equivalence relation for English speakers, but are not of course the same thing.

Just as rules describing the consequences of behavior can be transmitted among and reinforced by family members, equivalence relations can also become family practices. In an interesting application from basic research, current data suggest that once a relation like

$$\{\text{Tanya} \approx \text{the black sheep}\}$$

has been learned, it cannot simply be erased, and probably cannot be reliably broken up by cognitive disputation (for example, "You're not a black sheep"). Rather, what is required is the construction and reinforcement of a new, competing equivalence, for example:

$$\{\text{Tanya} \approx \text{delightfully high-spirited}\}.$$

Minuchin (1974, Minuchin & Nichols, 1993) often deals with such equivalences in his family work, for example in shifting the family from $\{$Susan $\approx$ anorexic $\approx$ sick$\}$ to $\{$Susan $\approx$ demands attention $\approx$ spoiled$\}$. Note also that simply stating the relation is not enough. The connection needs to be reinforced, often many times, before the equivalence emerges.

Another important antecedent involved in shaping behavior, including family practices, is *modeling,* a process in which one person observes what another does and what the outcome (consequences) may be, and may later imitate that behavior. Imitation is a basic human repertoire, important for development, and crucial for initiating people into family and other cultural groups. It is often important in working with families to carefully examine the models present. For example, aggressive, physically coercive parents are likely to teach those repertoires to their children (Latham, 1994; Sloane, 1976/1988). Peers, who often teach the practices of street culture, can model and reinforce violent acts (Canada, 1995). Highly visible sports figures who model such behavior as fighting and self-absorption are also likely to be quite influential with youths. Some of these models can be targets of intervention in social work practice; all of them need to be considered in assessment and case planning.

Structural antecedents, a final set of factors that influence behavior, are relatively stable factors in the individual and the environment. These conditions need to be considered in planning treatment, even when they cannot be directly changed. Personal factors, including biological and intellectual capacities of the person, and environmental factors like the physical neighborhood and agency eligibility standards, may set outer limits on what is possible. As explored in later chapters, however, it is essential not to move too quickly to judgments regarding what can and cannot be changed. For example, recent research (Lovaas, 1987; Maurice, 1993) indicates that up to 50 percent of autistic children can be mainstreamed if state-of-the-art intervention, with professionals and families working as a team, occurs early enough. Most of the remaining 50 percent can also be significantly helped by the approach. A few years ago, the standard understanding was that the cause of this developmental disorder was inadequate mothering; psychodynamic treatment of mother and child consistent with this paradigm was never demonstrated to be effective, however. Similarly, agency procedures are too often accepted as unchangeable, when a network of empowered workers and clients can frequently spark significant shifts.

All of these events and conditions, antecedents that precede and consequences that follow behavior, are relevant to understanding what happens in families, and in working with families to make lasting changes. The relationships among behavior, antecedents and consequences—technically termed *contingencies*—become geometrically more complex as the number of persons and relationships increases. Beginning social workers often find sitting in a room with several family members far more confusing than working with an individual. Under those circumstances, it is not surprising that transactions between the family and other environmental systems, which add further complexity, are often neglected. A few powerful dynamics, however, are commonly crucial.

BEHAVIORAL DYNAMICS AND FAMILIES

Research over several decades makes it clear that the best predictors of satisfaction and dissatisfaction in couples are the rates of positive and aversive exchanges present (Jacobson & Margolin, 1979; Karney & Bradbury, 1995). Not only do couples reciprocate such exchanges on a daily basis, but rates of positive and negative exchange tend to be relatively independent of each other and therefore often need to be separately addressed (see discussion in chapter 6). While the presence of additional individuals in a family complicates the patterns, the same general pattern tends to hold. The key to understanding the core dynamics within a family is, therefore, observing and inquiring about the rates of such exchanges.

For every family, and to some extent, for each family member, what is experienced as positive and what is experienced as aversive are likely to vary. Although basic reinforcers and aversives like food and warmth are fairly universal, preferences are extensively shaped by larger cultural factors (as noted later in this chapter), by personal constitutional factors and experiences, and by family culture as well. In some families, time spent sitting and talking is highly valued, for example, while others have learned to enjoy more active pursuits. In some families, dinner conversations that involve conflicting views are regarded as exciting, while in others such interactions are experienced as unpleasant. It is crucial, therefore, to discuss people's experiences and the personal meanings (equivalence relations) they carry, as well as to observe family transactions.

"Roles" within families (Satir, 1964) are also shaped by family culture; in identifying those roles it is important to think about the *functions* such roles play within family culture. Since each role interlocks with others, each may be filling a sort of ecological niche that needs to be considered. The family and worker may need to construct an alternative set of interlocking roles that in some way can fulfill similar functions while being less costly. Alexander's *functional family therapy* is an excellent statement of this principle; as Barton and Alexander (1991), note, "*The functional family model assumes that processes occur in circular and reciprocal ways, and an occurrence of a relational context creates the meaning of any behavior, not an individual focus.*" (p. 407, emphasis in original).

Another way of stating this is that the social worker is often interested not only in the occurrence of a particular practice, but rather in the incidence of a transactional *scene* involving a set of interlocking practices within the family. In such repetitive, reciprocal scenes, one individual may usually play out the same role or the players may be interchangeable. Each acts in part because of the consequences provided by others in the scene. In some families, for example, conflict may function to create personal space by lessening the intensity of contacts, which is experienced as aversive by one or more family members.

These overall patterns—positive exchanges, negative exchanges, and the configuration of reciprocal, transactional scenes—are key to understanding the behavioral dynamics of families. A number of graphic tools are available for capturing such patterns (Mattaini, 1993). One of the simplest and most useful is the intrafamily ecomap (see Figure 1-4).

A simple mapping of overall exchanges, with some of the common circumstances noted, provides the worker with a critical overview of who treats who, how, and on what occasions, in the family. Whatever decisions are made about addressing specific areas, it is this overall configuration that needs to be reshaped, "restructured," in families where major difficulties are found in the internal system.

Figure 1-4

An ecomap depicting exchanges within the family.

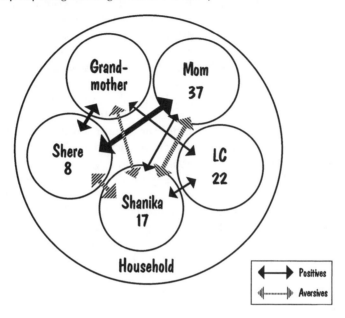

Ethnic and Cultural Diversity

Although overall patterns of exchange and transactions within the family and between family and environment are important for understanding all families, family practices vary enormously among different cultural, racial, ethnic, and religious groups, as well as in groups that vary by sexual orientation, social class, disability, age, and other factors. Variations occur in several interlocking areas, including valued elements (reinforcers), aversive elements, differing expectations (rules), and differing meanings (equivalence relations). At first, the most obvious differences among groups may involve the topography of practices—what the practices look like. This includes, for example, what people do when they socialize; the kinds of food, music, and recreation they enjoy; or traditional ways of earning a living and teaching children. At a deeper level, however, variations among what cultural groups teach people to value, and how they teach them to think, and the worlds they teach them to experience are at the core of understanding people and families in their diversity.

A few examples may clarify the enormous range of differences present. Members of a number of cultures, including several Asian groups, traditionally value the well-being of the group (family or community) more highly than individual identity and achievement. For members of such cultures, the personal ambition so highly valued among many white Americans may be seen as inappropriate, egocentric, and self-absorbed. For many African Americans, an extended kinship network is central to one's personal world, reflecting continuity with centuries-old practices originating in Africa (Black, 1996). High levels of education are valued by some cultural groups (and subcultural groups) more than by others.

What is experienced as aversive also varies enormously according to the culture. In many middle class European American families, assertiveness by children is valued; in a traditional Chinese family, however, if that assertive behavior were directed toward a parent or elder, it could be shockingly aversive (Sue & Zane, 1987). At the same time, every family and every individual has been shaped by unique circumstances, and therefore the social worker needs to be prepared for differing levels of assimilation and bi-culturalism (Gelfand & Fandetti, 1993). Family members themselves are the best source of specific information about what is valued and aversive. The more familiarity the worker has with the cultures from which most of his/her clients come, however, the more likely he or she will really hear what they are saying.

Cognitive factors (rules and equivalence relations) vary tremendously by culture. For example, spanking is frowned on among some groups, but others still operate from the rule, "Spare the rod and spoil the child." (Current research indicates that spanking is generally a poor practice; see chapter 7 for details.) At a broader level, Native Americans and Jewish people are members of cultures that have recently experienced genocidal persecutions (Rosen & Weltman, 1996; Tafoya & Del Vecchio, 1996), which naturally shape how one sees the world, what one expects, and the meaning of events (rules and equivalence relations). Native Americans have experienced a centuries-old effort to eliminate their cultures, and often to exterminate their people wholesale (Lowery, in press). This of course leads to negative expectations of the larger culture, based on historically, and often currently, accurate rules like, "White people cannot be trusted and will punish effective action on my part if they can." Other cognitive coping strategies, including irony and humor (for example, Vizenor, 1991), and raw artistic confrontations with reality (for example, Louis, 1989, 1995) have become common practices among Native Americans dealing with the results of this history.

Many Jewish parents want their children to marry other Jews. This expectation arises, not out of racism, but because they see the survival of their people as ever-threatened. Marriage outside the group, therefore, can be seen as disloyal:

{out-marriage ≈ loss of Jewish tradition ≈ disappearance of the group}.

The social worker needs both to learn as much as possible about practices within cultural groups, and to develop a sensitivity to hearing such nuances when they emerge with clients.

Transactions with Other Cultural Entities

As noted above, the boundary of a social work case is not the boundary of the family, because the family is embedded in larger cultural entities (for example, the neighborhood, and ethnic culture[s]), and members of the family are also usually participants in or have contact with other larger systems on an ongoing (schools, work sites), or limited-term (hospital, assistance payment systems) basis. Significant positive and aversive exchanges with those systems, in turn, typically affect both family dynamics and individual experiences. *The purpose of family-centered social work intervention is the co-construction of a family reality characterized by increased access to positives, decreased exposure to aversives, or both, consistent with the good of the collective.* The boundary of the case, therefore, needs to be drawn to incorporate those events, including transactions involving the larger environment.

Figure 1-5 is an ecomap portraying the overall situation experienced by a small family consisting of a single Latina mother living in an inner-city area. The mother is referred for services because she is feeling overwhelmed and depressed. Notice that her family experiences aversive contact with the school attended by her eight-year-old son, strong positive exchanges with extended family (which provides limited financial but substantial emotional support) and the Catholic church, limited connection with the social welfare system (food stamps only), and no connection with income-producing work. All of these factors fall within the boundary of "the case."

Ecomaps like this one are often crucial to understanding the dynamic, contextual networks of transactions occurring in a case; the next chapter further expands on their construction.

Dealing with the mother's emotional struggles is likely to require the co-construction by client and worker of ways to influence the overall transactional pattern defining the case. The process is of one of shared power (Lowery & Mattaini, in press) in which worker, client, and often others included within the case boundary all have strong voices in a process of deep

Figure 1-5

A simple ecomap tracing transactional events within the household, and between the household and others.

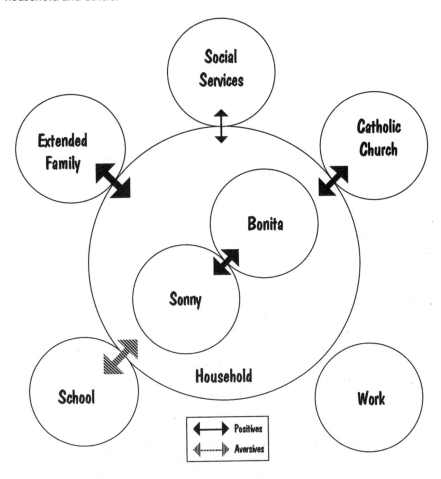

mutual respect, all make contributions from their available repertoires which are viewed as gifts rather than achievements, and all share responsibility for the outcomes. Learning to practice within a framework of shared power is an endless developmental challenge for social workers raised in competitive, egotistical western society, which often does not prepare the social worker to recognize the essential connectedness among people and their world. Such recognition may be the heart of spirituality, though it may be described differently in different traditions (Einstein, no date).

Transactions over Time

In addition to paying attention to the broad range of transactions affecting a family, competent family practice often needs to examine changes in these transactions over time. For example, a family that has just immigrated to this country from Haiti may have functioned very well there, but may find the racism and other oppressive conditions present in the United States overwhelming. Teenage children in the family, exposed to U.S. youth culture, may rapidly distance themselves from traditional practices, and in the process spark conflict in the family. Family history, operationalized in terms of changing transactional experiences, is important to explore, in order to determine with the family how the breakdown has occurred. Graphic tools are also useful here. For example, Figure 1-6 shows two sequential ecomaps, one portraying the contextual situation experienced by the family in Haiti, and the other the current situation.

It is even possible to extend such images back in time intergenerationally (see chapter 2). Such images can help the family and the worker make sense of what has changed, what the trajectory may be, and where to begin. As will be discussed in the next chapter, working with the family to envision a third image—portraying how the family members would like their lives to be—can be a powerful tool for engaging everyone in constructing solutions, participating in a practice culture of shared power.

CONCLUSION: UNDERSTANDING FAMILY CULTURES

An enormous body of literature discusses various ways to assess family functioning from many different theoretical perspectives. For example, Reid (1985) summarizes work related to communication and metacommunication, family rules of interaction related to control and involvement, alliances among family members, and flexibility in response to changing conditions. Minuchin (Minuchin & Nichols, 1993) looks for patterns of family structure and family myth. For work with couples, Jacobson and Christensen (1996) emphasize the answers to six questions:

1. How distressed is this couple?
2. How committed is this couple to this relationship?
3. What are the issues that divide them?
4. Why are these issues such a problem for them?
5. What are the strengths holding them together?
6. What can treatment do to help them? (pp. 71–72)

Figure 1-6

Sequential ecomaps tracing changes over time.

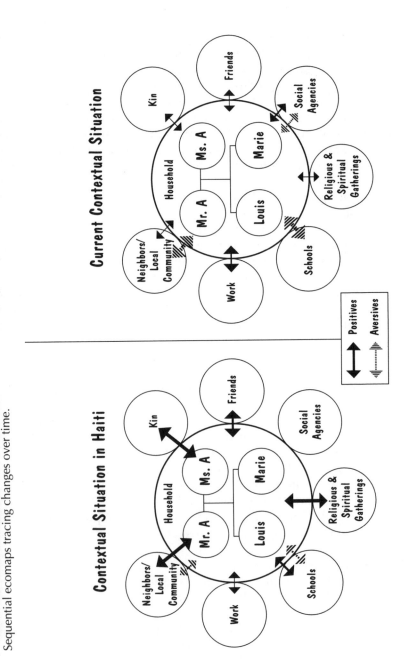

Contextual Situation in Haiti

Kin

Friends

Social Agencies

Household

Ms. A

Marie

Mr. A

Louis

Religious & Spiritual Gatherings

Neighbors/ Local Community

Work

Schools

Current Contextual Situation

Kin

Friends

Social Agencies

Household

Ms. A

Marie

Mr. A

Louis

Religious & Spiritual Gatherings

Neighbors/ Local Community

Work

Schools

Positives

Aversives

Many of these dimensions and questions are relevant to ecobehavioral work with families and will be considered in later chapters. However, the ecobehavioral approach is broader. It requires seeing the family as it is embedded in its world, and determining what is working for the family and what is not. While a predetermined system identifying what is "healthy" and what is "pathological" would simplify things for the social worker, it would do a disservice to the families, and would also be inconsistent with the variety of family cultures and larger cultural entities in which families are grounded.

For example, imagine a grandmother who feels shame for the actions of her granddaughter, perhaps related to substance abuse and lack of employment. If the grandmother is quite disturbed about this, a cognitive, Euro-American perspective might view her discomfort as reflecting excessive enmeshment, and work to change her thinking. If the client is a member of some Native American groups, however, the shame she experiences could be culturally normative, reflecting a set of cultural practices that have worked for that group for thousands of years. If the client were a member of some Asian groups in which family identity can be much stronger than individual identity, the experience of shame might be even stronger. Individual family cultures are just as variable; many different sets of interlocking practices may work successfully for particular families.

What is needed, then, is a framework that allows room for many types of satisfying family functioning, and still provides a coherent structure for practice with families consistent with the sharing of power. The ecobehavioral model, as outlined in the next chapter, offers an alternative that is grounded in current and emerging knowledge in science and in practice.

REFERENCES

Anderson, S. C. (1994). A critical analysis of the concept of codependency. *Social Work, 39,* 677–685.

Barton, C., & Alexander, J. F. (1991). Functional family therapy. In A. S. Gurman & D. P. Kniskern (Eds.), *Handbook of family therapy* (vol. 1) (pp. 403–443). New York: Brunner/Mazel.

Black, L. (1996). Families of African origin: An overview. In M. McGoldrick, J. Giordano, & J. K. Pearce (Eds.), *Ethnicity & Family Therapy* (2nd ed.) (pp. 57–65). New York: Guilford Press.

Canada, G. (1995). *Fist stick knife gun.* Boston: Beacon Press.

Einstein, A. (no date). *The world as I see it* (abridged ed.). Secaucus, NJ: Citadel Press.

Falloon, I. R. H. (1991). *Behavioral family therapy.* In A. S. Gurman & D. P. Kniskern (Eds.), *Handbook of family therapy* (vol. 2) (pp. 65–95). New York: Brunner/Mazel.

Gelfand, D. E., & Fandetti, D. V. (1993). The emergent nature of ethnicity:

Dilemmas in assessment. In J. B. Rauch (Ed.), *Assessment: A sourcebook of social work practice* (pp. 357–369). Milwaukee: Families International, Inc.

Glenn, S. S. (1991). Contingencies and metacontingencies: Relations among behavioral, cultural and biological evolution. In P. A. Lamal (Ed.), *Behavioral analysis of societies and cultural practices* (pp. 39–73). New York: Hemisphere Publishing.

Halford, W. K. (1991). Beyond expressed emotion: Behavioral assessment of family interaction associated with the course of schizophrenia. *Behavioral Assessment, 13,* 99–123.

Hayes, S. C. (1992). Verbal relations, time and suicide. In S. C. Hayes & L. J. Hayes (Eds.), *Understanding verbal relations* (pp. 109–118). Reno, NV: Context Press.

Jacobson, N. S. (1997). *The overselling of psychotherapy: What is a radical behaviorist to do?* Presidential Scholar Address, Association for Behavior Analysis Convention, Chicago, IL, May 24.

Jacobson, N. S., & Christensen, A. (1996). *Integrative couple therapy.* New York: Norton Press.

Jacobson, N. S., & Margolin, G. (1979). *Marital therapy: Strategies based on social learning and behavior exchange principles.* New York: Brunner/Mazel.

Karney, B. R. & Bradbury, T. N. (1995). The longitudinal course of marital quality and stability: A review of theory, method, and research. *Psychological Bulletin, 118,* 3–34.

Latham, G. I. (1994). *The power of positive parenting.* Salt Lake City: Northwest Publishing.

Lerner, S. (1997). Chemical Reaction. *Ms., 8*(1), 57–61, July/August.

Louis, A. C. (1989). *Fire water world.* Albuquerque: West End Press.

Louis, A. C. (1995). *Vortex of Indian fevers.* Evanston, IL: Northwestern University Press.

Lovaas, O. I. (1987). Behavioral treatment and normal educational and intellectual functioning in young autistic children. *Journal of Consulting and Clinical Psychology, 55,* 3–9.

Lowery, C. T. (in press). The sharing of power: Empowerment with Native American women. In L. Gutierrez & E. Lewis (Eds.), *Women and empowerment.* New York: Columbia University Press.

Lowery, C. T. & Mattaini M. A. (in press). Shared power in social work: A Native American perspective. In H. Briggs & K. Corcoran (Eds.), *Structuring change in social work practice.* Chicago: Lyceum.

Markman, H. J. (1991). Constructive marital conflict is NOT an oxymoron. *Behavioral Assessment, 13,* 83–96.

Mattaini, M. A. (1993). *More than a thousand words: Graphics for clinical practice.* Washington, DC: NASW Press.

Mattaini, M. A. (1997a). *Clinical practice with individuals.* Washington, DC: NASW Press.

Mattaini, M. A. (1997b). Visualizing practice with children and families. In J. T. Pardeck & M. J. Markward (Eds.), *Reassessing social work practice with children* (pp. 51–66). Amsterdam, Netherlands: Gordon & Breach.

Mattaini, M. A. & Meyer, C. H. (1998). The ecosystems perspective. In M. A.

Mattaini, C. T. Lowery, & C. H. Meyer (Eds.), *The foundations of social work practice: A graduate text* (2nd ed.) (pp. 3–19). Washington, DC: NASW Press.

Maurice, C. (1993). *Let me hear your voice.* New York: Fawcett Columbine.

Meyer, C. H. (1993). *Assessment in social work practice.* New York: Columbia University Press.

Minuchin, S. (1974). *Families & family therapy.* Cambridge, MA: Harvard University Press.

Minuchin, S., & Nichols, M. P. (1993). *Family healing.* New York: Free Press.

Minuchin, S., Lee, W.-Y., & Simon, G. M. (1996). *Mastering family therapy: Journeys of growth and transformation.* New York: John Wiley & Sons.

Patterson, G. R. (1976). The aggressive child: Victim and architect of a coercive system. In E. J. Mash, L. A. Hamerlynck, & L. C. Handy (Eds.), *Behavior modification and families* (pp. 267–316). New York: Brunner/Mazel.

Patterson, G. R. (1982). *Coercive family process: A social learning approach* (vol. 3). Eugene, OR: Castalia.

Petit, M. R., & Curtis, P. A. (1997). *Child abuse and neglect: A look at the states: 1997 CWLA stat book.* Washington, DC: CWLA Press.

Poppen, R. L. (1989). Some clinical implications of rule-governed behavior. In S. C. Hayes (Ed.), *Rule-governed behavior: Cognition, contingencies, and instructional control* (pp. 325–357). New York: Plenum.

Reid, W. J. (1985). *Family problem solving.* New York: Columbia University Press.

Rosen, E. J, & Weltman, S. F. (1996). Jewish families: An overview. In M. McGoldrick, J. Giordano, & J. K. Pearce (Eds.), *Ethnicity & Family Therapy* (2nd ed.) (pp. 611–630). New York: Guilford Press.

Satir, V. (1964). *Conjoint family therapy.* Palo Alto, CA: Science and Behavior Books.

Sidman, M. (1989). *Coercion and its fallout.* Boston: Authors Cooperative.

Sloane, H. N. (1976/88). *The good kid book.* Champaign, IL: Research Press.

Spickard, P. R., Fong, R., & Ewalt, P. L. (1995). Undermining the very basis of racism—its categories. *Social Work, 40,* 581–584.

Sue, S., & Zane, N. (1987). The role of culture and cultural techniques in psychotherapy. *American Psychologist, 42,* 37–45.

Tafoya, N., & Del Vecchio, A. (1996). Back to the future: An examination of the Native American holocaust. In M. McGoldrick, J. Giordano, & J. K. Pearce (Eds.), *Ethnicity & Family Therapy* (2nd ed.) (pp. 45–54). New York: Guilford Press.

Tolstoy, L. (1877/1997). *Anna Karenina.* New York: Penguin.

Vizenor, G. (1991). *The heirs of Columbus.* New York: Quality Paperback Book Club.

CHAPTER TWO

The Practice Process with Families

Family work can be confusing. So much is happening so quickly in work with families that it is easy to get lost in the details. Mastering a core framework to guide one's professional thinking throughout can offer significant advantages under those circumstances. This chapter outlines the overall practice process for ecobehavioral work with families. Four primary functions need to occur in such practice, as shown in Figure 2-1.

These four functions are (1) engaging the family, (2) constructing a shared vision of the goal-state to be constructed or maintained, (3) completing an ecobehavioral assessment, and (4) implementing an interventive plan or strategy. As shown in the figure, these four functions overlap. While a general conceptual order, as portrayed by the arrow, is present, more often than not the process is iterative and recursive; as intervention is occurring, for example, new assessment information may emerge that requires changes in the plan. Each function is discussed separately in the material that follows, but in reality each is always present to some extent in each of the others. It is crucial to bear this basic framework in mind throughout this book. Whether working with couples (chapter 6), doing parent education (chapter 7), or working with families living with serious mental illness (chapter 10), the basic framework still provides primary strategic guidance, and the central principles discussed in chapters 2–5 apply in various ways to all practice with families.

ENGAGEMENT

The social work practitioner needs to achieve a positive, trusting relationship with family members in order to participate with the family in constructing and stabilizing a satisfactory family configuration. Social workers often ask family members to share private information and to take steps that are unfamiliar and may feel risky. Family members will do so only if the so-

Figure 2-1

The practice process.

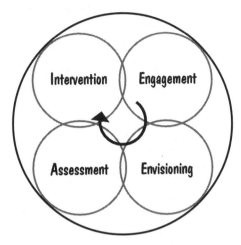

cial worker is seen as caring, authentic, trustworthy, and knowledgeable. Social workers often are also the only immediate source of support and reinforcement for clients as they begin to experiment with new repertoires (although if the repertoires are to be maintained, natural reinforcement from other sources needs eventually to be accessed).

"Engaging" a family, therefore, requires becoming a source of valued reinforcers and a trusted source of rules. The worker begins this process immediately by treating all family members with respect, authentically recognizing their strengths and what they have done and are doing well, and communicating empathy for what clients are experiencing—to some extent experiencing the emotions that the client does, and letting the client know that is happening. In addition, the worker provides a nonpunitive audience for clients who often are not used to being heard without subtle or overt punishment. By doing so, a social worker provides an important model for family members who may ordinarily criticize and argue with each other without first really listening. While the worker may at various points particularly attend to or support certain family members, ultimately the goal is to forge a genuinely reinforcing relationship with each member of the family. In a shared power paradigm, the social worker begins with the certain knowledge that every family member has something critical to contribute to the work, has real power; this framework necessarily involves deep respect.

In engaging the family, the social worker in fact becomes an important, but temporary, member of the family culture. This is one way of looking at the process Minuchin (1974) calls "joining" the family. As a member of the family culture, the worker will often act in ways that are familiar to the family ("mirroring" family patterns). In some cases, the purpose of joining the family is to work with family members to change that culture, and in others to work with them to modify transactions with environmental systems. In all cases, however, one of the worker's primary responsibilities is to find some way of connecting and developing a collaborative contract, even in situations where the family is referred for services involuntarily. The only other option is to rely on coercion, which for the reasons discussed in the previous chapter is usually a poor choice. A *constructional* process (Schwartz & Goldiamond, 1975), involving the collaborative construction of new repertoires and practices, can emerge only from reinforcement and authentic communication. The contract for work should be explicit, and the practitioner needs to honor it respectfully and completely.

Client "resistance" within an ecobehavioral model is viewed as a breakdown in this process. The apparently resistant behavior is viewed as functional in some way: to protect oneself or the family from aversive experiences, as perhaps the only available way to influence external systems, or a reflection of differing agendas, in which there is no clearly articulated, collaboratively developed agreement on what to work toward, or how to do so. Dealing with resistance, therefore, is a normal part of the social worker's job. Research in family therapy indicates that less experienced therapists often experience more resistance, and this appears to be related to higher levels of confrontation and lower levels of validating positive steps that the family members are taking (Patterson & Forgatch, 1985). Rather than responding defensively, the worker should view what people do as the best responses they have available under particular antecedent conditions (Falloon, 1991).

While there is no single way to engage all families and their members, a number of general stategies can be useful. First, social workers can and should make explicit their commitment to recognizing and supporting the power within the family, and they should mean it—they should look with the family for areas where each can contribute, and provide authentic reinforcement for those contributions. Efforts to resolve problems and move ahead should especially be recognized. Such recognition of positive aspects of what family members do and say has a triple function: it reinforces doing or saying more of those things among family members, it establishes the social worker as a source of valued reinforcers, and it models a process that is crucial to effective family functioning. Being heard is a valued source of reinforcement and supports the construction of equivalences like

{me ≈ worth taking time for ≈ valuable}.

In cross-cultural situations, achieving credibility with families may be particularly challenging (Sue & Zane, 1987). Some principles that may help with all families, but particularly in cross-cultural situations, include the following:

• Familiarity and experience with families of particular cultural groups may suggest some generally useful rules for work with families of those cultures (see, for example McGoldrick, Giordano, & Pearce, 1996). For example, in cultures where older persons traditionally receive particular deference and respect, the social worker may want to address him or herself first to those figures in the family.
• When possible, working on the family's "turf," in the family's natural environment, especially the home, often makes it easier for the family to be open to the worker. Work in the home also provides valuable assessment data, and minimizes generalization problems (both areas are discussed at greater length later in this chapter).
• If the worker resembles people whose advice and view of the world the family has come to trust, engagement may be easier. Considerations here may include choice of words, familiarity with topics addressed in early contacts, and even the way the worker dresses.
• Workers should attempt to describe client situations in words and in ways that are congruent with the family's experiences.
• If family members find that predictions the social worker makes prove to be true, the family members may come increasingly to trust the worker's description of the connections between actions and consequences.

Many clients have had aversive experiences with professionals, including social workers (for many clients, sadly, equivalences like {social worker ≈ coercive} are well developed), and some have never had a genuinely trusting relationship with anyone. Under such circumstances, there is no reason to expect that those clients would immediately engage deeply with social workers. The social worker then needs to provide opportunities for new experiences and learning by remaining consistent despite challenges, and acting creatively, nondefensively, and authentically. It is the worker's responsibility to find ways to communicate nonpunitive empathy, find ways to reinforce, and be seen as credible, while letting go of "ego" by refusing to personalize initial resistance and by caring more about the outcome for the family than about the way he or she looks to the family or anyone else. A social worker must in some cases come back to a family over and over again before finally being allowed to "join" in any significant way.

ENVISIONING

Elaborating on family members' visions of how they would like the situation to change is a powerful way to demonstrate a commitment to shared power and to move toward constructive work meaningful to the family. This process immediately shifts the focus away from pathology and what is wrong, and toward hopes and possibilities for what might be built, the goal-state to be achieved.

Family members' visions of possible outcomes of their work with the social worker may not always be consistent, of course, and it is important both to hear differing perspectives and to try to identify commonalities. Shared goals may need to be fairly abstract initially, like "improving communication" or "reducing conflicts," but even at that level, a common vision is useful. Although not always practical, conjoint interviews are often valuable for this purpose. It is important that everyone involved have a chance to participate in this process. Adolescents often prefer an initial individual discussion; everyone's visions can then be shared in a later joint session, followed by a process of work to identify common ground. Although some family therapy theorists insist that all family members be seen in every session, this is not always possible in family-centered social work, and in some cases may well be counterindicated (as in most cases of domestic violence— see chapter 4). In practicing from a shared-power framework, it is essential however that everyone with a stake in the outcome have a genuine opportunity to a meaningful voice in the process.

Table 2-1 suggests sample questions that may help family members elaborate on their visions of what they hope to construct in their work with the clinician. It is useful to begin by discussing the positive alternatives, the potential for "sculpting" an improved life, whenever possible, because constructing positive repertoires and practices can be achieved by relying primarily on reinforcement techniques rather than coercion. (As with sculpture, the available material places some limits on the final product, but something of beauty can emerge from a variety of media, of whatever shape or size).

In some cases, however, family members may find it more difficult to envision an improved goal-state than to describe current problems and issues. When necessary, the social worker and the family can begin with an exploration of each family member's perceptions of current issues, and gradually work toward a positive alternative vision. (Stopping problem behavior can be achieved either by constructing incompatible alternatives, or by using punishment and threats. For the reasons discussed in the previous chapter, the constructional life-sculpting alternative is clearly best when possible.)

Table 2–1

Sample questions that may be helpful to family members in envisioning the goal state of their work with the social worker. Not all questions would be used in a single case, but several may be necessary to move toward clarity. (Some have been adapted from solution-focused and behavioral authors.)

- If it were up to you, what would you like to see change in your family? (If client indicates doubt that change is possible:) If it were possible, though, what would you really like to see change?
- If we are successful, what is your vision of how your family and your life would be different?
- Who will be doing what differently?
- When did this issue come up? How did it develop? What was it like in the family before this happened? (Recalling happier times may establish hope that similar happier times can be rebuilt.)
- Imagine that your family story is a novel, and the next chapter is a happy one, what will happen in that chapter? (Furman & Ahola, 1992)
- If a miracle happened, and that when you wake up tomorrow your problems have disappeared, what would it be like? (de Shazer, 1985)
- If a Martian landed after your problems were solved, what would he see your family doing? (A Martian cannot interpret; he can only see behavior.) (Schwartz & Goldiamond, 1975)

ECOBEHAVIORAL ASSESSMENT

The vision of an improved life configuration or family situation constructed with the family then shapes and guides the next major practice function, the assessment. Individualized assessment is the hallmark of professionalism. While similar dynamics occur among many families, each is unique in ways that often make a difference in practice. Assessment is the process of working with family members to achieve an understanding of how the current situation differs from the desired goal-state, and to clarify the necessary steps to move from one to the other.

The assessment process with families is even less linear than with individuals (see Mattaini, 1997). A great deal is often happening when meeting with or working with several members of the family, and the complexity of the interpersonal and ecosystemic situations can become geometrically more difficult to grasp as the number of people involved increases. The social work consultation can easily become quite diffuse and unfocused, and rather than achieving a comprehensive and comprehensible ecobehavioral perspective on the family in context, there is a risk of focusing primarily on less important but easily accessed areas, or on apparent "pathology."

Table 2–2

Sample interview guide for completing family assessment. This is only a guide; not every area may be relevant in every case, but be sure to explore in depth any area that may be important either for understanding the current situation, or for providing possible resources later. Answers to many of these questions may simply emerge in the course of a natural dialogue. (Adapted from Mattaini, 1997.)

I. Ecobehavioral Scan
I'd like to ask you a few questions so we can develop a clear picture of your situation together, and so I can be sure I understand your life as it is now. (The social worker may wish to draw a transactional ecomap with the family during this stage.)

- Let's start with what's going *right* . . . what areas of your family life are currently going best?
- Let's begin with the connections you have outside the immediate family. How much contact do you have with relatives or extended family? On a scale of 0 (not at all) to 5 (a lot), how much satisfaction do you get from those contacts? Are there any struggles with those folks? One a scale of 0 to 5, how much pain do those struggles cause? (Use a similar scale with each area that appears to be salient below).
- Do you have many friends? How often do you see friends? How are those relationships going? Anyone else?
- What about work and school? What's going well there? So on our 0 to 5 scale . . . are there things that aren't going so well? About a __ on our scale?
- Tell me a little about where you live. How satisfied are you with your home and neighborhood?
- Any religious or church affiliation? Are you active?
- Is anyone in the family active in other groups or organizations?
- Any legal involvement?
- How is everyone's health? Any problems there?
- How much alcohol do people in the family use? Anyone take other medication or drugs?
- Now let's turn to your family itself. What's going right in the family? Who gets along best with who? Who have more struggles getting along? (Elaborate as necessary, and quantify, to explore the relationships within the family.)
- Does anyone else live in your home? How do you all get along with them? (Explore both positive and negative exchanges, and quantify if possible.)
- What would you like to do more of in your family? What would you like to do less of? (Suggest self-monitoring or observational measures to expand data.)

II. Identification of Focal Issues
(Remember that focal issues may involve the behavior of one person, but to the extent possible shift toward transactional definitions. Also, remember that focal issues need not involve only family members, but may involve transactions with other people or systems.)

- So, out of all of this, where would you like to begin? What's most important to you?
- I notice that you seemed to struggle a bit with ___. Is that one thing we should pay attention to?

Table 2–2   *Continued*

- What do you think would be a realistic goal here? (Expanding and becoming more specific, but building on the envisioning that occurred earlier.)
- Do you think that there is anything else we should work on at this point?
- So, specifically, one of our goals right now is. . . . (explicate in behavioral terms).

III. Contextual Analysis of Focal Issues

Now, let's see if we can get a really clear picture of our first goal (or focal issue), which is. . . . (General flow is from current undesirable situation to goal state; this kind of analysis should occur for each identified focal issue, although all may not be done at the same time. Focal issues left aside for later should be clearly stated and written down, however, so the family knows that they will be addressed later.)

- As near as you can tell, how did this problem start?
- When was that?
- Does this problem behavior ever pay off in any way for anyone—does it ever produce any advantages for anybody?
- Who else acts a little like this sometimes?
- Who or what supports the current pattern?
- What are the costs? What other problems does it cause?
- What seems to trigger the problem? Are there times when it doesn't happen? (Identify occasions.)
- Are there some times when this is not a problem? Tell me about those times. . . . When is the problem most likely to come up? (Search for motivating antecedents.)
- What do you think it would take to get from where you are to where you want to be? (Explore resources, including tangible, personal, and social.)
- Who would be willing to help you achieve this goal or resolve this problem?
- Who or what might stand in the way?
- How important is this to you? Why? How will reaching this goal enrich your lives? How quickly do you think that will happen? (Build motivation.)

IV. Identification of Interventive Tasks

(This part of the assessment process needs to flow from the information provided in earlier stages, and should emphasize tasks that will address the areas identified in the contextual analysis. It should include exploration of interventive options for mobilizing the resources and addressing the obstacles discussed in that analysis. Identify approaches with the best empirical support within the realities of the family situation. Careful specification of the multiple steps required to work toward the goal may be required. Explore possible reinforcers to be used along the way as well.)

It is therefore important that in the early stages the social worker have in mind a clear and relatively simple framework for family assessment. Information collected through transactions with family members and collaterals often does not emerge in an organized way, but needs to be aggregated in a way that enables the family and worker to develop a meaningful interventive strategy.

The four core assessment functions in an ecobehavioral model are (1) completing an ecobehavioral scan of the family situation, (2) identifying focal issues, (3) completing a contextual behavior analysis of those focal issues, and (4) identifying interventive tasks (see Figure 2-2).

Like the overall practice process (Figure 2-1), assessment is iterative and recursive, circling back as the data emerging suggest, but the ordered framework shown in Figure 2-2 gives the worker and the family a map for making sense of the family's situation, however confusing the presentation may be. One of the social worker's key contributions to this process is a clear understanding of the family culture and dynamics. Another is a coherent strategy for integrating the information gathered. An interview guide that may be useful for completing each assessment function is shown in Table 2-2. The sample questions shown should not, of course, be used literally or in a rote fashion with each family, but may provide useful guidance for structuring the process.

While the four functions discussed here should be used flexibly and creatively, they fall into a certain natural order; for example, deciding on interventive tasks would be difficult and probably ineffective before understanding the issues in depth, and except in the simplest of cases each of these functions needs to be addressed.

ECOBEHAVIORAL SCAN OF THE FAMILY SITUATION

Before moving toward constructive action, it is usually essential to understand the context within which the family members live out their lives, the

Figure 2-2

Four central assessment functions.

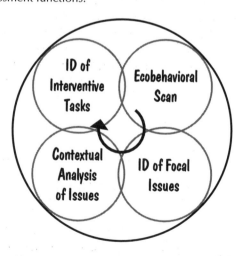

"sea of concurrent contingencies" (Malott, Whaley, & Malott, 1997, p. 367) that shapes their behavior, the interlocking practices that define both the family culture and the other cultural entities within which family members are embedded. At this point, an ecosystems perspective is crucial; only by observing the current family situation, and often knowing something about the way that situation developed, can one complete an adequate assessment. Exploring their situation also communicates a message to the family that the social worker is interested in trying to view the world from their perspective, which is crucial for engagement.

At this stage of assessment, the social worker should focus on processes, not attributes or dispositions. The goal is to develop an overall picture of transactions of family members with persons and cultures outside as well as inside the family. It is particularly valuable to attend to family member's own perceptions of these dynamics, since each has his/her own perspective, however biased it may be, which reflects experience with the operative contingencies. For example, Van Treuren (1986) had each member of a family draw the family as he or she saw it, showing the strength and type of connections among family members. This valuable technique could be even more useful from an ecobehavioral perspective if what were sketched were the level of positive and negative exchanges present among family members as observed by each.

Exchanges with External Systems

While traditional family therapy is concerned primarily with intrafamily dynamics, family-centered ecobehavioral practice recognizes the deep interconnectedness of families with their larger environments. The social and physical environment is involved in many of the most intense positive and negative exchanges that families experience and has a major impact on family and individual functioning (Mattaini, Grellong, & Abramovitz, 1992). Since understanding these external connections is often crucial to make sense of what is happening within the family, it is best to begin by examining them. For example, conflict between an adolescent and a parent may revolve around failure in school, an event that may need to be understood in depth in order to work with the family toward resolution of the conflict.

The major variables to consider in assessing the family's involvement with other systems and events with which the family comes into contact include positive and negative exchanges (for example, salaries or threats from employers, or support provided by peers), and conditions and events that may function as antecedents (for example, models of violent or peaceful behavior). Also valuable to consider is "What exchanges are not present that might be expected, or might be useful?"

Visual tools like the transactional ecomap are particularly useful here, not only to explore and elaborate specific positive and negative exchanges with environmental actors and systems but also to capture overall patterns present in the case. For example, Figure 2-3 portrays a family that is likely to be very stressed as a result of multiple aversive exchanges with other systems, and for which little environmental support is apparent (few positive exchanges occur).

Such ecomaps can be prepared with the family in the assessment process, and offer one way to operationalize the sharing of power, since family members can have the primary voices in determining what conditions and events to include, and in clarifying how they experience those fac-

Figure 2-3

A transactional ecomap depicting major features of a family's experiences.

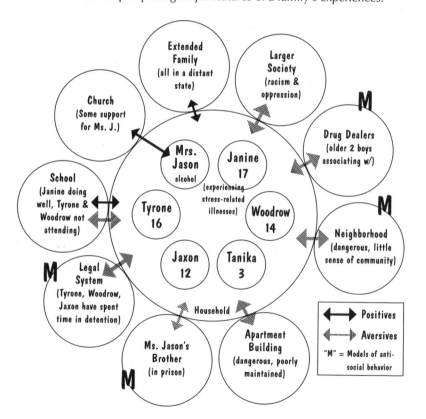

Figure 2-4

A blank Quick Scan form for use in assessment.

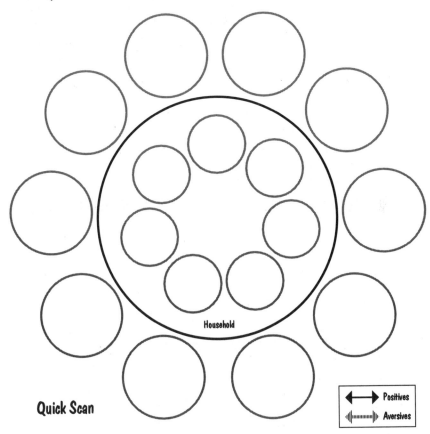

Quick Scan

Household

◄——► Positives
◄|||||||||||||► Aversives

tors. If the family-centered social worker keeps blank Quick Scan forms (like that shown in Figure 2-4) handy, completing them with the family can be an efficient process, requiring only that persons and cultures unique to the family be noted, and that common exchanges be portrayed with arrows.

Solid arrows can be used for positive exchanges, and red or cross-hatched arrows for aversives. Reciprocal exchanges can be portrayed by double-headed arrows, while unidirectional ones can use single-headed arrows. The thickness of the arrows can be used to reflect the power of the exchanges. Recognizing that a person or family may and often does experience both positive and aversive exchanges with another system, both should be noted. While such complexity may not always be desirable, it is also possible (Figure 2-3) to note sources of important antecedents, like the models of antisocial behavior identified by the letter M.

In Figure 2-3, in addition to the arrows, a good deal of specific data can also be noted. All of this information may be useful in developing a plan for work with the family, although finding a balance between capturing what is relevant and salient (Germain, 1968) without losing too much valuable time requires considerable professional judgment.

Key Family Repertoires

Transactions and exchanges within the family are the next major consideration in assessment. While events occurring within families can be very complicated, ecobehavioral theory clarifies the major dynamics that need to be considered. The core consideration is the level and quality of positive and aversive exchanges present. Several other dimensions, especially communication, acceptance, and repertoires for managing change and developmental transitions, in turn, support or fail to support functional patterns of exchange.

Positive Exchange

As clarified in chapter 1, positive exchange is the heart of life satisfaction, as well as the most powerful interpersonal force available for constructing positive change. Two useful ways to think about positive exchange in the family include the extent of "giving" present, and the extent to which family members reinforce each other's satisfying actions. In a healthy family, each member offers the others a rich level of positive experiences, which may include affection, entertainment, physical maintenance, opportunities for care giving, assistance with work, and many other events and conditions. In a well functioning family, such positive exchange is ongoing, with giving apparently occurring "freely," though it is important that an overall balance be present to avoid exploitation of one or more members who give more than they receive. Note that what is experienced as positive varies with cultural factors, with family culture, and according to individual tastes.

In addition to a high level of "giving," in healthy families people reinforce others for behaviors they like. If someone does something well or pleasing, others recognize this explicitly (in ways consistent with cultural variables), with a word, a smile, or a touch. In less well functioning families, it is common for positive events to go by unnoticed, while negative ones receive a good deal of attention. Positive exchange (giving and reinforcing) is the heart of a caring family, provides a sort of emotional "bank account" that can be drawn on during difficult times, and encourages the sharing of power within the household. Both giving and reinforcing repertoires can be explicitly enhanced (see chapter 4) if assessment indicates that they are too infrequent.

Aversive Exchange

The other crucial dynamic in families is the extent and severity of unpleasant or damaging exchanges present. Managing and minimizing such transactions is a key family repertoire. Any family in which there are many or very intense aversive transactions is likely to be a stressful and unpleasant environment for its members. Aversives include punishment, threats, and unpleasant conditions established to try to force change in other's actions. While some aversives are likely to occur in any human collective, families in which punishment and coercion are minimized tend to be happier and more productive.

One danger in a family in which coercive dynamics are embedded in the culture is that one aversive action tends to produce a reciprocal aversive response, and that these exchanges are likely to escalate over time. This pattern, which has been studied among parents and aggressive children, and in families of mentally ill individuals, among others, often requires explicit attention, emphasizing the construction of more functional alternatives.

Some conflicts occur in any family (and conflicts as defined in some ways can even be productive; Markman, 1991). Well-functioning families, however, have available repertoires for containing conflicts so that they do not escalate or spread into unrelated areas, and have developed problem-solving communication skills that enable them to move from issue to solution without damaging relationships through reliance on excessive aversives. Interventive strategies for reducing aversive exchange are discussed in chapter 4.

Communication

Effective communication is essential for clarifying what is experienced as reinforcing or aversive, and for helping family members to develop the empathy necessary for authentic intimacy (which most human beings value as deeply reinforcing). An enormous body of literature examines communication within families, but three essential repertoires capture most of the key dynamics. The first repertoire is the ability to really listen to and hear each other, as opposed to either refusing to listen or acting as if one is listening while really doing something else (like planning one's own response). The second repertoire involves the willingness and skills to express oneself authentically. The third repertoire, which relies on listening and authentic expression, is problem solving, which can be further disaggregated into a series of separate tasks. All of these communicative repertoires can be learned; strategies for constructing and enhancing them are presented in chapter 5.

Acceptance

While some transactional patterns can and should be changed in the course of family consultation, in recent years there has been increasing recognition of the need in well functioning families for members to have the skills to empathize with each other, and to accept aspects of themselves, each other, their relationships, and their world that may not be changeable, or that may be very costly to try to change (Hayes, Jacobson, Follette, & Dougher, 1994). For example, spouses may need to achieve a level of mutual acceptance of physical changes that accompany aging, and family members may need to accept temperamental differences and preferences among themselves that can be viewed alternatively as enriching or as aversive. Acceptance-based approaches are at the cutting edge of contemporary relationship theory and practice and appear to be useful in situations where nothing else works. Strategies for addressing issues of acceptance when they are identified as important in the assessment are explored in chapter 5.

Flexibility

Every family experiences changes as a result of both developmental transitions over the life course of individuals (children beginning school, for example), seasonal and cultural cycles, major individual or environmental changes (for example, illness or economic shifts), and day-to-day variations. There are several core repertoires required to manage these changes effectively and creatively. These include (1) acceptance (again), (2) problem-solving skills, (3) approaches for transmitting cultural practices useful for managing such transitions (for example, providing advice—rules—for dealing with particular developmental transitions), and (4) responsiveness to changing occasions. These social skills involve three dimensions: behavioral repertoires, the consequences for those behaviors, and the extent to which particular behaviors occur on occasions when they are likely to be effective. These domains can be viewed in a three-dimensional space as shown in Figure 2-5.

Flexibility requires that family members have a range of appropriate repertoires available, and that these repertoires be differentially applied on occasions when they are likely to produce positive family outcomes. For ex-

Figure 2-5

The three dimensional space within which social behavior occurs. In the most desirable situation, the client has the required repertoires available, those behaviors occur on appropriate occasions and produce adequately reinforcing consequences. In the sample case shown, the client has somewhat limited repertoires (for example, assertive skills); the repertoires she has tend to occur on appropriate occasions, but the level of available social payoffs is low. This case involves deficits in behavioral repertoires and environmentally available consequences, but strength in terms of appropriate stimulus control. (Sensitivity to available and socially sanctioned consequences could also be considered as a fourth dimension, which could be portrayed using different-sized spheres if desired.) Adapted with permission from Follette, W. C., Bach, P. A., & Follette, V. M. (1993). A behavior-analytic view of psychological health. *The Behavior Analyst, 16,* 303–316. Used with permission.

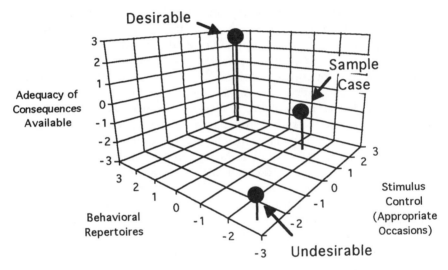

ample, effective parenting of young teens requires a range of repertoires ranging from limit setting to negotiation to ignoring. It is important that parents have these repertoires available, that they use them on appropriate occasions, and that family, friends, and community provide support for these actions. Work with the family may focus on any or all of these dimensions.

Families that are overly rigid tend to have serious problems dealing with change, and may begin to lock some family members, or groups of members, into ineffective roles. For example, family therapists often notice dysfunctional alliances that can develop in families, often involving triangles in which two members (for example, one parent and a child) may ally against another (for example, the other parent). Two family members may also team up to care for another (perhaps a developmentally delayed child), sometimes a useful pattern, but sometimes one that builds dependency, depending on how flexibly it is played out (Reid, 1985). Problems between parents can sometimes also be displaced on a child (the "identified patient"), although this pattern has sometimes been overemphasized (Jacobson & Christiansen, 1996). The patterns themselves are not so much the problem as is the rigidity with which they are maintained, regardless of situational factors.

At the same time, excessive flexibility can lead to chaos, a situation in which family members act randomly without regard to appropriate occasions. People are generally adapted to function best in relatively predictable situations, and family rituals (like rituals associated with other cultural groups) can therefore be very helpful in maintaining systemic equilibrium. These can be daily rituals (eating a meal together), seasonal rituals (around holidays, for example), or developmental rituals; in each case, the situation evokes repertoires that produce predictable reinforcers for family members. (Rituals can, of course, also be aversive, in which case they may appropriately become interventive focal issues.)

Ethnic and other cultural differences are also important here. Different cultures have developed varied strategies for managing changes and transitions; in fact, they have much to teach each other about possible alternatives. When some members of the family experience multiple and often conflicting sets of practices (for example, a woman from some traditional cultures exposed to the women's movement at work, or immigrant youths exposed to European American media and school systems), negotiating strategies for coping with change that are acceptable within both cultures is often a major focus of family work.

All of these repertoires are generally required for a family to function in a way that is satisfying for all members; most families will have strengths in some, which can then be used as resources in constructing others. While the social worker may be tempted to focus on everything at once, in most cases family work is time-limited (either because of funding mechanisms or due to family preference), and it is therefore usually necessary to identify with family members a small number of key repertoires on which to focus. Change in even a small number of repertoires may require extensive practice and refinement, so it is important to be realistic in planning interventive strategies and tasks.

Individual Factors

Family functioning is affected not only by exchanges with other systems and transactional events among family members, but also by individual factors.

For example, if one (or more) family members is experiencing serious physical or mental illness, or struggling with substance abuse, the impact on the
family can be enormous. It is important to distinguish, however, between
cause and effect. For example, schizophrenia is now recognized as an illness
with a biological basis (it is not caused by family dynamics), but its course
can be substantially affected by the way in which the family deals with it
(Falloon, 1991; Halford, 1991). Similarly, while all family members are
deeply affected by addictions to alcohol or drugs, popular literature related
to "codependency" often suggests that other family members (usually the
spouse) are in some way responsible for the continuing addictive behavior.
There is no empirical basis for this assertion, since addiction appears to be
the result of learning processes (Herrnstein & Prelec, 1997; Ainslie, 1992),
probably in concert with certain biological processes (Leukefeld, Miller &
Hayes, 1996). Under those circumstances, attribution of responsibility to
the spouse can be a serious injustice.

At the same time, within a shared-power frame, family members can do
much to contribute to moderating the effects, and in some cases to the solution, of such problems. Chapter 10 provides data-based examples of such
strategies. The stress associated with coping with individual issues can also
be debilitating and demoralizing, and family approaches like those discussed here, as well as individual approaches such as stress management, acceptance-based and cognitive work, and exposure to supportive networks
(see Mattaini, 1997, for detail) can be useful under such circumstances.

Collecting Data for the Ecobehavioral Scan

Where does the information required to complete the ecobehavioral scan
come from? Certainly, family interviews are often the most efficient
method, drawing on questions like those listed in Table 2-2. The most accurate data, however, often come from observations, which can be conducted as a collaborative effort between the social worker and family members. The most crucial observations include patterns of positive and aversive
exchanges among family members, which can be observed during the interview, in analogue tasks like a role play in which family members replay a
challenging episode that occurred at home, or can be self-monitored by
family members themselves (see below).

The observations most likely to be consistent with ordinary family functioning occur in the natural environment, particularly in the home. This is
one reason to use home visits whenever possible. There are many cues present in the home for family members to accurately recall events and to re-
experience emotional reactions. Replaying episodes may be more realistic
in the actual setting where they occurred. In addition, and crucially,

changes and solutions developed and practiced in the home are far more likely to be used by the family outside of the consultation setting, because there are no issues of transfer of training. Social work historically led the way in recognizing the importance of home visiting, of observing and intervening in the client's own world; while office visits may be less expensive and more convenient for the worker, home visits are often more consistent with excellence in providing services.

Observations of intrafamilial dynamics should involve not only the frequency of positive and aversive events, but also the circumstances under which they occur. Sequential patterns of exchange are often crucial. For example, Burman, John, & Margolin (1992) studied differences among physically aggressive, verbally aggressive, withdrawing, and nondistressed couples. Among their findings, the researchers observed that in all types of distressed couples, husbands tended to become more defensive if their wives made a critical statement (and their wives in turn tended to escalate), but in nondistressed couples husbands were generally nonprovocable. Also, the overall rate of offensive verbal statements (like criticisms) among wives in physically aggressive couples in a challenging discussion task was 29 percent. If their husbands made offensive statements first, however, that rate increased to 40 percent. In nondistressed couples, by contrast, wives' overall rate of offensive negative statements was only 12 percent, and this did not increase if their husbands made an offensive statement to the wives. Both husbands and wives in the nondistressed couples also made more positive statements to each other than did couples in any of the distressed conditions. More detail about this study is found in chapter 6.

In another example, in far too many families a stable culture of coercion develops. In these families, one person (a parent, a partner, or a child) makes a demand of another. A second family member then reciprocates with an angry refusal, because that person has learned that such a refusal sometimes results in the demand's being withdrawn. The first person may then back down, or may escalate, making an even more aggressive demand. The second person may then give in (reinforcing escalation), or may in turn escalate further. The only ways out of this coercive cycle are either for one party to give in, reinforcing the other's escalation, or for the conflict to continue to escalate to the point of physical aggression and violence. (See Patterson, 1976, for further detail.)

Some of the most useful observations of family processes can be completed by family members, using self-monitoring approaches. A number of these are discussed in later chapters, but some examples may be useful here. In the early stages of parent education, for instance, parents are often asked to keep track of how often they give their children instructions, and of how often the children comply. In addition to being useful for determining how serious an issue child compliance is, such data can help to reach a joint understanding of whether parents are also making demands too often (Sloane, 1976/1988). As another example, a calendar indicating the number of hours a couple spend together over the course of a week, and what they do during that time, can be useful both for clarifying the issues present, and for identifying positive areas that might be expanded.

Families can also provide valuable information by completing standardized Rapid Assessment Instruments, which can identify areas of satisfaction and dissatisfaction, while providing data for tracking progress or lack of it over time, very useful for practice monitoring. For example, I commonly use the Marital Happiness Scale (Azrin, Naster, & Jones, 1973) with couples. This simple instrument allows each member of the couple to rate their satisfaction with 10 common relationship dimensions (for example, communication, child rearing, money) as well as overall satisfaction, and can be used for each session. Similarly, the Index of Family Relations (Hudson, 1992) can be used for multigenerational work. Fischer and Corcoran (1994) provide a wide range of rapid assessment instruments that may be of use for family work. At the same time, it is crucial to remember that such instruments are often somewhat distal from actual events; the closer the data collected is to actual behavior, the more likely it will be both valid and clinically useful.

One tool that has been widely used in family-centered practice is the genogram (Hartman, 1978). There is some risk that clinical time spent completing a complex genogram could be better spent in more focused work, and generic genograms are not commonly used in ecobehavioral work, except in special cases like adoptions, where every bit of information available about the family of origin may be treasured later by the child. In general, however, I recommend the use of two forms of genogram:

1. Simple genograms that clarify complex family structures where it may otherwise be difficult to understand parental and sibling relationships and household compositions.
2. Behavioral genograms that explore particular focal issues relevant to the case, such as serious mental illness or substance abuse over multiple generations.

For example, in a case involving substance abuse, there are significant advantages to knowing how widely substances have been and are used in the family, to explore intergenerational patterns, and to begin to examine possible social and environmental determinants of the problem.

In addition to transactional patterns within the family and exchanges with others outside the family, the functioning of individual family members is also part of a broad contextual scan. Individuals with severe mental illness, children struggling with learning disabilities, substance abusers, and persons with serious physical illnesses or disabilities living with (or in frequent contact with) a family can both dramatically influence and be influenced by family practices and events, and these issues should certainly be explored as part of the assessment.

The outcome of an adequate ecobehavioral scan is a richly textured picture of the family in its world. Clinical research indicates the kind of image that may emerge. A study done to explore ecobehavioral patterns common among families in the caseload of a family mental health agency in a large urban area (Mattaini, Grellong, & Abramovitz, 1992), found eight relatively discrete family clusters, accounting for 95 percent of the client population studied. The largest group (21 percent) consisted of "multideficit families," characterized by very poor family functioning with low rates of positive exchange and high rates of aversives. These families also tended to have low incomes, to live in inadequate housing in crime-ridden neighborhoods, and to include family members with substance abuse, work performance problems, and acute chronic physical disabilities. Intervention with such a family should certainly be very different from that with the next largest group (18 percent), relatively middle income but "extremely isolated" families, which tended to be involved in quite limited positive or negative exchange either within or outside the household. (This study is discussed in more detail in chapter 3.)

IDENTIFYING FOCAL ISSUES

Once the social worker and family have clarified the current situation, the next step is to identify focal areas to move from that state toward the envisioned goal-state. This is a crucial assessment function, because it is not possible to directly address everything at once (although change in one area may, and often does, resonate in others as well). An agreement should emerge from this third assessment stage about a small number (generally one to three) of focal issues, specific goals to be constructed (Schwartz & Goldiamond, 1975), or problems to be addressed. These foci can be adjusted and recontracted later, but need at any point to be clear.

Clear focus is crucial to effective work, as well as to selecting what to monitor to determine whether clients are reaching their goals. While positive states or repertoires to be constructed are the ideal (for example, "To increase the amount of positive time we spend together"), clarification of problems to be addressed (for example, "To reduce the number and severity of arguments we have") usually also suggests the alternatives to be constructed, so either approach can work. To the extent possible, the focal issues selected should be agreeable to each member of the family with whom the worker is involved; sometimes defining such goals in somewhat global terms (like, "improving communication") can be a starting point, although more specificity is eventually required.

Selecting a small number of focal issues can be difficult, particularly when many challenges and hopes have been identified in the earlier stages of the assessment. The following are some criteria that can be used, although there is no invariant order among them; the final choices involve professional judgment and family values. Issues can be selected on the basis of:

- order of concern to the family
- order of salience—in some cases, major foci jump out from the ecobehavioral scan or ecomap
- difficulty of resolution—early progress on simpler issues can build hope and commitment for those that are more difficult.

Additionally, there are cases in which some issues must be addressed before others can be; for example, it may not be possible to improve parent-child relations in certain families until substance abuse has in some way been addressed. Families often are struggling with many issues, and it may be frustrating not to be able to deal with them all, but this is the reality of practice. Most family work is relatively short term; regardless of length of involvement, partializing the case situation is always crucial, because there is only so much that can be done at once without the work becoming diffuse and potentially confusing. Choices among focal issues must usually be made, therefore, and the family must always have the strongest voice in this decision.

At this stage, it is also essential to consider how the family and worker will know if the goals are being achieved, if progress is being made or maintenance achieved, if the problems are being solved. Doing so requires clear specification of what will change—in particular, *whose behavior will change in what ways*—if the goal-state is being approached. This clarity is essential for completing the next assessment function (contextual analysis), and also for monitoring purposes.

Note that the goals established need not relate only to the behavior of family members. In many cases the actions of other persons, or groups of persons, in the family's contextual situation may be the target issues—for example, inducing an eligibility worker to provide access to resources, or a school teacher to change her approach to a learning disabled child. Regardless of whose behavior is the focus of the work, the actions or exchanges targeted need to be as clearly specified as possible, and then made part of the contract established with the family.

Once focal issues have been identified, it is important to determine how they will be monitored, to track whether and how well they are being addressed. This can be done using simple graphs like the one shown in Figure 2-6, which shows satisfaction with three relationship dimensions included on the Marital Happiness Scale for each partner in a couple seen by the author. Communication, affection, and personal independence were among the areas identified by the couple as focal issues.

The general trajectories were positive over five sessions of treatment, and the levels at a later follow-up point demonstrated continued improvement. (Several booster sessions were provided on an "as-needed" basis at challenging points in between the block of treatment sessions and the follow-up point several months later.)

Another approach to monitoring, particularly useful for families struggling with multiple issues involving exchanges with other environmental systems, is the use of sequential, quantified transactional ecomaps like that shown in Figure 2-7. The intensity of positive and negative exchanges can be rated by the social worker, the family, or one or more family members separately, and plotted over time, thus portraying not only shifts in particular exchanges, but overall systemic transactional patterns as well.

Notice the two black "X"s found on the "intake" panel of this figure. One is located within the family, clarifying that high levels of internal aversive exchange is one of the focal issues identified; the other highlights the problematic school situation of the oldest child. The sequential ecomaps allow the worker and the family to trace progress in these areas, but also to notice other issues that may surface, like the intensifying conflict between the single mother and her ex-boyfriend, which is likely to have multiple effects that resonate throughout the case system. A shift in focal issues may be important under such circumstances.

COMPLETING A CONTEXTUAL ANALYSIS OF FOCAL ISSUES

The third assessment function moves to a different analytic level. Theoretical application and critical thinking are the crucial repertoires required as the social worker, in concert with the family, makes sense of the contextual factors that support problem behaviors identified as focal issues, or that will be required to shape constructive alternatives. Whether the focal issues involve family practices, stressful exchanges with an employer, or obtaining entitlements from governmental officials, this step is crucial to effectiveness.

Figure 2-6

Graphs tracing shifts in a couple's relationship during and following social work consultation.

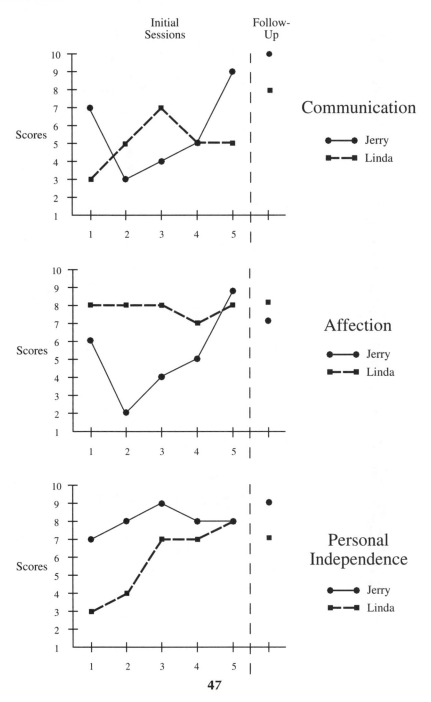

Communication

Affection

Personal Independence

Figure 2-7

Sequential ecomaps depicting changes in the case over time.

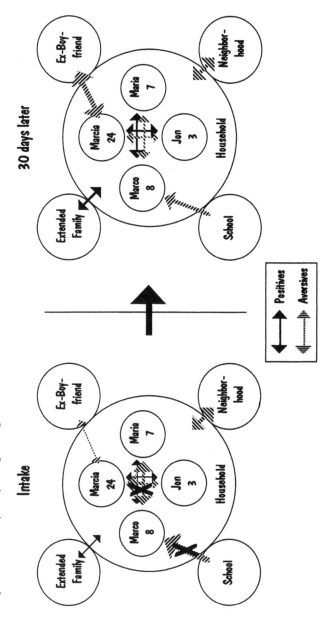

Professional social work practice does not move directly from problem to solution. Rather, understanding the issues in an individualized way enables the work to focus where it is most likely to be useful. Reid (1992) discusses a somewhat similar process of contextual analysis, in which the social worker considers the causes of the problem, the obstacles to resolving it, and the resources that may be required to do so. An ecobehavioral approach, however, can be deeper, providing specific guidance about important antecedents or consequences related to actions, practices, and repertoires identified as focal issues.

Recalling the three-dimensional space involved in social behavior shown in Figure 2-5, contextual analysis focuses in general on the following questions:

- Do family members, agency representatives, collaterals, or whoever else is involved in the focal issues, have the necessary skills in their repertoires?
- Do these players use these skills on appropriate occasions?
- What are the consequences when they do?

Answering these questions results in clear directions for intervention. Ordinarily, the first question is the easiest to answer and address, while the third is the most difficult and critical. In the sections that follow, we look at each, with special emphasis on the third.

If family members or others simply lack the skills required to address the issues, skills training can be very useful. Much intrafamily work, for example, focuses on training family members in areas like communication skills, parenting skills, and conflict containment. While the social worker often needs to provide modeling, opportunities to practice, and high levels of reinforcement for initial attempts that the family and worker can gradually refine through shaping, eventually using such skills should result in better outcomes in the natural environment.

The second relevant dimension in contextual analysis is the *discrimination of appropriate occasions* for behavior. Family members commonly have effective behaviors in their repertoires, but do not use them in the family. For example, many individuals know how to act nonprovocably and do so with their employers, but do not do so with family members. The goal in such cases is for the family and social worker to encourage and prompt such action in the family, and in the beginning to ensure that it is reinforced.

Another example of inappropriate discrimination of occasions is what is often called *enabling*. In families where one member is abusing substances, other family members often act in ways that make it easier to continue the problem behavior or protect the abuser from negative consequences (for example, buying liquor for the abuser, or bailing him out of jail). Under many circumstances, acting in helpful and protective ways can be very important and useful practices within a family. The outcome for both the individual and the family can be negative, however, if being "helpful" enables substance abuse. Learning new rules about the kind of occasions that call for specific actions is then a crucial step toward improving family life (see chapter 10 for more information). Overall, if contextual analysis produces accurate information about the family practices and behaviors that will be effective, and about the occasions when they will be, natural positive consequences can often maintain them.

Because consequences ultimately shape behavior (see chapter 1), attention to patterns of consequences that define family culture is always important. One useful consequence-based approach, when focal issues involve an excess of problematic exchanges, is *functional analysis*. This involves determining the function of problem behavior, in other words, what consequences, on what occasions, shape the behavior—why it occurs. With many developmentally delayed individuals, for example, practice researchers have discovered that problem behaviors (like self-injurious behavior—SIB) typically have one of several functions, and identifying the function leads to interventive options. If SIB functions to reduce "demand" in a situation, teaching new ways to ask for a break often is useful, for example. If SIB primarily increases attention received, teaching new ways to get attention can reduce the problem. This approach (called *functional communication training*) can produce dramatic results (Carr & Durand, 1985; Durand & Carr, 1992). A similar approach can be used with other focal issues. For example, if one member of a couple is using fights to produce some "space"—separate time and personal autonomy—and this function can be identified, it is often possible to construct less aversive ways to ask for a break.

An emphasis on the functions of behavior is one of the distinguishing features of *functional family therapy*, developed by Alexander and his colleagues (Barton & Alexander, 1991; Morris, Alexander, & Waldron, 1988). There are two critical considerations in this model: the function(s) of behavior themselves and the "meaning" (self-talk) that people use to describe the functions of behavior in the family. For example, a child may be tantruming to gain parental attention (the function), but the parent may describe the reason the child is doing so to herself and others as the child "trying to make her life difficult." Helping the parent to redefine the function of the behavior, then helping the family to find more satisfying ways to provide attention to the child, would be identified as important interventive tasks. As Falloon (1991) notes, people in general do the best they can, given the options they recognize having; family members, however, may need help in believing that about each other.

The functions of behavior, the consequences or outcomes of actions, may be intrapersonal (some self-stimulatory behavior among developmentally delayed children), intrafamilial (for example, arguments resulting in increased closeness when a couple makes up), environmental (youths who stay out late to be with friends), or a combination (a woman who works late, resulting in both satisfying a demanding boss and avoiding spending time with a critical partner at home). People may or may not be aware of the functions of their own behavior. Asking family members about the outcomes of actions sometimes is helpful; observation can also suggest reasonable hypotheses. In most cases, the social worker and family will begin with such hypotheses, then test them through interventions. If the interventions do not work, a closer look at functions may be necessary, as in the example above of the woman working long hours. If anxiety about satisfying work demands can be satisfied, but she still avoids spending time at home, clearly something more is going on.

Familiarity with empirical work in the field can be crucial in functional analysis. For example, serious depression is often a multidetermined phenomenon. Depressed persons often experience many aversives which contribute directly to depression; they do not experience many reinforcers due to lack of activity, and they may be biologically unresponsive to those they do experience. Often a social component is also involved. Biglan (1991) and his colleagues discovered that acting in depressed ways can be functional, protecting the individual from aggressive acts from other family members. When a person appears sad and vulnerable, others often do not criticize them or make many demands on them. When the depressed person begins to act less depressed, however, according to Biglan's research, other family members, by then quite frustrated, act more aggressively. This can result in increased depressive behavior both directly, because of the increase in aversives, and indirectly, since acting that way is protective. In other words, "depression" can be both a biological and an emotional outcome, and a functional pattern of behavior. (For more detail about multidimensional intervention with depressed individuals and their families, see Mattaini, 1997, chapter 7.)

Some questions that may be useful for understanding the functions of current behavior are shown in the Interview Guide (Table 2-2). The central issue in these cases is to determine the consequences present, and think through with the family other possible ways of obtaining those. When family members are not doing something useful that they know how to do, like recognizing positive steps taken by others, the crucial issues usually involve determining what reinforcers are missing, and how to construct them.

The reinforcers selected should be as easy to access and "natural" to the family environment as possible. For example, privileges like time spent playing a game with a parent or watching favorite videotapes may be easier, more natural, and healthier for a parent to provide than expensive toys or electronic equipment. Simply increasing the level of social reinforcers and recognition available can be a very powerful intervention. Chapter 4 provides more detail about increasing rates of reinforcement for positive action in the family, but a few crucial points should be clarified here. First, some people believe (self-talk) that other family members should act in positive ways simply because it is "right." People with highly developed rule-governed repertoires sometimes do, but acquiring such repertoires is a long-term process, and for children in particular a gradual one. In fact, learning to "do the right thing" occurs as a result of extensive external reinforcement in the beginning, and is later internalized as rules and equivalence relations. Second, it is often counterproductive to give everything noncontingently and without concern for reciprocation, since this can be a prescription for exploitation. Far better is a family culture that provides high levels of recognition and reinforcement for positive action, increasing those behaviors and improving the quality of life for everyone. This should be done explicitly and authentically, not covertly or manipulatively.

IDENTIFYING INTERVENTIVE TASKS

Given an adequate contextual analysis of focal issues, selecting appropriate interventions for the family situation is relatively straightforward. If that analysis suggests lack of skills, skills training is indicated, for example. If one focal issue identified is that the family lacks access to adequate nutrition, and contextual analysis indicates that the reason the family has not yet obtained food stamps is because an eligibility worker has not completed the paperwork, then attention to consequences affecting that worker and perhaps her supervisor, probably through advocacy, will be included in the intervention plan. Interventive tasks, following directly from the assessment, are not limited to issues in family dynamics, but may address any part of the ecobehavioral field.

A good deal of collaborative practice with families can be framed in terms of "self-management." The general model for self-management is (1) *identifying the overall goals* (focal issues), (2) *pinpointing* the behaviors to be changed and the occasions when they should occur (this takes place during contextual analysis), (3) *tracking* (monitoring) the incidence of the pinpointed actions, and (4) *providing adequate consequences* when the pinpointed actions occur on appropriate occasions. Clients can often implement most or all of these steps themselves, including tracking progress on goals and pinpoints; this tracking is a form of self-monitoring. Self-monitoring itself is an empowering strategy (Kopp, 1993), and self-management as an overall model is highly congruent with a shared power perspective on social work practice.

As an example, if a couple has an overall goal of "feeling satisfied" with their relationship, pinpoints identified in the contextual analysis might include increasing the incidence of positive exchange and active listening events. The couple might keep a record of how often these occur (say, on a chart on the refrigerator), and might recognize each other for taking the pinpointed actions; they might also track "recognizing" behaviors, as an additional level of self-monitoring. Self-monitoring may be difficult in certain circumstances, for example in cases where a family is currently living in a disorganized and aversive shelter for homeless families. In those cases, or where literacy is an issue, creative adaptations, including retrospective records constructed in meetings with the social worker, can be useful. If families are unwilling to participate in even simple self-monitoring, they may not yet have genuinely bought into the social work interventive process as partners, and more attention to engagement and envisioning is required.

When ongoing counting of events is not reasonable, another simple approach to tracking is the use of a *behaviorally anchored rating scale* (BARS) (Daniels, 1994). Figure 2-8 shows an example of a BARS in which members of a couple rate their experiences since the last session.

When constructing a BARS, the social worker and family members

Figure 2-8

A behaviorally anchored rating scale for level of positive exchange between a couple.

Level of Goal Attainment	Frequency of Positive Acts of "Giving" by your partner:
5	Positive acts of giving occur several times a day
4	Positive acts of giving occur at least once a day
3	Positive acts of giving occur once or twice a week
2	Positive acts of giving occur only occasionally
1	Positive acts of giving never occur

should specify the actions to be tracked in clear behavioral terms to the extent possible, because doing so is likely to lead to more valid tracking. In this case, if both the husband and wife originally indicated that their partner was functioning at level 2 on this scale, and at the present time the wife places an X on level 3, and the husband on level 5, this would suggest that some progress is occurring; however, the wife is perhaps observing fewer positive actions than is her husband. This may be an accurate statement of events, or may be a difference of perception, but either way it is important data. Multiple rating scales of this kind can be combined, and are then simply a different form of Goal Attainment Scaling (Kiresuk & Sherman, 1968). In couples or family work, it may also be useful to have clients rate themselves and each other on such scales to determine the extent of observational consistency among family members.

The more the worker and family know about the universe of possible interventions, the more likely they will choose well. There are in general two types of tasks, those that occur within the worker-family sessions, and those that occur at other times or places (see Reid, 1992, for extensive discussion of "session tasks" and "home/environment tasks"). Modeling and role-playing communication skills with the social worker are examples of the first, while practicing the same skills at home between sessions is an example of the second.

The chapters that follow describe a wide array of interventive tasks that can be selectively adapted to fit many different family situations. No listing can possibly capture all of the possibilities and permutations available, since every family is different. Still, some core principles provide critical strategic guidance:

1. Family-centered practice in a shared power frame is a co-creative process. Each of the parties involved and affected (family, worker, and sometimes collaterals) should have a strong, meaningful voice in designing the case plan, to which each makes contributions from his or her skills, knowledge, gifts—his or her unique powers. The social worker can provide information and support, recognize contributions and structure the process, but decisions and implementation in this approach are not unilateral. It is often far more important that a plan that is acceptable to all emerges from the collaborative assessment process than that it include any specific components. Those involved will generally provide each other with richer reinforcement within such an arrangement, and it is therefore more likely that behavior will change.

2. If the family members have participated throughout in the assessment, then they are well positioned to be deeply involved in developing interventive plans as well. In child welfare cases, for example, when informa-

tion has been shared among all parties, when the biological and foster families have had access to and contributed to the written assessment report, and everyone's perceptions of the ecobehavioral situation have been taken seriously, participants are far more likely to engage fully in developing and implementing interventive tasks (Lowery & Mattaini, in press).

3. The tasks selected should focus primarily on the construction of an improved reality (and not primarily on decreasing problems). Those tasks must be clear and behaviorally specific, but may allow substantial room for creativity. The responsibilities of everyone involved should be clearly spelled out—and everyone should have such responsibilities. The tasks will usually involve learning new repertoires, determining the appropriate timing for use of each repertoire, and somehow enriching the level of reinforcement available for positive behaviors and practices. The same principles apply to environmental exchanges as well. Advocacy and negotiating with a problem landlord may sometimes require the use of legal threats or public embarrassment, but this is ordinarily not the place to begin. It may be possible to facilitate an atmosphere of problem-solving, in which the worker and family can genuinely listen to the landlord's concerns, and he to theirs. When possible, a relationship based on such exchanges is more likely to be maintained than one built on threats. Therefore, in an ecobehavioral model, interventive tasks at all levels far more often emphasize the acquisition of prosocial skills and practices, and the construction of reinforcement networks for them, than the use of aversives.

4. One set of tasks inherent in an ecobehavioral approach is ongoing monitoring of the state of the case. Particular attention should be paid, of course, to whether progress (or maintenance where that is the goal) is occurring on focal issues. If it is not, more attention to assessment, and to the contextual analysis (third assessment function) in particular, is required. At the same time, other changes occurring in the family's ecobehavioral field should also be considered. In some cases, changes resulting from the intervention (say, increased communication between a teenager and one parent) may have unexpected effects in other areas (say, increasing tension between parents). In other cases, unrelated events (for example, a parent's being laid off at work) may dramatically change the situation for the entire family, and may require a reformulation of the case. Observational data, scores on rapid assessment instruments, self-monitoring data, sequential ecomaps, and other monitoring approaches discussed above can be used in whatever way makes sense to the worker/family team. The family can, and usually should, have the strongest voices in tracking progress. It is important to remember, how-

ever, that this is one of the areas of expertise that the social worker as a professional is expected to bring to the table. If a case is not being monitored, no one knows whether the family is moving toward its vision, whether its situation is improving or deteriorating.

CONCLUSION

The material covered in this chapter is relatively generic; work with families always requires some level of engagement and attention to their visions of the way their life might change, for example. Families that do not recognize that their voices and concerns matter, that do not (at least tentatively) agree to engage with the worker even in involuntary cases will not benefit from social work intervention. It is the social worker's job to find ways to authentically engage families in a shared power dynamic and to help them to elaborate their visions of success.

Similarly, effective intervention relies on an adequate assessment that takes into account the ecobehavioral field within which family members, and the family culture, are embedded. Clarity of work requires clarity about direction—the identification of focal issues. Changing the situation requires understanding the behavioral dynamics present—contextual analysis. Such an assessment process produces clear guidance about steps required to construct an alternative, more reinforcing, reality with the family.

The chapters that follow elaborate useful classes of interventive strategies and techniques in further detail, outlining approaches to work with problems with environmental systems and constructing more satisfying family cultures, for example. Later chapters in the book deal with approaches for work with special groups and issues—couples, parenting, violence, substance abuse, and serious mental illness in the family.

From the discussion in this chapter, the following key practice principles emerge:

- The four core processes in practice with families are engagement, envisioning, assessment, and intervention. While those processes tend to occur roughly in the order listed, they are overlapping and recursive in practice.
- Engagement involves joining the culture of the family in a co-creative process of shared power.
- Envisioning is a process of elaborating with the family an improved contextual reality to be constructed through the work the family and social worker do together. This strategy is incommensurate with thinking of practice with families as therapy to remediate pathology.

- Assessment itself involves four overlapping and recursive functions: completing a broad ecobehavioral scan of the family's situation in context, identifying focal issues (which may involve exchanges with external systems as well as within the family), contextual analysis of each focal issue, and the selection of interventive tasks.
- Interventions selected with the family may include constructing new repertoires and family practices, determining when to use those repertoires, and enriching the consequences for positive actions, as well as tasks involved in shifting the balance of positive and aversive exchanges with extrafamilial actors and systems.

REFERENCES

Ainslie, G. (1992). *Picoeconomics: The strategic interaction of successive motivational states within the person.* Cambridge: Cambridge University Press.

Azrin, N. H., Naster, B. J., & Jones, R. (1973). Reciprocity counseling: A rapid learning-based procedure for marital counseling. *Behavior Research & Therapy, 11,* 365–382.

Barton, C., & Alexander, J. F. (1991). Functional family therapy. In A. S. Gurman & D. P. Kniskern (Eds.), *Handbook of family therapy, Volume 1* (pp. 403–443). New York: Brunner/Mazel.

Biglan, A. (1991). Distressed behavior and its context. *The Behavior Analyst, 14,* 157–169.

Burman, B., John, R. S., & Margolin, G. (1992). Observed patterns of conflict in violent, nonviolent, and nondistressed couples. *Behavioral Assessment, 14,* 15–37.

Carr, E. G., & Durand, V. M. (1985). Reducing behavior problems through functional communication training. *Journal of Applied Behavior Analysis, 18,* 111–126.

Daniels, A. C. (1994). *Bringing out the best in people.* New York: McGraw-Hill.

de Shazer, S. (1985). *Keys to solution in brief therapy.* New York: W. W. Norton.

Durand, V. M., & Carr, E. G. (1992). An analysis of maintenance following functional communication training. *Journal of Applied Behavior Analysis, 25,* 777–794.

Falloon, I. R. H. (1991). Behavioral family therapy. In A. S. Gurman & D. P. Kniskern (Eds.), *Handbook of family therapy, Volume II* (pp. 65–95). New York: Brunner/Mazel.

Fischer, J., & Corcoran, K. (1994). *Measures for clinical practice* (volumes 1 & 2). New York: Free Press.

Follette, W. C., Bach, P.A., & Follette, V. M. (1993). A behavior-analytic view of psychological health. *The Behavior Analyst, 16,* 303–316.

Furman, B., & Ahola, T. (1992). *Solution talk: Hosting therapeutic conversations.* New York: W. W. Norton.

Germain, C. B. (1968). Social study, past and future. *Social Casework, 49,* 403–409.

Hartman, A. (1978). Diagrammatic assessment of family relationships. *Social Casework, 59,* 465–476.

Hayes, S. C., Jacobson, N. S., Follette, V. M., & Dougher, M. J. (Ed.), (1994). *Acceptance and change: Content and context in psychotherapy.* Reno, NV: Context Press.

Halford, W. K. (1991). Beyond expressed emotion: Behavioral assessment of family interaction associated with the course of schizophrenia. *Behavioral Assessment, 13,* 99–123.

Herrnstein, R. J., & Prelec, D. (1997). A theory of addiction. In Herrnstein, R. J., *The matching law: Papers in psychology and economics* (pp. 160–187). New York: Russell Sage.

Hudson, W. W. (1992). *WALMYR assessment scales scoring manual.* Tempe, AZ: WALMYR Publishing.

Jacobson, N. S., & Christensen, A. (1996). *Integrative couple therapy.* New York: Norton.

Kiresuk, T. J., & Sherman, R. E. (1968). Goal Attainment Scaling: A general method for evaluating comprehensive community mental health programs. *Community Mental Health Journal,* 443–453.

Kopp, J. (1993). Self-observation: An empowerment strategy in assessment. In J. B. Rauch (Ed.), *Assessment: A sourcebook for social work practice,* (pp. 255–268). Milwaukee: Families International, Inc.

Leukefeld, C. G., Miller, T. W., & Hayes, L. (1996). Drug abuse. In M. A. Mattaini & B. A. Thyer (Eds.), *Finding solutions to social problems: Behavioral strategies for change* (pp. 373–396). Washington, DC: American Psychological Association.

Lowery, C. T. & Mattaini, M. A. (in press). The co-construction of empowerment cultures in child welfare. In W. Shera and L. Wells (Eds.) , *International perspectives on empowerment practice.* New York: Columbia University Press.

Malott, R. W., Whaley, D. L., & Malott, M. E. (1997). *Elementary principles of behavior* (3rd ed.). Upper Saddle River, NJ: Prentice Hall.

Markman, H. J. (1991). Constructive marital conflict is NOT an oxymoron. *Behavioral Assessment, 13,* 83–96.

Mattaini, M. A. (1997). *Clinical practice with individuals.* Washington, DC: NASW Press.

Mattaini, M. A., Grellong, B. A., & Abramovitz, R. (1992). The clientele of a child and family mental health agency: Empirically-derived household clusters and implications for practice. *Research on Social Work Practice, 2,* 380–404.

Minuchin, S. (1974). *Families and family therapy.* Cambridge, MA: Harvard University Press.

McGoldrick, M., Giordano, J., & Pearce, J. K. (1996). *Ethnicity and family therapy* (2nd ed.). New York: Guilford.

Morris, S. B., Alexander, J. F., & Waldron, H. (1988). Functional family therapy. In I. R. H. Falloon (Ed.), *Handbook of behavioral family therapy* (pp. 107–127).

Patterson, G. R. (1976). The aggressive child: Victim and architect of a coercive system. In E. J. Mash, L. A. Hamerlynck, & L. C. Handy (Eds.), *Behavior modification and families* (pp. 267–316). New York: Brunner/Mazel.

Patterson, G. R., & Forgatch, M. S. (1985). Therapist behavior as a determinant for client non-compliance: A paradox for the behavior modifier. *Journal of Consulting and Clinical Psychology, 53,* 846–851.

Reid, W. J. (1985). *Family problem solving*. New York: Columbia University Press.

Reid, W. J. (1992). *Task Strategies*. New York: Columbia University Press.

Schwartz, A., & Goldiamond, I. (1975). *Social casework: A behavioral approach*. New York: Columbia University Press.

Sloane, H. N. (1976/1988). *The good kid book*. Champaign, IL: Research Press.

Sue, S., & Zane, N. (1987). The role of culture and cultural techniques in psychotherapy. *American Psychologist, 42*(1), 37–45.

Van Treuren, R. R. (1986). Self-perception in family systems: A diagrammatic technique. *Social Casework, 67*, 299–305.

CHAPTER THREE

Interventive Strategies: Enhancing Environmental Exchanges

Families that are unable to access adequate levels of positive exchange with their environments (social and interpersonal, physical, economic, and educational), or that consistently experience high levels of aversive exchange with those environments, are at particularly high risk for multiple problems. Unfortunately, many social workers tend to minimize attention to these issues in practice, preferring to focus narrowly on intrapsychic or intrafamilial issues (Rosen & Livne, 1992; Nurius, Kemp, & Gibson, in press). This may in part be a response to viewing work with environmental systems as somehow less "professional" than those that are considered "therapy."

This is a serious issue, because the most powerful interventions are those that take the environment into account in a meaningful way. Not only is work with environmental events and systems more consistent with a non-pathologizing shared power perspective, it is also often far more effective. For example, multisystemic family intervention (Henggeler, Schoenwald, Borduin, Rowland, & Cunningham, 1998), which takes environmental intervention seriously, is demonstrably effective for dealing with antisocial behavior of children and youths, while many traditional approaches (including individual treatment of the child and play therapy) do not usually make a significant difference with such children.

This is not to say that intrafamilial and individual issues should not be addressed. Rather, work with environmental exchanges can be crucial for addressing problems of fit between family members and other systems, and such work can dramatically affect individual behavior and family dynamics as well, as shown in examples discussed later in this chapter. For instance, changes made within the family (like the use of new parenting skills) are unlikely to be maintained if they are discouraged by family and friends. A solid argument can be made that practice with the family that encompasses the environment in a fundamental way is the most challenging, and the most professional, work a social worker can do. Labeling this work "just case management," for example, is a serious mistake. The environment is powerful; empowered action begins by influencing one's environment, which then reciprocally affects oneself differently. Understanding transactional exchanges among family members and environmental actors is often necessary to make sense of focal issues in a case (Henggeler, Schoenwald, Borduin, Rowland, & Cunningham, 1998). Delinquent behavior often has roots in the family, but may be primarily maintained through interactions with peers and the school system, for example, and work with only one of those components may not be powerful enough to turn the problem around. Environmental work, therefore, is important *both* for addressing specific issues and for changing the aggregate experience of family members. Social support (the availability of reinforcers from others) is demonstrably crucial for everyone (see chapter 7 of Rothman & Sager, 1998), and high levels of aversive experiences can lead to depression, aggression, and other undesirable outcomes (Sidman, 1989). The overall balance is important, since high levels of overall support can buffer the effects of aversives, while high levels of aversives over a long period of time can reduce sensitivity to reinforcers that are available (Dougher & Hackbert, 1994). Social isolation is associated with many family issues, including child maltreatment (Mattaini, McGowan, & Williams, 1996). Conversely, dramatic increases in positive exchange can affect mood and behavior in positive ways (Embry & Flannery, in press). One way to examine available supports with family members is to graphically depict the current situation. The Social Network Map (Gaudin, 1988), one tool for doing so, is shown in Figure 3-1.

Beginning with a blank map, family members individually or as a group plot individuals who are in some way important to them in the appropriate quadrant, with a dot and initials. The closeness of the relationship is depicted by distance from the self (or the family) in the center. Other forms of social support mapping can be found in Mattaini (1993b); a simple computer program that can help sketch exchanges between the household, other persons, and environmental systems can also be helpful (Mattaini, 1993c).

Differential family exposure to environmental events should clearly affect case planning. For example, Figure 3-2 summarizes some of the findings of a study of families who were being seen in a large, multisite outpatient family and child mental health program (Mattaini, Grellong, & Abramovitz, 1992).

In this study, eight separate clusters of families emerged. For example, cluster 1 families experienced moderate to high rates of aversives, not only within the family, but also from extended family, work, school, friends, and

Figure 3-1

Social Network Map. Source: Reprinted from "Treatment of families who neglect their children," by J. M. Gaudin, Jr., 1988, in E. W. Nunnally, C. S. Chilman, & F. M. Cox (Eds.), *Mental illness, delinquency, addictions, and neglect* (p. 180). Newbury Park, CA: Sage Publications. Copyright, 1988, by Sage Publications. Reprinted by permission.

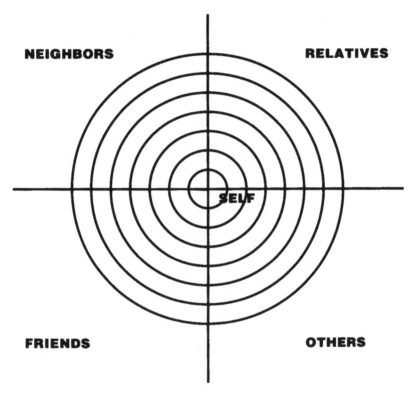

neighborhoods. As a result, plans for addressing these families' situations clearly need to include a broad focus on multiple transactional issues. By contrast, cluster 5 families were characterized by high levels of aversive exchange within the family (and extended family), but high rates of positive exchange with other systems. Intrafamilial dynamics are a natural focus under those circumstances. Cluster 6 families experience few positives from anywhere, within or outside the household; exposure to new sources of reinforcement from *somewhere* is a central issue for such families. (Note that cluster 2 households usually consisted of a single person living alone; exchanges with "each other" therefore are not applicable in that cluster.) The

Figure 3-2

Profiles of household clusters, showing median levels of positive and negative impacts on the household from various systems. Source: Reprinted from M. A. Mattaini, B. A. Grellong, & R. Abramovitz, (1992), The clientele of a child and family mental health agency: Empirically-derived household clusters and implications for practice, *Research on Social Work Practice, 2,* pp. 394–395. Copyright, 1992, by Sage Publications. Reprinted by permission.

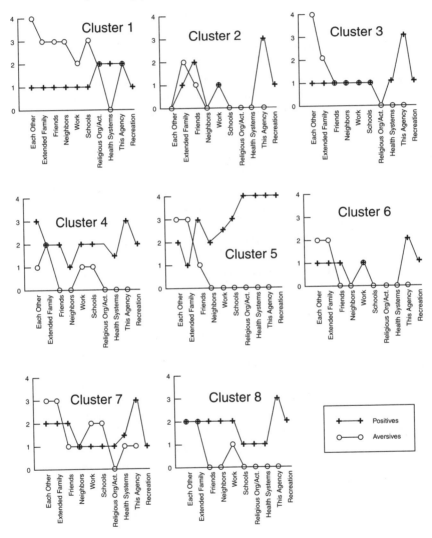

configuration characterizing each of the identified clusters, in fact, provides considerable information about the type and level of intervention that may be required.

THE TRANSACTIONAL ECOMAP

Given the central importance of such environmental exchanges, ecomaps tracing these events are particularly useful tools (Hartman, 1978/1995, Mattaini, 1993b). Transactional ecomaps as described in chapter 2 are particularly valuable for clarifying the family situation in ways that lead directly to interventive planning. These tools can be prepared jointly with families, since doing so helps the social worker and the family members to develop a shared view of the case. Once plotted, the general patterns to be explored include particularly:

• excesses of aversive exchanges with particular environmental systems or actors (which may be unidirectional or reciprocal)
• deficits of positive exchanges with environmental systems or actors (again, unidirectional or reciprocal)
• high rates of aggregate aversive exchanges
• low rates of aggregate positive exchanges.

The first two of these patterns may be important for identifying specific focal issues to be addressed, like a struggle with a school or an assistance payments office in the first case, or lack of close friendships in the second. The third and fourth issues on the list speak to possibly important interventive focuses at a higher level of abstraction, since a high overall rate of stressful and aversive transactions, a low rate of overall positives, or both may be problems in their own right. Each can contribute to individual problems within the family (for example, depression or substance abuse), as well as to collective struggles. On the ecomap, it is important to note not just the overall level of exchange, but also the relative levels of positive and negative exchange. For example, transactions with neighbors who are drug involved may produce stress, but may also offer the only friendships that some families experience. Similarly, a church may be a source of strength, but may also structure contacts with other members who may be judgmental and unsupportive. Personal or systemic relationships are almost never entirely positive or negative, so in most cases both should be examined.

The transactional ecomap can be used as a tool at many points in family work. In assessment, it is generally first developed during the ecobehavioral scan; focal issues are then identified and analyzed based on the image prepared. A goal-state ecomap can be used to refine the vision of the work to be done, and sequential ecomaps can be used as a monitoring tool. As the ecomap is used to identify potential intervention points, there are in general two clusters of possible interventive tasks: those involving exchanges with existing cultural entities and systemic actors, and those involving the construction of new environmental entities. Each of these interventive clusters is discussed separately below. Finally, the chapter concludes with a discussion of basic principles for effective work with environmental exchanges.

ENHANCING EXCHANGES WITH EXISTING SYSTEMS

Attention to transactions with people outside the family, and particularly with environmental groups that maintain their own cultures is a primary focus in assessment. In many cases, assisting clients to increase contact with such entities can be the most powerful of all interventions, and in other cases working with clients to decrease problem exchanges is crucial. The following listing is only partial, but may be useful for ensuring that a broad look at the client family's contextual situation is comprehensively taken.

Extended Family and Kinship Networks

For many individuals and family units, primary sources of positive and negative exchange involve the extended family. For example, high levels of criticism from kin are associated with problems in parent-child relations in the home (Dumas & Wahler, 1983). For some cultural groups, like African Americans, extended family and nonrelatives who are considered kin are often a main source of strength and support (emotional and tangible). Among some Native American groups, clan relations are crucial, many relatives of a certain generation may be regarded as grandparents, and particular relatives (uncles and aunts, for example) may carry particular responsibilities. Relatives who have passed away are sometimes regarded as continuing to play an active role in the life of the client family. It is valuable for the social worker to study common patterns like these (see, for example, McGoldrick, Giodano, & Pearce, 1996; Vargas & Koss-Chioino, 1992), while recognizing that differences of acculturation, generation, and family uniqueness may dramatically affect the extent to which common patterns are characteristic of a particular family (Gelfand & Fandetti, 1993). Work to improve or strengthen relationships with extended family, relying on many of the strategies presented in later chapters of this volume (for example, acceptance skills and augmenting positive exchange) and on creative collaboration with the family network, can be among the most powerful of interventive options.

Friends and Peers

A second area that should be discussed in nearly every case is the extent to which family members are connected with friends and peers. Friends play a different role than do family members, and the two are not usually substitutable. Informal support networks can buffer the effects of struggles and conflicts in the family (and can even actively reduce their severity as discussed later under self-help and support groups). Peer relationships are particularly important developmentally for children and youths but in fact can be essential supports or potentially stressful throughout the life cycle. One of the common issues with aging clients, for example, is the gradual loss of friends through death, illness, and accumulating limitations on travel.

Among youths, participation in antisocial peer groups can make change more difficult, and connecting to prosocial peers can conversely have a significant positive effect (Henggeler, Schoenwald, Borduin, Rowland, & Cunningham, 1998). The social worker has several options in cases where peers are an issue: working with a group of youths to shift their activities in more positive directions, working with families to increase parental monitoring and reduce contact with antisocial peers, or working with the family to assist the youths to access more positive networks (these options are discussed in detail in chapters 7 and 8).

Clients can experience social isolation and loneliness for a variety of reasons, including lack of resources and access, or skill deficits. Strategies and techniques for working with clients in such situations have been well developed (Gambrill, 1996). The table reprinted as Table 3-1 (Gambrill, 1996) provides an introduction to some of those options. Among the most commonly useful strategies are skills training and problem solving related to how and where to meet persons who may become friends; many of the systems described here may provide possible contacts.

Social isolation may be coercively enforced in violent or abusive relationships; in such cases, extensive formal and informal support may be required if the client is to construct a safe alternative. (Refer to chapter 4 for more information about work with violence in families.)

Table 3–1

Differential Interventions for Social Isolation and Loneliness

What Assessment Reveals	Intervention
Few opportunities to use social skills.	Increase opportunities to use skills in current social settings and create additional ones.
Lack of reinforcement for desired behaviors (e.g., initiating conversations).	Rearrange contingencies so that desired behaviors are reinforced.
Reinforcement of behaviors that interfere with desired behaviors (e.g., aggressive reactions).	Rearrange contingencies so that these behaviors are no longer reinforced.
Few models of desired behaviors.	Increase models of desired behaviors.
Models of undesired behaviors.	Decrease them if possible.
Behavior deficits.	Develop required skills through model presentation, coaching, instructions, practice and feedback.
Faulty discriminations.	Provide information about when to use skills; provide prompts and incentives to encourage use of skills in contexts in which they will be reinforced.
Inaccurate beliefs (e.g., rules) about the nature of social relationships.	Provide accurate information (e.g., regarding helpful rules) and increase constructive beliefs.
Not using social and self management skills.	Encourage use of skills by rehearsal, assignments; arranging prompts and incentives; and self-management training.
Behavior surfeits such as aggressive reactions.	Replace interfering responses with positive alternatives (e.g., via rearrangement of contingencies, anger management training, social problem-solving training).
Behavior surfeits such as high social anxiety; fear of negative evaluation.	Arrange exposure to feared situations; provide successful experiences in real-life, provide anxiety management training.
Unrealistic expectations such as excessively high performance standards.	Encourage realistic expectations (e.g., provide knowledge about social norms and rules).
Low sense of worth; hopelessness.	Offer positive social experiences; replace interfering behaviors (including thoughts and feelings) with positive alternatives.
Disinterest in other people.	Pair people with valued activities and consequences.

SOURCE: Reprinted from Gambrill, E. (1996). Differential interventions for social isolation and loneliness. In M.A. Mattaini & B. Thyer (eds.), *Finding solutions to social problems*: Behavior strategies for change (p. 357). Washington, DC: American Psychological Association.

Schools

Other than the family, no sector of life is more critical to the life success of children and youths than the education system. Nearly 30 percent of youths fail to graduate from high school (for some minority groups the rate is much higher), and many of those who do graduate have not achieved basic cultural literacy skills. Inner city and poor schools are a glaringly apparent national tragedy (Kozol, 1991). A child who is failing in school should be regarded as an *emergency*; the fact that millions are failing, even though we know how to prevent it (Crandall, Jacobson, & Sloane, 1997), can only be regarded as a cultural emergency. Educational success is important not only because the skills learned are crucial to individual and the family survival in the modern world, but also because success or failure affects how one thinks about oneself (equivalence relations). In addition, the overall culture needs the contributions of everyone to achieve the best collective outcomes.

Children (and their families) often find themselves in serious conflicts with schools, and social workers can and should help to resolve those problems. Social workers have developed a range of effective interventive strategies for work with families and schools, some of which can be implemented within the school (Ginsburg, 1990), and others in concert with parents and school personnel (Webster-Stratton, 1997). Establishing communication between school and home is particularly important, especially communicating identification of strengths and recognition of successes (rather than primarily notifications of problems). Constructing respectful contacts between families and school personnel is a powerful intervention (Henggeler, Schoenwald, Borduin, Rowland, & Cunningham, 1998), increasingly supported by community groups like Jessie Jackson's PUSH/Rainbow Coalition (Citizen Education Fund, approximately 1995).

Henggeler, Schoenwald, Borduin, Rowland, and Cunningham (1998), and the Jackson group list specific actions that parents can take with their children and school personnel to strengthen both academic work and inter-system connections, including asking to see the child's schoolwork, inquiring about tests, ensuring that children have quiet places to do homework, turning off the television, and sitting near the child at that time, recognizing children's effort and achievements, and having frequent contact with teachers. Social workers can prompt, encourage, and facilitate such actions. Social workers may also find that they need to become directly and personally involved with teachers, school counselors and administrators, and may need to return over and over to mediate changes and connections.

Once an adequate relationship with the school personnel has developed, the social worker may also be able to provide consultation regarding dealing with classroom management issues. For example, Ervin, Miller & Friman (1997) designed a strategy for encouraging classmates to make positive comments about a 13-year-old, socially rejected girl (involving other students receiving points toward privileges for providing positive recognition to the target child). While the details are important and should be studied before replicating this intervention, the overall approach is straightforward, and can foster a classroom situation in which everyone wins.

In another example, Ninness, Ellis, Miller, Baker, and Rutherford (1995) described ways to help youths learn to monitor their own behavior, an approach that has proven extremely effective for reducing problem behavior and increasing on-task efforts. The basic approach involves having both teacher and student rate the student's behavior for a period of time (at first, as short as 20 minutes if necessary, but building to an entire day), and arranging for the child to receive points for *both* good behavior and accurate monitoring. Since most teachers do not have much background in such approaches, consultation for such arrangements may be appreciated if offered in a respectful way. Children can also be rewarded at home for good behavior and effort at school. This is usually done using some form of "home note" signed by the teacher (or occasionally by phone, although that can be more time consuming for the teacher).

In some cases, the family and the social worker may need to respectfully and assertively advocate for changes in a child's school program. This may range from changes in the level of work the child is assigned, to shifts in teachers or classrooms, to transfers to other schools. It is never acceptable to simply tolerate an educational arrangement in which a child is failing.

Work and Adult Educational Settings

Adults derive much of their satisfaction with life, and some of their sense of worth, from what they do day to day, especially work or school. These activities provide access to financial resources, social contacts, and the possibility of success or failure experiences. Individuals share their successes or failures with their families on many levels (financially, emotionally, and socially). Assistance for achieving adequate rewards and minimizing aversive experiences from work or educational settings can, therefore, be a major social work contribution to both individual and family welfare.

In a time when entitlement programs are being dramatically reduced, family survival more than ever depends on occupational success. Many possible social work interventions can be useful in this area, including the following:

- simply encouraging and demonstrating faith that a client can succeed vocationally
- working with the client to develop and implement a job search strategy, or connecting the client with a job finding club (Azrin, Flores, & Kaplan, 1975), a particularly effective model discussed later in this chapter
- working indirectly through the client or directly with client and employer to resolve work-related issues to everyone's satisfaction
- assisting clients to think through an overall vision for changing their occupational situation
- accompanying the client where necessary to explore new possibilities (for example, visiting a college campus), or helping the client to identify someone else who could do so.

These and other strategies can be useful in many cases, and the creative worker can do a good deal in partnership with family members to open and explore new possibilities in work and education areas. At the same time, it is important to recognize the reality of overall community situations, since in many areas few employment opportunities may exist, especially for those with few skills and limited experience. Some clients, for example many African American males with a history of contact with the criminal justice system, may be in particularly difficult positions in terms of obtaining work, and empathy and advocacy (individual and class) are often required in addition to active engagement with the issue.

Religious and Spiritual Collectives

In addition to the personal strength that many draw from spirituality of one kind or another, social collectives grounded in religious belief or spiritual experience are an important life sphere for many families. Clients who carry strong beliefs but may have lost contact with churches, synagogues, mosques, prayer groups, and other related spiritual entities often benefit from reconnecting. These organized collectives may provide a place for family members to share experiences together, and with others in similar circumstances. Not only formal services and rituals, but also the many organizations associated with such churches can offer considerable opportunities for connectedness and support. Within the African American community, for example, both evangelical Christian and Muslim religious institutions are often centers of family and community life.

At the same time, families may experience pressure and stresses from religious groups; as with any other system, both positive and negative transactions should be recognized when present. For instance, some congregations strongly condemn gay and lesbian unions, and may therefore be experienced as seriously aversive by families that include gay relationships, as well as by others who recognize the oppression involved. The social worker needs therefore to explore religious connections with the family as possible resources, but without pressure. For example, while over 70 percent of Korean Americans belong to Korean Christian churches (Kim, 1996), others have maintained traditional beliefs rooted in panspirituality and sometimes feel that they share little with Korean American Christians. Respectful exploration of possibilities is often useful, and the more social workers know about multiple traditions, the more likely they will be able to do so in thoughtful ways.

Ethnic Communities

Ethnic communities and cultures provide another source of both positive and aversive experiences. Ethnic collectives are sometimes quite formal and structured; for example, some Orthodox Jewish communities are tightly interconnected not only in religious practice, but also in daily economic and social life. Among indigenous groups, tribes and clans may be the most important collective for many, even more than is the immediate family. Other ethnic collectives may be much more informally structured, consisting of loose-knit networks that meet frequently in a social club or a bar. People, and peoples, can draw enormous strength from association with others who share their history, values, and often language. Helping clients to connect, or reconnect, with such networks can therefore be particularly valuable.

A related approach is collaboration with traditional elders, spiritual leaders, and healers. Among many ethnic groups, certain problems are framed in epistemological terms that may be quite different from Anglo/European American understandings. Some personal and family issues may be viewed as emerging from biological imbalances or disturbed human or spiritual relations, for example, rather than as reflecting mental disorders. Social workers and other professionals often fail to ask about, much less honor, such understandings if they are not their own; this failure reflects an unjustifiable cultural arrogance. It is commonly valuable to refer to, or collaborate with traditional healers or those with deep cultural knowledge, particularly if discussion with the client indicates that doing so is more consistent with the client's world view than is a Western framework. While many social workers verbally agree with this approach, such referral and collaboration appears to be relatively uncommon.

Recreation

For many families, connections with recreational activities and social groups engaged in them are among their strongest positive transactions. Families as a whole, as well as individual members, can derive substantial benefit from such activities, which may involve less conflict than work, school, or other transactional networks. In families under stress, members often have gradually withdrawn from such contact; in some severely stressed families, satisfying recreation may never have been a feature of family life. Clinically, therefore, it can be very useful to think with the family about both potentially reinforcing activities in which the family, as a whole or as a subset, can engage, as well as about individual options for each family member.

This may at first glance appear simplistic, but even for serious issues of long standing, like addictions, recreation counseling has proven to be important (Azrin, 1976; Meyers & Smith, 1996). Many obstacles may also present themselves in this work, which may require a great deal of creativity on the part of both worker and family members to overcome. Lack of funds (including for transportation) is a common barrier, as is lack of experience— many people are hesitant to try something new, in part because they fear they may be embarrassed by lack of know-how, but also because until one actually has new experiences, the reinforcers involved may not be at all obvious.

While one advantage of certain forms of recreation is the human contact afforded, many people also draw great satisfaction from activities that connect them with other natural phenomena. Care of and involvement with animals, plants, and even the nonanimate world are intrinsically rewarding for many people and appear to be associated with positive mental health. People will often go to a good deal of trouble and expense to access such spiritual experiences, and there may well be an evolutionary basis for such attraction (Wilson, 1992). Active pursuits are also probably biologically more advantageous in many ways than are such passive activities as watching television for extended periods. Careful consideration of all of the possible options, therefore, is indicated. One way to encourage this is to ask clients who are unable to identify possible recreational activities to evaluate each item on a long written list (a *reinforcer menu*) on a 1 to 5 scale. Doing so may help to generate new possibilities and spark creative ideas for options that may not be on the list, but emerge from the exercise.

Volunteering

Many service organizations report that it is increasingly difficult to find volunteers, in part because many more women are now in the paid labor force than was true some decades ago, but probably also because competing activities (especially television and other recreational options) absorb an increasing proportion of people's time. Enormous satisfaction can be drawn from volunteer and service experience, however, and this is certainly an area for the social worker to explore with family members. In many cases, it is younger people, including teens, who have the most available time and energy. Guiding this energy toward community service can have synergistically positive effects for the individual, the family, and the community (Waterman, 1997; Finn & Checkoway, 1998).

Many clients who have never engaged in such activities before may need considerable encouragement to take such steps, as well as assistance in making the necessary contacts (for example, by rehearsing the phone calls involved, and then allowing the client to make the call while the social worker is present to offer support). Many more possibilities exist than may occur to the client immediately since a wide range of organizations may use and need volunteers—arts organizations, after-school tutoring programs, political action groups, social agencies, and hospitals, among many others.

Self-Help and Support Groups

Another area that social workers can consider with clients is joining any of the many (in some communities, there are hundreds) of self-help and support groups available. Some groups are problem-focused (like 12-step groups for gambling problems); some groups focus on ways to cope with problems that are primarily owned by another family member but have potentially enormous impact on oneself and others (like Alanon groups for the family of persons with drinking problems); and other groups are primarily enhancement oriented and may have larger social justice implications (for example, consciousness-raising groups).

A certain mythology has developed around some self-help groups. The 12-step groups are an example; although considered by some to be "the most effective" intervention available, the best available data suggest that while they are particularly powerful for some persons, they are not nearly so good a fit for some others (Longabaugh, Wirtz, Zweben, & Stout, 1998), so the social worker needs to be familiar with multiple alternatives. There is clear evidence that some groups can be enormously helpful; for example, support groups for battered women not only provide emotional assistance, but also reduce the incidence of battering—even among those who choose not to leave their batterers (Tutty, Bidgood, & Rothery, 1993). (The mechanism here may be that involvement in the group makes potential battering a more public phenomenon, which may make it more aversive to the batterer.) Many forms of parent support groups can be useful (see discussion later in this chapter). The challenge for social workers is to learn about the availability of such groups in the community, which changes often, and to gradually sort out which may be of most use to which kinds of clients. It is also often essential to discuss with the client that some experimentation should be expected, since the first group tried may not be the one that they will find most satisfying.

Neighborhood and Community Groups

Client families live in geographic communities, of course, and there is often potential to become involved in neighborhood or block associations, in local party politics, or in activist groups around local or even global issues. Participation in such cultural entities can have several positive outcomes, including social connectedness and awareness of empowerment on an individual level, and enhancing overall sense of community (which in turn has an impact on perceived quality of life, fear of crime, and evaluations of other specific facets of the community; Citizens Committee for New York City, 1989). Parent-teacher associations, parent advisory boards, and other formal connections with the school system can have similar effects.

Communities of Interest

Communities of interest may have little or no connection to geography, ethnicity, or many of the other dimensions discussed thus far. If members of client families have specific interests (computers, meditation, sports, martial arts, or investing, for example), there are often organized groups of people with similar interests available. As with many of the other possibilities discussed above, the two biggest challenges are first to identify and locate such groups, and then to assist the client to make the initial connections. Both the social worker and family members can and should share responsibility for locating possible networks with which to connect family members, not in a high-pressure way, but rather as an ongoing challenge. To address the second issue, problem-solving discussions and connecting with individual members of such groups who can smooth introductions, provide initial exposure, and when necessary offer to accompany the client to a meeting or two, can be useful.

The cultural entities listed above are not an exhaustive list. They do, however, offer beginning possibilities to examine for assisting client families to connect with networks that may offer higher levels of positive exchange and may support family members in reaching their goals.

CONSTRUCTING NEW SUPPORT NETWORKS

Connecting families and family members with existing cultural entities is often the most efficient way to work and has the advantage of using naturally existing networks that require no attention from the social worker to maintain. In some cases, however, organizations or networks that fit the needs of the case may not be available, and an individual social worker, or often an agency may then work with the clients to construct such entities. The social work and related professional literature offer many such examples, and many opportunities exist to creatively extend what has already been done. In most cases, these alternatives should focus on constructing networks that shape and reinforce healthy, fulfilling action, rather than dwelling on problems and pathology—once again focusing on the construction of positive alternatives.

Working with staff of one's own agency, staff from other agencies, and client families to construct such networks involves specialized skills in program development and group and community practice that are beyond the purview of this book (see Mattaini, Lowery, & Meyer, 1998 for introductions to these areas). A thorough knowledge of practice with families, however, requires familiarity with the basic approaches to this work. The paragraphs that follow, therefore, introduce a number of useful strategies and suggest further reading for details. The examples that follow include family support programs, self-help and mutual aid groups, job-finding clubs, and multifamily groups. These are only a sampling, providing some notion of the range of possibilities; there are many others as well, some of which will be described in detail in later chapters of this book.

Family Support Programs

Although professionals in child development and other disciplines, rather than social workers, have often taken the lead in constructing family support programs, they are a very useful model, and one that social workers should be more familiar with. Such programs are generally based in local communities, often serving a particular neighborhood, and in some cases blend into "parent resource" programs. Core elements of family support programs include home visiting, child development screening, parent training, and social and other support arrangements for parenting (Comer & Fraser, 1998). In a study by Comer and Fraser (1998), such programs also provided a number of other related services, including child care, educational programs for children, organized activities, and adult education opportunities. Family support programs are generally interdisciplinary, including educational, medical and social service staff, with a strong representation of natural helpers and trained paraprofessionals. Program goals generally involve reducing child maltreatment and enhancing child development, enhancing family relations, and enriching the lives of parents. When Comer and Fraser looked at evaluation data from six such programs, they found that the programs "can be effective in strengthening families and promoting the well-being of children," producing a range of positive behavioral, medical, and educational outcomes for both parents and children (results for adolescents are not so clear).

In describing a successful child maltreatment program, Wolfe (1991) discusses social support groups offered in a community setting that have much in common with family support programs. The emphasis in Wolfe's program is on building friendships among parents and offering opportunities for positive activities with children. This approach is particularly important given the relationship between social isolation and child maltreatment (Mattaini, McGowan & Williams, 1996; Moncher 1995). These factors are discussed further in chapter 9. While many parent education groups primarily emphasize learning parenting skills, they function in fact in several ways, also providing a supportive environment where parents learn from each other about available resources and provide each other with general emotional support and mutual aid (Brunk, Henggeler, & Whelan, 1987), thus blending into the next category of mutual aid. One model with outstanding empirical support is Carolyn Webster-Stratton's, in which there has been an "evolution from an initial goal of improving parenting skills in order to reduce children's conduct problems and promote their social competence to the broader goals of strengthening parents' social support and increasing their school and community involvement" (p. 156, 1997). This program and others like it will be discussed further in chapter 7.

An important observation in the Comer and Fraser study was that strong family-support programs typically treat clients as "colleagues" in the work. In the terms used in this book, these programs emphasized shared power and maintained organizational cultures of empowerment. Lightburn and Kemp (1994) make this explicit in their description of one such program, in which family members were actively engaged in learning collectives. In this network, parents served as learners, teachers, and mentors for each other, and the development of community among participants was a core goal, along with enhancing family relations, education, and mediating with other community systems.

Self-Help and Mutual Aid Groups

Social workers often refer clients to self-help or mutual aid groups. A "self-help" group, in the terms used here, is led by group members, and the social work role lies in referral and outside consultation; a "mutual aid" group, by contrast, has a professional leader. Such groups provide existing cultures which clients can join, and which in turn can reinforce positive steps and discourage negative ones. In many cases, however, an appropriate group may not be available, and the social worker or agency may want to initiate or sponsor one. In the case of self-help groups, the social work role in general is to contact existing groups or national offices of, for example, 12-step groups like Alcoholics Anonymous, and explore steps required to establish a local affiliate.

Social workers can also establish and lead mutual aid groups of many kinds (Gitterman & Shulman, 1994). In fact, several of the other options discussed elsewhere in this book can be seen as special cases of such groups. Establishing a general mutual aid group requires identifying the population to be served, clarifying the purpose of the group to the extent possible, recruiting members, and working with the members in a shared-power framework to further refine the group's purpose and activities. The most common pitfall in beginning such a group might be a failure to be clear about the group's purpose since people who gather in a room are unlikely to effectively group if they have incompatible agendas.

An example in which beginning a mutual aid group could be useful is found in many family service agencies. Commonly, many single-parent clients being seen at the same time by different agency workers report problems with social isolation and loneliness. A group of such clients can be formed, who can work together to develop solutions to this common issue, model and role-play new repertoires, and explore possibilities for accessing new social connections. The group itself may also become an important source of valued reinforcers.

Job-Finding Clubs

At a time when even disabled single parents are being asked to support their children with limited or no help from the society at large, social workers can in some cases help to increase the likelihood that clients will locate at least some form of employment that may help them to support their families. Before discussing this, however, it is crucial to remember the social justice dimensions involved. It would be ethically problematic for a social worker to accept employment in programs that participate in maintaining oppressive society practices more than they do in helping those in need. If the worker determines that there is a need for assistance in locating and maintaining employment, and that there are opportunities available that are consistent with human dignity, then "job-finding clubs" are one approach that has excellent empirical support. Those clubs that have demonstrated their effectiveness, not surprisingly, are structured as empowerment cultures, where clients and staff collaborate, using their respective talents and strengths, toward a mutual goal of stable employment. Note that this is *not* the same thing as a "class" in which welfare recipients are lectured that they need to take responsibility for themselves—an approach rooted in coercion.

Given the right approach and available opportunities, early research on voluntary job-finding clubs indicated that most or all of those who attended regularly found jobs, and that those jobs paid better than those found by controls who did not attend (Azrin, Flores, & Kaplan, 1975). This approach has been replicated in various settings, and the results tend to support the early findings. Components of such programs include daily group meetings, which facilitate a range of support including a buddy system, shared automobile transportation, role playing of interview skills, consultation on telephone skills, mutual resume review, shared job leads, and mutual recognition of positive steps taken. Job-finding clubs can also enlist family support and provide models of persons who had previously attended and successfully obtained employment. Other job-readiness skills (grooming, promptness, ability to resolve conflicts effectively) are also commonly included in such programs (see the original reference for considerable detail about procedures). An additional procedure with empirical support that has been vastly underutilized is offering a financial reward (a "bounty") to anyone who locates a position that is subsequently filled by a program participant (Jones & Azrin, 1973). This procedure can have a much higher payoff in cost-benefit terms than many traditional ways of assisting clients to find employment.

It is sometimes asked whether developing efforts like job-finding clubs is professional social work. Thinking back to the purpose of social work, if such programs help families achieve financial independence, thereby accessing a substantively higher level of reinforcers, and reducing exposure to aversives, they clearly fit. Many program activities can be carried out by paraprofessionals, but program design and supervision (and usually initial testing for implementation as well) are clearly professional functions.

Multifamily Groups

Several of the program models discussed already have included arrangements in which one or more members of several families participate with others in groups. In this section, we will look briefly at "multifamily groups" in which two or more members of families participate in group meetings with members of other families. There are many variations of such groups (see Meezan & O'Keefe, 1998, for a summary), and both familiarity with the literature and creativity are useful in developing them. A multifamily group is an ideal setting for shared power, since such a setting brings together a larger number of people with varying and unique repertoires, and the social worker is only one of many strong voices present. Two types of multifamily groups will be briefly discussed here as examples: psychoeducation groups for families with mental illness, and prevention and education groups for families at risk for child maltreatment.

For families in which one member struggles with a severe mental illness like schizophrenia, the research consistently indicates that family psychoeducation (usually in conjunction with appropriate medication) is a crucial factor in reducing relapse and rehospitalization. Multifamily groups appear to be a superior modality for this work (Anderson, Reiss, & Hogarty, 1986; McFarlane, Link, Dushay, Marchal, & Crilly, 1995). Useful content for such groups includes education about the causes and effects of mental illnesses, medication, and skills for living with mental illness. The "all in the same boat" (normalization) phenomenon tends to build mutual support, and group members can serve as resources to each other for problem solving. In addition, groups can help to link patients and families with advocacy organizations like the National Alliance for the Mentally Ill, which are additional empowerment cultures from which families themselves and the larger community can benefit. (Psychoeducation and other behavioral work with families living with mental illness is discussed in further detail in chapter 10).

Given what has already been said about the importance of social support versus insularity in preventing child maltreatment, it is not surprising that multifamily and extended-family groups are also an emerging force in child welfare work (Lowery, 1998). Multifamily groups like the Family-to-Family Program conducted by Friends of the Family in Van Nuys, California, are an excellent example (Meezan & O'Keefe, 1998). In this program, groups of six to eight families met weekly with teams of four professionals. While including a variety of activities (only some of which are overtly behavioral, although all are involved in creating a culture that reinforces effective parenting), the program identified a small number of core practices that workers and families attempted to incorporate into their group and individual lives, and consistently prompted, modeled and reinforced those practices. Both family functioning and child behavior improved more in the experimental group than in a control group receiving traditional family therapy, an outcome consistent with the power of constructing empowerment cultures. (Such groups are discussed in detail in chapter 9.)

Overall, in each of these examples, whether multifamily psychoeducation groups, job-finding clubs, or family support programs, the core concept is the creation of an empowerment culture in which positive actions and practices are richly reinforced, and that rely on the identification and use of the multiple talents and repertoires that groups can bring to a task. Like the earlier examples of linking clients with existing networks, these interventions have real power and should often be considered as the first line intervention with families, rather than as adjuncts to the "real practice."

CORE PRACTICE PRINCIPLES FOR ENHANCING ENVIRONMENTAL EXCHANGES

Several core practice principles emerge from the discussion in this chapter:

1. It is essential to look at the overall case configuration to understand the family's situation. The transactional ecomap is a key tool for this work, since it helps social workers and family members make sense of problems and emotions and understand (1) the network of contingencies within which the family lives and (2) the kinds of behaviors and practices those contingencies support and punish. For example, some families' situations provide high levels of noncontingent aversives, others may encourage undesirable behavior (like drug use), and others may not provide enough reinforcement for positive action from family members or environmental actors (teachers, for example).
2. Effective practice usually involves increasing family members exposure to networks and empowerment cultures that will support positive actions and practices desired by the family—the environment is a *powerful* shaping force for everyone.
3. Assisting the family to enhance environmental transactions requires a commitment to shared power, in which the social worker respects and encourages all voices, and explicitly works with the family to use the strengths of everyone involved to shape a new reality. The social worker must be willing to share responsibility with the family for outcomes, as opposed to either abdicating responsibility and blaming the family, or appropriating all accountability and refusing to share this with the family.

4. The social worker operating from a shared power stance is willing to take an active role, to intentionally and explicitly engage actors and systems in the family's environment, to operate in the home, on-site in other agencies, and on the street.
5. Environmental engagement often requires "experimenting with life" and reinforcer sampling; what works will not always be immediately evident.
6. Multisystemic therapists (Henggeler, Schoenwald, Borduin, Rowland, & Cunningham, 1998) have found that an active stance in which everyone involved commits explicitly to taking some kind of action every day leads to better outcomes than general, abstract plans.
7. Referrals to other agencies and organizations are a central feature of environmentally oriented practice. A referral should not be considered to be complete, however, until the client has actually made contact with and accepted services from the entity to which he or she was referred.
8. The case management literature provides considerable guidance for effective referrals, including involving and preparing the client, accompanying the client when indicated, determining the appropriate point of contact, and evaluating the success of the referral with client and agency (Rothman & Sager, 1998). Clearly, much more than providing a phone number is involved!
9. Environmental intervention often requires case or class advocacy. If an individual family or a class of families are not receiving adequate services, if required resources that could be provided by the community are not made available, the social worker carries an ethical responsibility to advocate for social justice. Involving clients in such advocacy can also be empowering, so long as possible risks to clients are carefully evaluated and determined to be acceptable (Mattaini, 1993a).

Once environmental factors have been addressed, or concurrently with that action, family-practice social workers will often work with family members to make shifts in family culture (intrafamily structure and dynamics). The next two chapters review interventive strategies for doing so.

REFERENCES

Anderson, C. M., Reiss, D. J., & Hogarty, G. (1986). *Schizophrenia and the family*. New York: Guilford Press.

Azrin, N. H. (1976). Improvements in the community-reinforcement approach to alcoholism. *Behaviour Research and Therapy, 14*, 339–348.

Azrin, N. H., Flores, T., & Kaplan, S. J. (1975). Job-finding club: A group-assisted program for obtaining employment. *Behaviour Research and Therapy, 13*, 17–27.

Brunk, M., Henggeler, S. W., & Whelan, J. P. (1987). Comparison of multisystemic therapy and parent training in the brief treatment of child abuse and neglect. *Journal of Consulting and Clinical Psychology, 55,* 171–178.

Citizen Education Fund (approximately 1995). *The national Reclaim our Youth Crusade "Back to School" pledge campaign.* Citizen Education Fund, 1700 K Street, NW, Suite 802, Washington, DC 20006.

Citizens Committee for New York City (1989). *Nurturing the grassroots: Neighborhood volunteer organizations and America's cities.* New York: Author.

Comer, E. W., & Fraser, M. W. (1998). Evaluation of six family-support programs: Are they effective? *Families in Society, 79,* 134–148.

Crandall, J., Jacobson, J., & Sloane, H. (Eds.) (1997). *What works in education.* Cambridge, MA: Cambridge Center for Behavioral Studies.

Dougher, M. J., & Hackbert, L. (1994). A behavior-analytic account of depression and a case report using acceptance-based procedures. *The Behavior Analyst, 17,* 321–334.

Dumas, J. E., & Wahler, R. G. (1983). Predictors of treatment outcome in parent training: Mother insularity and socioeconomic disadvantage. *Behavioral Assessment, 5,* 301–313.

Embry, D. D., & Flannery, D. J. (in press). Multi-level prevention and intervention to reduce youth violent behavior. In D.J. Flannery and C. Ronald Huff (Eds.), *Youth Violence: Prevention, Intervention and Social Policy.* Washington, DC: American Psychiatric Press.

Ervin, R. A., Miller, P. M., & Friman, P. C. (1997). Feed the hungry bee: Using positive peer reports to improve the social interactions and acceptance of a socially rejected girl in residential care. *Journal of Applied Behavior Analysis, 29,* 251–253.

Finn, J. L., & Checkoway, B. (1998). Young people as competent community builders: A challenge to social work. *Social Work, 43,* 335–345.

Gambrill, E. (1996). Loneliness, social isolation, & social anxiety. In M. A. Mattaini & B. A. Thyer (Eds.), *Finding solutions to social problems: Behavioral strategies for change* (pp. 345–371). Washington, DC: American Psychological Association.

Gaudin, J. M., Jr. (1988). Treatment of families who neglect their children. In E. W. Nunnally, C. S. Chilman, & F. M Cox (Eds.), *Mental illness, delinquency, addictions, and neglect* (pp. 167–188). Newbury Park, CA: Sage Publications.

Gelfand, D. E., & Fandetti, D. V. (1993). The emergent nature of ethnicity: Dilemmas in assessment. In J. B. Rauch (Ed.), *Assessment: A sourcebook for social work practice* (pp. 357–369). Milwaukee: Families International, Inc.

Ginsburg, E. H. (1990). *Effective interventions: Applying learning theory to school social work.* New York: Greenwood Press.

Gitterman, A., & Shulman, L. (Eds.). (1994). *Mutual aid groups, vulnerable populations, and the life cycle.* New York: Columbia University Press.

Hartman, A. (1995). Diagrammatic assessment of family relationships. *Families in Society, 76,* 111–122. Originally published in 1978.

Henggeler, S. W., Schoenwald, S. K., Borduin, C. M., Rowland, M. D., & Cunningham, P. B. (1998). *Multisystemic treatment of antisocial behavior in children and adolescents.* New York: Guilford Press.

Jones, R. T., & Azrin, N. H. (1973). An experimental application of a social reinforcement approach to the problem of job-finding. *Journal of Applied Behavior Analysis, 6*, 345–353.

Kim, B.-L. C. (1996). Korean families. In M. McGoldrick, J. Giordano, & J. K. Pearce (Eds.), *Ethnicity and family therapy* (pp. 281–294). New York: Guilford Press.

Kozol, J. (1991). *Savage inequalities.* New York: Harper Perennial.

Lightburn, A., & Kemp, S. P. (1994). Family-support programs: Opportunities for community-based practice. *Families in Society, 75*, 16–26.

Longabaugh, R., Wirtz, P. W., Zweben, A., & Stout, R. L. (1998). Network support for drinking, Alcoholics Anonymous and long-term matching effects. *Addiction, 93*, 1313–1333.

Lowery, C. T. (1998). Social work with families. In M. A. Mattaini, C. T. Lowery, & C. H. Meyer (Eds.), *The foundations of social work practice: A graduate text* (2nd ed.) (pp. 165–187). Washington, DC: NASW Press.

Mattaini, M. A. (1993a). Behavior analysis in community practice. *Research on Social Work Practice, 3*, 420–447.

Mattaini, M. A. (1993b). *More than a thousand words: Graphics for clinical practice.* Washington, DC: NASW Press.

Mattaini, M. A. (1993c). *Visual ecoscan for clinical practice.* Washington, DC: NASW Press.

Mattaini, M. A., Grellong, B. A., & Abramovitz, R. (1992). The clientele of a child and family mental health agency: Empirically-derived household clusters and implications for practice. *Research on Social Work Practice, 2*, 380–404.

Mattaini, M. A., Lowery, C. T., & Meyer, C. H. (1998). *The foundations of social work practice* (2nd ed.). Washington, DC: NASW Press.

Mattaini, M. A., McGowan, B. G., & Williams, G. (1996). Child maltreatment. In M. A. Mattaini & B. A. Thyer (Eds.), *Finding solutions to social problems: Behavioral strategies for change* (pp. 223–266). Washington, DC: American Psychological Association.

McFarlane, W. R., Link, B., Dushay, R., Marchal, J., & Crilly, J. (1995). Psychoeducational multiple family groups: Four-year relapse outcome in schizophrenia. *Family Process, 34*, 127–144.

McGoldrick, M., Giordano, J., & Pearce, J. K. (1996). *Ethnicity and family therapy* (2nd ed.). New York: Guilford Press.

Meezan, W., & O'Keefe, M. (1998). Multifamily group therapy: Impact on family functioning and child behavior. *Families in Society, 79*, 32–44.

Meyers, R. L., & Smith, J. E. (1996). *Clinical guide to alcohol treatment: The community reinforcement approach.* New York: Guilford Press.

Moncher, F. J. (1995). Social isolation and child-abuse risk. *Families in Society, 76*, 421–433.

Ninness, H. A., Ellis, J., Miller, W. B., Baker, D., & Rutherford, R. (1995). The effect of a self-management training package on the transfer of aggression control procedures in the absence of supervision. *Behavior Modification, 19*, 464–490.

Nurius, P. S., Kemp, S. P., & Gibson, J. W. (in press). Practitioners' perspectives on sound reasoning: Adding a worker-in-context component. *Administration in Social Work.*

Rosen, A., & Livne, S. (1992). Personal versus environmental emphases in formulation of client problems. *Social Work Research & Abstracts, 29*(4), 12–17.

Rothman, J., & Sager, J. S. (1998). *Case management: Integrating individual and community practice* (2nd ed.). Boston: Allyn & Bacon Press.

Sidman, M. (1989). *Coercion and its fallout.* Boston: Authors Cooperative.

Tutty, L. M., Bidgood, B. A., & Rothery, M. A. (1993). Support groups for battered women: Research on their efficacy. *Journal of Family Violence, 8,* 325–343.

Vargas, L. A., & Koss-Chioino, J. D. (Eds.)(1992). *Working with culture: Psychotherapeutic interventions with ethnic minority children and adolescents.* San Francisco: Jossey-Bass.

Waterman, A. S. (Ed.),(1997). *Service-learning: Applications from the research.* Mahwah, NJ: Lawrence Erlbaum Associates.

Webster-Stratton, C. (1997). From parent training to community building. *Families in Society, 78,* 156–171.

Wilson, E. O. (1992). *The diversity of life.* Cambridge: Belknap/Harvard.

Wolfe, D. A. (1991). *Preventing physical and emotional abuse of children.* New York: Guilford Press.

CHAPTER FOUR

Interventive Strategies: Modifying Exchanges within the Family

Behavioral research has consistently found that the relative rates of positive and negative exchanges within the family are the best predictors of family health and satisfaction and of the development of individual family members (for example, Karney & Bradbury, 1995; Patterson, 1982). Attending to these transactions is a central focus of an ecobehavioral approach to the family. The extent of needless and destructive hurt in families has reached tragic dimensions in our society—with battering and abuse as the endpoint of an aversive continuum (Sidman, 1989). (Violence within families, which is sadly common in social work cases, will be briefly considered at the end of the chapter.) Reinforcers and aversives vary from culture to culture, from family to family, and from person to person, based on shared and individual meanings and experiences, but the basic principles are robust. Other dimensions, like communication (discussed in the next chapter), may in fact be important primarily because of their effects on behavior exchanges. For example, Sloane (1976/1988) has clarified that many parents' efforts to "communicate" with their children, especially older children and teens, actually punish children's communicative behaviors. Questions asked of children, for instance, often include obvious or subtle evaluative and punitive dimensions (for example, "Are you really sure you want to go there?" or "Is that Jim going to be there?"). Under such circumstances, it is not surprising that youths learn to provide as little information as possible. Similar patterns are often present in couples and in adult child-parent relationships. Strategies for working with such dynamics will be elaborated in the next chapter, but it is useful to recognize the connections between communication and behavior exchange.

It has now been clearly established that positive and negative exchanges among family members tend to be reciprocal (Jacobson & Christensen, 1996). For example, intimate partners tend to provide each other with

85

highly correlated rates of reinforcers and highly correlated rates of aversives on a daily basis (Wills, Weiss, & Patterson, 1974). Gottman and colleagues found in several studies that couples establish a sort of long-term "bank account"—when there has been a high rate of positive exchange, negative events are not necessarily reciprocated, but when few "good faith" deposits have been made, negative reciprocity is often immediate (Gottman, Markman, & Notarius, 1977; Gottman, Notarius, Markman, Bank, Yoppi, & Rubin, 1976).

Similar dynamics play out in parent-child relations. In an extended program of research working with families of aggressive youths, Patterson and his colleagues have described a coercive spiral that can develop between parent and child, where an aversive from one is in turn reciprocated by an aversive from the other in a recursive way (Patterson, 1976b, 1982). Each then tends to escalate his or her demands, until eventually one side or the other backs down. Naturally, this pattern teaches family members that the way to escape from unpleasant demands is to punish, and to escalate to more severe punishment if demands are not immediately met. Over the long term, such coercive cycles became part of family culture. In the same studies, parents of problem children tended to offer reinforcers noncontingently (whether the child's behavior was positive or negative), while among non-problem comparison children desirable behavior was rewarded, but undesirable behavior was not. Non-problem children therefore became sensitive to reinforcement, while problem children became somewhat insensitive to both punishment and reinforcement.

Perhaps nonintuitively, rates of positive and negative exchange in families tend to be relatively independent (Bornstein & Bornstein, 1986; Mattaini, Grellong, & Abramovitz, 1992). In other words, within a family, there may be high rates of positives and low rates of aversives, or the converse, but there may also be high rates of both positives and aversives, or low rates of both. (For example, cluster 6 families in Figure 3-2 experienced relatively low rates of any kind of exchange from each other, as compared with the other clusters.) Interventive planning certainly needs to involve increasing rates of positive exchange if these are low and may *also* independently need to target decreasing aversives if those are high. Negative events tend to be more reliably reciprocated than positives, and may have a stronger "valence" than positives (Stuart, 1980), so they usually must be addressed.

INCREASING MUTUAL REINFORCEMENT IN THE FAMILY

While "tit-for-tat" contracts can be useful in the short term to resolve serious parenting problems (see chapters 7 and 8), the results of three decades of work suggest that over the long term, families need to aim at increasing the rate of positive exchange "holistically." For couples work, in fact, simple contracting has generally not proved very useful. The most important goal is to embed practices of "giving" and "recognition" in the family culture, so that each party provides reinforcers to the others on a rich and regular basis. These reinforcers should often be provided contingently, when one member does something that the other appreciates. Constantly giving non-contingently is a prescription for oppression. As mentioned above, children do not achieve the necessary developmental socialization if they receive what they want regardless of their behavior. Similarly, giving without expectation in couples or other family relations can result in one person being "taken for granted" and disrespected, giving a great deal but receiving little in return. Traditional sexist cultural practices support such dynamics, and this pattern is also associated with depression. Follette and Jacobson (1988, p. 280) suggested that oppressive relationships probably are causally related to many cases of depression seen by clinicians; data summarized by Biglan (1991) also indicate that couples and family dynamics can reliably shape depression.

Why Is Adequate Reinforcement Often Missing?

Relationships cannot be sustained without effort, and the primary effort required is reinforcement. There is a common misconception in U. S. society that love and family relationships should be easy. Several related and natural processes make sustaining rich relationships within the family challenging. The first is that providing reinforcers requires effort, and people naturally tend to minimize effort. When a couple is courting, for example, partners commonly offer each other a rich range of reinforcers. Over time, they tend to cut back due to the effort involved. This is a natural process, and avoiding it requires specific effort. The second phenomenon, labeled "reinforcer erosion" by Jacobson and Margolin (1979), involves a process of satiation. In the beginning of a relationship, the reinforcers exchanged are novel and exciting; over time, they naturally become somewhat less so. (Jacobson and Christensen, 1996, suggest that in successful relationships this phenomenon can be attenuated through conscious attention to maintaining variety in the relationship, and through individuals taking actions to keep themselves interesting.) A third factor commonly occurs in relationships in which high levels of aversives are present. In such cases, the person who acts in aversive ways comes to be experienced as aversive him or herself, and other family members then may refuse to act positively toward that person until he or she changes first. Similar processes also occur in troubled parent-child relationships.

On the other hand, predictability of reinforcers, if institutionalized in family culture, provides a level of stability that can immunize family members from aversives in other spheres of life. "Rituals," for example, regular predictable family events and ways of coping with challenges (Hartman & Laird, 1983), are important because they help family members to access reinforcers and avoid aversives. Many family rituals and practices also evolve special "meanings" for family members, meanings that in ecobehavioral terms involve shared equivalence relations (for example, presence at Christmas ≈ caring, or refusing to attend a "mixed marriage" ≈ loyalty to group) and shared rules. Not all predictable events and rituals, however, are reinforcing; many persons go home for holidays because they feel too guilty to break family rules ("guilt" is a self-generated aversive), but being home may also involve exposure to other aversives. Ritual itself, therefore, is not necessarily positive, but rituals that involve adequate levels of reinforcers can be.

The practices that need to be embedded in and supported by family culture to achieve adequate outcomes are not mysterious or complicated. The first are high levels of mutual "giving," and recognition for doing so. Family members often know what other family members would like, and interventive tasks in which they do more of those things (detailed later in this chapter) are potentially powerful. Of course, very few reinforcers are shared by everyone; different cultural groups, different families, and different individuals, through a combination of biological and experiential factors, come to value different reinforcers; so universal prescriptions are not nearly as useful as custom designed tasks. In parenting as well as in couples' relations, institutionalizing the practice of recognizing and effectively rewarding actions that one appreciates is particularly important.

In family relations, reinforcement is the closest thing we have to magic; every effective parenting, family treatment, and couples approach addresses this point in some way, either explicitly or implicitly (Jacobson & Christensen, 1996; Latham, 1994, Sloane, 1976/1988; Stuart, 1980). The use of praise and encouragement to bring out the best in the child is among the essential parenting practices emphasized in Webster-Stratton's (1997) well supported parenting program. The first modules in Polster and Dangel's (1989) effective parent training program are praise and attention, and rewards and privileges. The first steps in Patterson's empirically solid parenting program involve understanding and using reinforcement effectively (Patterson, 1975, 1976a). The first focus of Stuart's (1980) couples treatment package involves increasing the rates of positive exchange, and Jacobson and Christensen (1996) also recognize this shift as central to couples' satisfaction, although they commonly pursue active change in the ratio of positive to negative exchange at a somewhat later stage in treatment than do some other authors. The acceptance-based strategies they employ early in treatment (see chapter 5) also involve reducing levels of mutual (and self) punishment and building empathy, a core reinforcer for most people.

Active steps can be taken to increase levels of positive exchange in the family; several are discussed in the next section. A parent, for example, can learn to praise her child contingently and consistently while minimizing noncontingent consequences (see actual case data shown in Figure 4-1, from Mattaini, McGowan, & Williams, 1996, for an example), and these steps will reliably have a profound effect on child behavior.

In the case portrayed, the child's behavior changed so dramatically that the mother shifted from consistently describing him as a "bad boy" to describing him in almost exclusively positive terms; once reinforcement became predicable, the child would even remind his mother to recognize his positive behavior, establishing a self-perpetuating, mutual "reinforcer trap."

Strategies for Increasing Positive Exchange

Before describing specific options for working with family members to increase positive exchange, it is important to emphasize that the examples presented here are only examples. The overall strategic direction of increasing positive exchange is useful whenever the rates are low, but the social worker and family often need to work together creatively to design approaches that fit the family's situation and style. Several principles are useful in planning such work. First, to the extent possible, exchange programs should be designed and implemented in the family's natural environment. If possible, the social worker and family should meet and work together in the home and other places where the family lives out its life. Certainly plans should include tasks that will be completed in such settings, even if some are first completed in the social worker's office.

Second, it is important that family members enter such tasks with a somewhat collaborative set, and this should be openly and honestly discussed with them. It is common for each person in a troubled relationship to wait for the other to change before acting, but positive exchange tasks require each actor to commit to the "Change First" principle—"I will make the first effort, and will continue it until the next meeting with the social worker, whether you take active steps or not, although I certainly hope you will" (Stuart, 1980). Under some circumstances, conflict and emotions may be too high in the beginning to obtain such an agreement, and positive exchange tasks should be deferred until somewhat later, but in most cases positive experiences build commitment for further work. For example, Stuart

Figure 4-1

The results of parent education around how to use praise and other social reinforcers to shape cooperative, positive behavior by a child. "Treatment 1" involved modeling, coaching, and reinforcing appropriate consequences. "Treatment 2" involved the mother watching videotapes of her interactions with her child. Not shown in this figure is that the level of physical affection, which did not occur at all during treatment 1, dramatically increased with the introduction of treatment 2.

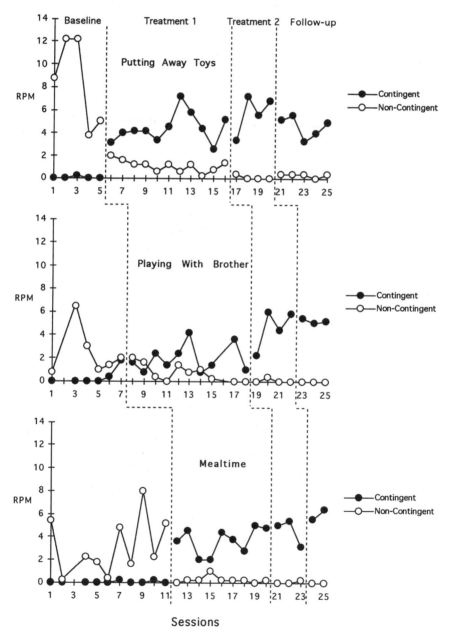

Sessions

(1980) and others, including the author, have had excellent success beginning couples work with the "caring days" task. If the social worker and the family have begun their work together looking at and perhaps acting with regard to larger systemic transactions as outlined in the last chapter, an adequate collaborative set often exists, and positive intrafamily experiences can build hope and commitment to take on the more challenging issues many families face. While there is a great deal of flexibility regarding timing and details, some active intervention of this type should be seriously considered with every family in which even only some members agree that the rate of positive exchange is inadequate.

One straightforward task that can be extremely useful for families who are not currently enjoying each other very much is what Reid (1985) called, simply, "planning mutually enjoyable activities" (p. 210). As Reid notes, there are many reasons why families may not do things together. Conflict may make contact aversive in general; schedules may have evolved that leave time for the necessities, but not for enjoyment; or people's interests may have changed as a result of normal developmental processes, and the family may not have taken this into account. Examples of activities that can be done together include recreational activities that were previously enjoyed, activities that one family member is very interested in but that others haven't seriously considered, "dates" for a couple, sporting events, or a joint shopping trip. Reid's approach to the task (which can be modified as necessary) offers considerable flexibility, and it is recommended in a shared power framework. He begins with a session task; in the session with the social worker, the family is asked to discuss possibilities for mutually rewarding activities and to see if they can reach a consensus. If they struggle, the social worker can participate in the discussion, using only the minimum intervention necessary. If the family cannot agree, the task is framed as providing a good deal of information about communication, but the social worker should propose and participate in the task with the strong expectation that it will succeed, at least partially (the family may identify some possibilities, but not yet be ready to commit, for example).

If well done, this task allows all participating family members a voice and communicates a message of shared responsibility ("it is up to all of us to make this work"). The task also provides guided practice in problem-solving communication, so that not only the activities ultimately planned but the process of planning as well constitute steps toward constructing an enriched family culture. In the normal course of family life, this task can and should happen often, so that it is a "natural" rather than a contrived task. Keeping the issue of reinforcer erosion in mind, experiments involving trying new activities or doing things in new ways need to be pursued on a regular basis. Plans need not always include all family members; a parent/child activity can be used to reconnect an adolescent with a parent who has become quite distant, for example, while other family members make plans to contribute to the family situation in other ways. All participating family members should usually have something to do between meetings with the social worker, but they need not all do the same thing (recall that shared power involves differential contributions).

Another general strategy for enhancing positive exchange involves variations of what Jacobson and his colleagues call "behavior exchange" (BE) procedures (Jacobson & Margolin, 1979; Jacobson & Christensen, 1996). Although these will be discussed in terms of work with a couple here, such procedures with variations are applicable to troubled relationships within couples, between parents and older or adult children, and among adult siblings, as well. The general BE approach is for each person to independently identify a list of things they could do that would be pleasing to the other. First, clients are asked to identify large or small actions that they might take that would please the other, but not to act on the list immediately. They share this list with the social worker in the next meeting. The partner is present and listens, but is not to respond in any way (even nonverbally), while the social worker helps the first person to elaborate his or her list, and be behaviorally specific about the items listed. The social worker then does the same with the other partner. Note that this task is intentionally different from asking each person what the other could do (although there is a place for such tasks, see chapter 6). It is each person's responsibility to work out what he or she could do to improve the relationship.

For the next task, Jacobson and Christensen (1996) give the clients the following instructions, both orally and in writing:

> I would like each of you to use your lists to enhance your partner's relationship satisfaction between now and the next session. Specifically, each of you is to go through your lists, pick one or more items that you choose to increase or decrease, and observe the effects of these changes in your behavior on the other's marital satisfaction. So, you [to the wife] pick some items from your list. Don't tell him what items you have chosen. Just implement them, and see what happens. Your goal is to increase his happiness this week. But don't tell him what you are doing or why you are doing it. And you [to the husband] are simultaneously doing the same thing with your list. Decide today or tomorrow which items you're going to work on; don't tell her what they are—just do them and see how they work.
>
> Now listen carefully. At no time between now and the next session should you discuss these lists in any way or discuss the assignment. Neither of you is under any obligation to choose any particular item from the list. I don't care what you do, as long as you do something. And most impor-

tantly, don't choose any item that will be difficult for you to do. Keep it simple and low cost. That's it. Then next week, bring the lists back to the session and we will discuss how things went. Questions? Now let's go over the assignment. (pp. 158–159)

Each person is to take active responsibility for enriching the relationship, in other words; there is no discussion about what is being done yet. The giver has "free choice" as to what he or she will do, which may make the procedure feel less burdensome (less aversive). Clients are specifically told not to attempt actions that would be too unpleasant, since those tasks would probably not be done graciously, and might be done so poorly that they would sabotage the overall effort. In the next session, all of these procedures are opened for discussion, and the worker and family members together can refine the next steps to take.

While tasks involving mutual positive exchange are critical arrows in the ecobehavioral quiver, carefully targeted unilateral reinforcement is an essential strategy in some cases. One example applies to work with a client whose partner or some other close family member is struggling with substance abuse. Recent research indicates that she (it is usually but not always a woman) can take certain steps to increase the likelihood of the substance abuser taking action, if that is her goal. Before taking those steps, though, it appears to be critical that she first act to make herself and the relationship as valuable as possible to the substance abuser, particularly by offering authentic reinforcement for positive behavior. (Extensive detail about the set of integrated procedures of which this is a part is found in chapter 10.)

In many couples cases, not just those involving substance abuse, the social worker may see only one partner; unilateral procedures for improving the relationship by increasing levels of authentic reinforcement is valuable for many such cases. Self-management techniques in which one partner self-monitors his or her own rate of social reinforcers offered to the partner are also often used to enhance solid, positive relationships; many behaviorists track such behaviors of their own, at least periodically, as one way to keep their relationships strong.

Another circumstance where most of the effort initially comes from one or two family members is parenting, especially with small children. Children who grow up in a highly reinforcing environment naturally learn to reinforce, and it clearly is the parent's responsibility to begin this process. Effective reinforcement is the core of every empirically supported parenting program. After discussions with the social worker, parents may decide to keep track of how often they recognize positive behaviors on the part of their children for a period of time. If upon monitoring the rate seems too low, the parent may then set a target to increase it. Such self-monitoring tasks are sometimes reactive, meaning the rate may increase due to monitoring, but this is not necessarily a clinical problem. A small piece of tape on the wrist or on a watch, a check-chart on the refrigerator, or some other simple record keeping device can ease recordkeeping and simultaneously act as a prompt. While more comprehensive and structured systems of reinforcers are sometimes required to address specific child behavior problems, as discussed later, simply increasing the rate of social reinforcers provided can be a powerful unilateral contribution to family life. It is important to be specific about the behavior being recognized, and to be sincere about one's appreciation in using this strategy. Everyone (including children) senses the difference between authentic recognition and manipulation, but everyone does some things that can be sincerely recognized every day.

The form of recognition offered may be culturally and personally different for different clients. For many groups and families, explicit verbal praise is appropriate, and its value should not be dismissed lightly. For other groups, however, a pointed smile or touch from a grandmother for a job well done may be more powerful. Many children, teens, and adults, find sincere questions without any punitive edge reinforcing, especially if follow-up questions asking for more detail are also asked. In effective organizations, for example, one of the most useful forms of recognition for a difficult job well-done is for a supervisor to sincerely ask the worker, in detail, about how he or she met the challenges involved (Daniels, 1994).

Notice that in none of the examples discussed above is a reinforcer exchange task simply "assigned." In every case, clients are active participants in deciding on and designing these strategic interventions, and shape them in ways that are consistent with their own repertoires and values. Problems with "compliance" therefore are less likely—even the terminology doesn't really apply. There has also been research on additional steps that can be taken the increase the likelihood that tasks will be completed. Reid's (1992) task implementation sequence includes the following steps that are associated with task completion:

- generating multiple task possibilities in ways that allow creative adaptation
- establishing motivation (consideration of rationale, likely consequences, and importance of the task)
- planning with the client for precisely how (when, where, etc.) tasks will be implemented
- identifying and resolving possible obstacles that may arise

- making an explicit agreement on the task
- summarizing the task plan (usually in writing)
- following up on the plan in the next contact.

Jacobson and Christensen (1996) suggest quite similar strategies, including explaining the rationale for a task, emphasizing its importance, involving clients in developing the specifics, anticipating and preempting reasons not to complete the task, and making sure it is clearly understood. They also suggest exaggerating the aversiveness of the task, so it turns out not to be so bad; this approach, however, is not consistent with the honesty required in a shared power paradigm. It is true that many clients have trouble completing many kinds of "homework" assignments, and I believe that an honest discussion of that fact is better than exaggeration. Jacobson and Christensen also discuss the power of a follow-up telephone call between sessions to remind clients of the task and monitor any difficulties; Stuart (1980) routinely suggests this with couples, especially in the early stages of work.

DECREASING AVERSIVES IN THE FAMILY

People often experience more needless pain from their families than from anywhere else. Family members often threaten, punish and coerce each other as a matter of course in our society. While some of this coercion is generally recognized as abusive (child abuse and battering, for example), those actions are only the extreme end of a continuum of aversive exchange in families: Those exchanges commonly occur at higher rates than reinforcers in families, as well as nearly everywhere else in society. Why do we turn so quickly to punishment and threats of punishment? According to Murray Sidman, "We punish people in the belief that we are going to get them to act differently. Usually, we want to stop or prevent particular actions. We punish someone whose conduct we consider bad for the community, bad for some other individual, or bad even for the person who is misbehaving. We want to put an end to undesirable conduct" (1989, p. 58). Aversives sometimes stop undesirable behavior, at least temporarily. As discussed in chapter 1, however, the change is often temporary. Aversives teach nothing about what might be done instead, and can damage relationships. Children who are diagnosed as meeting the criteria for "conduct disorder" or "oppositional defiant disorder," for example, elicit particularly high rates of aversives from the family, but the research indicates that they become increasingly immune to the effects. Over time, many couples also increasingly demand change from each other and simultaneously grow accustomed to those demands. Jacobson and Christensen (1996) discuss the way that couples thereby teach each other to "turn up" the aversive volume until they obtain a response; given that this works on some occasions, but not on others, an intermittent schedule of reinforcement is established—and behavior patterns learned on such schedules are particularly difficult to change. Some aversives are also delivered to family members for reasons that have nothing to do with that family member; for example, people experiencing job stress sometimes take it out on a partner or child.

The coercive cycle studied by Patterson and discussed earlier is a common result of reciprocal threats and punishments. In many families that social workers see, the level of aversives has been so high for so long that there is little commitment to trying to resolve the situation, and there are often high levels of anger, hurt, and depression. Environmental aversives (see chapter 3) contribute to the problem in an additive way. Reversing adversarial, coercive relationships therefore is a major task in work with troubled families. In the past three decades, there has been increased recognition of how important this is. For example, a few years ago it was common for parent training programs to include material on "how to spank" in non-abusive ways (for example, Polster & Dangel, 1989; Sloane, 1976/1988). More recently, however, with the general recognition of the potential damage associated with relying on punishment (Sidman, 1989), and in particular with physical punishment (Gunnoe & Mariner, 1997; Straus, Sugarman, & Giles-Sims, 1997), there has been a significant shift. Behavioral parent education materials now generally say, "Regarding Spanking: Don't!" (Latham, 1994, p. 195). Better alternatives are now well established (see chapter 7). Interestingly, some research indicates that occasional physical punishment may cause more problems in some cultural groups than others, perhaps because of how it is done (Gunnoe & Mariner, 1997). This area is discussed further in chapter 7, but in general, it is clear that high rates of aversives in the family are a problem in themselves and can make it more difficult to gain commitment for other changes as well.

Several general strategies for reducing aversive exchange in families are outlined here; more detail and other alternatives are also found in subsequent chapters. General strategies include increasing self-awareness, functional analysis, enhancing conflict resolution skills, and building mutual acceptance of differences. They are generally discussed here in ascending order of difficulty, but giving up coercion is always challenging, since aversives do often produce an immediate short-term response; it is important to honestly acknowledge this, while also helping the family to recognize the costs involved.

Increasing Self-Awareness of Aversives

As human beings, we often are not aware of our own behavior or of its effects on our world. Just as psychoeducation is important in work with families coping with mental illness, education of other kinds is useful in many areas of family work. Education about the negative effects of aversives and the value of nonprovocability is often a useful start because it sensitizes clients to notice their own behavior. The first step is to actually notice when one acts punitively or coercively. There are many ways to increase such self awareness. In some cases, simply asking clients to notice when they rely on these practices is a beginning, but it is often useful to ask people to actually keep track of how often they disagree, threaten, or criticize each other for a few days (this can also be a useful task for one person—partner or parent—who is seen for unilateral work). Cases where aversives in other areas of life (for example, at work) appear to be contributing to the situation need to be addressed either in terms of actively working to change the situation using approaches like assertiveness, or in terms of learning ways to cope with them cognitively (see chapter 3, and Mattaini, 1997, for additional strategies for dealing with systemic problems that may primarily involve one family member but may affect others as well).

Increasing awareness can often be done within a family session. In communications training sessions with families, discussed in detail in the next chapter, the social worker can use a two sided card (4" × 6" or larger), with one green side and one red side. The practitioner can place the card on a small table in the middle of the room, green side up. Any time a family member feels punished during the subsequent discussion, they turn the card to the red side—a nonverbal way of giving the person speaking an opportunity to rephrase their statement. When the statement is made nonpunitively, the card is turned back to the green side. If handled with some humor and flexibility, such techniques can increase awareness without feeling punitive themselves.

Clients (especially adults, but sometimes also older children) can also learn to respond nonprovocably to undesirable situations. The first step is identifying current and alternative self talk (for example, shifting from saying to oneself, "She has no right to do that," to "We all have times we say things we don't mean; cut her some slack"), followed by practicing those shifts either in imagination or in role plays similar to real life situations in the home. (Simultaneous practice in physically defusing arousal—relaxation skills—may also be needed.) Note that nonprovocability does *not* at all mean agreeing with everything or giving in to any demand. It means maintaining an emotional equilibrium while responding honestly, and it represents an active decision to forego the payoffs involved in getting back at someone in a hurtful way.

Functional Analysis

While some aversive exchange in families is related to external stressors, much of it is functional—family members treat each other punitively or co-ercively to get each other to change. Parents spank (and adults batter each other) to stop things they do not like, to assert control, or to coerce others to take action. Understanding why someone in the family (or everyone in the family, when a culture of coercion has been established) acts aversively, what the function of that behavior is, can often be very useful. Many parents, for example, resort to severe and sometimes abusive punishment for behavior that they see as very important or involving children's safety, especially when they don't know any other way to get their children to obey them. Helping parents to learn new ways to be "in charge" can remove the need to use highly aversive, power-assertive discipline which we now know can lead to many problems later in life (Biglan, 1995). This strategy is extensively discussed in chapter 7. Here are some core points related to decreasing aversives:

• It is nearly always possible to use reinforcers to build alternatives to the problem behavior (for example, for following instructions, or for playing in the yard rather than in the street).

• Some parents, partners, or other family members make a high level of demands on others in the family, even though the demands are not really important. Sloane (1976/1988) suggests a task in which parents keep track of how many demands they make for a few days, then decide whether that may be an excessive number (in which case they can work to reduce the number). Controlling demands, as opposed to respectful requests are never appropriate in intimate adult relationships. Where such demands are being made with the function of establishing and maintaining control, a commitment to give them up is essential to improving the family situation. See the later section on violence, and Chapter 6 on couples work for further information.

• In work with aggressive or oppositional children and youths in families where a coercive culture has been well established, both social reinforcers and back-up reinforcers (for example, privileges and tangibles that can be earned) are often needed to shift the oppositional behavior (Patterson, 1976b, 1982). In the beginning, social reinforcers by themselves may not be powerful enough to restructure the overlearned culture but should always be paired with backup reinforcers so that they ultimately come to be more influential, and the need for the backups can be phased out.

In some cases, aversives may have other functions, for example to gain some distance in a relationship that is temporarily experienced as stiflingly close. In such cases, less hurtful ways to request some space can be useful. Acceptance-based strategies (discussed later in this chapter) can also be helpful. In other cases, for example in couples where one partner has already privately decided to leave, the function of aversives may be to maintain distance, and even to induce the other partner to leave.

It is therefore crucial to work with clients to complete an honest functional analysis. A mother may be treating an older adolescent daughter very aversively, for example, for any of a number of reasons (or several). She may be so stressed at work that she strikes out an available target (her daughter); she may believe that she is "losing control" of her child and may be trying to reestablish it; or she may wish to drive the young woman, a constant reminder of the child's abusive father, out on her own. Differing functions clearly call for different interventions, ranging from problem solving around the work situation to education about developmental processes, to assisting the daughter to find new alternatives if the home situation cannot be resolved. Note that the mother in this case may be aware of her behavior and its reason, or may not be. In the instance where the child reminds the mother of the man who battered her, acting aversively may create more distance; however, the mother may keep acting in that way without realizing that distance is the function of her behavior. One way to identify possible functions is to ask about or observe what follows the behavior. The answers may (but do not always) suggest the functions.

Conflict Resolution Skills

Conflict is a major precipitant of aversive exchange in families. As defined by Patterson (1975), conflict occurs when one actor makes a demand for immediate change, and the other person involved refuses to comply. The power struggle that may emerge can escalate to a point where serious emotional or physical hurt occurs, and this may happen quite rapidly in families where such conflict has become part of family culture. In these cases, the function of coercive actions is to resolve the conflict to one's satisfaction— to get one's way. In this book and in much of the literature, problem-solving and conflict resolution is viewed as one facet of effective communication. This is discussed in detail in the next chapter. Several approaches to conflict resolution as a means to reduce aversive exchange are worth mentioning here, however.

In many communities, one or more agencies offer mediation services, including parent-adolescent mediation. Parent-adolescent mediation is a short-term approach, usually consisting of perhaps four sessions, in which parents and youths meet individually and jointly with one or two mediators (sometimes one adult and one teen mediator) to reach a respectful agreement around a particular issue in a way that satisfies everyone involved (Umbreit & Kruk, 1997). While mediation is not a solution to long-standing, multidimensional family conflicts, it is a useful alternative for families in which one major conflict is disrupting a previously reasonably good relationship. Social workers should explore the availability of such services in their community, in order to be prepared to refer when appropriate.

More extended, structured problem-solving models can be of use even to quite severely conflicted families. Serna, Schumaker, Sherman, & Sheldon (1991) reported on the development of the "Family Conference" approach with three very challenging families where conflicts regularly escalated to suicide threats, promiscuous acts of defiance, severe physical fights among adolescent siblings (where one broke another's arm, for example), and refusal to talk. This study is noteworthy for the tenacity it demonstrated, which is often crucial to effective social work practice. The professionals first taught the family members communication skills in a group setting. Everyone learned the skills, but home observations and reports indicated that they were not being used in naturally occurring conflicts. In-home skill reviews and practice were then tried, but still, there was no evidence that family members used the skills in everyday life; their conflicts continued to be played out in the old ways. Finally, the professionals developed a structured problem-solving approach that involved family members sitting down at a scheduled time, and using a structured format where family members wrote down issues that needed discussion, identified the skills required to deal with them, and then used these skills to work on the problem. (Details of this approach, which with creative variations has broad applicability, are found in the next chapter.)

Power considerations are important in conflict resolution. The author recently led a workshop in which social workers trained in mediation emphasized the need for "equal power" in parent-adolescent work, while those trained in family therapy emphasized the need to "put parents in charge." It was quite difficult for those operating from one stance to hear the other. If one thinks of power only in coercive terms, achieving a "balance of coercion" within the family is clearly not healthy, nor should any member of the family exercise coercive control through high levels of aversives. A shared power perspective redefines the issue altogether (Lowery & Mattaini, in press). Parents and adolescents each have their own strengths and powers. Power is not limited; if one gains, the other need not lose. The mediation stance might be phrased as, "You both are responsible for working toward a solution, and each of you has intelligence, emotions, experience, and creativity to bring to this process. You can also each respect the other's thoughts and feelings." The family therapists might say to both parent and child, "The parent has a responsibility to protect the child and to choose from his or her greater experience what to recognize, what to honor, and what to allow. The child, on the other hand, has a responsibility to honestly try to construct a life that works for him or her. And you both have the responsibility to respect each other's efforts." Notice that there is no power struggle implied in any of this, nor are the two stances contradictory. Nothing is "equal" or "unequal" either; each person's power and responsibility is essential—and different. Only if power is viewed as a limited resource that must be taken from someone else does a problem emerge.

One final point: Recall that Patterson's definition of conflict includes a demand for *immediate* change. One major step toward conflict resolution is the recognition that a solution to every problem need not always be discovered and agreed upon instantly. It is helpful for social workers to keep in mind that immediate solutions are necessary only in life-threatening circumstances; clients, too, can be reminded that it is often necessary for issues to be discussed, but a period of thinking-time may need to elapse before a solution acceptable to all emerges. Respectfully agreeing to disagree, for now, is often, paradoxically, an important skill for reaching agreement.

Building Acceptance of Differences

People are different. What they prefer and value is different, and what they dislike is different. At present, the cutting edge of family and couples work involves procedures to increase acceptance, rather than change, within the family (Hayes, Jacobson, Follette, & Dougher, 1994; Jacobson and Christensen, 1996). Acceptance-based strategies are explored in depth in the next chapter, but it is important to open the discussion here, because increases in acceptance naturally lead to decreases in aversive exchange. These new models are nuanced and carefully defined; it is important not to oversimplify what they are saying. For example, no one believes that clients should be encouraged to tolerate abuse, or that everything and anything should be accepted. Acceptance, in fact, often proves to be a first step toward change, rather than an alternative to it. In addition, acceptance-based strategies can be viewed as "change first" approaches, that have much in common with behavior-exchange procedures discussed earlier in this chapter.

When two people live together as a couple, some predictable processes tend to play out over time. In the beginning, both tend to show the parts of their own repertoires that the other finds attractive and to attend to parts of the other's behavior that they like. Over time, other less desirable behaviors emerge, and habits or approaches to life that once seemed intriguing and attractive sometimes also may come to be experienced as being at least somewhat aversive. For example, a man may choose a partner who is very lively and spontaneous because this companion encourages him to loosen up a bit. Over time, however, that spontaneity may become tiresome. What first attracts often is what ultimately causes struggle. Similarly, parents often have particular (and high) expectations of their children. However, as they grow up, children come to value things and deal with the world in ways that the parent did not expect and finds aversive. Children, in turn, over time come to see that the parents they once idealized have weaknesses, sometimes very significant ones.

Accepting differences like these in honest ways, including acknowledging the pain they may cause, leads to far better outcomes than does punishing others just for being different from what one would want. There is pain in relationships; there are inevitably gaps in intimacy, and it is both unreasonable and unrealistic to expect others to change repertoires that may define who they are and may have been all their lives. When balanced with a personal commitment to take action to improve relationships to the extent possible, acceptance of these realities leads to mature relationships.

Acceptance and commitment therapy (ACT) (Hayes & Wilson, 1994) emphasizes the need to accept rather than fight truths about oneself, one's life, and other people, as a precondition to committing to take steps that may in the long run lead to change. A couple who came to see the author about their relationship illustrates this point. Many areas were troublesome to the wife, including a very judgmental and demanding mother-in-law, financial concerns, and lack of time together. The husband, however, indicated in the beginning that he did not believe there were any very serious troubles. From an ACT perspective, he needed to hear her struggles, and accept that his marriage was not as ideal as he had convinced himself, before committing to taking steps to make it better. He also needed to accept that this awareness would sometimes make him uncomfortable. Both partners needed to accept that his mother was as she was (for all sorts of developmental reasons, which they could identify to some extent). This is where the nuances are important, however. Accepting that the mother was who she was did not mean tolerating abuse. It meant honestly facing what they had to deal with, and then committing to work together to manage their contacts with her so she would not poison their relationship.

Acceptance can fortify family members for the hard work to come, but can also help them to honestly engage each other as they are, which can be one of the most enriching experiences in life. While sometimes frightening, in the long run honest acceptance is a far better practice to establish in the family than those in which everyone attempts to coerce each other to give them some small satisfaction, while denying the pain and challenges. More detail regarding strategies for enhancing communication, conflict resolution, and acceptance is found in the next chapter. First, however, we turn to the extreme end of coercion in the family, violence and abuse, and what is known about the best practices for work with violence in the family.

VIOLENCE IN THE FAMILY

Violence, often quite severe, occurs very frequently in families, although hard numbers are difficult to establish. Acts of physical coercion may occur in half the homes in the United States each year, with spouse abuse occurring in at least 15 percent (and perhaps many more) (Fagan & Browne, 1993). About 3 million cases of child maltreatment (about one-third involving physical abuse) are reported each year. Perhaps one-half to two-thirds of these are "unfounded"; but given the many definitional and measurement issues in child maltreatment, many cases, possibly a majority, are not reported (Mattaini, McGowan & Williams, 1996; National Research Council, 1993). Little definite data are available about violence against the elderly, but it appears to affect at least 3 to 4 percent of that population (Reiss & Roth, 1993). The incidence of sibling violence, which can be very severe, is apparently higher than any other form of family violence.

Despite the difficulty in estimating precise numbers, the number of families seen in social work settings where violence occurs is very high. Because the question is often not asked, and because of the social stigma associated with family violence, it is frequently not recognized even when it is present. Many estimates indicate that some physical violence occurs in half of adult intimate relationships over the lifetime of the relationship, although some is low-level physical aggression whose function is not coercive control, and that may involve different dynamics than does battering (Jacobson & Christensen, 1996). In this chapter, we focus particularly on battering between spouses and intimate partners, and to some extent among other adult family members; violence toward children will be examined in chapter 8. Violence toward women by men is sometimes accompanied by reciprocal violence by women toward men. In general, however, the data suggest that men do more damage and usually do not experience the emotional terror that women do when they themselves are threatened or attacked; in addition, women's violence apparently usually involves self-defense (Fagan & Browne, 1993).

Issues at larger social levels, including histories of oppression and the effects of severe economic and educational deprivation, are related to family violence in many ways. Poverty and its associated stresses, for example, increase risk for child maltreatment (although it occurs at a significant rate in all socioeconomic and cultural groups). In the past decade or so, battering partners and beating children have been increasingly recognized as human rights issues, and not simply "family matters" (Lowery, 1998). Among the rights guaranteed by the Universal Declaration of Human Rights promulgated in 1948 (United Nations, 1993) is "the right to life, liberty and security of person" (p. 5); societies have an obligation in justice to recognize and ensure these rights to all, and to protect their members from "patriarchal terrorism" (Johnson, 1995). Whether torture occurs for "political" reasons or within the family, it is still torture. Family violence not only causes profound emotional and often physical damage (including death) within the family itself, but it also damages us all. Violence and coercive threats have no place in intimate relationships.

Despite the importance and ubiquity of family violence among social work clients, identifying best practices for intervening has so far proved difficult, perhaps in part because acceptance of such behavior is deeply ingrained in a coercive sociocultural matrix. A number of major examinations of the available research have struggled with the lack of definitive data (for example, Crowell & Burgess, 1996; Fagan & Browne, 1993). Unfortunately, as is true with substance abuse, practitioners often develop very strong opinions about "best practices" with little data to support them. Those strong opinions sometimes stand in the way of collecting the data we need (Brannen & Rubin, 1996). The material that follows reflects the state of the art to the extent that seems possible at the moment, but it is essential that social workers continue to follow and contribute to the gradually emerging literature in this area.

When the data are not determinate, well-established theory can also be useful in identifying possible interventive strategies. Violence is a behavior. It is not caused by anger, by substance abuse, or by mental illness, although in some cases such factors may decrease inhibitions. Repetitive violence (in the family or elsewhere) occurs because it pays off in some way, largely by establishing coercive control, and sometimes by relieving negative emotional states (Mattaini, Twyman, Chin, & Lee, 1996). While a honeymoon period often occurs after a violent episode, during which many noncontingent and reciprocal reinforcers are exchanged, the pattern of coercive control typically returns eventually, because it is the most reliable strategy the person involved currently has for maintaining control. Despite promises and often abject apologies, in most cases the evidence suggests that battering does not stop on its own, but rather tends to escalate over time. Understanding battering in this way has substantial interventive implications.

Work with Victims and Survivors

Whether the victim of battering is a legal spouse, a domestic partner of the same or the opposite sex, or a child, parent, or sibling, a first concern must always be safety. Self-determination is also a critical consideration; while the social worker may personally believe that a client absolutely should leave the batterer, that decision needs to be the client's; denying her (it is usually but not always a woman) that right, even if it were possible, would be profoundly disempowering. The research has clarified that there are many costs, financial and emotional, associated with leaving, and in fact a woman who leaves a batterer is at significantly higher risk of injury and death for some months after leaving than she was before (Fagan & Browne, 1993). The social worker therefore has several important functions. One is to listen nonpunitively and nondemandingly, to let the victim find her voice, without which she cannot move ahead.

A second function is to help the victim carefully consider each of her options, and the positive and negative, short and long term consequences associated with each. It is common for a battered woman to need a period of weeks to years before being ready to take active steps, and it is her right to take the time she needs. The social worker can inform her of available options (including shelter possibilities), and how to access them, but clearly should not replicate the coercive processes the victim has already experienced. It is essential to recognize what a major and often costly shift leaving can be. It often includes giving up one's home and many possessions that one has worked for for years. Facing friends, family, and coworkers often also produces substantial shame and embarrassment. And of course enormous risks are often involved if the batterer pursues the victim to a friend or family member's home, to a shelter, or (as commonly happens) to work after she leaves.

Social workers can in some cases develop resources like support groups (discussed later in this chapter) that have proven to be useful. And finally, social workers can help clients to make "safety plans." It is critical to discuss safety planning early on in discussions of battering, usually in the first session. For a victim who for now chooses to go back home, it is useful to plan ahead for the times when she (and perhaps her children) may be at risk.

While such a plan clearly needs to be individualized, it will usually include considerations like the following:

- Keeping a bag of items that will be needed if a quick escape is necessary packed and in an accessible place (for example, near the door, in the trunk of the car, or with a relative); items packed may include car keys, money, medicines, necessary clothing, and items needed for the children.
- Planning ahead how she will leave the home, and where she will go if she has to leave; there should be more than one option (family, friends, shelters), and these options should be cleared in advance so the client will feel prepared.
- Setting aside money, if possible, that she can use to manage immediate needs if she decides to leave.
- Consideration of warning signs for battering is often helpful; in some cases a victim may be able to leave before the situation escalates to the point where she is in imminent danger.

Because recent research indicates that batterers often physically abuse their children as well (and because being forced to watch abuse can be abusive in itself), child protective issues often intertwine with those of domestic violence. In some situations, there can be legal or ethical obligations to report family situations that place the children at risk. This is complicated, because it may involve breaking a parent's confidentiality, so that it is essential to have consultation available to help clarify options and obligations when such decisions need to be made.

One intervention that appears to be valuable in work with victims of battering is support groups which can help the client move from the position of victim to that of survivor. In an important study by Tutty, Bidgood, & Rothery (1993), women who participated in support groups showed improvements in many emotional and cognitive areas (for example, perceived stress and locus of control). They also reported better family functioning and lower incidence of both emotional and physical abuse even among those who stayed with their batterers. While intervention with the victims appears to have made a difference in the behavior of the batterers, it is important to note that this does not mean that the women were "responsible for" the abuse, or somehow were bringing it upon themselves. It may be that in addition to providing new coping skills, participation in the groups opened up the rigid boundaries that batterers often attempt to enforce, making future instances of battering more public, and therefore more risky legally and personally.

The content of the time-limited groups examined by Tutty, Bidgood and Rothery included safety planning, recognition of the coercive nature of battering, reduction of self-blame and learned helplessness, explorations of larger sociocultural practices that support battering, opportunities to express anger (and loss, if the relationship ended), and the development of support networks to reduce social isolation. While there is much unknown about how to make such groups maximally effective, the existing data suggest that referral to, or establishment of such groups should be a standard part of social work intervention for battering.

Work with Batterers

Even more than in the case of work with victims, there is little consensus regarding the most effective interventions for batterers, and even less clear data. Some in the field believe that "nothing works," but this is probably an excessively negative view given accumulating data (Tolman & Edleson, 1995). Given what little data is available, current practice wisdom suggests that individual treatment is often not effective, in part because the drop-out rate is very high, and that couples work is usually counterindicated because of the possible risk to the victim. Group interventions are commonly recommended, along with coordination with the legal system. Social workers who work with batterers should read the major sources in this area (for example, Fagan & Brown, 1994, Crowell & Burgess, 1996; Edleson & Tolman, 1992); the material that follows only summarizes some critical points that should be core knowledge among all social workers.

The "Duluth Model" for work with batterers (Pence & Paymar, 1993) is the most commonly used in practice, and is highly consistent with an ecobehavioral approach to practice. This model recognizes that battering is simply an extreme manifestation of an overall pattern of coercive control. The Power and Control wheel (see Figure 4-2) identifies several related strategies, including intimidation, emotional abuse, isolation, assertion of male privilege, and others.

The core of the approach is a group intervention within which a culture that fails to support the practices of power and control emerges, which instead supports the alternative practices shown in the Equality Wheel (Figure 4-3).

Note that the Duluth model not only identifies practices to be reduced but is also constructional—it makes clear what should be done instead. (As might be expected in a culture that relies heavily on coercion, the Power and Control Wheel is much better known than the Equality Wheel, although theory tells us that *both* are clearly crucial in a constructional model—we must know what to construct.) The Duluth Model exposes the

Figure 4-2

The Power and Control Wheel. Source: E. Pence & M. Paymar (1993). *Education groups for men who batter: The Duluth model* (p. 185). New York: Springer Publishing Company, Inc. Used with permission.

client to a group culture where other men like himself do not accept coercion, but do support its alternatives, offering modeling, respected sources of rules, and valued reinforcers. The literature emphasizes the importance of developing such a group culture, since groups of batterers could instead support traditional sexism and coercive practices. It appears that court-ordered treatment of this kind may be more successful than is voluntary treatment. This may occur primarily by reducing dropouts, although many court systems do a poor job at following up on such orders. There may also be some clients for whom entirely different models may be more appropriate (Bennett, 1998; Moore, Greenfield, Wilson, & Kok, 1998).

The justice system is a major player in dealing with battering, but there are no simple solutions there. While initial research conducted in Minneapolis suggested that mandatory arrest reduced battering, those results were not supported in other areas of the country or with lower socioeconomic groups (for some of whom arrest may be a more normative experience) (Sherman, 1992). By itself, mandatory arrest is at best a weak intervention, as are many other legal remedies including court orders of protection and court-ordered referrals (Crowell & Burgess, 1996). It is theoretically likely that integrated cultures among police, judges, prosecutors, and agencies where battering is viewed as an unacceptable, terroristic vio-

Figure 4-3

The Equality Wheel. Source: E. Pence & M. Paymar (1993). *Education groups for men who batter: The Duluth model* (p. 186). New York: Springer Publishing Company, Inc. Used with permission.

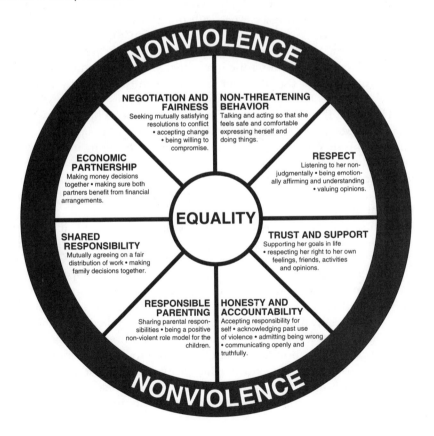

lation of human rights could have a profound impact, however, and this should be the policy and advocacy goal of concerned social workers.

Other forms of intervention are controversial, but the data are beginning to show that in some cases they may be effective. In a controlled study reported by Brannen and Rubin (1996), couples in which less severe battering was occurring were referred by the court to one of two conditions. All couples involved in the study indicated their intention to stay together. The first condition was gender-specific groups: the women attended support groups like those discussed above, and the men attended batterers' groups similar to those just described. The second condition used couples' groups that focused on clarifying the batterer's responsibility, contracting for change and safety, explorations of alternative ways of problem solving, and related cognitive and behavioral interventions. Both conditions produced nearly identical results, with more than 90 percent of couples in each group reporting no further violence at the 6-month follow-up.

An even more controversial intervention, and one that may be dangerous under many conditions, is work with the individual couple. The issues raised may increase risk to the victim, and the format may suggest to those participating that the members of the couple somehow share responsibility for the problem, perpetuating the injustice done. Some family approaches may eventually prove useful under certain circumstances, however. Cloé Madanes, a major player in family therapy, recently presented an intriguing model in which the closed system of the violent family is opened up in dramatic ways (Madanes, Keim, & Smelser, 1995), not only by involving the courts and protective services, but by, for example, bringing in the *batterer's mother* (telling her that her job is not completed), along with other members of the social network. This "therapy of social action" works with an extended social network to protect the safety and human rights of the woman and children.

Because this model has not yet been rigorously tested, it is not yet part of the state of the art. The parallel development of many of these emerging approaches is interesting, however. All clarify that violence is a serious collective problem involving human rights, and all clarify that coercive violence in intimate family relations is absolutely unacceptable. All are also constructional, emphasizing the need to develop cultures within the family, and the networks within which the family is embedded, that shape and maintain alternative practices like respect, honesty, accountability, shared responsibility, nonthreatening behavior, and the others shown on the equality wheel. In other words, the goal in practice with persons who choose to live within families, even the most dysfunctional, is to work toward the construction of shared power cultures, as opposed to cultures of coercion.

REFERENCES

Bennett, L. W. (1998). In defense of batterer-program standards. *Families in Society,* *79,* 93–97.

Biglan, A. (1991). Distressed behavior and its context. *The Behavior Analyst, 14,* 157–169.

Biglan, A. (1995). *Changing cultural practices.* Reno: Context Press.

Bornstein, P. H., & Bornstein, M. T. (1986). *Marital therapy: A behavioral-communications approach.* New York: Pergamon.

Brannen, S. J., & Rubin, A. (1996). Comparing the effectiveness of gender-specific and couples groups in a court-mandated spouse abuse treatment program. *Research on Social Work Practice, 6,* 405–424.

Crowell, N. A., & Burgess, A. W. (Eds.),(1996). *Understanding violence against women.* Washington, DC: National Academy Press.

Daniels, A. C. (1994). *Bringing out the best in people.* New York: McGraw-Hill.

Edleson, J. L., & Tolman, R. M. (1992). *Intervention for men who batter.* Newbury Park, CA: Sage Publications.

Fagan, J., & Browne, A. (1993). Violence between spouses and intimates: Physical aggression between women and men in intimate relationships. In A. J. Reiss, Jr. & J. A. Roth (Eds.), *Understanding and preventing violence: Volume 3: Social Influences,* (pp. 115–292). Washington, DC: National Academy Press.

Follette, W. C., & Jacobson, N. S. (1988). Behavioral marital therapy in the treatment of depressive disorders. In I. R. H. Falloon (Ed.), *Handbook of behavioral family therapy* (pp. 257–284). New York: Guilford Press.

Gottman, J. M., Markman, H., & Notarius, C. (1977). The topography of marital conflict: A sequential analysis of verbal and nonverbal behavior. *Journal of Marriage and the Family, 39,* 461–477.

Gottman, J. M., Notarius, C., Markman, H., Bank, S., Yoppi, B., & Rubin, M. E. (1976). Behavior exchange theory and marital decision making. *Journal of Personality and Social Psychology, 34,* 14–23.

Gunnoe, M. L., & Mariner, C. L., (1997). Toward a developmental-contextual model of the effects of parental spanking on children's aggression. *Archives of Pediatrics and Adolescent Medicine, 151,* 768–775.

Hartman, A., & Laird, J. (1983). *Family-centered social work practice.* New York: Free Press.

Hayes, S. C., Jacobson, N. S., Follette, V. M., & Dougher, M. J. (Eds.) (1994). *Acceptance and change: Content and context in psychotherapy.* Reno, NV: Context Press.

Hayes, S. C., & Wilson, K. G. (1994). Acceptance and commitment therapy: Altering the verbal support for experiential avoidance. *The Behavior Analyst, 17,* 289–303.

Jacobson, N. S., & Christensen (1996). *Integrative couple therapy.* New York: Norton Press.

Jacobson, N. S., & Margolin, G. (1979). *Marital therapy: Strategies based on social learning and behavior exchange principles.* New York: Brunner/Mazel.

Johnson, M. P. (1995). Patriarchal terrorism and common couple violence: Two forms of violence against women. *Journal of Marriage and the Family, 57.* 283–294.

Karney, B. R., & Bradbury, T. N. (1995). The longitudinal course of marital quality and stability: A review of theory, method, and research. *Psychological Bulletin, 118,* 3–34.

Latham, G. I. (1994). *The power of positive parenting.* North Logan, UT: P & T Ink.

Lowery, C. T. (1998). Social justice and international human rights. In M. A. Mattaini, C. T. Lowery, & C. H. Meyer (Eds.), *The foundations of social work practice: A graduate text* (2nd ed.) (pp. 20–42). Washington, DC: NASW Press.

Lowery, C. T., & Mattaini, M. A. (in press). Shared power in social work: A Native American perspective. In H. Briggs & K. Corcoran, *Structuring change in social work practice.* Chicago: Lyceum.

Madanes, C., Keim, J. P., & Smelser, D. (1995). *The violence of men: New techniques for working with abusive families: A therapy of social action.* San Francisco: Jossey-Bass.

Mattaini, M. A. (1997). *Clinical practice with individuals.* Washington, DC: NASW Press.

Mattaini, M. A., Grellong, B. A., & Abramovitz, R. (1992). The clientele of a child and family mental health agency: Empirically-derived household clusters and implications for practice. *Research on Social Work Practice, 2,* 380–404.

Mattaini, M. A., McGowan, B. G., & Williams, G. (1996). Child maltreatment. In M. A. Mattaini & B. A. Thyer (Eds.), *Finding solutions to social problems: Behavioral strategies for change* (pp. 223–266). Washington, DC: American Psychological Association.

Mattaini, M. A., Twyman, J. S., Chin, W., & Lee, K. N. (1996). Youth violence. In M. A. Mattaini & B. A. Thyer (Eds.), *Finding solutions to social problems: Behavioral strategies for change* (pp. 75–111). Washington, DC: APA Books.

Moore, K., Greenfield, W., Wilson, M., & Kok, A. (1998). Moore and colleagues respond. *Families in Society, 79,* 97.

National Research Council (1993). *Understanding child abuse and neglect* [Report of the Panel on Research on Child Abuse and Neglect]. Washington, DC: National Academy Press.

Patterson, G. R. (1975). *Families.* Champaign, IL: Research Press.

Patterson, G. R. (1976a). *Living with children.* Champaign, IL: Research Press.

Patterson, G. R. (1976b). The aggressive child: Victim and architect of a coercive system. In E. J. Mash, L. A. Hamerlynck, & L. C. Handy (Eds.), *Behavior modification and families* (pp. 267–316). New York: Brunner/Mazel.

Patterson, G. R. (1982). *Coercive family process.* Eugene, OR: Castalia Press.

Pence, E., & Paymar, M. (1993). *Education groups for men who batter: The Duluth model.* New York: Springer.

Polster, R. A., & Dangel, R. F. (1989). Behavioral parent training in family therapy. In B. A. Thyer (Ed.), *Behavioral family therapy* (pp. 31–54). Springfield, IL: Charles C. Thomas.

Reid, W. J. (1985). *Family problem solving.* New York: Columbia University Press.

Reid, W. J. (1992). *Task Strategies.* New York: Columbia University Press.

Reiss, A. J., Jr., & Roth, J. A. (Eds.), (1993). *Understanding and preventing violence.* (Vol. 1). Washington, DC: National Academy Press.

Serna, L. A., Schumaker, J. B., Sherman, J. A., & Sheldon, J. B. (1991). In-home generalization of social interactions in families of adolescents with behavior problems. *Journal of Applied Behavior Analysis, 24,* 733–746.

Sidman, M. (1989). *Coercion and its fallout.* Boston: Authors Cooperative.

Sherman, L. W. (1992). *Policing domestic violence: Experiments and dilemmas.* New York: Free Press.

Sloane, H. N., Jr. (1976/1988). *The good kid book.* Champaign, IL: Research Press.

Straus, M. A., Sugarman, D. B., & Giles-Sims, J. (1997). Spanking by parents and subsequent antisocial behavior of children. *Archives of Pediatrics and Adolescent Medicine, 151,* 761–767.

Stuart, R. B. (1980). *Helping couples change: A social learning approach to marital therapy.* New York: Guilford Press.

Tolman, R. M., & Edleson, J. L. (1995). Intervention for men who batter: A research review. In S. M. Stith and M. A. Straus (Eds.), *Understanding partner violence: Prevalence, causes, consequences, and solutions* (pp. 163–173). Minneapolis: National Council on Family Relations.

Tutty, L. M., Bidgood, B. A., & Rothery, M. A. (1993). Support groups for battered women: Research on their efficacy. *Journal of Family Violence, 8,* 325–343.

Umbreit, M. S., & Kruk, E. (1997). Parents and children: Parent-child mediation. In E. Kruk (Ed.), *Mediation and conflict resolution in social work and the human services* (pp. 97–115). Chicago: Nelson-Hall.

United Nations (1993). *The International Bill of Human Rights.* New York: United Nations.

Webster-Stratton, C. (1997). From parent training to community building. *Families in Society, 78,* 156–171.

Wills, T. A., Weiss, R. L., & Patterson, G. R. (1974). A behavioral analysis of the determinants of marital satisfaction. *Journal of Consulting and Clinical Psychology, 42,* 802–811.

CHAPTER FIVE

Interventive Strategies: Enhancing Communication and Acceptance in Families

Clear, respectful, honest communication and effective problem solving have long been recognized as essential to adequate family functioning and relationship enhancement. Family therapists and behavioral social workers interested in family work often therefore make work with communication a central focus of practice. Recently, strategies based on "acceptance" of each other (and other realities) have received increasing attention, although early communication theorists also recognized the importance of acceptance as a prerequisite to communication (for example, Gordon, 1970). In mainstream United States culture, people often talk about communication and breakdowns in communication, but this culture commonly does not prepare people well to actually communicate. Communication and acceptance are essential to any genuine relationship, including parent-child and adult-adult relationships. In raising small children, parents also rely on other strategies (see chapter 7), but need to establish effective communication channels early, since they become increasingly important as children grow up. A point comes in every child's life when parents' main influence comes through the power of relationship, at a time (usually in adolescence) when others, especially peers, become increasingly powerful factors. And among adults, relationships are maintained and deepened only through respectful, accepting communication.

Communication was a central focus of the family therapy movement as it developed from roots like the work of Bateson and his colleagues (for example, Bateson, Jackson, Haley, & Weakland, 1956) which evolved into the Mental Research Institute (MRI) in Palo Alto, California, in the late 1950s and 1960s (see, for example, Watzlawick, Beavin, & Jackson, 1967). Virginia Satir (a social worker) emphasized identifying and shifting communication patterns in the family in her classic *Conjoint Family Therapy* (1967). Strategic, structural and systemic family therapists often work particularly with communication processes (Jay Haley [strategic] worked at MRI for a time, and he later worked with Salvador Minuchin [structural]). Behavioral family work has always recognized the importance of constructing effective communication repertoires (Stuart, 1980; Thomas, 1977). Client-centered therapy (Rogers, 1951) relied on "active listening" skills and provided some of the underpinnings of the approach to listening skills discussed here. Some of the basic tenets of crisis intervention practice (Parad & Parad, 1990) also evolved from communication models, including a reliance on active listening and structured problem solving.

Work on family communications offers two particular advantages. First, it is usually relatively easy for family members to agree that they have a "communication problem" and that the family might benefit from improved communication. This agreement not only provides a starting point for contracting, but also shifts the focus from a single "identified patient" in the family who may be assigned the blame for family struggles, to an emphasis on family process. (Note that family process is only an appropriate target for work when that is where the primary issues lie; if environmental stresses are the primary issue, it is poor practice to focus on intrafamily dynamics.) The second major advantage of communication work is that this process can make a rapid and meaningful contribution to changing families' experiences, either actively by constructing new transactional patterns, or indirectly by increasing mutual acceptance.

DIMENSIONS OF COMMUNICATION

Gordon, in his book, *Parent Effectiveness Training* (1970), identifies three major clusters of behavior associated with communication: (1) listening (receptive) repertoires, (2) expressive repertoires, and (3) problem-solving repertoires. Although some of Gordon's examples are dated, three decades later there is still great wisdom in his work, and more recent statements (for example, Ginsberg, 1997) rely on Gordon through no more than one or two degrees of separation. (Gordon in turn relied on Rogers and others; progress always involves building on the work of others.) We will also rely on that basic framework here. The constructional aspect of this framework is particularly useful; rather than focusing primarily on identifying "what people are doing wrong" (pathology) and helping them to stop, Gordon's approach assumes that communication repertoires are skills that can be learned, and that if they haven't been, they can be. Once family members experience success with those repertoires, they will no longer need to turn to coercive strategies, which are always costly. While it is often helpful to sensitize family members to their own behaviors that may block communication, the primary emphasis should clearly be on learning and using new repertoires.

Contemporary behavioral science has clarified that in the development of verbal cultures, "[t]here must be a listener before there is a speaker" (Skinner, 1989, p. 36), and the same is true in families. There is often a tendency to jump to "how can I express myself so they will hear me," but if no one is listening, communication cannot occur. Communication training, for families, for social workers, in business, or in any other setting needs to begin by teaching participants how to really listen to and hear each other. Many times, for example, people interrupt others; even if they don't they often are thinking about what they will say when their turn comes, rather than truly listening to the other person.

A second set of critical skills is learning how to express oneself to make it as easy as possible for the other person to listen nondefensively, and to respond positively. Only when all parties to a discussion are listening and expressing themselves well and respectfully is it likely that they will be able to reach an agreement when they do not immediately concur about an issue. Although some people have learned to enjoy arguing for the attention it produces, in general the reinforcer for conversation is agreement (Skinner, 1989). If a family consistently fails to achieve agreement, they are likely to either try to avoid one another, to switch to coercive strategies to obtain what they want, or both.

Channels of Communication

Communication consists of more than just the words said. A message involves nonverbal and *paraverbal* channels in addition to the verbal. Nonverbal communication involves "body language"—how one sits and moves while listening or expressing oneself. For example, it is common in conflicted families for family members to turn away, roll their eyes, smile at inappropriate moments, or otherwise communicate emotions through facial expression and body position. Paraverbal dimensions involve tone of voice, volume, and the use of sounds that may not be words but still communicate. It is usually important to begin communication skills training by clarifying the importance of these dimensions (demonstration and modeling are usually important here), even before practicing what to say (and what not to say).

The goal is to help family members communicate "openness" to each other. In many but not all cultures in the United States, a body position in which people are sitting at a comfortable distance for close communication;

are leaning toward and looking at each other; do not construct obvious blocks with arms and legs, hair, or furniture; and "look interested" is an important beginning. In some cultural groups, however, variations are present. For example, for some traditional Native American groups, constant eye contact may feel intrusive; in the author's mental health work in rural Alaska, for example, some of the best communication occurred when people were sitting parallel to each other, looking out over the Yukon River. For some Filipinos, it is respectful to look at someone when they are speaking ("paying attention"), but not to look uninterruptedly at them when you are speaking ("staring"—which is experienced as aggressive). In one such family, the wife would reach out and touch her husband to get eye contact if he looked away when she was speaking; she was almost certainly unaware that she did this.

At the same time, it is crucial not to stereotype; some Native Americans maintain especially intimate eye contact at emotionally important moments, for example. General knowledge of diverse practices in this area is certainly useful, but it is also often necessary to discuss how people communicate interest and respect nonverbally in their family. Family members may be able to articulate this immediately; if not, family patterns are likely to be recognized later as a result of the sensitivity raised by the discussion.

"Tone of voice" is one of the most common complaints family members raise about each other. There are several strategies for addressing this, and a creative mix may be useful in any particular case. First, family members often attenuate their aggressive and coercive practices at least in the beginning when meeting with the social worker, providing a window of opportunity to teach new repertoires. Patterson (1975) indicates that in areas like voice tone, it can be useful to begin with the principle that "the victim is always right"—if one feels hurt, it is best to practice a different way to say something that is more likely to be heard. It is crucial to do this in a matter-of-fact way, normalizing such conflicts and indicating that it is not a major problem to modify these patterns. Humor can help.

In families where this kind of pattern is an issue, a red/green prompting card is a useful first approach. When the worker or family identifies a pattern of using an adversarial tone of voice (often even when the words expressed, the "content," is positive), the social worker can suggest that learning how to say things in a way more likely to be heard could work better and elicit the families' agreement. Then, a two-sided card, with one side a bright red and the other side green (as mentioned in the previous chapter) can be placed on a small table in everyone's reach (note that this may also require sitting close together, which can increase intimacy). The card begins with the green side up. Anyone who experiences an expression as a "zap"—as hurtful verbally, paraverbally, or nonverbally—can turn the card to the red side. Whoever is speaking then makes a second attempt to express him- or herself more respectfully. If successful, the card is turned back, and the conversation can continue without major interruption. If the restatement is not successful, it may be necessary to interrupt the process and discuss and practice alternatives.

When using this approach with a family, the author begins by practicing in a light way, modeling a statement or two that he might make to someone; that person turns the card over, and the author makes a restatement. The approach is particularly engaging for families with latency-age or adolescent children. The card need not be used for more than part of a session or two and can always be brought out again. It is important when using this (or any other technique) that it be presented as a simple tool that can be helpful in doing something important, and not as something that feels too much like a game. A similar process can, of course, be structured without the card, through discussion.

For some cases, an alternative approach is a better fit; this consists in teaching one or more family members to respond to the overt, verbal content, and not to the nonverbal or paraverbal message. This is useful when the function of the nonverbal message is to get a reaction, to "push someone's buttons," as often happens when there is a lot of anger present. In this case, the goal is to teach alternative, verbal ways of communicating anger. If coercive expressions are a common problem in the family, responding to content technique should only be used over the short term, while alternatives are constructed; no one should be asked to tolerate ongoing abuse. On the other hand, in generally well functioning families, it is useful for everyone to be willing to be nonprovocable on occasion, since, as a common maxim in the field says, "everyone is crazy once in a while."

The Content of Communication

In functional family communication, people are able to express and to hear several kinds of messages, all of which are important. They are able to describe events and experiences honestly; they are able to request what they would like; they are able to share their responses to and opinions about situations; and they are able to suggest possible solutions to issues that come up. They are also able to express what they are feeling emotionally, and to empathize with each other's emotions. Negative emotions are neither the only ones nor the most important ones that need to be communicated in this way. Expressing positive statements of caring, appreciation, and joy is even more critical to developing a satisfactory and reinforcing family life; this is one of the most frequently missing repertoires in families that are in conflict or have struggled with each other. Just as doing reinforcing things together is critical (see the previous chapter), so is expressing positive emotions. Examples of all of these types of content are found in the material that follows.

BARRIERS TO COMMUNICATION

Families often agree immediately that they are experiencing communication problems, or would like to enhance their communication. If this is not immediately apparent, however, the worker can ask a series of questions, prefaced by a statement such as, "One of the areas that is often important for families is improving their communication. Let me ask, do people in your family ever do any of the following?"

- Ordering or commanding ? ("Just do what I say!")
- Warning or threatening? ("If you don't, you'll be grounded for the summer.")
- Moralizing or preaching? ("The grown-up thing to do would be. . . .")
- Advising or giving solutions without knowing the whole story? ("Just walk away. . . .")
- Lecturing or giving "logical" arguments? ("Now, let's be logical about this. . . .")
- Judging or blaming? ("You never care what happens to me!")
- Name-calling? ("You little slut. . . .")
- Analyzing or diagnosing each other's problems? ("The real problem is, you're jealous of your brother. . . .")
- Probing or interrogating? ("Who else was there? What exactly were you doing for all that time?")
- Giving false reassurance or patronizing? ("I'm sure you're just exaggerating—I bet you're one of the most popular kids in the class")
- Withdrawing, distracting? ("Let's just forget it and talk about something else. . . .")

These are some common communication blocks; see Gordon (1970) for more detail and other examples. In some cases, it is useful to go through a full list like this; about halfway through, family members are often smiling or laughing, saying "Oh, yes . . ." or otherwise indicating that these kinds of exchanges resonate with their experiences. In other cases, the social worker can select a few communication blocks that seem likely, based on contacts so far, to be obstacles in the family, and ask about those. The questions can be followed by a brief discussion of the kinds of situations where these blocks tend to happen.

This exercise confirms that obstacles to effective communication exist in the family; the discussion can give some guidance regarding the kinds of situations where learning new skills might be particularly helpful. The social worker should guide discussion away from extensively blaming individuals for these patterns and move toward discussion of the importance of everyone learning new skills so that these problems are minimized.

Sloane (1976/1988) has identified perhaps the most important block to communication in families: family members often inadvertently punish each other for talking. He gives the following examples:

Mother: Where did you go after school?
John: Oh, a couple of us went over to Brad's to listen to CDs.
Mother: Was Milt [another adolescent the parent feels is a "bad" influence] there? (p. 307)

Parent: How's your job going?
Mary: Oh, I don't know, it's really getting to be a drag—I've been thinking about quitting.
Parent: Can't you stick to anything for over a week? (p. 308)

In both cases, the parent punished the young person for talking; in the first case subtly, in the second more directly. Not surprisingly, youths who experience such interactions are likely to stop talking. Notice that the situation here puts the youth in a double bind: He or she will be punished for talking but will also be punished ("You never tell me anything") for not talking. Adults punish each other in similar ways. For example, imagine that one partner (Louise) tells the other (Maria), "I'm feeling burned out. . . . Would you like to go somewhere for a romantic weekend?" and Maria responds, "I thought you had a lot of work to do." Maria has punished Louise's description of her feelings, as well as her effort to reach out in an affectionate way. The function of Maria's statement may be distancing (many couples struggle with distance and closeness—see chapter 6), or may be avoiding a weekend that Maria doesn't expect to enjoy. Alternatively, Maria may be worried about Louise getting work done that's important to their financial situation, or there may be some other message present. Whatever the function or motivation, effective communication is not occurring here.

Obstacles and barriers to communication may occur on any of the three dimensions shown in Figure 2-5. Looking with the family at their situation along each of the three dimensions can help to identify what's missing in communication, and what needs to be constructed. It may be that family members do not have the necessary skills (the behavior dimension); contemporary society often does not provide many models of effective communication, and it is common for people to be doing the best they know how, and still not be able to really communicate with each other. Skills training in listening, expressing, requesting, and other repertoires, as presented in the next sections of this chapter, is the key in those situations. In other cases, clients may know how to listen respectfully and may do so with employers or friends, but may not do so with each other (a problem along the "occasions" dimension). In those cases, it is important to help family members use those skills more often with each other. In some cases, simply increasing statements of appreciation and recognition when another family member acts will reciprocally increase positive exchange in both directions, as discussed in chapter 3, and communicating in this way is central to family functioning. People will continue to do so, however, only if they get a positive response—if reciprocal reinforcement is provided (the consequences dimension). Often, therefore, work to enhance communication involves concurrent work along all three dimensions: learning new skills, learning to use those skills consistently within the family system, and learning to reinforce each other for doing so.

CORE COMMUNICATION SKILLS

It is often valuable to engage the family (or whatever family member or members you are working with) in direct skills training. Under some circumstances, skills can be taught "on the fly" as problems are addressed; this is particularly useful in crisis intervention or very short-term (one or two sessions) work. In most cases, however, it is useful to spend one or two sessions specifically on communication-skills training (often after one or two meetings devoted to increasing positive exchange). The discussion that follows will assume that this is the structure being used, but alternatives will be discussed later in the chapter.

Listening Skills

Receptive communication—listening—is the first communication skill to emphasize. In fact, if all families members learn to listen well in a context of positive exchange, many issues can be resolved without requiring much else. If no one is listening, however, no communication is possible.

Listening skills exist in a hierarchy. A person needs first to learn the basics, and then can move to more advanced levels. Just the most basic skills by themselves are helpful, and some people may find those challenging enough. Some family members may already have reasonably strong existing repertoires and can improve further during the social work consultation. Probably no one always uses advanced "active listening" skills (see below) at all times in their families, but if people consistently use the basic skills and have the higher level skills available when needed, the family will probably cope quite well. In skills training, the social worker will ordinarily begin with the simplest skills and move to others if time, motivation, and capacity allow.

The general skills training process begins by describing the skill and giving several examples. The social worker can then role play simple examples (examples that do not involve high conflict issues in the family) with family members, then give them opportunities to role play with each other. It is often also useful to work out home tasks with the family so that they can practice on their own in their natural environment. Examples of these strategies are presented in the discussion of clusters of listening skills that follows. These clusters are generally progressive and probably easiest to learn in roughly this order, but the order is not absolute.

Cluster 1: Nonverbal Listening Skills

The first and most important listening skills require only that the listener sit quietly, not talk, and show nonverbally that he or she is paying attention to what the other person is saying. In presenting this skill, it is important to mention the common tendency to think about what one is going to say in response, thus not really paying attention to the speaker. Family members are reassured when told that listening does not necessarily mean agreeing, and that later they will have opportunities to say what is on their minds. In the beginning, however, just listening communicates respect, and only if everyone in the family is willing to listen to each other can they work things out. In some cases, listening quietly may be very challenging, and the social worker should be prepared to confidently and respectfully interrupt interruptions, stating again that this is practice for listening and that everyone will get a chance to speak.

Sloane (1976/1988) suggests a strategy for such practice: family members make up situations and tell each other about them, selecting scenarios that they would expect to be very upsetting to the person to whom they are talking. The idea is to give people practice with difficult situations, which they may then be able to transfer to easier, but real-life ones. The listeners' role is to indicate interest and respect nonverbally—just by how they sit and look at the speaker. Once everyone has had a chance to practice this, the family and worker should discuss whether they are satisfied with their progress and ready to move on to the next level.

Cluster 2: Furthering Responses

In the next set of role plays, the listener continues to communicate interest nonverbally and can also use simple furthering responses (those that move communication along), including paraverbal sounds, words, and phrases like:

- "I see. . . ."
- "Uh-huh. . . ."
- "Umm. . . ."
- "Good grief. . . ."
- "Tell me more. . . ."

Giving responses like these is a small, but significant step, since people tend to feel heard if the listener gives simple feedback—these replies are reinforcers for talking (Sloane, 1976/1988).

An additional set of furthering responses are short, noncritical questions to clarify what the speaker is saying, for example:

- "What happened then?"
- "Who else heard that?"
- "What did you say?"

Finally, brief paraphrases of what happened can also reinforce talking, for example, "So first you went downtown, then back home, then . . . ?" The trick with all of these furthering responses is to ensure that they are delivered in nonpunitive and reinforcing ways; a paraverbal sound or a question can be reinforcing, but with a small shift in tone or wording, it can be experienced as critical or skeptical. (The two-color card can be useful at this stage.) Note that at this point, no personal opinions or concerns on the part of the listener are yet being expressed; the purpose of the exercises is to practice listening first. Since there are several subgroups of furthering responses, it may be useful to practice each separately.

Cluster 3: Reflecting Feelings

For many people, the most difficult part of listening is to listen not only for events and the way they happened, but also for the associated feelings. Not all families will be ready to take on this final and most challenging level of listening skills, but many can. Reflecting feelings may involve directly restating what the other person said ("You were really angry"), inferring feelings from what the other person said and the way it was said ("You must have been pretty angry by then"), or asking about feelings experienced ("Did you find yourself getting angry at that point?"). There are many levels of emotion, and the closer the listener can come to the experience of the speaker, the more communication is facilitated (Hepworth, Rooney, & Larsen, 1997). For example, if the speaker is very animated, and clearly furious, asking, "Are you a little upset?," would not be very responsive. It is useful for the social worker to develop several imaginary reflecting-feelings scenarios, to role play making statements based on those scenarios, and to ask family members to practice making statements reflecting those feelings. In this training, listeners learn to listen empathically, to some extent feeling themselves the emotions the speaker experiences. The skilled social worker will also have been modeling all of these listening skills, including empathic listening, during all contacts with the family.

Training in reflecting feelings is a step toward "active listening" (Gordon, 1970), which involves the listener paraphrasing what the speaker is saying, including as appropriate both the feelings involved and the events or conditions that contributed to the feelings. In active listening, the listener replies to a message using one of innumerable variations of "It sounds like you are feeling _____ because _____." (Many variations are necessary to avoid sounding like an active listening robot!) Examples of full active listening statements include:

- "It sounds like you are really frustrated with the way your boss is treating you."
- "It seems like you're really tired, and maybe pretty frustrated, after trying so many times to talk to your daughter."
- "So when he asked you to go out, you were really thrilled!"

It is unrealistic to expect a full active listening statement that includes the emotional dimension as well as the situation associated with the emotion in every conversation, but having this repertoire available can greatly facilitate communication at challenging times. Notice also that reflecting feelings and active listening can and should be used when positive events and emotions are experienced, not just when there is a problem. Listening well reinforces talking; if family members can both listen and avoid punitive responses, people will share more with each other, and what is shared is more likely to be honest, rather than shaded to avoid punishing reactions.

Once family members can fairly reliably listen to each other at whatever level is possible given their current skills and the available time, training can turn to expressive skills—effective ways to tell others thoughts and feelings, and to express requests.

Expressive Skills

Communication depends on more than listening, of course; expressive skills are the other side of the process. Family members can talk about their experiences and desires in ways that either distance or engage others. Perhaps the most important principle for effective expression is that each speaker respectfully and honestly talk from his or her own perspective, rather than focusing on blaming others or attributing motivation to them. A simple but powerful device for doing so is the "I-Statement" (Gordon, 1970). Sentences that begin with the word "you" often express blame ("You always . . . "), judgment ("You are not really trying"), or motivational attribution ("What you really want to do is to hurt me"). In each case, the expression creates distance and is likely to be experienced as an aversive attack, which is likely to spark counteraversives. Far better is to begin with "I"; for example, "I am very distressed about how little time we have together." It is important to help people learn "clean" I-statements; for example, the statement, "I am very sad that you don't love me anymore," is really a you-statement disguised as an I-statement. The ideal statement talks about one's own emotions:

- "I feel very sad because we seem not to be able to enjoy being with each other."
- "I am really worried that you may be doing something dangerous."
- "I really appreciate your efforts to spend more time with the kids."

What is expressed should not be limited to descriptions of negative emotions; far more statements of positive recognition should be present in any relationship than aversive ones. While I-statements are usually less aversive than you statements, partly because they provide cleaner opportunities for the other to respond, expressions of negative affect are somewhat unpleasant, and the emotional bank account concept remains important here.

Very young children need to learn to respond to directions given by parents (this repertoire can be developed in enjoyable ways) for their own safety and development. In the normal developmental process, however, there is a shift toward self-determination; in intimate adult relationships, no one has the right to coercively demand that someone else comply with his or her wishes, nor are such demands likely to produce a satisfactory relationship. The extreme end of this continuum is battering (Pence & Paymar, 1993), but even between parent and child, requests are often a more desirable communicative option. Learning to make requests rather than demands, therefore, is a valuable skill. The heart of a request is again an I-statement:

- "I would like you to be home by 10:00 p.m."
- "I would appreciate it if you don't discuss this matter with my parents."
- "I would really appreciate it if you would call me when you are going to be late."

These statements can be combined with statements of one's reasons for the request, for example, "I worked really hard to prepare you a special meal last night and was disappointed when you came home so late that it was ruined. I would really appreciate it if you would call me when you are going to be late." Note that other family members need to make a commitment to use their listening skills to really hear such messages as non-defensively as possible. All of the evidence suggests that a family culture in which such listening and expressive practices are well established is more reinforcing than one in which coercion and punishment are the norm.

The shift from demands to requests does not mean that there are no consequences for actions, however. One young man (J) I saw as a client hit his wife when she went out drinking and left their young children alone at home while he was working. He indicated that he was at the end of his rope and felt that this was the only way he could "teach her" what her responsibilities were. I believe that no one has a right to batter, even under circumstances like these, but this does not mean that J could only say, "I'd prefer that you not leave our children alone." Some variation of the following would be appropriate: "I am very concerned about our children being home alone. I feel very strongly that someone needs to be with them when I am at work. If you choose to leave them alone, I will have to take steps to protect them. I may need to leave you and move with the children to my mother's home. What I really want, though, is to have a serious talk with you about this." Similarly, in parenting, it is possible to recognize that youths have choices, while still expressing one's own wishes, and in some cases clarifying the consequences of each option.

Several other rules of thumb are useful for effective expression (the principles discussed in this paragraph were suggested by Stuart, 1980, and Stuart, personal communication, February 1978). Some phrases are likely to evoke defensive responses. For example, the words "always" and "never," according to Stuart, can be thought of as a double-barreled shotgun, only to be used when one wants to draw blood. Statements like "You always . . . " or "He never . . . " are likely to elicit denials and examples of times when whatever is alleged was not true. Whatever is said should also be true. Deception has no place in family relationships; what appears to be a small "white lie" can have profound effects on trust and do significant damage. Timing is important; times when people are under stress (like getting ready for work, or preparing for a party) are high-risk times for conflict, and poor choices for expressing serious concerns. (Another high-risk time is driving home from couples counseling!) Choosing a time when people are reasonably relaxed, or even "making an appointment" to talk later is much more likely to be useful. It is important not to extend this time too far, however, because some stress may also be associated with waiting for the "appointment." What is said should also be productive; some experiences are better left untold. For example, if one partner in a committed gay union suddenly remembers a particularly happy time in a previous relationship, he need not describe the episode to his partner if it may be experienced as aversive.

Once family members have learned how to express themselves effectively and to listen to each other, they are ready to move toward problem solving. As described by Gordon, when "you have a problem," the important skill for me is listening; when "I have a problem," the important skills are expressive; but when "we have a problem," some form of problem-solving communication is required.

Problem Solving

When family members have a mutual problem or are in conflict about an issue, problem-solving skills are crucial for finding or constructing a solution that works well enough for everyone so that they can move on and avoid getting stuck. The specific solution developed is not usually as important as healing whatever damage the issue has caused in the relationship, and avoiding even more serious damage. The process of mutual problem solving, therefore, is more crucial than the outcome in most cases. Real problem solving requires a commitment to shared power, in which the voices of all of those involved are important, and mutual contribution and responsibility are assumed. This does not mean that everyone has "equal power," or "equal responsibility"—as discussed previously, people have different developmental and personal gifts that they bring to the table. Parents do not give up their power or responsibility by engaging in problem-solving work with their children; rather, they bring their strengths and help their children discover and create their own. Just because parents listen to what their adolescents say, they are not obligated to do what the child wants them to. They are, however, communicating respect and making it more likely that a solution that works for everyone can emerge. The way people initially express their experiences and desires also often moderates if they feel genuinely heard.

In an emergency, decisions sometimes need to be made immediately (and doing so is often a parental responsibility). Most family issues, however, are not emergencies of this type. What time curfew is set for in a family where a young person has run away several times, or whether to go to the in-laws for the Jewish holidays, usually need not be decided at this moment, and often not in a single session. It is useful to give everyone an opportunity to present his or her view of the problem, and then to allow some time to elapse before a decision is made. Temporary or experimental decisions are often possible, and sometimes people need to experience an impasse to develop motivation for problem solving. The social worker can help defuse a tense situation by pointing out that improving the process of communication is most important, and that the issue being discussed may not need to be finally decided right now. Families will often return to the next session having reached a creative new solution after having time to think about what they have heard from each other.

There are two general strategies for teaching problem-solving communication. One is to teach communication skills needed for problem solving (including listening and expressive skills) in the course of active work, while discussing a "representative issue" (one that is typical of family struggles, Reid, 1985). The other is to teach the skills first, and then move toward applying them to current problems. Each of these strategies has advantages, and one need not be used to the exclusion of the other. Four approaches to improving family problem solving will be briefly outlined here; there are many others, but those presented clarify the general range and principles. Details of others can be found in standard texts that review models of work with families (for example, Gurman & Kniskern, 1991a, 1991b; Jacobson & Gurman, 1995). The four approaches are discussed here in an ascending order of structure; in general, the more serious and long-standing the conflicts in the family, the more structured the solutions may need to be.

Problem-Solving Communication

The task-centered model of social work practice (Reid & Epstein, 1972; Reid, 1985, 1992) is a well established approach for work with families that often emphasizes communication skills. The general model begins with establishing a problem-solving set involving several guidelines (Reid, 1985, p. 195):

- Family members should focus on the problem and solutions, rather than on personal qualities.
- Each family member should be willing to make some concessions.
- Family members should make active efforts to find positives in other's proposals.
- Each family member should be willing to take constructive action.
- Family members should work for specificity of problems and solutions.

The subsequent steps include (1) problem identification, (2) problem exploration, and (3) generating, evaluating, and selecting solutions. During each phase, the worker prompts, teaches, and recognizes important skills. During the problem identification process, listening skills and effective ways to express problems are emphasized, as each family member has an opportunity to discuss the issue(s) present as he or she sees them. During the second—problem exploration—stage, family members clarify details about one selected issue, examine contextual factors involved, and explore related feelings. Skills emphasized during this phase include a willingness to take some responsibility for the situation and its solution, focusing on present factors that can be modified rather than history that cannot be changed, and staying on track. The third phase involves identifying and weighing the consequences of the (usually multiple) solutions that may be possible, building on and improving each other's ideas, willingly taking personal action, recognizing positives in each other, and compromising.

This approach can be used very flexibly; only those skills and actions that are relevant to the family's struggles may need to be discussed, and this can occur during relatively fluid discussions within only the very broad structure outlined above. For families that will be seen only one or two times, or who are struggling with a definite and limited issue, this model can be very useful. For example, in a family with two adult daughters whose elderly parent is hospitalized and temporarily cognitively impaired as the result of anesthesia, and who are in severe conflict about discharge plans, a discussion that begins with ensuring that each of the sisters hears the other's perspective, followed by a more detailed exploration of the issues involved, and finally a search for solutions that includes all possible options is a very useful rough structure to work within. (The parent's voice also ultimately needs to be heard and respected in such situations as well.) The goal in a situation like this is not to "fix" the relationship between the sisters (which is neither their request nor the function of the social worker in this setting, although referral can be offered), but to help them work through a particular issue. This process, however, can offer the clients a model and framework for future conflict resolution, particularly if the worker clearly labels each stage.

Family Mediation

A recent approach that appears to have much to offer especially for clearly delimited issues (like many involving developmental transitions between parent and teenager, or adult children and their aging parents) is family mediation. Mediation is time limited (often between about two and four sessions), and provides an opportunity for the voice of each family member involved to be heard. Since each is also encouraged by the process to take responsibility for the outcome, there are many opportunities for shared power in mediation. Mediation is formally seen as fundamentally different from clinical work, and the two roles should not be confused; in fact, there are serious ethical concerns about shifting between them (Gold, 1997). The mediator is expected to remain neutral and to simply guide a structured process, rather than engaging the family in an emotionally deeper way. In such situations as parent-child mediation, there are substantial challenges in dealing with power; mediation should not undermine parental authority, but needs to help the child be genuinely and respectfully heard (Umbreit & Kruk, 1997). Sorting out issues of power imbalances and "equal partici-pation" within a mediation structure can be complicated, but an explicit shared power perspective can go a long way toward that aim. Specific train-ing in mediation as a model is generally required, because it is a different process than the clinical work most social workers have been trained to do. In many cases, mediation is carried out in community settings by volunteers, with professionals like social workers or attorneys providing supervision and consultation. Co-mediation (sometimes involving an adult and a youth me-diator) is common.

The mediation process is generally structured into phases, much more so than in Reid's model above, for example. Although different programs involve somewhat different structures, the structure that will be used should be explained and closely adhered to. In one model (Umbreit & Kruk, 1997), the five phases are: (1) setting the stage; (2) defining the is-sues; (3) processing the issues; (4) resolving the issues; and (5) making an explicit agreement, often in writing. In some mediation models, all or nearly all of the work occurs in joint sessions, while other models rely heav-ily on private sessions between mediator and individual clients or family subsystems (a "shuttle diplomacy" approach); some programs use these strategies flexibly depending on the level of emotion and depth of conflict present.

Contingency Contracting

Contracting within families has a long and somewhat controversial history. A contract is an explicit agreement that clarifies expectations and conse-quences. In early work with pre-delinquents, Stuart and his colleagues first found (Stuart, 1971) that contracting seemed to be useful, but later con-cluded that the "quality" of the contracts (the extent to which they seemed to include the necessary features) did not appear to make much difference; rather involvement in a negotiation process may have been the crucial fac-tor (Stuart & Lott, 1972). In a later review, Stern (1989) suggested that con-tingency contracting may be of less use than commonly believed, since par-ents often have lost control of important consequences for adolescent children, and because contracts were often "imposed" in ways that left no real voice for some participants.

This critique raised important issues, but the data suggest that adequate contracts can be powerful tools in work with children and adolescents. Most effective models for working with disturbed parent/adolescent relations and other family issues incorporate agreements and contracts of various kinds, and extensive data support them. Both Reid's approach and mediation, discussed above, include contracting processes. On the other hand, and not at all surprising from a shared power perspective, imposed contracts (which are not clean agreements) tend to produce resistance. Schools, families, and the legal system often establish lists of imposed expectations paired with the punishments for violating them and call these "contracts"; these typically do not produce strong, lasting results. A contract in which people's values and wishes are mutually respected and that spells out actions and consequences *with emphasis on positive consequences* is quite different (DeRisi & Butz, 1975; Falloon, 1991). Contracts tend to be most useful and important when serious issues involving well-established mutual aversive repertoires that may be difficult to change without ongoing attention are present.

Falloon (1991), whose work will be discussed extensively in the chapter on families living with mental illness, describes the use of contracts in the following way:

> A contract is drawn up by two or more family members that specifies the behaviors each desires the other to perform more frequently. The rewards that the recipient is willing to provide for the performance of the specific behaviors that are included in the contract are clearly specified. In this way, each person agrees both to give and receive pleasing behaviors. A written agreement is signed by all persons involved. Implementation of the contract is reviewed at each treatment session and amendments are added where necessary. (p. 84)

Note the strong emphasis here on a constructional approach that relies on incentives. Although contracts can include some sanctions, only if the agreement is primarily constructional can it be expected to be useful. The reinforcers involved need to be meaningful to the recipient, and opportunities to reexamine and renegotiate need to be provided. While it is possible to use verbal agreements, written agreements (which may or may not be called "contracts") are very useful for their clarity. We will return to contracting in the chapters on work with seriously antisocial youths, and mental illness.

The Family Conference

A final approach, and the most structured, is the *Family Conference* as developed and tested by Serna and her colleagues (Serna, Schumaker, Sherman,

& Sheldon, 1991). An outline of this approach will complete the continuum from the less to the more structured approaches to problem-solving communication. In the Serna study, families including adolescents presenting with severe conflicts were first taught communication and problem-solving skills in groups, and subsequently received individualized and family coaching both in a training setting and at home. This process was quite intensive, and lasted for some months. At the end of all of this, family members could use the skills relatively well in a structured practice situation, but still did not use them often or reliably in unstructured interactions with each other at home.

The clinicians therefore moved to a very structured procedure, in which first the clinician, and later the parent, chaired a scheduled family meeting. Between meetings, each family member completed cards identifying issues that should be discussed at the family conference. At the beginning of the scheduled family conference, the completed cards were collected, and each family member was asked to say something positive to someone else. One card was then selected by the moderator, and family members discussed their views of the situation described on the card. Family members next identified the communication skill required to resolve the situation, then used that skill to try to reach a solution. Other issues were handled in the same way. Finally, family members evaluated their effectiveness in the conference, and closed by again each saying something positive about someone else present. All of these steps were guided by a written framework.

Initially, the procedures were followed very precisely. Once the specified skills were used reliably, more flexibility was introduced. In each of the research families, positive results were maintained at a nine-month follow-up. The message here seems to be clear: Even families that do not respond to intensive skills-building approaches may be able to resolve their difficulties and learn to address problems that arise constructively. A structure that teaches, reinforces, and stabilizes a new set of family practices consistent with problem resolution is required in such cases. (See chapter 8 for detail about using this approach with antisocial youths.)

STRATEGIES FOR ENHANCING COMMUNICATION SKILLS

There are many ways to work with families to build and bolster communication skills. Several have been mentioned in the material above, and it is often useful to mix and phase multiple approaches in a creative way. While the consultation should not feel like a game in which family struggles are not being taken seriously, it is helpful to use humor and clarify that learning new ways to hear and speak to each other need not be deadly serious at all times. General strategies for skills development include the following:

- Skills training, in which skills to be learned are labeled, modeled, and then practiced in simulated situations. Such skills training can be conducted individually, in partial or full family sessions, or in groups (see below). The social worker will often find it useful to have developed a series of examples in advance, going from less to more difficult. The worker and family members can then take on some of those roles to practice before moving into their own issues.
- *In vivo* training, in which the worker labels, models, and prompts the use of helpful skills during the course of ongoing discussions about focal issues for the family. The worker should clarify in advance that he or she will be doing this, so that the family does not find themselves being unexpectedly interrupted (which can feel mildly punitive). Either skills training or *in vivo* work can be (and ideally is) conducted in the family home. Thus there is less difficulty in generalizing the skills to the natural setting.
- Enactment, in which the family replays an episode that has occurred at home, then practices alternative ways to handle it ("new way replays," Embry, Flannery, Vazsonyi, Powell, & Atha, 1996, p. 92), or enacts possible future scenarios. Affect is often somewhat attenuated when such scenes are reenacted in the presence of the social worker, which may make it easier than in the original situation for people to look at their own part in the episode and to consider alternatives. Family members should be prepared by being told that reenactment can be mildly embarrassing, but that people can learn a lot from it; family members can often identify for themselves alternative ways to handle things in this process. Enacting possible future events is often combined with skills training; it can be useful to inoculate family members so that relatively predictable slips and conflicts need not be as difficult to manage as they might be if participants were not prepared. The social worker's primary task and that of the family members', with the worker's support, is to reinforce strengths that emerge in the enactments and to make constructional suggestions to enhance the process, rather than to focus on what was done wrong. In families for which communication is an issue, there are no doubt areas where enhancement would be valuable, but there often are also significant strengths, which can be recognized and reinforced. For example, some family members may be more skilled in assertive communication than the social worker him or herself, and this can be acknowledged—a shared power perspective requires recognition of such strengths, which can contribute to an improved family situation.

- The use of home assignments (homework), in which family members practice what they have learned in session when they are on their own in their natural setting. One or more scheduled "practice sessions" between sessions with the social worker can be very helpful. In some cases these sessions can be taped to be replayed in the next formal session. Family members can listen to their tapes and also discuss how their homework session went at home or in the session, and identify both strengths and areas for improvement. Family members may also find it helpful to commit to observing and recording their own behavior; for example, in couples work simple counts of the number of times one partner "recognizes" the other can be a powerful intervention (see chapter 6).

- Multifamily groups can be particularly useful for learning and practicing communication skills, as well as for other purposes such as parent education and psychoeducation, as discussed in other chapters (Falloon, 1991; Meezan & O'Keefe, 1998). In some cases, youths and parents are separated into separate multifamily groups for skills training, then brought together as individual families to practice applying what has been learned. In other cases, members of multiple families may all be seen in a single group. The approach leads to extensive interfamily support, new perspectives on better alternatives, and opportunities to practice skills with members of other families while one's own watches. Other group members also can often be helpful in identifying and building connections with other needed community resources (Brunk, Henggeler, & Whelan, 1987). Communication skills training relies heavily on an educational model as opposed to a medical or pathology-rooted model, and it is often better to present it as family life education, for example, rather than "group therapy" which suggests inner pathology. All participants in a multifamily group bring their own gifts and talents to the work, including but not only the social worker.

- Tools and prompts may make it easier to clarify what is to be learned and the process of doing so. A simple list of skills to be hung on the wall, notations to remind the family of practice sessions on a calendar, the green/red card described above for giving ongoing feedback about the effects of one's statements without interrupting, checklists on which family members note steps they have taken, graphs showing progress, and any number of other creative tools can help to concretize the work, and also can be seamlessly incorporated into practice monitoring efforts.

Improvements in communication are among the central tools for intrafamily work. A related strategic direction is enhancing "acceptance" among family members. Over the past five years in particular, behavioral researchers and practice theoreticians have recognized the limits of active intervention and the important place of acceptance in healthy family functioning. This is not to say that active approaches like communication skills training are not important, but rather that there is an additional dimension that needs to be considered. In fact, genuine acceptance requires certain component skills, in particular empathic listening.

ACCEPTANCE IN FAMILIES

While some dysfunctional patterns certainly need to be actively challenged and addressed, it is unrealistic and often counterproductive to suggest to family members that each try to get other family members to change well learned (and often in some ways functional) patterns in all areas. For instance, those repertoires that first attracted a couple to each other sometimes become issues over time. In recent years it has become clear that asking others to change basic patterns of behavior will often fail, and that unrealistic expectations of relationships and people is a common factor in many distressed families (Bornstein & Bornstein, 1986; Ellis, Sichel, Yeager, DiMattia, & DiGiuseppe, 1989). For example, in family relationships people commonly believe rules like:

- If my partner really cared, he would know what I want and feel without needing to be told.
- It's terrible if a real disagreement occurs in my family.
- If my daughter really cared about me, she would do what I ask her to do at all times.

Accepting the realities of real-world relationships is important to achieving satisfaction in families.

While the importance of acceptance has long been known (the Serenity Prayer states a willingness to "accept what can't be changed"), in recent years helping professions have increasingly recognized the broad importance of acceptance for personal and family health and satisfaction. It is important to clarify that acceptance theorists do not advocate that *everything* be accepted; obviously, battering and other forms of oppression should never be accepted. Even in such situations acceptance has a place, but in a way that is almost paradoxical. A battered woman may need to accept that her husband or boyfriend is likely to continue to hurt her (and probably to escalate the level of abuse) before she is ready to take action. Denying this reality ("He's not really like that; he doesn't mean to hurt me") may stand in the way of effective action.

There are three classes (domains) of events or conditions relevant to acceptance: (1) those situations in which action is useful and that need not or should not be accepted; (2) those that need to be accepted for now but that may ultimately change if one takes action now; and (3) those that will not change and must simply be accepted (see Table 5-1).

The first class or domain, in which action is useful, includes one's own actions and self-talk, which can be changed immediately. The third class (those areas in which acceptance rather than action are useful) include historical events, memories, the physical world, and actions of other people that really have no negative impact on oneself or others; in many cases, such factors can be denied, but the denial carries a substantial price.

The second class is slightly more complicated than either of the others. One's own emotions result from one's current situation and historical learning experiences. Some people, for example, become quite nervous if an intimate is angry at them, while others become angry in return. Those emotions are real and should therefore be accepted, as should the emotion of the other person involved. One often *can*, however, take action now that will result in change later. Acceptance and commitment therapy (ACT) (Hayes & Wilson, 1994; Mattaini, 1997) is an approach that emphasizes both accepting the current situation while committing to action that may ultimately shift that reality.

Table 5–1

Domains in which acceptance, acceptance with commitment to change, and change strategies may be useful in enhancing quality of life.

Domains in which an emphasis on change is often useful:
- self-talk and beliefs that prove inconsistent with events
- one's own undesirable overt behavior
- aversive situations, except those that are inherently unchangeable.

Domains in which current acceptance, with commitment to act to achieve change, can be useful:
- one's own emotions (which are responsive to current life events and conditions)
- others' unpleasant emotional experiences
- firmly held beliefs of others
- behavior of others over which one has potential influence, and which has a genuinely aversive impact on one's own or others' lives.

Domains in which acceptance is useful:
- events and memories from one's own and others' histories
- one's own past acts
- actions of others over which one has no influence, or which have no genuinely aversive impact upon oneself or others
- the physical world.

One simple ACT technique that is useful in individual work as well as with family members is to help the client shift from statements like, "I would like to try to get closer to her, but I am too afraid"—which often result in inaction, to statements like, "I am going to try to get closer to her [commitment], *and* I am afraid [acceptance]"—which can lead to action. Note that one is willing, in taking this approach, to accept the discomfort that accompanies action, rather than avoiding or denying it. ACT is among the current cutting edge approaches for work with individuals, and acceptance is also now recognized as useful and important for work with families as well. Neil Jacobson and his colleagues (Jacobson & Christensen, 1996; Koerner, Jacobson, & Christensen, 1994) have extensively explored acceptance in work with couples (discussed in detail in chapter 6 of this book).

In families in general, including couples, acceptance often involves and requires honest communication, which is why this material is included in the communication skills chapter. Unless individuals in the family can take the risk of radical honesty, and others can take the risk of really hearing what is said, acceptance is impossible. One of the techniques that Jacobson and his colleagues recommend for work with couples involves "empathic joining." In this process the therapist or social worker assists each partner to explore his or her honest emotions, while the other partner participates as an observing audience.

Griffee (1994) indicates that families are usually seeking two things when they turn to consultation: (1) understanding each other better and (2) an often conflicting pull toward greater intimacy while maintaining personal autonomy and independence. Since each individual's life experience has been different, each inevitably has somewhat different values, and sees and responds to different aspects of events. Griffee indicates, therefore, that successful family work requires family members to act to try understanding each other better (empathic listening), while accepting that they will never completely understand anyone else's view (a somewhat existential acceptance). In her approach, the helping professional explicitly surfaces the core conflicts and assists the family to see and accept them. Putting into words the desire for understanding and the necessarily imperfect extent to which it can be achieved, as well as the conflicting and concurrent reinforcers involved in intimacy and independence, and helping family members to see that these core conflicts are an inevitable part of relationships can be particularly useful in shifting self-talk away from unrealistic expectations, as can explicit recognition that difference is inevitable and in itself is not bad; it can even enrich family life by opening one's eyes to other ways of seeing.

The basic techniques for facilitating the deepening of acceptance in families include the following:

• Modeling and assisting family members to learn and use deep empathic listening and expressive skills, so that family members can really listen nonpunitively to each other's emotional experiences and at least to some extent "feel with" the other.

• Educating family members about the core conflicts, about the realities of relationships, and about realistic expectations based on many factors that have shaped people to be who they are at any time (past history, developmental repertoires, conflicting current pressures, and emotional state, for example) to help shift self-talk towards acceptance and away from blame.

• Having family members practice (in role plays or in home assignments) identifying and cognitively processing situations in which these core conflicts play out in family life.

• Assisting family members to take action to experience the world in ways that increase empathy, for example by having family members reverse roles in a role play, or try to put into words what they think another family member is experiencing, then providing the other an opportunity to refine this.

• Assisting family members to recognize what they do value and experience in common (attending to areas of difference can lead to neglect of the many things family members have in common, which can be crucial in holding the family together).

These strategies and others creatively developed to help achieve a family culture of empathic acceptance, can assist family members to live gracefully with, and even value certain nonharmful qualities of other members of the family that might otherwise become issues, and to focus on areas of appreciation. Such acceptance can potentiate change in areas of the relationship where such change is appropriate.

REFERENCES

Bateson, G., Jackson, D. D., Haley, J., & Weakland, J. H. (1956). Toward a theory of schizophrenia. *Behavioral Science, 1,* 251–264.

Bornstein, P. H., & Bornstein, M. T. (1986). *Marital therapy: A behavioral-communications approach.* New York: Pergamon Press.

Brunk, M., Henggeler, S. W., & Whelan, J. P. (1987). Comparison of multisystemic therapy and parent training in the brief treatment of child abuse and neglect. *Journal of Consulting and Clinical Psychology, 55,* 171–178.

DeRisi, W. J., & Butz, G. (1975). *Writing behavioral contracts.* Champaign, IL: Research Press.

Ellis, A., Sichel, J. L., Yeager, R. J., DiMattia, D. J., & DiGiuseppe, R. (1989). *Rational-emotive couples therapy.* New York: Pergamon Press.

Embry, D. D., Flannery, D. J., Vazsonyi, A. T., Powell, K. E., & Atha, H. (1996). PeaceBuilders: A theoretically driven, school-based model for early violence prevention. *American Journal of Preventive Medicine,* Supplement to Volume 12, Number 5, 91–100.

Falloon, I. R. H. (1991). Behavioral family therapy. In A. S. Gurman & D. P. Kniskern (Eds.), *Handbook of family therapy, Volume II* (pp. 65–95). New York: Brunner/Mazel.

Ginsberg, B. G. (1997). *Relationship enhancement family therapy.* New York: John Wiley and Sons.

Gold, L. (1997). Marriage and family: Mediation in couple and family disputes. In E. Kruk (Ed.), *Mediation and conflict resolution in social work and human services* (pp. 19–35). Chicago: Nelson-Hall.

Gordon, T. (1970). *Parent effectiveness training.* New York: Wyden Press.

Griffee, K. (1994). Acceptance and the family context. In S. C. Hayes, N. S. Jacobson, V. M. Follette, & M. J. Dougher (Eds.), *Acceptance and change: Content and context in psychotherapy,* (pp. 223–233). Reno, NV: Context Press.

Gurman, A. S., & Kniskern, D. P. (Eds.), (1991a). *Handbook of family therapy: Volume I.* New York: Brunner/Mazel.

Gurman, A. S., & Kniskern, D. P. (Eds.), (1991a). *Handbook of family therapy: Volume II.* New York: Brunner/Mazel.

Hayes, S. C., & Wilson, K. G. (1994). Acceptance and commitment therapy: Altering the verbal support for experiential avoidance. *The Behavior Analyst, 17,* 289–303.

Hepworth, D. H., Rooney, R. H., & Larsen, J. A. (1997). *Direct social work practice: Theory and skills* (5th ed.). Pacific Grove, CA: Brooks/Cole.

Jacobson, N. S., & Christensen, A. (1996). *Integrative couple therapy.* New York: Norton.

Jacobson, N. S., & Gurman, A. S. (Eds.),(1995). *Clinical handbook of couple therapy.* New York: Guilford Press.

Koerner, K., Jacobson, N. S., & Christensen, A. (1994). Emotional acceptance in integrative behavioral couple therapy. In S. C. Hayes, N. S. Jacobson, V. M. Follette, & M. J. Dougher (Eds.), *Acceptance and change: Content and context in psychotherapy,* (pp. 109–118). Reno, NV: Context Press.

Mattaini, M. A. (1997). *Clinical practice with individuals.* Washington, DC: NASW Press.

Meezan, W., & O'Keefe, M. (1998). Multifamily group therapy: Impact on family functioning and child behavior. *Families in Society, 79,* 32–44.

Parad, H. J., & Parad, L. G. (1990). *Crisis intervention: Book 2.* Milwaukee: Family Service America.

Patterson, G. R. (1975). *Families.* Champaign, IL: Research Press.

Pence, E., & Paymar, M. (1993). *Education groups for men who batter: The Duluth model.* New York: Springer.

Reid, W. J. (1985). *Family problem solving.* New York: Columbia University Press.

Reid, W. J., & Epstein, L. (1972). *Task-centered casework.* New York: Columbia University Press.

Rogers, C. R. (1951). *Client-centered therapy.* Boston: Houghton Mifflin.

Satir, V. (1967). *Conjoint family therapy* (rev. ed.). Palo Alto, CA: Science and Behavior Books.

Serna, L. A., Schumaker, J. B., Sherman, J. A., & Sheldon, J. B. (1991). In-home generalization of social interactions in families of adolescents with behavior problems. *Journal of Applied Behavior Analysis, 24,* 733–746.

Skinner, B. F. (1989). *Recent issues in the analysis of behavior.* Columbus, OH: Merrill.

Sloane, H. N. (1976/1988). *The good kid book.* Champaign, IL: Research Press.

Stern, S. B. (1989). Behavioral family therapy for families of adolescents. In B. A. Thyer (Ed.), *Behavioral family therapy* (pp. 103–130). Springfield, IL: Charles C. Thomas.

Stuart, R. B. (1971). Behavioral contracting with the families of delinquents. *Journal of Behavior Therapy and Experimental Psychiatry, 2,* 1–11.

Stuart, R. B. (1980). *Helping couples change: A social learning approach to marital therapy.* New York: Guilford Press.

Stuart, R. B., & Lott, L. A. (1972). Behavioral contracting with delinquents: A cautionary note. *Journal of Behavior Therapy and Experimental Psychiatry, 3,* 161–169.

Thomas, E. J. (1977). *Marital communication and decision making: Analysis, Assessment, and Change.* New York: Free Press.

Umbreit, M. S., & Kruk, E. (1997). Parents and children: Parent-child mediation. In E. Kruk (Ed.), *Mediation and conflict resolution in social work and human services* (pp.97–115). Chicago: Nelson-Hall.

Watzlawick, P., Beavin, J., & Jackson, D. D. (1967). *Pragmatics of human communication: A study of interactional patterns, pathologies, and paradoxes.* New York: Norton.

SECTION II

STRATEGIES FOR WORK WITH PARTICULAR FAMILY CONFIGURATIONS AND ISSUES

CHAPTER SIX

Work with Couples

A strong couple bond (whether the relationship is straight or gay, and involves traditional marriage or some other variation) can provide the most stable and important source of mutual reinforcement available to most adults, at least in many cultural groups represented in the United States. In a society where the influence of the extended family has substantially declined due to mobility, time constraints, and changing values, the couple relationship has become if anything more crucial than ever before, providing economic stability, emotional intimacy, a context for parenting, and fulfilling many other functions large and small. At the same time, nearly half of marriages (and probably more nontraditional relationships) do not endure, and among those that do, many provide only limited satisfaction and security. In some social groups divorce is the norm; some friendship networks in fact tend to reinforce talk and action related to ending couples relations (Medved, 1989).

While not all couple relationships should endure (many characterized by physical or emotional abuse, for example, probably should not), Stuart (1980) argued that there are reasons to try to maintain the bond in many cases, and his arguments are perhaps even more persuasive today, as the social safety net has become increasingly weak. Divorce is the most common route for women (and often their children) into poverty and can be emotionally devastating; among men, divorce is associated with physical illness and higher risk for death. (Perhaps men are socialized to avoid talking about the stresses of divorce more than are women, but there clearly are still costs.) Children also may pay an emotional price for divorce (Kalter, Kloner, Schreier, & Okla, 1989; Wallerstein & Corbin, 1989). The price of staying together, of course, can be even higher in some cases, but there is certainly reason to carefully consider all of the alternatives.

Social workers often see clients involved in troubled couple relationships, whether this is the reason for their seeking service, or they come for others problems like parenting. While the basic principles presented

143

throughout this volume apply to work with couples as well, certain distinct strategies and techniques are particularly useful because the couple relationship is different from any other family arrangement. A couple can be viewed as the confluence of two family cultures (see Figure 6-1); each of those cultures has its own well established practices, which in some way contact each other in the newly formed couple.

Each of those family cultures may also be embedded in other cultures; interethnic relationships, which are dramatically increasing (Spickard, Fong, & Ewalt, 1995), can be particularly challenging, but also particularly enriching for that reason. Extended family and other cultural groups often provide less guidance in forming the new microculture of the couple than was true in earlier times, placing an additional strain on often inexperienced young people. For all of these reasons, along with sexist, oppressive practices supported by many of the impinging sociocultural entities, couple relationships which could be the richest source of reinforcers available are often, instead, the most painful source of aversives for their members.

The relationship between members of a couple does not fit the definitions of a "culture" as used by Glenn (1991) or Harris (1989) discussed in chapter 1, because those definitions require the presence of multiple generations. A couple does qualify as a culture in Skinner's terms ("the contingencies of reinforcement maintained by a group," 1987, p. 74), however. Couples typically develop regularized networks of interlocking behaviors, their own ways of doing things (often even specialized languages), and those sets of practices commonly are maintained over extended periods of time and passed on to the next generation if children are involved. The goal in work with couples is not so much to change single behaviors as to assist the members of the couple to make and maintain long-term shifts in whole

Figure 6-1

The couple as the confluence of two family cultures.

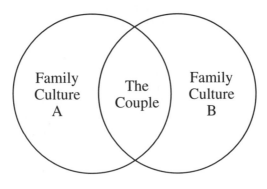

sets of practices. For these reasons, it is useful to think of couples as micro-cultures, and I will do so in this chapter.

UNDERSTANDING THE MICROCULTURE OF THE COUPLE

"The most powerful and consistent predictors of marital satisfaction and stability are positive and negative behaviors by husbands and wives and the reciprocity in these positive and negative behaviors" (Jacobson & Christensen, 1996, p. 37). Although there is enormous personal and cultural variation in what constitutes "positive and negative behaviors," transactions in conflicted and nonconflicted couples are characteristically different. The state-transition diagram in Figure 6-2 shows data from a study by Burman and her colleagues (Burman, John & Margolin, 1992) mentioned in chapter 2.

This study provides rich information about some of these differences, and the social worker beginning work with couples can benefit from looking at it closely. (While this figure is based on a single study of 79 couples, the data are highly consistent with the extensive literature on couple dynamics.)

Look first at the upper left quadrant, which traces interactions within physically aggressive couples. Even though the couples knew they were being observed, as they discussed an issue of importance to them, husbands made offensive and defensive comments often, 18 percent of the time for each type of negative comment; their wives made offensive comments 29 percent of the time, and defensive comments 10 percent of the time (these probabilities are shown inside the circles; see the original study for definitions). In other words, these couples were characterized by high rates of negative exchange (about 50 percent of exchanges if "intellectualizing" comments—morality lessons and demands of the other—are included). Rates of positive statements were only 13 percent for wives and 14 percent for husbands. (Neutral comments are not shown in the figure.) Partners in these physically aggressive couples were also highly provocable; the probabilities shown on the arrows between circles show the probability of the type of statement pointed to, given the occurrence of the type from which the arrow originates. If a husband made an offensive comment, for example, the probability that his wife would reciprocate with an offensive comment rose to 40 percent, while the probability that she would respond with a positive comment dropped to 7 percent.

Compare these figures to the nondistressed couples in the lower right quadrant. The rates of positive comments, even during discussion of a conflicted issue, were over 20 percent, while the rates of offensive comments averaged only about half the rate of positives. Levels of provocability were also

Figure 6-2

"State transition diagrams for the four conflict style groups. Mean unconditional probabilities for each spouse are given inside state circles, and mean conditional probabilities are displayed near arcs for those transitions with a significant t test for the z-score index of contingency. OFF = Offensive Negative, DEF = Defensive Negative, INT = Intellectualize, POS = Positive." Reprinted from Burman, B., John, R. S., & Margolin, G. (1992). Observed patterns of conflict in violent, nonviolent, and nondistressed couples. *Behavioral Assessment, 14,* 15–37, with permission from Elsevier Science.

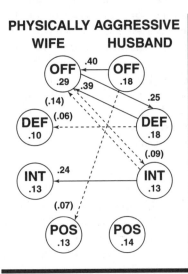

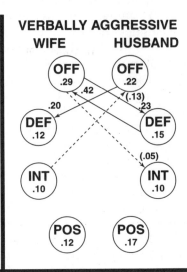

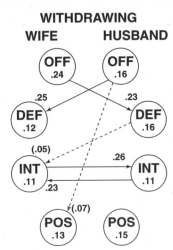

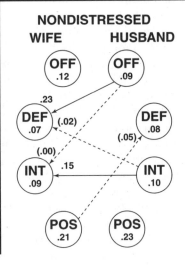

much lower here. For example, if a wife made an offensive comment, there was no change on average in the likelihood that her husband would respond differently. Data for the verbally aggressive and withdrawing couples, similarly, show higher rates of negative exchange and lower rates of positive exchange than in the nondistressed couples.

The available data indicate that rates of positive and aversive exchange, while not completely independent, are not highly correlated. As with other family configurations, couples may exchange relatively high rates of both, relatively low rates of both, or high rates of one and low rates of the other (Bornstein, Anton, Harowski, Weltzien, McIntyre, & Hocker, 1981; Bornstein & Bornstein, 1986; Bornstein, Hickey, Schulein, Fox, & Scollati, 1983; Gottman, Markman, & Notarius, 1977; Gottman, Notarius, Markman, Bank, Yoppi, & Rubin, 1976). As a result, it is often necessary to specifically work with the couple both to increase the rate of positives present, *and* to decrease the rate of negatives. While building awareness of negatives (through discussion or self-monitoring, for example) by itself can be a useful intervention for reducing aversives, more active intervention may be required. As always in an ecobehavioral approach, however, this is usually done by constructing functional alternatives—for example, by finding new ways to ask for more "space" or learning new ways to resolve conflicts that arise.

The problem of "reinforcer erosion" and the usual gradual drop in the rate of reinforcers exchanged in couples (see chapter 4) needs to be addressed in the majority of couples seen for consultation, since the relationship will really be satisfactory to the partners only if each experiences adequate levels of genuinely reinforcing events. The question of reinforcers exchanged should be raised in ways that help the couple to notice positives in the relationship that they may not be paying attention to at the present time. Jacobson and Christensen (1996), for example, suggest asking:

• How did the couple get together?—including what they liked about each other, what attracted them to each other
• What was their courtship like?—what they did together.

These questions often elicit a good deal of positive affect and even affection. The social worker may need to help the couple stay focused in these discussions while assuring them that they will get to the issues later. Jacobson and Christensen then suggest moving to questions about what the relationship is like now on the good days, and how the relationship would look like if current problems were resolved (note the move toward envisioning here). Those authors suggest that asking questions like these is part of a "hidden agenda" for the early sessions, providing some relief by improving the relationship at least temporarily. A shared-power approach discourages hidden agendas, however. Questions about previous and current reinforcers can be asked in the context of a direct message that mutual positive exchange is crucial in a relationship. Clients can see the benefit of such questions and discussions as they occur; nothing need be hidden from them.

Additionally, it is generally useful to spend at least some time individually with each partner early in the work, usually as part of the first session. While the social worker seeing the couple needs to clarify that it is important that there be no secrets between either partner and the worker, it is useful to explore the level of commitment to the relationship with each partner before beginning the work. In some cases, one partner has already decided to leave, in which case the direction of the consultation needs to change. When commitment is not clear, Stuart (1980) suggests asking each person to "give the relationship" six sessions, during which each partner will make an effort to make the relationship as good as it can be. At the end of that time, they can decide whether that is good enough—and they will at least feel that they have given themselves a fair chance. Most change that occurs with couples typically happens in the first few sessions, so a contract for five or six sessions, with the possibility of extending to an additional five or six sessions, is usually adequate unless there are serious issues of substance abuse, mental health, or external aversives involved. In some cases, the existence of an extramarital or outside affair with a third party will emerge in either joint or individual sessions, which may dramatically change the direction of the work with the couple. These cases are discussed in detail later in the chapter.

Well-established patterns of positive and aversive exchange can be viewed as cultural practices that help to define the couple as a couple. Coercive escalation, for example, as described in earlier chapters, is quite characteristic of distressed couples; nondistressed couples, by contrast, at some point stop fighting and move toward problem solving (Jacobson & Christensen, 1996). It is common for such practices to have been modeled and shaped within the family of origin. It is often useful to spend some time discussing how the couples' families of origin dealt with the focal issues present in the couple (for example, distance and closeness, substance use, expressing satisfaction or dissatisfaction with the behavior of the other, or making financial decisions). This can help to identify why the members of the couple act (and think) as they do, and why change may be more difficult than the partner might expect. At the same time, it is important to move from that understanding to a plan to cope with the differences, which may involve efforts to change, willingness to accept behavior that may not be preferred, or a mix of the two.

Each partner brings his or her family culture (or lack thereof in the case of "under-organized" or "underritualized" families, as they are sometimes called) into the relationship, and it can be useful to discuss the differences, and how they may be balanced in the new family formed by the couple. Specific focal issues can be different for each couple, but there are some common areas of struggle, including relationships with families of origin and extended families, specific financial decisions and the process of arriving at them, the amount and types of transactions with friends, the kinds of things and actions that are valued or devalued, and religious and other cultural traditions. Each of these clusters of issues and many others faced by couples are often embedded in differences in the family cultures of origin. These differences can be recognized and respected; the couple can then move toward actively considering how they want to build their own practices in these areas.

Over time, couples (and families in general) commonly work out a microculture that produces acceptable outcomes for both partners, but a dramatic shift in the context within which the couple is embedded can disrupt that balance. If one or both partners experience a major change in employment or financial situation, if an aging parent moves in or otherwise requires much more time and attention, if a child is born, or other major changes occur, the transition can be difficult because individual patterns and couple practices that previously produced adequate consequences may no longer do so. The social worker under such circumstances, returning to the core ecobehavioral framework, can help the couple to mourn the losses involved, then to move on to elaborating a new vision and beginning to shape repertoires consistent with the new circumstances.

Before leaving the discussion of positive and aversive exchanges, the possibility of domestic violence which was extensively discussed in chapter 4 should be mentioned. It is important to inquire during the initial individual sessions about the presence of physical violence in the couple before moving actively into couples treatment, since risks may increase if the work being done raises the level of stress or conflict within the couple. Refer to chapter 4 for guidelines in cases in which battering may be present; the strategies suggested in the present chapter are counterindicated in those cases.

SELF-TALK AND COUPLE RELATIONSHIPS

As in other areas of human behavior, it is not only events and conditions that are important in couples, but also the "meanings" that people associate with such events and conditions (equivalence relations), and how consistent they are with a person's expectations (rules). In conflicted couples, one or both partners commonly construe things in the worst possible terms—for example, "If she is late coming home, she doesn't love me anymore," or, "The reason he is working so much is to avoid me." In some cases, such equivalences may be accurate, but in many cases they are not. Many times neither partner understands all of the motivations and meanings of his/her own, much less the other's, actions. One common strategy in couples work, therefore, is to assist partners to consider more positive explanations for each other's actions. While some therapists encourage putting the most positive spin possible on everything, this approach is not consistent with an ecobehavioral commitment to honesty. A willingness to consider more positive interpretations of one's partner's actions, however, which may well be real, can be a meaningful gift for each partner to offer to the other.

Rules (which include beliefs, assumptions and expectations) are also crucially important and often need to be explicitly discussed with the couple. Unrealistic beliefs about marriage or couple relationships are common in U.S. culture (Bornstein & Bornstein, 1986; Ellis, Sichel, Yeager, DiMattia, & DiGiuseppe, 1989), including, for example:

- The level of romance and excitement is constant in a good relationship.
- My partner would know what I think and feel if he or she really loved me.
- If we are ever angry with each other, there is something drastically wrong with our relationship.
- Out-of-control anger (and even violence) is a fact of life, even in the best relationships.
- Love means always wanting to be together.

Such beliefs (both unrealistically positive and unrealistically negative) are supported in popular literature, media, and among friendship networks. Individuals also often carry rules that come from negative family experiences, such as, "Women are always unfaithful, so it is only a matter of time until you betray me," or "Battering is a woman's lot in life; there is nothing I can do about that."

Helping the couple to articulate and clarify equivalences and rules that may be guiding their actions and to determine the extent to which those are accurate are among the social worker's functions in couples consultation. Shifts in equivalence relations occur primarily by constructing alternative meanings, which are subsequently reinforced in one's world. If one partner has accepted the equivalence {partner working late ≈ not loving me}, constructing an alternative like {partner working late ≈ partner very anxious about job situation} can be enormously helpful in building empathy and avoiding hurt—assuming the alternative is true (Mattaini, 1997).

When the issue involves inaccurate rules, there are two general strategies for working toward a shift. The first is *disputing of irrational beliefs*, developed by Albert Ellis (Ellis & Dryden, 1997), in which faulty assumptions are directly challenged, often using humor—for example, "So if she won't go out of town with you this weekend, it's *terrible*? It's a *tragedy*?" This technique aims at having the client recognize the extent to which his or her thinking involves exaggeration, overgeneralization, excessively rigid demands of self or others, or selective attention.

The second strategy for working with inaccurate rules, *collaborative empiricism*, was developed by Beck and his associates (Beck, Freeman, & Associates, 1990; Beck, Rush, Shaw, & Emery, 1978). Beck's approach involves asking the client(s) to work with the therapist to test their rules (assumptions, expectations). For example, the social worker might say to one partner:

> So, you believe that your family will not accept Jocelyn because she is Jewish. Since this is a very important question in your lives, would you be willing to test this? For example (and you may be able to think of even better experiments), would you be willing to talk first with one of your sisters, and see how she reacts?
> Or:
> You said you believe that in happy marriages there are almost never any disagreements. Would you be willing to test that? I would like you to identity three of your friends that you believe have a good relationship. . . . Now, would you be willing to ask at least one of them whether he or she experiences disagreements in his or her relationship?

The idea here is to encourage clients to at least consider alternative descriptions of reality, and to test those, rather than to blindly act based on rules they have learned earlier in life that may not be accurate. Changes in self-talk can lead to changes in behavior, and ultimately what is important for couples is that rates of reinforcing behavior increase and often that rates of aversives decrease. Several core repertoires typically lead to those outcomes.

CONSTRUCTING POSITIVE MICROCULTURES WITH COUPLES

In the ecobehavioral approach, the central focus is on constructing and maintaining new practices in the family, and this is true for couples work as well as intergenerational and other family work. A number of repertoires are consistent with the research currently available related to couples' relationships, and perhaps the most useful approach is to share that information with the couple as part of the assessment, and to return to it through-out intervention. The social worker can begin this process by listing the core repertoires on a white board, discussing them with the couple, and giving the clients copies of the list to take home for further discussion. This process shifts the focus away from what's wrong, and toward what needs to be built. The list of empirically supported repertoires that the author shares with clients is shown in Table 6-1.

Because of the wide personal and cultural variations present among couples, the specific actions that each cluster of skills includes are far from universal. For some couples, explicit verbal description of actions that one takes and that the other appreciates (for example, "I appreciate so much that you work with me to make dinner, it's really fun to do together") is an ideal form of recognition; while for others that may be embarrassing, and a simple, intimate smile may be more meaningful. In some Native American and Pacific cultures, teasing one's partner is commonly experienced as af-fectionate (and therefore as "giving"), while among European Americans, some forms of teasing have a veiled aggressive function. In some cultures, one is seen as "listening" only if one maintains direct eye contact, while in others that is rude. It is therefore crucial to *discuss with the couple* the actions that should be included in each cluster of skills, from their unique per-spective.

The general process for constructing these repertoires and stabilizing them as features of the couple's microculture is one of skills training. This is a far less threatening and aversive way of framing work with the couple than defining and "treating" their "pathology." It is also more respectful and communicates the message that the worker realizes that each has been doing the best he can given current skills and circumstances. In some cases, the partners may not have these skills in their repertoires, and in other cases they may not use them with each other (an issue of discriminating occa-

---

Table 6–1

Essential Couples Skills

- give
- recognize
- accept
- listen with respect
- use "I" statements
- make requests rather than demands
- problem-solve
- contain conflict
- tell the truth.

sions). Often clients have not reinforced each other for approximations of these skills. Assuming that case assessment (chapter 2) indicates that the couple relationship is the primary focal issue to be dealt with, the basic process is straightforward and consistent with the approach discussed in chapter 5 for enhancing communication skills:

1. Identification of priority skill areas that the couple wishes to enhance to reach the improved relationship they envision.
2. Clarification and modeling of each skill.
3. Contextual analysis, including appropriate occasions for using the skill and obstacles that the couple may face in doing so.
4. Practicing the skill in the session.
5. Practicing the skill at home when the social worker is not present.

For some of the skills listed, other specialized techniques have been developed, which are discussed with the descriptions of the skills. The suggestions offered are a sampling of the many ways that couples can experiment to construct and stabilize healthy practices in their families. Other creative approaches, so long as they are consistent with constructing these essential repertoires, can often be developed with clients. For example, every couple needs to regularly experience positive times with each other, but this can happen in innumerable ways.

Giving

If a couple relationship is to be satisfying, there is no substitute for a rich, mutual exchange of valued reinforcers. Each partner must commit to *giving* to the other often, and giving what matters to the other. Couples should also be encouraged to give themselves, as a couple, experiences that are reinforcing for both. It is common in distressed couples for each to wait for the other to make the first step, and to withhold reinforcers until that happens. This is, of course, a set-up for failure. Stuart (1980) indicates that each partner must commit to the "change first" principle, agreeing to begin to give to the other first, regardless of whether the other responds immediately or not (to reduce sensitivity to momentary variations).

The social worker needs to clarify that a commitment to giving is core to a satisfying relationship, not only during the time the couple is working with the social worker, but continuously. Complications like satiation, reinforcer erosion, and changing preferences need to be elaborated. Partners in successful relationships put considerable effort into identifying and providing reinforcers that are meaningful to each other. Given the enormous variability among cultures and individuals, there is no substitute for open discussions of what each appreciates about and from each other.

There are at least three stages in couples work in which an explicit emphasis on giving is useful. The first is in the beginning of the work; a procedure like Stuart's *caring days* (see below) can jump-start positive exchange and begin to rebuild commitment to the relationship. Early discussions should also include what the partners liked about each other when they got together and what they like and appreciate about each other even now, despite the struggles they may be having. A focus on giving is useful again somewhat later in the work, after the couple has begun to make some progress at accepting each other (see below), and may be ready to take additional steps to build intimacy. At that point, a procedure like Jacobson and Christensen's (1996), which is outlined in detail in chapter 4, can be particularly valuable. Finally, an emphasis on giving is crucial when planning for maintenance as consultation draws to a close. A discussion of the natural process of declining positive exchange and the need to make active plans to prevent this can be helpful at that point. For example, on the first Sunday of every month, the couple may wish to discuss actions they have appreciated and other behaviors that they would appreciate. An individualized maintenance plan should be developed with each couple.

Caring days (Stuart, 1980) is a procedure that is best used in the very beginning of couples work; it is generally assigned as homework in the first session, after initial assessment has been completed. The purpose of caring days is to increase mutual positive exchange quickly, setting a positive tone for the subsequent work, and reminding the couple of the reasons why the relationship has been valuable to them. The general steps involved are as follows:

- The social worker briefly describes the procedure and the "change first" principle and indicates his or her belief, based on hundreds of cases in which it has been tested, that the procedure is potentially *very important*. The importance of completing this procedure, no matter what obstacles may arise, is stressed.
- The social worker lists actions each partner would appreciate, if the other performed them during the next week, down the middle of a sheet. (Leave room on each side for the partners to make checkmarks, or insert small dates.) The items on the list should be small things that are not deeply conflicted. It is almost always necessary to give examples to begin the process, like:
  —Call me at work.
  —Give me a two-minute neck rub.
  —Go to a movie with me.

—Sweep the kitchen floor.

—Bring me a little gift.

The couple can usually then identify their own reinforcers. Begin by asking one partner (whoever appears most cooperative and positive about the other) to identify several. Reassure the couple that no one needs to do any specific thing on this list: these are only starting points.

- Collect at least 15 to 20 ideas for the list, making sure to get at least some from each partner. Leave room on the bottom for more items that can be added during the week.
- Ask each partner to commit to trying to do at least a couple of things from the list every day until the next session, *regardless of whether his or her partner does this*. Indicate that if one partner does not complete the assignment, this will be discussed at the next session, but should not be discussed at home.
- Each time one member of the couple notices that his or her partner has done something on the list, the *recipient* should note this with a checkmark (or the date). Note that it is the recipient who determines whether what is done is pleasing (reinforcing). During the week, each can also add other things that the other has done for them that they appreciate, to the bottom of the list.
- The social worker will usually find that it pays to call the couple (both members if possible) two or three days after the session to be sure they remember to do the task and to address any problems experienced in completing it.
- The worker should then go over the list with the couple at the beginning of the next session. If the assignment has not been done, it may be necessary to review and reassign the task, and end the session early, which emphasizes its importance. (This can usually be avoided if the social worker makes clear in the first session that this data will be necessary for the next session to happen, and makes the follow-up phone call.)
- In almost every case, the caring days procedure produces noticeable progress and builds hope for the potential of the joint work. If there is some progress, but more seems possible, the procedure can be assigned for a second week. If there is no progress, especially after trying for two weeks, individual sessions to reexamine commitment to the relationship and the process may be indicated. Formal caring days are generally structured for a maximum of two weeks, but should be followed by discussion of ways to maintain high levels of giving, which may include periodic record keeping or scheduled discussions of what each appreciates in the other's behavior.

Obviously, Jacobson's behavior exchange and Stuart's caring days procedures represent only two examples of the many possible ways to build positive exchange. Open discussions with couples regarding the way they might structure such exchange into their relationships may produce creative new approaches. It is important to reassure people that while the procedures may feel somewhat artificial, what they are giving each other is genuine. If putting up a note on the refrigerator that says, "What can I do for you today?" helps someone remember to give, that does not at all mean that what is given is not real. (Such prompts need to be changed—or moved—periodically, or people stop noticing them.)

Recognizing

Giving is crucial; like any other behavior it will be maintained only if it is reinforced, so providing recognition for what the other does that is valued is essential for maintenance. In fact, if recognizing becomes a habit, less attention will need to be paid to giving, because it will occur more and more naturally. There are many ways one can recognize one's partner, including:

• Verbal expressions of appreciation for what one does for the other.
• Putting into words things the partner does that one values (including, for example, achievements at work, acts of committed parenting, etc.).
• Paying attention to what one agrees with in what the other says (many couples slip into a pattern of finding things to contradict or disagree with, a mildly or even severely punitive repertoire that gives a message of devaluing and can do considerable damage over time).
• Asking follow-up questions that indicate that one really finds what the other person is talking about to be interesting and worth discussing.
• Nonverbal expressions of affection, reinforcing proximity and presence.

Increasing rates of recognition is usually the most powerful intervention one can make in a relationship

The deep power of this strategy cannot be overemphasized; in fact, in terms of intrafamily dynamics, this is perhaps the most important statement in this book. It is crucial to seriously discuss this point with couples throughout the consultation process because they commonly will not see its importance until they have extensively tested it for themselves. Self-monitoring procedures, in which one keeps track of at least how often, and perhaps in what ways, one recognizes one's partner, are therefore powerful interventions. Keeping a simple record like that shown in Figure 6-3 for a few days or weeks can be helpful for this purpose.

Figure 6-3

A recognition self-monitoring chart.

What my partner did:	How I recognized it:

Using such a record, or even a simple tally sheet, occasionally can be a useful maintenance procedure as well.

Accepting

Early behavioral approaches to work with couples placed heavy emphasis on active techniques like behavior exchange and communication skills training (for example, Jacobson & Margolin, 1979; Stuart, 1969, 1980; Thomas, 1977). Consistent with shifts in individual work (Hayes, Jacobson, Follette, & Dougher, 1994; Mattaini, 1997), in recent years there has been increasing recognition of the need to construct acceptance skills in couples work as well. Neil Jacobson and his colleagues have been at the forefront of this work (Koerner, Jacobson, & Christensen, 1994). Jacobson was a pioneer in behavioral couples work. His original work emphasized change-oriented strategies, but his research has indicated that for many couples, acceptance strategies may be even more important and that both acceptance and change are often required. *Integrative couple therapy* (ICT) (Jacobson &

Christensen, 1996) is the result. The book by Jacobson and Christensen is a seminal work, which should be read by all social workers seeing couples.

As discussed in chapter 4, "acceptance" does not mean that everything—for example, the oppression associated with violence—should be tolerated. What acceptance does mean, however, is recognition that people are who they are, and do what they do for reasons deeply rooted in their history, biology, and situation; they often will not change in basic ways (even if they may want to). This is particularly true with older couples, those who are more traditional, less emotionally engaged, or who disagree about what is to be valued in a couple relationship; in such cases, Jacobson and his colleagues found that change-oriented techniques were often inadequate to significantly shift marital or couple satisfaction. For these couples, acceptance-based work appears to be especially important.

Acceptance involves "letting go of the struggle," and accepting that differences between the partners are real, but need not ruin the relationship. This is a strategy rooted in changing self-talk; the equivalence {differences ≈ unacceptable ≈ doomed relationship} is shifted to {differences ≈ inevitable ≈ livable}. Jacobson and Christensen's approach also couches problems as possible "routes to intimacy" (1996, p. 12)—again a very significant shift from {problems ≈ disaster ≈ distance} to {problems ≈ routes to closeness}. Helping each partner to recognize and accept that there may be areas of major difference, even in central values, but that such differences need not lead to unmanageable pain or the breakup of the relationship, is also central to acceptance.

The integrative couple approach emphasizes several specific techniques (some of which may be more consistent with an honest, shared power approach than others, see below), but the strategy is about more than technique; rather it involves shifts in fundamental ways of thinking about each other and the relationship. Helping couples to learn to talk to themselves, each other, and others in terms of different equivalences and rules is the core. Acceptance also involves a commitment to giving up coercion; neither partner has the right to force the other to change. Perhaps paradoxically, the other is often more willing to change once coercion is abandoned.

The first technique emphasized in ICT is *empathic joining around the problem* (Koerner, Jacobson, & Christensen, 1994, p. 114). The social worker using this technique explores central issues with which the couple is struggling (closeness-distance, control and responsibility, or conventionality-unconventionality), by interviewing each, in as much emotional depth as possible, in the presence of the other. The observing partner remains quiet. The goal here is to assist each partner to listen to and really hear the other's struggles with the issue; these struggles are typically painful for both, but this may not be recognized "in the heat of battle." Expressions of fear, disappointment, hurt and pain, if they are heard and not used as ammunition for future battles, can build empathy.

A second acceptance-based technique is to turn the problem into an "it" (Koerner, Jacobson, & Christensen, 1994, p. 115), in ICT terms, depersonalizing the issue, and helping the couple to join against a common enemy, the problem. The technique appears to work well, although it may be that turning the problem into an enemy may be less consistent with acceptance than seeing it as a reality, not necessarily something good or bad, just a fact, which may change over time but currently is real.

A third technique recommended by ICT is "enhancing self-care" (Koerner, Jacobson, & Christensen, 1994, p. 116), which in the terms used here refers to ensuring that each partner receives adequate levels of reinforcement and avoids severe deprivation. Some of this reinforcement may come from the couple relationship, and some from other sources.

Building tolerance (Koerner, Jacobson, & Christensen, 1994, p. 116), a final technique, can be done through role playing in the session or at home, when the problem scenes are replayed often enough to desensitize the partners to them, perhaps in conjunction with empathic joining discussions. In some cases, the social worker can also help the couple identify some positive aspects of the behaviors that they find difficult to tolerate, so long as this is real and not an unbelievable reframing. For example, many behaviors may create distance between the partners; if the partner who desires more closeness then uses the free time to do something productive, it is not a total loss. At the same time, Jacobson and Christensen (1996) indicate that it is essential to acknowledge the unpleasant effects as well. In other words, "This bothers you, but it is not a total tragedy." Since the behaviors at issue are often the ones that first attracted the couple to each other (for example, the "free spirit" is now seen as "irresponsible"), a reminder of this may also increase tolerance.

An additional tolerance-building technique recommended in ICT, but which I see as inconsistent with the honesty and shared power characteristic of an ecobehavioral approach, is to ask the partners to "fake the problem" (p. 116). For example, someone who is seen by his partner as unsympathetic would be asked to withhold sympathy even when he feels like giving it, then later would tell the partner he was faking, and actually did experience sympathy. There is an extensive rationale for this technique (Jacobson & Christensen, 1996, p. 143 ff), but it does not appear to be constructive of honesty in the relationship, and I believe it is likely to prove empirically to be counterproductive.

Acceptance-based strategies and techniques consistent with an ecobehavioral model are deeply respectful. They are inconsistent with messages that one partner is wrong, weak, or must change to meet the requirements and wishes of the other. Instead, these techniques and strategies convey clearly that one partner needs to take seriously what is important to the other and has no right to demand that the other change to please him or her, much less to force the partner to do so.

Listening with Respect

Listening skills were a major emphasis in chapter 5, and that material will not be repeated here. It is important to note, however, that listening respectfully is one of the most crucial repertoires for couples, and one that is commonly missing. Partners, especially if they have been together for some time, often stop really listening to each other; this "tuning out" may be particularly common among men, but it is a general problem. Listening *respectfully* involves the specific listening skills discussed previously (nonverbal skills, furthering responses, and the reflection of feelings and content), but also a commitment to avoid acting punitively and critically. Many couples evolve a microculture in which both engage in reciprocal punitive or competitive exchanges. Being "right" or being "the winner" offers a form of reinforcement often supported by the larger culture, but these low-quality reinforcers are not nearly as satisfying over time as recognition and respect.

Listening well involves quietly attending to what the other is saying, even if the message is one that the listener does not want to hear, for example, dissatisfaction with or criticism of one's own actions. One of the best ways to immediately defuse tension is to be willing to really listen to the other's perspective and feelings, and to respond nondefensively with a willingness to honestly look at oneself and one's behavior. If the listener can at least to some extent let go of the culturally shaped, egotistical need to defend one's own behavior and can really hear his or her partner, the relationship will improve, and the listener may also learn something important about him- or herself.

It is usually more important that partners really listen to and try to understand each other (acceptance) than that they agree. Listening well means attending to what the other is saying, rather than planning how one will respond when one's turn comes (even while the other is speaking)). Listening well also involves asking follow-up questions, seeking clarification and detail, which shows real interest. "How was your day? . . . I think I'll go turn on the news," is quite different from, "How was your day? . . . Boy, that must have been fascinating! What did she say then?"

Expressing Oneself Using I-Statements

As in all family relationships, communication requires both respectful and attentive listening and respectful expression of feelings and opinions. (This area was covered in detail in chapter 5.) Unfortunately partners often blame each other; "take out" frustrations from other life spheres, like work, on each other; and punish each other for honestly expressing feelings and opinions. The larger culture commonly models and shapes these repertoires and often does not prepare people (especially men) well to share their feelings or to state their opinions as personal thoughts rather than universal absolutes.

Extensive practice in making I-statements is an excellent way to develop and deepen the expressive repertoires that contribute much to a solid relationship. Once both respectful listening and I-statements have been discussed, modeled, and practiced in the session, a particularly useful home assignment is for the couple to practice these skills for at least 20 minutes once or twice before the following session. Such an assignment has many variations, but one way to structure it is as follows:

> You both seem to be doing well at listening and making I-statements. Would you be willing to pursue this a bit further at home before our next meeting? What I would like you to do is to set aside two 20-minute "appointments" this week, when you can practice. During those times, I'd like each of you to make at least five (and hopefully more!) I-statements about your thoughts, your hopes, your feelings, your likes, or your interests. I'd like the other one to listen very carefully and respectfully, to repeat what your partner said, and to ask questions for more detail. While you are making I-statements, I would like you to use a piece of paper and a pencil, and mark each time you make an I-statement. This is to emphasize your awareness of when you are doing this. How does that sound? Is there anything you would want to change about it?

The task then is given in writing to the couple after a discussion in which details are worked out, obstacles are discussed and planned for, and commitments are made. Unless these skills have just been practiced in the session, it is also usually best to do so at least briefly at the conclusion of this task discussion.

Expressions should not, of course, only involve problems; there need to be high levels of expression of positive sentiments as well. When there is an issue, however, it is crucial that it be expressed in clear behavioral (rather than attitudinal) terms, that only the current issue be discussed, and that it not be treated as an issue on which the entire relationship hinges unless it truly is. For example, "I was very hurt last night when you spent so little time with me at the party; I felt left out, and I was embarrassed to be seen standing by myself so much" is a clear expression, including three I-statements. Contrast this with, "You abandoned me last night and spent all your time flirting with other men at the party. Maybe it's time for me to find someone else. You've been screwing around like this ever since we were married. And your mother before you was just the same." This second statement involves blame, expands the issues dramatically, and is almost certain to lead to escalating conflict. It is also often best to clarify, by making a request, what it is that one partner wants the other one to do, rather than just identifying the unwelcome behavior. This should be done in a respectful rather than demanding way.

Making Requests Rather than Demands

In couples relationships in particular, coercive demands really have no place. A healthy couple consists of two adults who have the freedom to do what they think is best and who freely choose to be together and to contribute to each other's lives. Coercive demands damage relationships, lead to counteraggression, withdrawal, and avoidance, and tend to escalate often to the point of abuse (Sidman, 1989). Partners are also often much more responsive to respectful requests (which certainly may involve a good deal of emotion) than to demands. Compare the following examples:

1. I was very worried and frankly pretty angry last night when I rushed home from work to spend time with you, and you did not get home until three hours later. I would truly appreciate it if you would call me when you are going to be late like this in the future. Experiences like this make me very unhappy.
2. The next time you are going to be late like last night, you call me, do you understand? I'm not going to put up with your crap anymore. You really treat me like dirt, and if you keep this up, I'm out of here!

The first example, which involves I-statements and respectful requests, while perhaps not easy to hear, may have a positive outcome. The second example, which includes you-statements of blame, profanity, demands, and escalation from the current issue to a global relationship threat, almost certainly will not. This is not to say that partners may not have a "bottom line," a limit regarding what they will tolerate. For example, in most cultures fidelity has proven to be useful, and many people expect that their partners will be sexually and emotionally faithful to them. A person cannot force the partner to be faithful, and efforts to do so could escalate into abuse. They can, however, clarify the consequences of infidelity: "I love you and want this relationship to work out. However, I am not willing to live in a relationship where my partner is unfaithful. If you decide you want to be with someone else, I'd prefer you be honest about that. But if you decide to be with someone else, I will not stay with you." This leaves the decision to the partner but treats both with respect.

Of course, the desires and interests of two partners are sometimes different, and negotiation is often required to reach solutions to issues. If both partners are prepared to use the repertoires described thus far (giving, recognizing, accepting, listening and expressing respectfully, and request-making), the problem-solving process can go much more smoothly.

Problem Solving

When dealing with couples, the social worker will commonly discover that the "problems" that appear to cause conflict are not the real issues; rather they are reflections of more encompassing dynamics, usually cultures of reciprocal coercion and inadequate levels of high-quality reinforcers, accompanied by ineffective communication and lack of acceptance. In other words, if all of the practices discussed thus far are well established in the family, problem solving involving collaboration and compromise is usually relatively manageable, partly because each partner genuinely wants the other to be happy. For example, a decision about whether to make a major move when one partner has an excellent opportunity is challenging, but given a commitment to each other and the relationship, it is likely that the couple can make either decision work. In most cases, paradoxically, the decision reached is in itself not really critical; the fact that the couple has institutionalized a process of decision making where each feels respected and heard is.

When a problem does come up, the steps discussed in the last chapter (problem identification, problem exploration, and generating, evaluating, and selecting solutions) for general problem-solving can provide a flexible but structured way to work toward solutions. It is also useful to remind the couple, when immediate decisions do not emerge from the process, that very few decisions need to be made immediately, and that is often useful to take a break for a few hours or days and come back to the problem after each partner has had some time to think it through. Some decisions, such as whether to have a child, may not need to be reached for a considerable period of time. Many decisions are also reversible, and thinking about decisions as experiments that can be revisited at a later time is often helpful. Even apparently major decisions, like making a geographic move, are often reversible; they may involve considerable effort, but it is important not to exaggerate this. Most people move several times and generally survive the experience! (Note that this is an example of paying attention to self-talk, in particular avoiding "awfulizing" [Ellis & Dryden, 1997] things that may be undesirable, but not tragic.) In problem solving, another rule of thumb often useful to follow is: If no alternative clearly emerges as the best, choose the least final one, since one can then try something else if the first choice does not work out.

Containing Conflict

Some conflicts are inevitable for every couple, even when strong relationship and problem-solving skills are present. Conflict (defined in some ways) can, in fact, be healthy, but only if it is well handled. Markman (1991) in reviewing a series of studies, suggests that couples that handle conflicts constructively have learned to "(a) express negative feelings about specific behavioral events, and (b) receive and respond constructively to (i.e., hear and validate) one's partner's expressions of negative feelings" (p. 91). Markman also indicates that the research suggests that wives are more likely to bring up negative feelings and that husbands' skills in responding to those expressions are therefore particularly predictive of marital satisfaction. Note also that, consistent with material presented earlier in this chapter, negative affect should be expressed in terms of specific events (not in general, attitudinal, or global terms) if conflict is to be handled constructively.

In many couples, however, conflict tends to escalate, and each may at some point say and do things whose primary function is to hurt the other (a natural response to aversives—all animals tend to strike out when in pain). In couples where this pattern is deeply rooted, new skills for containing conflict are required. Several repertoires are useful for this purpose, depending on the couple. It is essential that the couple discuss and agree in advance on whatever strategies they decide can be useful. It is often best to role play actually using the strategies selected in a reenactment of an actual conflict, so that the couple knows what to expect and how it may feel emotionally.

Commonly useful strategies include:

• Doing more of whatever works for the couple sometimes (a strategy that has been elaborated by solution-focused practitioners). The social worker can help identify such processes by saying, "Sometimes, when you are in conflict, you don't get into a serious fight. Can you give me some examples? What made the difference? What did you do that was different from times when things got out of control?"

- Making a commitment to simply listen respectfully, no matter what the partner says: for some couples, this results in gradual moderation of the level of affect.
- Suggesting a change of scene, moving to a different room, or sitting down together.
- Moving physically closer together (so long as there is no danger of violence), which often increases intimacy and results in lowering voices. Note that this is different from one partner pulling the other toward him or her and trying to kiss him or her to keep the partner quiet!
- "Owning" and acknowledging one's own anger. For example, "I am very angry right now and I may not be completely reasonable. But I really want to see a change. . . ."
- Asking for modest, reasonable changes, rather than extreme and unrealistic changes.
- Stating a willingness to compromise, so long as this is reciprocal and does not result in oppression of one partner by the other.
- Taking advantage of the moments of "reflex fatigue" (Stuart, 1980), when things settle down a bit after an initial flare, to move into problem-solving discussion.
- Requesting that both partners speak respectfully, repeating this (respectfully!) as often as necessary until reasonable discussion begins. For example, "I would like to talk with you about this, but I can only do it if we are both willing to speak quietly and respectfully."
- Requesting that the discussion be limited to the current issue, or to one issue at a time. This can be valuable (so long as the couple has previously agreed to it) to avoid letting the conflict bleed into many other areas in the relationship; instead it is kept present-focused, behaviorally specific, and bounded.
- Requesting a time-out. For example, "I think we are getting pretty hot now and we might say things we do not mean. I would like to take a break for five minutes [or ten, or thirty, depending on the couple] and cool off, then come back to this." It is important to plan to finish the discussion; otherwise this becomes a strategy of refusing to hear the partner's issues and complaints, which is counterproductive. It is particularly important to agree on this strategy ahead of time and for the partner to agree not to "pursue" the other to try to keep the discussion going instead of allowing the timeout.
- Leaving the situation. A last-ditch strategy when nothing else is working, leaving the situation can prevent even further escalation, but involves considerable relationship cost, since it clearly gives a message that, "I am

not going to listen to you." Some couples, however, may need this as a backup, for example where one or both partners are afraid that they may become physical if they can't interrupt the process somehow.

When the level of affect has settled down (which eventually happens, if for no other reason than fatigue), and the couple is at the stage of potential *rapprochement*, often one or both may be able to acknowledge what they have learned as a result of the conflict, and one or both may be ready to commit to reasonable changes to avoid similar conflicts in the future. Many conflicts can be prevented through effective problem solving and the other skills discussed throughout this book. When discussing the realities of conflicts with an objective third party, those involved may recognize the often childish and "primitive" behaviors likely to emerge at times of high emotion; this can lead to a commitment to learn to handle conflict differently.

Tell the Truth

Dishonesty and deception can do tremendous damage to relationships. Many individuals have learned in the course of their early developmental, family, and other experiences that honesty is often punished. As a result, they may shade the truth, tell outright lies, or simply omit talking about things that their partner would want and expect to know. In a successful relationship, what each says to the other must be the truth (as defined by what the partner would expect one to say). Even in extreme cases, say when someone loses a job, has made a serious financial mistake, or has become romantically interested in someone else, only honesty can work in the long run; social workers can sometimes help provide a setting where people can talk about such difficult issues. Techniques outlined above to assist with acceptance can be useful for establishing a context for such discussions. One partner does not need to tell the other about everything in the past; not everyone is well prepared to deal with such disclosures, and it can be hard on the person telling the story as well. In some cases, a person may need to assertively indicate a preference to not go into those matters. The elements disclosed to one's partner, however, should always be true. Truth can be painful, but deception is potentially much more devastating.

SPECIAL ISSUES: INFIDELITY AND SEXUAL PROBLEMS

Infidelity and sexual problems often surface in couples consultation. Each of these issues is common. It is a mistake not to recognize them, although in some cases, social workers inexperienced in these areas may feel uncomfortable. Attention to these issues when they are present can make the difference between a positive outcome and an unsatisfactory one.

Infidelity

Sexual relationships outside of marriage are common in the United States, with about half of married men and a third of married women involved in such relationships over their lifetimes. (Most of the research done relates to married, heterosexual couples; although not much is known about incidence among other couples, it is probably not lower.) These numbers can be misleading, however, since a substantial proportion of affairs occurs in the final year of marriage when the relationship may already be dying (Pittman & Wagers, 1995). Rates among stable marriages are much lower. Well known scholars in the marriage counseling field indicate that outside involvements are common, however, in couples that seek help (Jacobson & Christensen, 1996). If one includes "emotional infidelity" (intimacy with someone other than the partner to an extent that the partner would experience as a violation of the couple's contract), the rate is even higher. Pittman and Wagers (1995), specialists in the area, suggest that extramarital affairs (announced or not) are usually present when established marriages end in divorce.

Two decades ago, many counselors working with couples indicated that they approved of "open" (but not secret) relationships for their clients (Stuart, 1980). Open relationships are apparently difficult to maintain, however, probably because the exchange of intimate reinforcers is diluted, with the partners having less to give each other. The larger culture also provides little social support for such arrangements. Extra-couple relationships usually produce jealousy, anger (based in part on equivalence relations like {affair ≈ giving what is mine to someone else}) and fear of loss. Perhaps the most powerful aversive dimension for most people is the deception involved, which then leads to a loss of trust. If the partners cannot trust that they will receive the reinforcers agreed to in the couple's contract, they may naturally be unwilling to invest in providing reinforcers themselves, and the relationship can wither very quickly. Repeated deception can be particularly deadly. For all of these reasons, while a couple certainly has the right to try to forge a relationship in which the boundaries are different from those espoused by common cultural values, affairs involving secrecy are usually serious problems, or symptoms of serious problems, and can pose enormous obstacles to couple counseling.

Still, many couples will come to the social worker for help when one partner (or occasionally both) is involved in an affair. The question then is how the social worker should deal with this. First, it is absolutely critical that the social worker not participate in deception. The worker should inquire about extra-couple involvement during initial individual contacts, and if an affair surfaces at any point, the worker should make clear that the client must disclose the affair, or the worker cannot continue to work with the couple. It is easier not to ask, of course, but that is a mistake. It is also difficult for a social worker to ask the individual involved in the affair to tell his or her partner that he or she is not committed enough to continue couples work (or for the social worker to say this if necessary), but this also needs to be done if the client refuses to disclose. (Note that the worker does not violate a confidence here.)

If the individual involved does agree to the disclosure, although it may not come as a complete surprise to the partner, the subsequent session is likely to be difficult, and the social worker should be prepared to do considerable crisis intervention. If the partner involved chooses to disclose and end the affair, Jacobson and Christensen (1996) provide guidelines for proceeding, generally as a joint effort (perhaps involving a joint letter) by both partners. Contact should be broken off completely, and the partner should be able to ask for whatever proof he or she wishes that this has actually happened. (Some variation may be needed when the affair occurs at work.) If the involved partner chooses at this point not to end the outside relationship, the social worker can make clear the risks to the relationship, but current state-of-the-art practice suggests that the consultation continue, with emphasis on honest communication of the emotions involved and work to build as much empathy as possible (Jacobson & Christensen, 1996). Some relationships do survive affairs, when active support is provided and there is an adequate history of positive exchange on which to build. Pittman and Wagers (1995), as well as Jacobson and Christensen, offer extensive guidance for this work.

From an ecobehavioral perspective, what happens within the couple—including infidelity—affects more than the two partners. Children, extended family, friendship networks, and—in the contemporary world—often work settings can be dramatically affected. This is also true in cases of separation or divorce. The social worker, or the partners with the social worker's support, should intervene in these interconnected systems to stabilize them during the crisis, to reduce the amount of damage done, and ultimately to help everyone involved envision and move toward a new, adequately reinforcing and minimally aversive balance. Responses to such crises can involve counseling, mediation, and even ritual. Divorce counseling goes beyond the scope of this chapter, but social workers working with couples should be prepared to move in that direction if necessary and should be familiar with that literature as well (for example, Everett & Volgy, 1991; Levine & Levine, 1996; Walsh, Jacob, & Simons, 1995).

In cases of infidelity in particular, however, whether the couple chooses to try to work out their relationship or to end it, it is important to discuss with them how to handle the emotional strains experienced by others who are affected, especially children, in the least damaging ways. Children (particularly adolescents) are often already aware of the situation; they certainly recognize the level of conflict present. In one case, a 15-year-old girl and her parents came to see the author about conflicts between the mother and daughter. In meeting with the parents, they indicated that their marriage was in serious trouble because of a recent affair between the husband and a young woman who worked for him, but that their daughter did not know about it. In a meeting with the daughter, however, she told the social worker about the affair, and indicated that she had become a good friend of her father's lover; but she also stated that her parents were unaware that she knew what was going on. This family needed enormous healing, and it was certainly unfair to the daughter to leave her to resolve her emotions on her own.

Sexual Difficulties

Some studies indicate that up to three-quarters of couples seen for counseling have some level of sexual difficulty, although this is an area that is often neglected (Stuart & Hammond, 1980). Sexual activity can undoubtedly provide important reinforcers for couples, and some kinds of sexual problems can be serious sources of aversives. It is important, therefore, for social workers working with couples to become comfortable discussing this topic. In some cases, clients may need to be referred for specialized services, but that cannot happen unless the issue is first surfaced. Social workers who are uncomfortable discussing sexuality, whether they are embarrassed to talk about it due to their own inexperience, or because sexuality offers particular personal challenges to them, need to prepare themselves through consultation, training, and in some cases personal therapy, if they are going to provide adequate services to clients.

Not every social worker needs to be trained as a sex therapist, and reading this short section will certainly not prepare the reader to become one. Many sexual issues, however, do not require specialty training. As in medicine, the generalist can do much with basic training. Clients can be told that most sexual problems have a solution and that some first efforts can be tried with the social worker. If these are not adequate, the social worker can refer to a specialist. Note that many social workers' clients may not have the resources to see specialists, however, so it is important to offer whatever services one can without overstating one's expertise. In some situations, using a co-consultant may prove valuable (for example, someone of the opposite sex when working with heterosexual couples). Note that under no circumstances, however, is it within the bounds of professional ethics for the social worker to have sexual contact with clients, to act as a sexual surrogate, or to observe clients' sexual behavior.

There are four levels of intervention for sexual problems, each progressively requiring increasing intensity and increased need for specialized training. Some additional reading should certainly be done before proceeding with any of this work; the higher the level of intensity, the more preparation is required. In a significant number of cases, situations that present as sexual problems actually involve deeper relationship issues. In such cases, relationship enhancement using the strategies outlined in the earlier sections of the chapter will usually need to be completed first. It is then often relatively easy to deal with remaining sexual issues using the spectrum of techniques that follow.

Level 1: Permission

In many cases, all that is needed to move toward an improved sexual adjustment is permission to communicate about sexuality, including each partners' likes and dislikes, and to experiment. Many couples do not discuss sexuality at all, and permission to do so can be a great relief. One partner (often the woman in a heterosexual relationship) may find current sexual exchanges unsatisfying or even aversive, but may not know how to raise the issue. If the social worker simply includes questions about sexuality in individual and joint interviews and demonstrates that it is natural to talk about sex in couples counseling, many couples can quickly reach an improved adjustment.

Level 2: Education

Many couples know very little about sex and may hold unrealistic or inaccurate beliefs about it that can be shifted through simple education. Many clients come into marriage having learned self-talk like:

• Women do not enjoy sex as much as men.
• It is natural to stop enjoying sex by age 40 (or 50, or 60, or 70 . . .).
• If a man has trouble getting an erection once, he is well on the road to impotence.

- In an adequate sexual relationship, both partners should attain simultaneous orgasm.
- Only immature women require clitoral stimulation to reach orgasm.

Discussion and education about what is "normal," about physiological facts, and about differing values regarding sexuality within the couple as well as those coming from families of origin can be particularly useful in these cases. The social worker, of course, needs a solid base of knowledge for this work.

Level 3: Simple behavioral changes

Discussions of the couple's current sexual patterns and desires often suggest specific, simple behavioral changes that can improve the sexual relationship. For example, many men do not really understand the need to take time for foreplay (and many women feel guilty asking for what they may erroneously believe is excessive time). Education that it is normal to require 30 to 60 minutes of intimate contact prior to intercourse to reach maximum levels of arousal, and discussion of the kinds of contact each finds arousing, is a start; a commitment to experiment with extended contact is the next step. Changes in timing and place that are more conducive to romance and arousal can also be useful. Variations of many kinds can be helpful to avoid satiation and keep interest in sexual contact high by ensuring novel reinforcers.

Many people (both men and women) often do not know that it is normal for a woman to require manual stimulation to reach full arousal; once they know this, the couple may need to experiment to learn how to do so. Some clients struggle with "spectatoring" (Stuart & Hammond, 1980), paying too much attention to "how they are performing" rather than to the way either their partner or they themselves are responding. This tends to be a particular issue with men who are concerned about impotence. Such clients may need to be taught to focus on either subtle changes in their partner's responses, or on their own physical experiences, instead of on performance.

Perhaps the most advanced technique that a social worker without further training might try is "sensate focus." Sensate focus, developed by Masters and Johnson (1970), involves the couple spending an extended period of time (60 to 90 minutes) having sensual physical contact with each other, with no expectation or demand for sexual arousal. Sensate focus is particularly useful for cases where there is clear performance anxiety, but it also seems to be valuable as a general technique for helping couples to experience physical togetherness as reinforcing (Stuart & Hammond, 1980);

and with variations even for more complex issues like lack of sexual desire (Heiman, Epps, & Ellis, 1995). The general procedure is as follows (to be flexibly applied depending on the couple):

• The couple preplan how to "set the mood"—selecting timing, place, and contextual conditions (for example, music, candles, showering together).
• The couple get completely undressed (except in cases of extreme inhibition, when this may be a goal to approach gradually), and relax in bed.
• The couple take turns touching each other in interesting ways (kissing, caressing, licking, etc.). The person receiving attention is to simply relax and experience, taking responsibility for giving continual feedback about what is pleasant, and how to do things in a way that would be more pleasant (rather than what not to do). The giving partner, meanwhile, is to focus only on the other's pleasure. After an agreed-upon amount of time, the two partners switch places. During this time, the effort is to really focus on physical experiences and to avoid letting the mind wander to the extent possible.

The couple should be instructed not to have sexual intercourse while doing this exercise, to reduce any performance anxiety. (Failure to comply with this instruction, however, is not a major issue.) The couple should ideally try this experiment about three times during the week when it is assigned and should try to avoid discussing it outside the sensate focus sessions until they return to the social worker. If it is realistic, each should try to write down their reactions as soon as possible after the sessions. According to Stuart and Hammond, fear of failure or rejection tend to be the main obstacles to sensate focus, and in the few cases where it is not pleasant for the couple, such obstacles should be explored.

    In cases where simple behavior changes and assignments do not resolve the issue, clients should be referred to trained specialists in sex therapy. While not every family social worker will become a sex therapist, it is useful to know something about what clients should expect from such therapy to prepare them for a referral. The next section sketches some of the approaches used. A good deal of other literature may also be helpful (for example, Kaplan, 1974, 1995; Rosen & Leiblum, 1995a; Stuart & Hammond, 1980).

Level 4: Sex therapy and treatment of severe sexual disorders

In recent years, significant shifts have occurred regarding both the kinds of cases that are referred for sex therapy and the approaches used for treatment. In the 1970s, the most common issues were premature ejaculation for men, vaginismus (painful intercourse), and anorgasmia (lack of orgasm) for women. Relatively straightforward behavioral interventions, like the squeeze technique for premature ejaculation and dilation exercises for vaginismus (Stuart & Hammond, 1980) can work quickly in such cases. At the present time, however, other problems are predominating (Rosen & Leiblum, 1995b). Erectile failure (impotence) seems to be increasing among men 40 and over. While a range of behavioral and cognitive techniques can help in such cases, currently the momentum is clearly toward medical treatments, especially medication and sometimes surgical intervention. The movement toward a medical model of treatment is increasingly common with many sexual dysfunctions and complaints, and some issues that once appeared to be exclusively psychological are now seen as having substantial physiological substrata. Disorders of sexual desire, cases where the client has little interest or even aversion toward sexuality and sexual contact, are now receiving a great deal of attention and appear to be increasingly common (Kaplan, 1995; Levine, 1995). "Hypersexuality," where the level of sexual behavior is excessively high by some standard, and the related so-called "sexual addictions," where sexual behavior appears to be compulsive and damaging to self or others (Nathan, 1995; Wincze, 1995), are also receiving increased attention. The strength of the positions held in this area often has little correlation with the evidence; much still remains to be learned here. Many of the more complex disorders currently appear to be related to histories of sexual trauma and abuse.

Because of the complex histories involved in the development of such emerging sexual complaints, it is not surprising that much more than sex therapy with the couple may be required. If sexual behavior is involved in equivalence relations with scenes of sexual abuse, if early sexual behavior was severely punished in childhood, or if first efforts at intimate connection by an already fragile youth were ridiculed, in-depth individual cognitive and behavioral work aimed at shifting these meanings (Mattaini, 1997) sometimes accompanied by medical intervention (Kaplan, 1995) may be needed before much movement can be expected within the couple. This may be particularly true for clients whose life experience has taught them to trust neither themselves nor anyone else (and who are often then pejoratively labeled as having "personality disorders"—"pathologies of the entire person" as defined by Davis and Millon, 1994, p. 43; see Mattaini, 1997, for an alternate perspective).

Many couples who come to social workers for consultation on improving their relationships, however, are not struggling with personal issues of this depth, and social work practitioners can offer relatively straightforward assistance in constructing more reinforcing sexual practices and experiences.

A couple is a family, if a small, one-generational one. Many couples, as well as some single persons, move on to another family developmental milestone at some point, bringing children into the family by birth or adoption. Parenting is an area that behavioral and ecobehavioral practice has examined particularly closely, and one in which the state of the art is very advanced. We examine strategies for constructing an effective, multigenerational culture in the family and the community of families in the next chapter.

REFERENCES

Beck, A. T., Freeman, A., & Associates. (1990). *Cognitive therapy of personality disorders.* New York: Guilford Press.

Beck, A. T., Rush, A. J., Shaw, B. F., & Emery, G. (1978). *Cognitive therapy of depression.* New York: Guilford Press.

Bornstein, P. H., Anton, B., Harowski, K. J., Weltzien, R. T., McIntyre, T. J., & Hocker, J. (1981). Behavioral-communications treatment of marital discord: Positive behaviors. *Behavioral Counseling Quarterly, 1,* 189–201.

Bornstein, P. H., & Bornstein, M. T. (1986). *Marital therapy: A behavioral-communications approach.* New York: Pergamon.

Bornstein, P. H., Hickey, J. S., Schulein, M. J., Fox, S. G., & Scollati, M. J. (1983). Behavioral communications treatment of marital interaction: Negative behaviors. *British Journal of Clinical Psychology, 22,* 41–48.

Burman, B., John, R. S., & Margolin, G. (1992). Observed patterns of conflict in violent, nonviolent, and nondistressed couples. *Behavioral Assessment, 14,* 15–37.

Davis, R. D., & Millon, T. (1994). Can personalities be disordered? Yes. In S. A. Kirk & S. D. Einbinder (Eds.), *Controversial issue in mental health,* (pp. 40–47). Boston: Allyn and Bacon.

Ellis, A., & Dryden, W. (1997). *The practice of rational emotive behavior therapy* (2nd ed.). New York: Springer.

Ellis, A., Sichel, J. L., Yeager, R. J., DiMattia, D. J., & DiGiuseppe, R. (1989). *Rational-emotive couples therapy.* New York: Pergamon.

Everett, C. A., & Volgy, S. S. (1991). Treating divorce in family-therapy practice. In A. S. Gurman & D. P. Kniskern (Eds.), *Handbook of family therapy: Volume II* (pp. 508–524). New York: Brunner/Mazel.

Glenn, S. S. (1991). Contingencies and metacontingencies: Relations among behavioral, cultural, and biological evolution. In P. A. Lamal (Ed.), *Behavioral analysis of societies and cultural practices,* (pp. 39–73). New York: Hemisphere.

Gottman, J. M., Markman, H., & Notarius, C. (1977). To topography of marital conflict: A sequential analysis of verbal and nonverbal behavior. *Journal of Marriage and the Family, 39,* 461–477.

Gottman, J. M., Notarius, C., Markman, H., Bank, S., Yoppi, B., & Rubin, M. E. (1976). Behavior exchange theory and marital decision making. *Journal of Personality and Social Psychology, 34,* 14–23.

Harris, M. (1989). *Our kind.* New York: HarperCollins.

Hayes, S. C., Jacobson, N. S., Follette, V. M., & Dougher, M. J. (Eds.), (1994). *Acceptance and change: Content and context in psychotherapy.* Reno, NV: Context Press.

Heiman, J. R., Epps, P. H., & Ellis, B. (1995). Treating sexual desire disorders in couples. In N. S. Jacobson & A. S. Gurman (Eds.), *Clinical handbook of couple therapy* (pp. 471–495). New York: Guilford Press.

Jacobson, N. S., & Christensen, A. (1996). *Integrative couple therapy.* New York: Norton.

Jacobson, N. S. & Margolin, G. (1979). *Marital therapy: Strategies based on social learning and behavior exchange principles.* New York: Brunner/Mazel.

Kalter, N., Kloner, A., Schreier, S., & Okla, K. (1989). Predictors of children's post-divorce adjustment. *American Journal of Orthopsychiatry, 59,* 605–618.

Kaplan, H. S. (1974). *The new sex therapy.* New York: Brunner/Mazel.

Kaplan, H. S. (1995). *The sexual desire disorders.* New York: Brunner/Mazel.

Koerner, K., Jacobson, N. S., & Christensen, A. (1994). Emotional acceptance in integrative behavioral couple therapy. In S. C. Hayes, N. S. Jacobson, V. M. Follette, & M. J. Dougher (Eds.), *Acceptance and change: Content and context in psychotherapy,* (pp. 109–118). Reno, NV: Context Press.

Levine, S. B. (1995). The vagaries of sexual desire. In R. C. Rosen & S. R. Leiblum (Eds.), *Case studies in sex therapy* (pp. 96–109). New York: Guilford Press.

Levine, S., & Levine, O. (1996). *Embracing the beloved: Relationship as a path of awakening.* New York: Anchor Books, 1996.

Markman, H. J. (1991). Constructive marital conflict is NOT an oxymoron. *Behavioral Assessment, 13,* 83–96.

Masters, W. H., & Johnson, V. E. (1970). *Human sexual inadequacy.* Boston: Little, Brown.

Mattaini, M. A. (1997). *Clinical practice with individuals.* Washington, DC: NASW Press.

Medved, D. (1989). *The case against divorce.* New York: Donald I. Fine.

Nathan, S. G. (1995). Sexual addiction: A sex therapist's struggles with an unfamiliar clinical entity. In R. C. Rosen & S. R. Leiblum (Eds.), *Case studies in sex therapy* (pp. 350–367). New York: Guilford Press.

Pittman, F. S., III, & Wagers, T. P. (1995). Crises of fidelity. In N. S. Jacobson & A. S. Gurman (Eds.), *Clinical handbook of couple therapy* (pp. 295–316). New York: Guilford Press.

Rosen, R. C., & Leiblum, S. R. (Eds.) (1995a). *Case studies in sex therapy.* New York: Guilford Press.

Rosen, R. C., & Leiblum, S. R. (1995b). The changing focus of sex therapy. In R. C. Rosen & S. R. Leiblum (Eds.), *Case studies in sex therapy* (pp. 3–17). New York: Guilford Press.

Sidman, M. (1989). *Coercion and its fallout.* Boston: Authors Cooperative.

Skinner, B. F. (1987). *Upon further reflection.* Englewood Cliffs, NJ: Prentice-Hall.

Spickard, P. R., Fong, R., & Ewalt, P. L. (1995). Undermining the very basis of racism—its categories. *Social Work, 40,* 581–584.

Stuart, F. M., & Hammond, D. C. (1980). Sex therapy. In R. B. Stuart, *Helping couples change: A social learning approach to marital therapy* (pp. 301–366). New York: Guilford Press.

Stuart, R. B. (1969). Operant-interpersonal treatment for marital discord. *Journal of Consulting and Clinical Psychology, 33*, 675–682.

Stuart, R. B. (1980). *Helping couples change: A social learning approach to marital therapy.* New York: Guilford Press.

Thomas, E. J. (1977). *Marital communication and decision making: Analysis, Assessment, and Change.* New York: Free Press.

Wallerstein, J. S., & Corbin, S. B. (1989). Daughters of divorce: Report from a ten-year follow-up. *American Journal of Orthopsychiatry, 59*, 593–604.

Walsh, F., Jacob, L., & Simons, V. (1995). Facilitating healthy divorce processes: Therapy and mediation approaches. In N. S. Jacobson & A. S. Gurman (Eds.), *Clinical handbook of couple therapy* (pp. 340–365). New York: Guilford Press.

Wincze, J. P. (1995). Marital discord and sexual dysfunction associated with a male partner's "sexual addiction." In R. C. Rosen & S. R. Leiblum (Eds.), *Case studies in sex therapy* (pp. 380–392). New York: Guilford Press.

CHAPTER SEVEN

Parenting

One of the best-researched areas in the human services is parent education. Decades of research in child development, child behavior, and parenting practices have resulted in clear guidelines for practice. "Best practices" for parent education can be outlined at this point (although further advances are certain), and every social worker should be prepared to provide or connect parents with resources for parent education. The kind of child behavior that is valued, the way it is reinforced, and other factors vary among cultural groups. For that reason, single prescriptions are not very useful. The basic principles, however, are applicable across cultures because they are grounded in the science of how human behavior develops. The *content* of behavior varies dramatically across cultures, but the *behavioral processes* involved are common (Lee, 1988). Examples of both the differences and the underlying commonalities will be provided later in this chapter. The basic principles also apply to all children, regardless of their levels of intellectual functioning. In the case of children with developmental delays, however, more precision and concurrent professional services are often required.

Human services staff and educators often refer to "parent training" or "parenting classes." While those alternative terms are acceptable, "parent education" may be preferable because it does not suggest that experts train parents in precisely what to do, but rather that parents learn the basic principles and can then apply them to novel situations in a thoughtful way. Resources are available (for example, Azrin & Foxx 1989; Latham, 1994; Sloane, 1976/1988) that provide specialized programs for working with specific child behavior issues. While these materials are useful for reference and ideas, the preferred primary strategy is in-depth sharing of our knowledge with parents to increase their power to shape events in their families. In addition, parent education often includes more than skills training; information and problem solving around the rights of children and families, and about advocacy strategies, for example, are often critical components of parent education, as is the construction of parenting communities. Social work practice in this area, as in others, is not primarily concerned with changing the behavior of the client, but rather working with the parent in the full ecobehavioral context to produce better outcomes. What the parent does is one dimension, but only one dimension, of this work.

Parent education can be useful for everyone, not only for situations where child abuse or seriously antisocial behavior is present. In those serious cases, additional services (see chapters 8 and 9) are required, but the basic parenting repertoires outlined in this chapter are foundational even for that work. Parenting education can be included in "family life education" in high schools, and probably should be, routinely. Fathers often do not participate in parent education, for a variety of reasons. In some cases, the fathers do not see parenting as their role, due to traditional or sexist values. In some cases, scheduling can be tricky, although this assertion is often more a diversion. In the organizations where I have provided or supervised parent education, I have found that fathers are often uncomfortable if they believe they will be the only, or one of a few, men in a group of women. All-fathers groups, particularly those where fathers themselves can take on leadership roles, can be effective under those circumstances, as can groups where the expectation is that parents will participate as couples (when two parental figures are present). Many families, of course, include only a single parent, and it is important to ensure that adequate services are provided to these often overwhelmed and "overemployed"—a term Minuchin (1974; Minuchin & Nichols, 1993) often uses—individuals. Parent education clearly can be effective regardless of social class; even in poverty populations where there are few supports, parents can learn and use new skills (Polster & Dangel, 1989). However, parents who are socially isolated (insular) often do not benefit from parent education alone, and those who are both poor and socially insular are almost certain not to (Dumas & Wahler, 1983). More is needed in these cases (see below).

Some parent education is conducted individually with one or both parents. This structure has the advantage of simplifying work in the home, which reduces generalization problems and provides opportunities for the social worker to actually work in a hands-on way with the child, to test and model interventions in the family's ongoing stream of life events. Parents and social workers can collaborate in this way to develop the most effective approaches to problems specific to particular families and children. With very severely behavior disordered or developmentally delayed children, this level of individualization is often essential.

Most parent education, however, is offered in groups. In addition to making efficient use of professional time, groups offer other advantages. Participants in parenting groups report improvements in larger system problems as well (Brunk, Henggeler, & Whelan, 1987), apparently because of group members' sharing of resources with each other in the course of the group sessions and the socializing that tends to accompany the meetings. Groups offer particular opportunities for the sharing of power; group members each have individual strengths that they can share with each other (Lightburn & Kemp, 1994; Webster-Stratton, 1997). Group members can bring their own data and present it to the group, for example. This can be reinforcing for the presenter and inspiring for other members—it is one thing for a professional to say that something works, but something else altogether to see it work in a family like one's own. In addition, members of at-risk groups (who are often social work clients) can share experiences with oppression (for example, institutionalized racism or class discrimination); sharing experiences with these aversives can help group members to develop strategies for addressing, or at a minimum support them in managing, such conditions.

One caution about the use of parenting groups needs to be mentioned, however. In working with abusive parents, Goldstein and his colleagues (Goldstein, Keller, & Erné, 1985) found that, for this population, skills learned in parent education groups often did not transfer to the home unless specific additional supports were provided. In some cases, it may therefore be necessary to provide at least some home-based services in addition to agency-based group sessions. These requirements are addressed in chapter 9, which examines work with families where child maltreatment is present.

One important discovery in the past two decades is that videotapes can be a very effective parent education tool (Polster & Dangel, 1989; Webster-Stratton, Hollinsworth, & Kolpacoff, 1989). Groups organized around such videotapes can be at least as clinically effective, and may be more cost-effective, than those that rely on expert trainers. For standard parent training with nonclinical families or those that are not severely damaged, videotaped parent education accompanied by group discussions is clearly consistent with the state of the art. Webster-Stratton's videotapes have particularly strong empirical support. For information on their availability, contact the Parenting Research Clinic at the University of Washington School of Nursing.

Those involved in parent education often report that some parents do not know what to expect from their children, what is developmentally normal, or what kinds of behavior are common to all children. Some parenting programs have focused primarily on teaching about child development; this approach has not proven to be effective in changing parenting behavior or in producing better outcomes for the family. In the context of a skill-building parent education program, however, learning accurate self-talk about child behavior can be helpful. Understanding, for example, that infants do not cry in order to defy their parents, and that two-year-olds and teenagers often test limits, can reduce parental anger and make it easier to calmly use new skills. Hearing and seeing that other parents are struggling with similar issues can also be helpful in normalizing parents' experiences.

It is crucial that new skills learned in parent education be supported by other members of the family network, particularly those who are living in the home. It is common to discover, for example, that a single mother and her children are living in the maternal grandmother's home, and the grandmother may be the central authority in the family. Under those circumstances, while work with the mother may be of benefit, if the parent education program and the grandmother are working at cross-purposes, the program is likely to have at best weak effects. The grandmother's involvement should therefore be sought, either through participation in the program, through special "grandparent" groups, or in family-level consultation. Similarly, partners, whether they are parents of the children or not, and whether they are generally seen in parental roles in the family or not, can provide tremendous support to a struggling parent, or can make parenting much more difficult. As discussed earlier in this chapter, fathers' groups can also be useful in ensuring that everyone is working from the same script. Webster-Stratton's program encourages all participants to bring someone (partner, parent, friend) with them to meetings. In discussing the importance of partners, Webster-Stratton indicates:

> During parent groups, partners are helped to define ways they can support each other when one is feeling discouraged, tired, or unable to cope. We help parents generalize the principles learned in the parenting program to relationships in general: the importance of having fun together; the value of praise in all relationships; the feeling of support that comes from communication that is nonjudgmental, empathic, and collaborative; the value of sharing feelings; the necessity of setting limits and complying with others' requests and limits; and the need to give and receive support. (p. 168)

There is little doubt that a village can raise a child more effectively than can one person, but only if all the people in the village are working together.

Personal and couples issues in the home, of course, can complicate parenting dramatically. Depression and other major mental illnesses, for example, reduce the energy available for child care and can disrupt parent-child relationships and child development significantly (Feldman, Stiffman, & Jung, 1987). Strain in the couple can affect children in several ways. A parent experiencing a high level of aversive exchange with his or her partner may strike out at the nearest available victim, which is often the

child (Sidman, 1989). A parent who is worried about the couple relationship is less likely to be available for prosocial involvement with children.
And parents who are in conflict in one area often generalize conflict behaviors to other domains, including parenting.

Webster-Stratton reports that in her research, children whose families
had received services and "were still maladjusted . . . shared the common
features of a family characterized by marital distress or single-parent status,
maternal depression, lower social class, high levels of negative stressors, and
low levels of social support" (1997, p. 160). Social workers working with families around parenting, therefore, should attend to other possible issues in
the household, and either offer services or refer as needed for help with
those issues identified. A good deal is known about effective intervention
with depression (see Mattaini, 1997), with couple issues (see chapter 6),
and with many other possible family issues like substance abuse and schizophrenia (see chapter 10 for strategies and resources). Parents who are both
"insular" (socially isolated, see below) and also poor, for example, are very
unlikely to make use of new skills they may learn in parenting classes without additional supports (Dumas & Wahler, 1983).

PARENTING AND THE COMMUNITY

Effective parenting apparently cannot occur in isolation. Social support is
critical to prevention of child maltreatment (Polansky, Gaudin, Ammons, &
Davis, 1985), to use of parenting skills that have been learned (Dumas &
Wahler, 1983; Wahler, 1980), and to improvement of child and family outcomes in many domains (Webster-Stratton, 1997). Insular mothers (Dumas
& Wahler, 1983; Moncher, 1995; Wahler, 1980; Wahler, Williams & Cerezo,
1991) in particular demonstrate difficulties in parenting. Insularity in those
studies is defined as experiencing relatively high levels of coercive social exchanges (for example, with critical kin and agency representatives), concurrent with low levels of positive exchange, particularly with friends. A
number of promising strategies and programs for enriching social networks
and connections have been developed that can reduce insularity and improve parenting outcomes.

One approach, as described above, is the use of multiple family groups
and parenting groups. The need to construct more supportive networks can
also be explicitly included in the content of parenting courses and groups
(Webster-Stratton, 1997). In some cases, groups may not be readily available, and the social worker may need to work individually with a parent.
Under these circumstances, as in every other type of case discussed in this
volume, the best beginning involves an honest discussion. An example is the

work with a young African American mother receiving public assistance whose young son was enrolled in a special needs school. She completed basic parent education, but her social situation was highly insular. She had almost no positive social contact, lived in almost complete isolation in a small, largely white community where she knew almost no one and in which very little transportation was available, and had significant aversive contact with social service agencies and some family.

The social worker, who had built a relationship with the client through parent education, explained what is known about the struggles of insular mothers, and the two agreed to work together to see if they could find some ways to connect the client more tightly to a supportive community. There were no obvious starting points for this work, so together the two developed a list of all the possible categories they could imagine (church, volunteer work, paid employment, contact with relatives, etc.), and then worked together to see if they could come up with specific possibilities from each of those domains. The social worker and the young mother developed a plan that included self-monitoring of contacts on a daily basis, with weekly goals. Ultimately, the mother became involved in regular contacts at the library, volunteer work that advanced to paid employment at a nearby hospital, and other social transactions to the extent that she experienced positive contacts nearly every day. Videotaped data indicate that she continued to use skills she had learned in parent education, even though in the beginning she had fallen into Dumas and Wahler's (1983) highest risk group, in which none of their poor, insular subjects maintained gains in parenting skills during follow-up.

Similarly, in the evolution of Webster-Stratton's work, the focus has expanded from the learning of parenting skills only, to developing a support community within the group, to ultimately facilitating the connections of parents to schools and other systems in the larger community. Webster-Stratton and others have also worked with teachers, so that both sides of the parent-teacher connection can collaborate in building bridges of support for raising children—a challenging task under any circumstances. The Fred S. Keller School in Yonkers, New York, has pioneered a particularly empowering strategy for enhancing these connections. Each spring, parents who have participated in the parent education program (which includes group and individual components), prepare posters for a poster session where each parent presents data for, and a discussion of, a program that they have developed and implemented with their special-needs child. School staff, other parents, and community representatives attend and discuss the parents' projects with each other.

A larger-scale program, the "Back to School Pledge Campaign," has been designed by Reverend Jesse Jackson's Rainbow/PUSH Coalition. The campaign, which constitutes one part of the "Reclaim Our Youth" project, is organized at a community level, with particular emphasis on work through church communities. Parents who participate in the program pledge to take a number of specific actions, including taking children to school, meeting with teachers, and turning off the television for three hours in the evening while the children do homework. (Teachers, of course, are asked to assign that homework as part of the program.) The church, or other support group, can then prompt and reinforce participation in the campaign, moving toward the construction of a positive parenting community. Family support programs (Comer & Fraser, 1998; Lightburn and Kemp, 1994), which were discussed in chapter 3, are a final example of strategies for building communities of effective parenting. Such programs often develop a strong sense of community, support, and shared power among the parents participating in the programs. Many communities also have parent resource centers, often volunteer run, which offer, or can connect, parents with parent education, provide written and audiovisual materials, and connections with advocacy groups as well.

In fact, any of the parent/community strategies discussed here can also serve as bases for advocacy efforts, which sometimes are even more crucial than parent education. For example, in communities where the schools are entirely inadequate (one form of oppression that often interlocks with others, like housing and employment discrimination, and economic and political exclusion; Briggs & Paulson, 1996), the most important practice to mutually construct and support may be effective advocacy for adequate schools. (Some of the repertoires required for such advocacy are outlined in a later section of this chapter.) In many cases, the most important and powerful interventions that ecobehavioral social workers can effect, whether they are working in family support, parent education, community center, or other programs, are helping parents to organize such advocacy campaigns.

POSITIVE PARENTING PRACTICES

Given the presence or construction of an adequate parenting support community, the other central goal for parenting education is to increase the incidence of effective parenting practices. Parents' actions have a profound impact on their children's behavior and development. Gerald Patterson and his colleagues have studied aggressive children and youths for over two decades, and Webster-Stratton summarizes their findings: "Parents of children with conduct problems exhibit fewer positive behaviors; use more violent disciplinary techniques, are more critical, more permissive, less likely to monitor their children's behaviors; and are more likely to reinforce inappropriate behaviors while ignoring or even punishing prosocial behavior" (1997, p. 159). On the other hand, the skills necessary for positive child outcomes are also well established. For example, in Webster-Stratton's demonstrably effective program the core parenting skills to be learned and practiced are:

- How to play with your child and help your child learn.
- Using praise and encouragement to bring out the best in your child.
- Effective limit setting.
- Handling misbehavior. (1997, p. 159)

(Note that these are in addition to community and support-building practices discussed earlier in this chapter.)

In the material that follows, 12 clusters of data-based parenting practices are considered. In some cases, these practices have been extensively discussed in earlier chapters; in those cases the discussion here is abbreviated. Those practices are still listed here, however, because they are core to effective parenting. This discussion emphasizes principles of positive parenting which apply broadly, rather than "prescriptions" for specific problems. Books are available that provide such specifics (for example, Latham, 1994; Sloane, 1976/88), which may be useful in particular cases, and are often useful for parents themselves to work from. The goal here, however, is to offer general strategies that the social worker and family can adapt creatively for almost any sort of parenting issue.

Parenting practices are presented here in a rough conceptual order; for example, it is generally important to pinpoint desired child behaviors in order to reinforce effectively. The listing here is not necessarily in order of importance, however. (The most important skills to learn well are probably effective reinforcement, establishing clear consequences, monitoring, and advocacy.) The *process* for teaching these skills is the same as in other forms of skills training discussed in chapters 5 and 6, and will not be repeated here.

Communication

Specific parenting practices as discussed below are far more likely to be useful in an overall environment of effective parent-child communication. Even for very small children, clear communication about what the parent approves, what limits will be enforced, and about the extent to which the parent values who the child is and what he or she does is crucial for later healthy development. As children get older, parents control fewer and fewer consequences of the child's behavior; by mid-teenage for most families the primary influence the parent has emerges from respectful, caring communication, rather than manipulation of more concrete consequences. (There are some exceptions in the case of seriously antisocial youths coming from families where parenting has often been significantly disrupted; those families are considered in the next chapter.) Communication skills are the primary emphasis of chapter 5 and will therefore not be further discussed here.

Pinpointing

Pinpointing refers to being clear about desirable and undesirable behaviors. Practically every parenting program developed in the last several decades emphasizes pinpointing (although sometimes using different terms). For example, saying "Good boy!" is not nearly as effective as providing recognition for specific positive behavior ("You did a very careful job of drawing that horse. It's lovely!"). The first suggests to a child that he or she is "all good" (Good boy!) or "all bad" (Bad boy!)—and typically the global evaluation changes based on current behavior or often a parent's mood. This approach does not give specific guidance about what is valued. In cases of global negative evaluations in particular, the child is not given information about what to do instead. Global evaluations also complicate the establishment of clear equivalence relations. The equivalence

$$me \approx good \approx bad$$

is simply incoherent, and children who learn such muddy equivalences may have trouble later in life knowing "who they are." Such inconsistency may contribute to severe personal and relational problems in later life that are often labeled "personality disorders." Other parenting patterns that may be associated with severe problems later include extreme variation in the consequences of similar behaviors (if the same action is sometimes praised, sometimes punished, and sometimes ignored depending on parental mood, confusion is to be expected) and inconsistent labeling of the child's emotions (Kohlenberg & Tsai, 1991, Mattaini, 1997).

    A clear pinpoint, by contrast, identifies desirable and undesirable behaviors clearly and consistently. Parents should state specifically what they like (and do not like) in behavioral terms, because this gives a clear message to the child. In cases of undesirable behavior, both the problem behavior *and the desirable alternative* should be stated. Pinpointing is also essential when the parent is trying to resolve a specific child behavior issue, for example tantruming, putting away toys and clothes, etc. In such programs, it is essential that both parent and child know "what counts" as a tantrum, what "putting away clothes" means, and so forth. It is very common for children and parents to have different understandings; this interferes with actual or perceived consistency.

Record Keeping

While it is certainly not necessary (or possible!) to keep track of everything a child does, when a parent has pinpointed a particular behavior to increase or decrease, record keeping can be essential. Nothing is more motivating to the parent of an autistic child than seeing graphs demonstrating that the child is gradually but consistently able to name people or things ("tacting"), to ask for what he or she wants ("manding"), or to follow instructions. Since most behavior change occurs gradually, it is difficult and often impossible to know for sure if a change is taking place unless one keeps track. For example, a young child who is not completely toilet-trained might have 30 "accidents" one week, 32 the next, then 25, 18, 25, and 15. In such a case, improvement is probably occurring, but it may not be at all apparent on a day-to-day basis. Accurate records can make a crucial difference under such circumstances, because if a clear trend toward the goal-state in the data emerges, present arrangements should usually be continued; if there is not, a change is probably required (compare the upper and lower panels of Figure 7-1).

A second reason why records are often essential to achieve behavior change is that they can play an active motivational role. Look, for example, at the chart in Figure 7-2, from Latham, 1994, on which a parent and child can keep track of instances when a child uses the toilet.

A picture of the child on the toilet or potty chair is attached at the top, reminding the child of the desired behavior. Smiling faces (or stars, or stickers, or whatever symbol is meaningful to the child) can be drawn or attached—often best by the child—each time he or she uses the toilet. Whenever a row is completed (in this case every five times) the child can be rewarded with something he or she enjoys, for example, having a story read to him or her. (Latham notes the importance of reserving the reward chosen, for only this purpose.) More detail about toilet training is provided later in this chapter; of note here is that the chart itself can become an active ingredient in the intervention plan.

The two general types of records that are most useful for parenting are charts (like Figure 7-2) on which detailed data are kept, and graphs (like

Figure 7-1

Graphs of a child's toileting accidents. In the top panel (A), the dry-pants procedure being used appears to be effective; the downward trend is visually apparent and is significant at beyond the .01 level ($Z = 3.29$) using the C statistic (Tryon, 1982). In the lower panel (B), the procedure is not clearly effective; although there are some good weeks, there is no stable visual or statistical trend, and a change of program should probably be instituted.

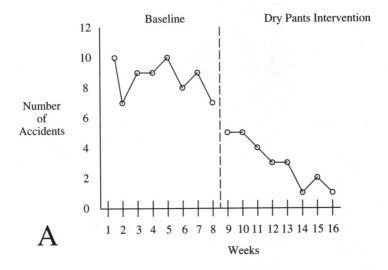

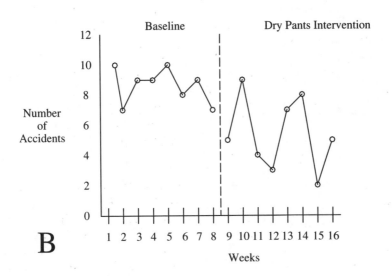

Figure 7-2

A chart of toileting successes. Source: G. I. Latham (1994). *The power of positive parenting.* North Logan, UT: P & T Ink.

Figure 7-1) on which data over time are summarized. Charts can often involve a lot of creativity; there is no reason why bedtime records cannot be fun, for example. In "The Bedtime Game" (Sloane, 1976/1988, p. 157 and following), the parent prepares a game board similar to those the child is familiar with. The child is allowed to make up to three moves a night, for (1) getting ready for bed with no more than one reminder, (2) using "relax time" (a 15- to 30-minute period of quiet or relaxing activity), and (3) being in bed with lights out on time. On some squares on the board, there are prize marks; when landing on one of these, the child can draw from a "Surprise Pack." A larger prize can be earned for completing the entire board. (Rewards can be privileges and activities, see below, and can be faded fairly quickly over time in this game.) There are many ways that charting can be both fun and useful at the same time.

In drawing graphs, the standard is to use the X axis (the horizontal one) to keep track of time, and the Y axis (the vertical one) to keep track of the number of behaviors per unit of time. In specialized behavioral programs, cumulative and even logarithmic graphs are sometimes used, but a simple graph showing daily or weekly counts is usually best for basic parent education.

Some social workers are concerned that their clients may not be able to read charts and graphs, that such tools may be "over their heads," particularly for people with limited education and literacy skills. The data available overwhelming demonstrate that this need not be a concern, so long as the record-keeping tools used are carefully designed. Nearly every parent and nearly every child over a few months old, except for those that are severely mentally limited, can make sense of "star charts" or charts on the refrigerator on which the child or parent puts a sticker for desirable behavior. Graphs can be slightly more complicated, but the experience of the Keller School (as reported earlier in this chapter) indicates that even parents with very limited education and literacy skills quickly learn to read ascending and descending lines, though the social worker may need to help with plotting data in some cases. Involvement in record keeping can be deeply empowering (Kopp, 1993) because services evaluation and intervention planning naturally emerge from record reviews. Many parents can quickly learn to keep and use their own records.

Prosocial Involvement

While both parents and professionals may slip into a pattern of thinking primarily about the way to reduce problem behavior when they consider "parenting skills," the most crucial ones are preventive in nature. Prosocial involvement, clarity of instructions and consequences, and reinforcement are the most powerful parenting practices and, if effectively used, will often entirely eliminate the need for separate strategies to decelerate problem behaviors. At a minimum, these practices will dramatically reduce that need. The most common pattern, however, is for people to quickly agree with that, but move immediately into, "But what do I do when. . . ." The first answer should always be the building of preventive repertoires. (Some behavioral programs even avoid teaching about time-out despite its efficacy and although it is a far better alternative than spanking, because it is too easy to slip into overusing it.)

Biglan (1995) summarizes a large body of work on the need for prosocial involvement between parent and child in the following way:

> Parents who fail to engage in positive activities with their children are particularly likely to develop unskilled, aggressive, uncooperative children. A young child whose parents get down on the floor and play with him or her is likely to learn many important things such as the names of objects and colors and words for relations such as "in," "under," and "on." More subtly, the child learns to manipulate the toy and develops the tendency to stay with the activity for longer periods of time." (p. 261)

In their longitudinal study of children from professional, working-class, and poor families, Hart & Risley (1995) found that children from poor families were exposed on average to about 13 million words in conversations with family in the first four years of life, compared to 26 million in working-class and 45 million in professional families. Children in professional families received about six encouragements (reinforcers) for every discouragement (punishment), while those in poor families experienced one encouragement to two discouragements. Not surprisingly, a follow-up at age 9 or 10 indicated that children's academic performance correlated highly with the way their parents treated them in the first three years of life. Those who were talked to more and received more encouragement naturally did much better than those for whom those factors were absent.

When young mothers, particularly those of lower socioeconomic status, are asked if they talk to their children very much, they often respond, "No, of course not, (s)he doesn't know how to talk yet." The same is also often observable on videotapes of normal daily interaction. Talking to children, reading to and with them, and encouraging them are crucial to optimal child development. Parental responsiveness and sensitivity to children is associated with cognitive development, social development, sense of self, and many other developmental tasks (Wolfe, 1991).

Positive interaction with parents is important at all ages; for older children and adolescents, positive exchange is important to improving relations with parents, as discussed in chapter 4. With younger children, it is important not only to further their development, but also to build attachment; such engagement also appears to be preventive of child abuse (Wolfe, 1991). Numerous studies indicate that relatively simple changes in parent behavior produce substantial differences. Among the interventions reviewed in Wolfe (1991) for parents with infants are the following:

- using a "facing position"—positioning themselves on the floor facing the child (Crittenden & Snell, 1983)
- using "Watch, Wait, and Wonder" (Mahrer, Levinson, & Fine, 1976)—an approach in which the parent is encouraged to and reinforced for getting on the floor with the infant and paying sensitive attention to what he or she is doing
- acknowledging child behavior verbally or with a smile
- imitating the child, and then elaborating and expanding (which enhances reciprocity)
- engaging with the child at a pace that is responsive to the child's developmental and momentary interests and needs.

For older children, Wolfe emphasizes repertoires like watching what the child is doing without interfering; commenting in a narrative way on the child's activities; and providing positive feedback by smiling, showing enthusiasm, and providing praise and physical affection. Many of the programs that work with parents to develop such sensitivity are conducted in groups; parents and social workers can then model new alternatives and support each other in those activities. Occasionally student social workers leading such groups are unaware of their value and indicate that it seems as if they are "just playing" with the children and their parents; it is essential that the purpose of such programs be clear to those conducting them so that they can optimize learning opportunities. Social workers who will be doing this work should read widely in the related literature, but the material here may be of use in guiding those explorations.

Clarity of Instructions and Consequences

Parents often give instructions that their children do not understand. Learning to follow instructions is a critical skill; very young children need to learn to respond to directions given by parents for their own safety and development. (This can often be done in enjoyable ways; practicing "following directions" can be done as a game.) With young children, instructions need to be very simple: they need to be behaviorally specific ("clean up your room" is much too broad, for example) and well timed, and only gradually build to multistep directions. A clear instruction should be brief and exclude extraneous words. For example, "Please bring me that book" is clear, while "I'm feeling like reading something . . . might be fun . . . I wonder if you would bring me something to read, like that one over there . . . would you do that? . . . would you do that, please? . . . and then maybe you could look at TV for a bit . . . are you listening to me? . . . would you do that?" is not. The second is confusing, involves multiple steps, does not state clearly the behavior required, and is repeated too quickly in inconsistent ways. Learning to follow instructions is a developmental progression; only when a child has learned to consistently follow one-step instructions should the parent work on two-step instructions, for example. Following instructions should, especially in the beginning, also be richly and consistently recognized.

One very powerful way to reduce the aversiveness of instructions is to provide some choice (with very young children, usually only two choices are offered, but more may be useful with older children). For example, a child may be asked whether he would rather do his homework or do his chores now (continuing to watch TV or quibble with a sibling are not offered as choices!); if a child is disturbing others by being noisy, she might be asked, "Tanika, I am trying to read, and it is too noisy. Would you rather sit down and read too, or would you rather go outside where you can make as much noise as you like?" The response may be more cooperative than if the parent instead merely tells the child to be quiet. This technique is particularly useful if the child is angry, when, for examaple, the choices may be to sit down and talk about it now, or to go to his or her room and cool off first.

Establishing clear consequences is also critical, particularly with more challenging children (and some children are temperamentally more challenging than others, Thomas & Chess, 1977). "Setting limits" is part of this process, but by itself may sound unnecessarily punitive and coercive. The consequences of available choices, both positive and negative, should be made clear to children in a matter-of-fact way and should then be immediately and consistently provided. Many parents slip into a pattern of making verbal threats, then not carrying them out. When the child stops paying attention to those threats, the parent often escalates to stronger threats, but may still not actually provide consequences. For example, in an incident I observed, a mother noticed her very bright two-year-old across the room playing with something breakable. The interaction went like this:

"Jason, put that down." (Child ignores.) "Jason, if you don't put that down now, I'm going to have to come over there!" (Child ignores.) "Jason, you little devil, you're going to get a spanking!" (Child ignores. Mother starts to stand up.) "I'm going to kill you—damn it listen to me!" Child responds, "Damn you!" and runs out of the room, dropping the breakable item.

Clear, predictable consequation was not customarily present in this family; both parents tried to maintain control through abusive, loud verbal threats. Had they quietly clarified consequences (positive and negative) of the child's options and enforced them without exception, the child would have quickly learned to respond (as the author later demonstrated with the same child). While doing so takes more effort than raising one's voice in the beginning, in the long run it is far more pleasant for both parent and child.

One way to clarify consequences, discussed in detail in chapter 5, is contracting: a contract is basically a clear statement of mutual desires and consequences. Recall, however, that contracts are most likely to be effective if they are genuinely mutual, and that so-called contracts that emphasize only punishments and sanctions are generally ineffective in the long run. Only contracts that provide positive motivation are likely to be really useful. If consequences are clear and certain, as Latham says, the parent can "let consequences do the talking" (1994, p. 268). There is no need, and no point, to engage in escalating conflicts about behavior if consequences are clear. The parent can calmly restate as often as necessary what the agreed upon consequences are; children learn very quickly to accept this and, in fact, like the security associated with such clarity.

Reinforcement

The most basic law of behavior is that overall, people do what works for them. (Some behavior may both pay off in some ways in the short term and be costly in others, of course.) The most crucial parenting skill of all is providing an adequate level of reinforcers for desirable behavior; this is the primary way that children learn adaptive behavior. Recently, some issues have been raised about the use of "rewards" and reinforcement. Alfie Kohn, for example, has been richly rewarded for publishing a book entitled, "Punished by Rewards" (1993). A number of careful reviews and original research have been conducted to test Kohn's assertions. The general results indicate that if reinforcers offered are genuinely "reinforcing, noncompetitive, based on reasonable performance standards, and delivered repetitively" (Dickinson, 1989, p. 1) the alleged problems do not appear (see also Carton, 1996, and Carton & Nowicki, 1998, for further detail regarding this controversy).

There are certainly times when privileges, tangible items, and even money may be of use as reinforcers, for example in contracting, but for most people the most important reinforcer is recognition, positive attention, and praise. As Latham (1994) indicates: "Without a doubt, the key to developing high quality human behavior is through the selective, positive reinforcement of appropriate behavior. . . . Look for opportunities to pay attention, in a very positive way, to a few select, appropriate behaviors, and do it intermittently, i.e., at times children least expect it." (p. 52) (And, it is important to add, much more often than one reprimands the child.) High rates of such recognition not only shape positive behavior on the part of the child, they also lead to strong affective attachment between parent and child. Recent studies confirm the observations that those in the field have recognized for some time: successes, contributions, hard work and effort, concentration, and other *behavior* should be recognized. General statements about the child being a "good boy" or "good girl" do not teach in the same way. According to studies recently reported in *The New York Times* (July 14, 1998), praising a child for attributes like "intelligence" can be counterproductive; it creates anxiety for the child, and he worries about making mistakes. Praise for behavior and effort, on the other hand, is strengthening (Reuters, 1998).

When a parent wishes to increase a desirable behavior that is difficult for the child, there are certainly times when such recognition can be paired with other conditions or things that a child values to increase motivation; this extra reinforcement then needs to be faded over time. For example, in cases where toilet training is the goal, there are several demonstrably effective approaches, all of which rely on reinforcement. A graduated series of approaches for toilet training is listed below. Note the use of reinforcers in each of them:

- For daytime bladder control with small children, Latham (1994) begins by taking the children to the potty chair and thanking them for sitting in it (reinforcer). If it appears likely to be important with this particular child at this moment, he might pair it with a morsel of a favorite food (reinforcer), which also associates the potty chair with reinforcement. If the child voids, the parent again praises enthusiastically (this really is a big achievement for the child!), and perhaps another morsel of food. This (and the other approaches below) work best if the child has been drinking a lot of liquids (which may seem counterintuitive, but provides more opportunities for positive behavior and reinforcement). If the child wets his diaper at other times, change it without scolding, caressing, or other response—neither punishment nor reward should be associated with "accidents."
- The second, somewhat more intensive approach used with older children (Latham, 1994), adds roleplaying and the use of a chart like the one

shown in Figure 7-2 and discussed above. In this case, praise, smiley-face drawings, and backup reinforcers like reading a story can be used.

- A third approach is "dry-pants" training (Foxx & Azrin, 1973), which combines a number of techniques including reinforcement for going to and using the toilet with periodic pants checks, and reinforcement for having dry pants. (This approach also can be expanded to include restitution training in which the child cleans up after himself, and other more intensive procedures if necessary, but only if reinforcement-based procedures on their own are ineffective after about 2 weeks.)

In Latham's extensive experience, the first two approaches have worked consistently with children of average developmental abilities. The third, more intensive approach works even with seriously developmentally delayed children and those for whom toilet training has turned into a battle ground. The key is effective reinforcement, which can gradually be faded by checking pants less and less often and providing recognition only intermittently for appropriate toileting. (Nighttime toilet training is more complicated, but relies ultimately on the same principles; see Latham, 1994, for detail).

Unfortunately, undesirable behavior is just as sensitive to reinforcement as is desirable behavior, and this is true even at a very young age. It is very common for caretakers to shape fussiness in babies by picking them up, cuddling them, and entertaining them every time they cry or fuss (Latham, 1994). Once a baby has been trained to be fussy, parents need to stop reinforcing him or her for fussing, and begin reinforcing for calmness. Latham's strategy is to first ensure that the fussing baby's needs are met (hunger, thirst, clean diaper, comfortable temperature, health). Then, lay the child in bed until he or she stops crying (which can take up to 45 minutes for a baby that has been well trained to cry, but usually less). When the child has been quiet for a brief period of 30 to 45 seconds, *then* pick him or her up and play. (It's crucial not to "give in" before the child stops, or you are training the baby to persist in crying for long periods). The level of crying may increase for a brief period (an extinction burst), but will settle down. Even for colicky babies, which can create enormous stress on parents, reinforcement is the key. Larson and Ayllon (1990) discovered that playing music and playing with a colicky child when the child is not crying, but gently placing the child in bed for a restful period without stimulation when he or she cries, then picking the child up again after about 30 seconds of quiet, reduces crying by about 75 percent—a dramatic shift for the family!

What reinforcers should be used? One principle is to use "natural" consequences to the extent possible. For example, if staying up a bit later is something a child values, this could be used as a reinforcer for going to bed without a struggle at the decided time. If the child does not do so, he or she will naturally get less sleep and be more tired, so bedtime the next night should be earlier. This form of consequation not only is easy to explain in a coherent manner to the child, it costs nothing. Praise and recognition should be natural in every setting (otherwise, these practices need to be constructed); they are not costly and they are helpful in developing an enriched family environment. It is often helpful to use natural consequences like these in systematic ways (precision reinforcement) to construct new repertoires particularly when a problem has to be resolved. At those times, pinpointing and record keeping should be combined with reinforcement.

Other forms of reinforcers can also be used, but should *always* be paired with social reinforcers for two reasons. First, this pairing increases the conditioned power of social reinforcers. Second, maintenance will usually depend on occasional social reinforcers, since contrived reinforcers should be withdrawn gradually over time, to move toward a more natural condition. Privileges and activities are often accessible and powerful reinforcers and can include time spent watching television or on the computer, time spent playing a preferred activity with a parent, the opportunity to decide what to have for dinner, or any of a wide range of others. Reinforcing activities are those that are "preferred"—those that a child prefers to engage in if given the opportunity. The Premack Principle (also know as Grandma's Law) can be useful here. It suggests using a high-probability activity (eating dessert) to reinforce a low-probability activity (eating broccoli). This principle is the heart of many self-management programs (for example, when I finish this report, I can go for a walk), and is enormously useful in parenting. Playing outside, for example, can be made contingent on completing homework, or watching TV made contingent on completing chores.

When other approaches are not powerful enough to resolve a serious problem, it may be necessary to use tangible reinforcers, at least temporarily. In teaching young autistic children receptive and expressive language, for example, it is often necessary to begin with preferred food reinforcers, pair them with socials, and only very gradually shift away from tangibles. Points toward a CD or a preferred toy can be offered to help motivate a child who has found school work highly aversive, but it is important to also ensure that the work is pitched at an appropriate level so that success is possible. In many families, spending money is contingent on completing certain responsibilities, rather than given freely. This is probably useful training for adulthood, when one typically must meet certain demands, fulfill responsibilities, and contribute in meaningful ways to get paid. Reinforcers provided in a such a systematic way are no more bribes than paychecks are. If a parent waits for a child to behave badly, then "pays" him or her to stop, that is a bribe. If a parent provides promised consequences when a child performs as they have agreed, that is not. (Note that either adults or children can be exploited by receiving short term rewards for behavior that in the long run will hurt them or others; for example, some poor children receive money, social support, and other reinforcers for acting as "runners" in the drug trade. This is a different issue.)

It sometimes takes some work to identify powerful reinforcers for a child, but with some attention and ingenuity, it can be done, even in families who have very few economic resources. The power of parental time and attention should not be forgotten; high-probability behaviors are often available to use, and children can also very often identify reinforcers that they would like to earn. Involving the child in determining the kind of behaviors to construct and the kind of reinforcers to work for is one more way of sharing power. What the parent or social worker thinks should be a reinforcer may not be, however, and sometimes surprising things are reinforcers. Children who get little other attention, for example, often find parental scolding and even spanking reinforcing (this can be determined by tracing whether the problem behavior escalates after the supposed "punishment"). The only way to be sure what is and what is not a reinforcer is to try it and see if the rate of behavior increases.

Actively Giving Up Coercion

Coercive, power-assertive discipline is associated with a wide range of child behavior and developmental problems; the data demonstrate increasingly that heavy reliance on coercive punishment and threat does more harm than good. Parents need to make an active decision, therefore, to give up this approach and rely on alternatives. It is essential that they have such alternatives available, however, or it is unrealistic to ask parents to give up what may seem like their only tool. The other repertoires discussed so far, and those presented in the next several sections can, it is increasingly clear, eliminate the need for highly coercive discipline.

A common concern on hearing this statement is that there may be exceptions. There may be a very few situations where coercive methods are essential, but not those that are routinely suggested. For example, one case was reported of a severely developmentally disabled infant who did not keep food or liquid down (rumination) and was as a result dehydrated, malnourished, and at risk of death. Squirting lemon juice into her mouth when she began the motions associated with rumination quickly ended this pattern, and she made a complete recovery (Sajwaj, Libet, & Agras, 1974). The procedure in this case was life-saving, and therefore justifiable. The most common type of situation in which parents believe coercion is required, however, relates to issues like "running out into the street." Latham (1994, p. 21) describes a procedure that works much more quickly and effectively than spanking the child under exactly those circumstances. When his 15-month-old grandchild ran into the street, Latham picked him up and told him that he could not run into the street. He placed him on the sidewalk, said "Play here," and touched the sidewalk. Four repetitions occurred, with the child running into the street; each time Latham used the same procedure, very calmly (but not affectionately). The child was not able to enjoy the reinforcers of being in the street. On the fifth opportunity, the child went to the curb, but stopped and looked at Dr. Latham, who was then able to give him considerable attention and affection for remaining on the sidewalk. A couple of more repetitions and intermittent reinforcement for playing on the sidewalk eliminated the problem completely, as the child learned "self-control." In contrast, Latham's next door neighbor relied on severe physical punishment and verbal abuse under the same circumstances; this kept the child out of the street only while his father was watching, and taught him nothing except to avoid his abusive father. Consistency in discipline is critical; coercive punishment and threat are ultimately counterproductive.

A pioneer in this area is Gerald Patterson of the Oregon Social Learning Center. Patterson and his colleagues discovered in the 1970s that coercion breeds coercion, and that coercive discipline teaches children to be aggressive (Patterson, 1976). This has been reconfirmed over and over in a research program extending over more than two decades (Patterson, 1982; Patterson, Reid & Dishion, 1992). Sidman (1989) clarifies the serious side-effects of coercion which include aggression, depression, and efforts at counter-control and escape, and indicates that the overall conclusion of hundreds of studies suggests that coercion begets coercion. It is perhaps easy to agree that abusive treatment and violence are counterindicated in parenting, but what about everyday spanking? Spanking is clearly a coercive, punitive approach, but it is very common, and many people who were spanked believe it did not hurt them any. Spanking has historically been part of many of the cultures found in the United States (although not all; see Deloria, 1996). Social learning theory suggests that the use of coercion would teach children themselves to rely on coercion (which seems to be supported by Patterson's work), but some argue that the way spanking is used matters most. Is it done explosively out of anger, or in a carefully controlled way meant only to teach? And does this matter? As recently as Sloane's (1976/1988) book, he recommended controlled spanking under some circumstances and provided instructions for how to do it (p. 165).

Practice is rapidly changing in this area, however, based on emerging data. Latham (1994), after careful review of the literature and extensive practice with normal and high risk children entitles chapter 12 of his book, *Regarding Spanking: Don't* (p.195). He indicates, "Spanking is intended to hurt a child, and by that hurt to communicate some lesson or message. But it is a poor tool, a barbaric method, for teaching good behavior . . . physical punishment modifies behavior only in the short run" (p. 195). Even more recent research, however, suggests that Latham is wrong—physical punishment modifies behavior in the long run, but *in the wrong direction.*

Two studies published in the August 1997 issue of the *Archives of Pediatrics and Adolescent Medicine* provide critical data. In the first, Murray Strauss (a noted researcher in family violence) and his colleagues found that, "When parents use corporal punishment to reduce [antisocial behavior], the long-term effect tends to be the opposite" (Strauss, Sugarman, & Giles-Sims, 1997, p. 761). The more children were spanked, the more antisocial behavior they exhibited two years later, even when controlling for many other variables that people have suggested may be important including culture, socioeconomic factors, and other parental deficiencies. A second article in the same issue (Gunnoe & Mariner, 1997) appears at first to suggest something different, indicating that, according to children's self-reports, spanking predicted more fights for some groups (whites and older children), but fewer for some other groups. A closer look at the study, however, indicates that for all groups, the more they were spanked the more overall antisocial behavior increased. "Antisocial behavior" included bullying and cruelty to others, cheating, lying, disobedience at school, lack of contrition, trouble with teachers, and associating with troublemaking peers. Self-reports of fewer fights may not be honest since children may be punished for admitting fights; even if accurate, increases in the many types of problem behavior listed here can only be viewed as very serious. There is good reason to rely on alternatives to coercive punishment; the first step, however, is a commitment to do so.

Prevention and Redirection

As in many other areas of life, the best investment of parental time is often to prevent problem behavior from emerging. One way to do so is to redirect the child's behavior before it becomes a problem. Running into the street is one example; Latham's grandchild never really had an opportunity to play in the street. In another common example, siblings often argue and fight, particularly when few obvious competing reinforcers are present at the moment. A parent, or the children themselves, can often describe the usual progression that leads to these episodes. They may often happen just before dinner, when the parent(s) are busy in the kitchen, and the children are tired, hungry, and unsupervised. And the problem may begin when one starts teasing the other. This is an example where keeping records for a few days may be helpful to pinpoint the issue and the way it commonly develops.

Several preventive approaches are possible here. One or more of the children might be engaged in meal preparation, thus preventing the children from being together unsupervised at a vulnerable moment, and incidentally building responsibility and providing opportunities to reinforce contributions. At the first sign of teasing, the children can be separated by asking one or more to do something else. One or more of the children can self-monitor (for example, "How many days this week can we go without an argument before dinner? If the record we keep on the refrigerator reaches 6, we can watch a favorite TV show"). Children themselves can also be engaged in a family conference to develop a creative plan for resolving the issue. While there are strategies for dealing with such fights and teasing when they occur (Sloane, 1976/88, recommends sending the responsible child to his or her room for 10 minutes if a responsible party is immediately obvious, and otherwise sending everyone involved to separate rooms for 10 minutes, for example), it is far better to prevent the problem in the first place.

Prevention is worth thinking about with children of any age. Toddlers are likely to "get into" things that are available; developmentally, curious exploration is a toddler's job! Prevention, in this case, means ensuring that dangerous and breakable things are not accessible (but other interesting things should be). It is common practice in work with parents of young children to help them conduct a physical audit of the home, identifying both hazards and possible prompts for mischief. Children and adolescents may get into trouble at school during unstructured times; while school staff may be able to design interventions themselves, parents and/or the social worker may need to consult with those staff to design ways to limit that unstructured time. For example, organized playground games dramatically reduce behavior problems (Murphy, Hutchinson, & Bailey, 1983), and teens can learn to self-monitor during unsupervised periods (Ninness, Ellis, Miller, Baker, & Rutherford, 1995).

Sometimes preventive measures are immediately evident. When they are not, the first step is to take careful records, using a simple chart like that shown in Figure 7-3. Each time the problem behavior occurs, the parent can begin by carefully describing that behavior. The next step is to complete the occasions box ("Occasion for Behavior"): What was going on before the problem occurred? Who was there, what were they doing, and what were they saying? Then, complete the postcedents box ("Situation After Behavior"): What happened after the behavior? Events and changes after

Figure 7-3

An analytic chart for identifying possibly active antecedents and consequences of a problem behavior.

Date	Behavior	Occasion for Behavior	Situation After Behavior	Possible Motivating Antecedents	Models

the behavior may be active reinforcers for the behavior; for example, if the child gets his or her way about what TV channel to watch after a trantrum, his or her tantrums may be maintained by such outcomes. Also, were there any obvious motivating antecedents, like deprivation, that made the behavior more likely? Finally, are there models for the problem behavior (for example, do others in the family model aggressive behavior)?

Possible preventive or interventive strategies may well emerge from looking at the chart. Changes in antecedents, if possible, are often the easiest to institute; if such changes do not seem realistic, then attention to consequences, if well done, will help to resolve practically any child behavior issue. Patience and "endurance" (Latham, 1994, p. 95) may be required, however, and one of the social worker's most important roles is to build hope that if the parent remains consistent, eventually the situation will improve. (It may also help to remind the parent that eventually many child behavior problems will disappear in the natural development process.)

Ignoring

One of the most difficult, and one of the most powerful, strategies for reducing problem behavior is ignoring it. Behavior that is maintained by parental attention will eventually extinguish if consistently exposed to planned nonreinforcement. The problem is, however, that it is easy to give in every so often, rather than ignoring consistently. If this happens, the parent is providing intermittent reinforcement, which produces a behavior that is very hard to eliminate. A behavior that is ignored tends to escalate before declining; this phenomenon is called the "extinction burst"—see Figure 7-4 for an example. Ignoring (planned nonreinforcement) therefore requires consistency and resolve. With small children who use tantrums coercively to get attention and their way, the first strategy, which works nearly all the time is, as Sloane suggests, obvious ignoring: "The instant (not even three seconds later) that your child starts to have a tantrum, shout at you, or talk back loudly, turn around and go to another room. If it occurs outdoors, leave the area. . . . Do this every time this behavior occurs. . . . Make absolutely no comment at all." (1976/1988, p. 287)

Parents are instructed that they may return after five minutes (if the tantrum has stopped). Certain other details are important; for example, if the tantrum occurred when the parent gave the child a direction or instruction, this then needs to be repeated so that the tantrum does not result

Figure 7-4

An "extinction burst"—the problem behavior first increases when it is ignored, but eventually fades due to nonreinforcement.

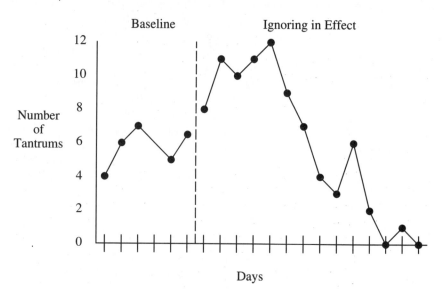

in the child escaping parental demands. Other creative procedures may need to be developed to deal with specific variations, but the general strategy is surprisingly robust. It is often necessary to make a specific plan and to write it down to ensure consistent application. (Sloane suggests that this procedure may take up to a couple of weeks to be effective, so persistence will be required.)

Many small, irritating behaviors occur primarily to obtain parental attention, and if the parent does not give attention to those, *but gives plenty of positive attention for desirable behavior,* those small irritations will commonly disappear. If others in the family, however, continue to pay attention, ignoring is less likely to be effective; so other adults and children may need to be included in a plan to ignore problem behaviors. Even very bizarre behaviors are reliably eliminated in special behavioral schools in this way, and there is no reason why the procedure cannot be equally effective in the home. Ignoring, paired with attention to positive actions, also leads to a far more congenial home atmosphere than does attending to every possible small issue that may come up. One very useful technique— commonly used by skilled teachers and parents—is to use the occurrence of an undesirable behavior as a cue to pay attention to a *positive*, incompatible behavior in which another child is currently engaged. The misbehaving child will then often imitate the other child, and can be noticed behaving appropriately.

Time-Out

Richard Foxx, a behavioral scientist who has made major contributions to the parenting and developmental disabilities literatures, has often described *time-out* as one of the great successes of the 20th century science of behavior. A majority of parents and teachers in the United States appear to be familiar with the term, even though the procedures as applied are often implemented in less than optimal and sometimes even entirely ineffective ways. The central strategy in time-out is to consequate an undesirable behavior with a brief (and it must be brief) period when reinforcers are not available—time out from positive reinforcement. Time-out, correctly used, can substitute for spanking when other procedures require more time and endurance than the parent can muster.

Unfortunately, time-out is usually used incorrectly, as a highly punitive strategy. Some excellent parent education programs refuse to teach time-out at all, since proper use of pinpoint reinforcement for positive alternatives and ignoring the undesirable behavior will ordinarily resolve most problems (eventually) without the use of even mild aversives like time-out. As Latham (1994) indicates:

> Whether I am observing parent or teachers, it is only rarely, so rarely in fact that I can't even think of an instance right now to the contrary, that time-out is used appropriately and in the appropriate context. What I typically observe is mountains of appropriate behavior going totally unrecognized, totally unacknowledged. Then a child misbehaves, and WHAM, the kid gets thrown into time-out. And I mean that quite literally! The youngster is grabbed by the arm, marched across the room, shoved into time-out and told, "Now you better behave yourself or you're going to stay in there all day long!" (p. 204)

The "procedures" Latham describes here are not time-out.

The question of whether to teach time-out, then, is complicated. Certainly, the social worker has an ethical obligation to work with the family first to construct a positive family environment (time-out from positive reinforcement can work only if there is an environment of reinforcement to begin with). The importance of this principle cannot be emphasized enough in print. If such an environment is really being constructed, well executed time-out can be a useful tool. The following are requirements for effective use of time-out:

- A record of the problem behavior should be kept, so that it will be clear if progress is being made. Time-out should be used only for predetermined problem behaviors, not everything that is troublesome or irritating. Time-out should be an exceptional procedure, not an everyday experience, in the life of a family.
- A program for reinforcing behavior incompatible with the problem behavior must be in place.
- As soon as the child performs the targeted behavior, the parent should escort the child to time-out *with a complete lack of emotion*; parental upset is often either paradoxically reinforcing to a child, or excessively punitive (which can border on abuse). The parent should begin by telling the child calmly and firmly to go to time-out. If the child does not immediately comply, the parent should provide the minimum amount of physical guidance required to move the child into time-out. The parent should think about doing the procedure as if he or she were a robot. While the procedure may seem to work better in the beginning if the parent is clearly angry, this effect will soon backfire.
- A safe, nonreinforcing environment should be used. For some children, the bathroom is a good choice. Alternatives include a laundry room or a corner of the kitchen. (The point is that it should be a nonreinforcing

place. In many cases, therefore, a child's bedroom may not be effective, since it may be full of toys and entertainment equipment.) The parent must take whatever steps are necessary to ensure that the place selected is safe for the child, of course. Some creativity may be required to find a space that is not dark, scary and dangerous, and also not reinforcing. (If a child makes a mess in the time-out space, he or she is allowed to come out only after it is cleaned up.)

- The child should remain in time-out for no more than one to two minutes for toddlers, and no more than three minutes from ages about three to six. Time-out is not as effective with children older than about six as are other procedures such as withholding privileges. (Older children may benefit from brief periods alone to cool off and think about the choices they want to make, however.) Brief time-out is both more effective and more humane than more extended periods to which children acclimate. The time, however, should usually begin to be counted only when the child is quiet. For example, if a three-year-old child is taken to time-out while having a tantrum, he should remain in time-out for no more than three minutes, once the tantrum has stopped. There are exceptions, however, when it may not be necessary to wait for a child to stop crying so long as it is not disruptive.
- After time-out is completed, the child should be seen as "having paid his debt to society" and should quickly be allowed to return to potentially reinforcing activities without residual resentment from the parent.
- If the time-out procedure has not produced a change after a week or so (according to the records being kept), the family and social worker should revisit the situation and examine other alternatives.

Parental Monitoring

Substantial evidence now shows that parental monitoring is important for preventing antisocial behavior (Patterson, Reid, & Dishion, 1992), and that improving parental monitoring is one important step for reducing antisocial behavior once it has become a problem (Henggeler, Schoenwald, Borduin, Rowland, & Cunningham, 1998). In many struggling families, parents maintain a good deal of control when the child is in the home (and it may be that a higher level of authoritative, vigilant control in the home is valuable for children who are living in high risk neighborhoods; Steinberg, Lamborn, Darling, Mounts, & Dornbusch, 1994), but this monitoring sometimes ends at the door of the home. The data are now incontrovertible, however: Parental monitoring of activities outside the home including at school, and of people with whom children and youths spend time, is important to preventing antisocial behavior in adolescence.

Parents can intervene to resolve problems early in school and other life spheres, as explained in the next section, "Advocacy." Parents can also exercise a good deal of control and influence over friends when their children are young. It is crucial, of course, as children become adolescents, to avoid the kind of punitive communication discussed in chapter 5, where parents interrogate their children and block communication when discussing friends. At any age, parents can express interest in their children's activities, encourage them to spend time with positive friends, prompt and reinforce positive activities (and help arrange them); parents can also honestly and nonpunitively express concern when it is indicated. If the child is becoming involved in serious problem behavior, stronger steps may be necessary (see chapter 8), but monitoring need not be aversive. The social worker can open this area for discussion, clarify that monitoring is a normal part of parenting (some parents are confused about whether they are "interfering" by monitoring), and help parents think through the obstacles and possibilities involved.

Advocacy

Although social workers and other professionals can often function as advocates for children and youths, parents are potentially the strongest advocates for their children. Special needs children, who may require special education services for part or all of their school careers, are much more likely to receive them if a parent is consistently and assertively involved in developing the periodic Individual Education Plans required by law. Children of color often face discrimination in schools as well, and nothing can turn such situations around as well as a strong parent who will not accept excuses for the use of racial epithets, or for artificial grade ceilings. When one Native American teenager who had always received A grades in English consistently received much lower grades from a new teacher, her mother (knowing that the quality of the girl's writing had not changed) took the papers to the teacher and asked, "What does my child need to do to get an A from you? Do you have a problem working with Indian children?" The mother would certainly have gone next to the principal if necessary. Such action can help resolve the current problem and also gives the child a powerful message of caring and valuing.

Advocacy skills include not only those involving assertive protection, but also such important steps as meeting and having regular contact with a child's teachers, working *with* teachers to resolve any educational issues that come up, and becoming educated about what the needs of one's child may be. Parents of autistic children, for example, need to know that the state of the art requires early and intensive behavior analytic treatment, and need the skills to inquire about the exact way such treatment is being provided (Maurice, 1993). They need to learn the elements to consider to evaluate the quality of programs (for example, Are data consistently taken? Are programs changed as indicated by the data? Does the program emphasize reinforcers rather than aversives?). Parents in this situation also commonly need to have the major voice in intervention planning and often provide at-home supervision to paraprofessionals who may be doing much of the treatment. While a highly skilled behavior analyst should be working with the parents to design programs, as should staff of the school system, the parents' role is central in such work.

In addition to individual advocacy, parents' collective advocacy is often required to help construct a world in which their children are safe and enjoy the opportunities they deserve. Parents of developmentally disabled and seriously mentally ill children and adults, for example, often are organized in associations that may negotiate and advocate with school systems, and may also partner with those systems to lobby for necessary resources for funds, including governments and insurance companies. Parents (and often grandparents) sometimes find that they need to organize to ensure their children's safety, for example by establishing and supervising safe corridors to and from schools in dangerous areas, as well as advocating collectively for better police protection. Parents also have potentially strong voices, often partnering with other advocates, in campaigns to improve schools, to establish youth programs, and otherwise to have their children's needs met by other systems.

While some of these activities may sound more like community organizing than clinical practice with families, all of these spheres work together to create a child's world. Social workers dealing with families can, and should, teach parents to evaluate schools and other programs their children rely on, can teach assertive and organizing skills, can assist in establishing and strengthening groups and organizations working on family issues, and can work with parents in a shared power framework to improve the world in which their children live. Agencies can organize information-sharing sessions bringing together parents and special education staff from school districts. They can sponsor "meet-the-candidates" evenings where local and state representatives can be asked about their support for programs important to children. Agency representatives can accompany individual parents or representatives of parent groups to meet with school and police administrators to discuss concerns. If social workers and parents recognize that they share responsibility for what happens to the children, and that they each bring important gifts and resources to the effort, enormous collective power will emerge from their joint efforts.

REFERENCES

Azrin, N. H., & Foxx, R. M. (contributor) (1989). *Toilet training in less than a day.* New York: Pocket Books.

Biglan, A. (1995). *Changing cultural practices: A contextualist framework for intervention research.* Reno, NV: Context Press.

Briggs, H. E., & Paulson, R. I. (1996). Racism. In M. A. Mattaini & B. A. Thyer (Eds.), *Finding solutions to social problems: Behavioral strategies for change* (pp. 147–177). Washington, DC: American Psychological Association.

Brunk, M., Henggeler, S. W., & Whelan, J. P. (1987). Comparison of multisystemic therapy and parent training in the brief treatment of child abuse and neglect. *Journal of Consulting and Clinical Psychology, 55,* 171–178.

Carton, J. S. (1996). The differential effects of tangible rewards and praise on intrinsic motivation: A comparison of cognitive evaluation theory and operant theory. *The Behavior Analyst, 19,* 237–255.

Carton, J. S., & Nowicki, S., Jr. (1998). Should behavior therapists stop using reinforcement? A reexamination of the undermining effect of reinforcement on intrinsic motivation. *Behavior Therapy, 29,* 65–86.

Comer, E. W., & Fraser, M. W. (1998). Evaluation of six family-support programs: Are they effective? *Families in Society, 79,* 134–148.

Crittenden, P.M., & Snell, M. (1983). Intervention to improve mother-infant interaction and infant development. *Infant Mental Health Journal, 4,* 23–31.

Deloria, E. C. (1996). *Waterlily.* New York: Quality Paperback Book Club.

Dickinson, A. M. (1989). The detrimental effects of extrinsic reinforcement on "intrinsic motivation." *Behavior Analyst, 12,* 1–15.

Dumas, J. E. & Wahler, R. G. (1983). Predictors of treatment outcome in parent training: Mother insularity and socioeconomic disadvantage. *Behavioral Assessment, 5,* 301–313.

Feldman, R. A., Stiffman, A. R. & Jung, K. G. (1987). *Children at risk: In the web of parental mental illness.* New Brunswick, NJ: Rutgers University Press.

Foxx, R. M., & Azrin, N. H. (1973). Dry pants: A rapid method of toilet training children. *Behaviour Research and Therapy, 11,* 435–442.

Goldstein, A. P., Keller, H., & Erné, D. (1985). *Changing the abusive parent.* Champaign, Il.: Research Press.

Gunnoe, M. L., & Mariner, C. L., (1997). Toward a developmental-contextual model of the effects of parental spanking on children's aggression. *Archives of Pediatrics and Adolescent Medicine, 151,* 768–775.

Hart, B., & Risley, T. R. (1995). *Meaningful differences in the everyday experience of young American children.* Baltimore: Paul Brookes.

Henggeler, S. W., Schoenwald, S. K., Borduin, C. M., Rowland, M. D., & Cunningham, P. B. (1998). *Multisystemic treatment of antisocial behavior in children and adolescents.* New York: Guilford Press.

Kohlenberg, R. J., & Tsai, M. (1991). *Functional analytic psychotherapy: Creating intense and curative therapeutic relationships.* New York: Plenum.

Kohn, A. (1993). *Punished by rewards: The trouble with gold stars, incentive plans, A's, praise, and other bribes.* Boston: Houghton Mifflin.

Kopp, J. (1993). Self-observation: An empowerment strategy in assessment. In J. B. Rauch (Ed.), *Assessment: A sourcebook for social work practice* (pp. 255–268). Milwaukee: Families International.

Larson, K., & Ayllon, T. (1990). The effects of contingent music and differential re-inforcement on infantile colic. *Behaviour Research & Therapy, 28*(2), 119–125.

Latham, G. I. (1994). *The power of positive parenting.* North Logan, UT: P & T Ink.

Lee, V. L. (1988). *Beyond behaviorism.* Hillsdale, NJ: Lawrence Erlbaum Associates.

Lightburn. A. & Kemp, S. P. (1994). Family-support programs: Opportunities for community-based practice. *Families in Society, 75,* 16–26.

Mahrer, A., Levinson, J., & Fine, S. (1976). Infant psychotherapy: Theory, research, and practice. *Psychotherapy: Theory, Research, and Practice, 13,* 131–140.

Mattaini, M. A. (1997). *Clinical Practice with Individuals.* Washington, DC: NASW Press.

Maurice, C. (1993). *Let me hear your voice: A family's triumph over autism.* New York: Fawcett Columbine.

Minuchin, S. (1974). *Families and family therapy.* Cambridge, MA: Harvard University Press.

Minuchin, S., & Nichols, M. P. (1993). *Family healing: Tales of hope and renewal from family therapy.* New York: Free Press.

Moncher, F. J. (1995). Social isolation and child-abuse risk. *Families in Society, 76,* 421–433.

Murphy, H. A., Hutchinson, J. M., & Bailey, J. S. (1983). Behavioral school psychology goes outdoors: The effects of organized games on playground aggression. *Journal of Applied Behavior Analysis, 16,* 29–35.

Ninness, H. A., Ellis, J., Miller, W. B., Baker, D., & Rutherford, R. (1995). The effect of a self-management training package on the transfer of aggression control procedures in the absence of supervision. *Behavior Modification, 19,* 464–490.

Patterson, G. R. (1976). The aggressive child: Victim and architect of a coercive system. In E. J. Mash, L. A. Hamerlynck, & L. C. Handy (Eds.), *Behavior modification and families,* 267–316. New York: Brunner/Mazel.

Patterson, G. R. (1982). *Coercive family processes.* Eugene, OR: Castalia Publishing Company.

Patterson, G., Reid, J., & Dishion, T. (1992). *Antisocial boys: A social interactional approach, Volume 4.* Eugene, OR: Castalia Publishing Company.

Polansky, N. A., Gaudin, J. M., Jr., Ammons, P. W., & Davis, K. B. (1985). The psychological ecology of the neglectful mother. *Child Abuse and Neglect, 9,* 265–275.

Polster, R. A., & Dangel, R. F. (1989). Behavioral parent training in family therapy. In B. A. Thyer (Ed.), *Behavioral family therapy* (pp. 31–54). Springfield, IL: Charles C. Thomas.

Reuters (1998, July 14). Praise children for effort, not intelligence, study says. *The New York Times on the Web.* Retrieved July 14, 1998, from the World Wide Web: http://www.nytimes.com.

Sajwaj, T., Libet, J., & Agras, S. (1974). Lemon juice therapy: The control of life-threatening rumination in a six-month-old infant. *Journal of Applied Behavior Analysis, 7*, 557–563.

Sidman, M. (1989). *Coercion and its fallout.* Boston: Authors Cooperative.

Sloane, H. N., Jr. (1976/1988). *The good kid book.* Champaign, IL: Research Press.

Steinberg, L., Lamborn, S. D., Darling, N., Mounts, N. S., & Dornbusch, S. M. (1994). Over-time changes in adjustment and competence among adolescents from authoritative, authoritarian, indulgent, and neglectful families. *Child Development, 65*, 754–770.

Straus, M. A., Sugarman, D. B., & Giles-Sims, J. (1997). Spanking by parents and subsequent antisocial behavior of children. *Archives of Pediatrics and Adolescent Medicine, 151*, 761–767.

Thomas, A., & Chess, S. (1977). *Temperament and development.* New York: Brunner/Mazel.

Tryon, W. W. (1982). A simplified time-series analysis for evaluating treatment interventions. *Journal of Applied Behavior Analysis, 15*, 423–429.

Wahler, R. G. (1980). The insular mother: Her problems in parent-child treatment. *Journal of Applied Behavior Analysis, 8*, 27–42.

Wahler, R. G., Williams, A. J., & Cerezo, A. (1991). The compliance and predictability hypotheses: Sequential and correlational analyses of coercive mother-child interactions. *Behavioral Assessment, 12*, 391–407.

Webster-Stratton, C. (1997). From parent training to community building. *Families in Society, 78*, 156–171.

Webster-Stratton, C., Hollinsworth, T., & Kolpacoff, M. (1989). The long-term effectiveness and clinical significance of three cost-effective training programs for families with conduct-problem children. *Journal of Consulting and Clinical Psychology, 57*, 550–553.

Wolfe, D. A. (1991). *Preventing physical and emotional abuse of children.* New York: Guilford Press.

CHAPTER EIGHT

Constructing Alternatives
to Antisocial Behavior

Antisocial behavior among children and youths is an increasing social concern, and one that social workers deal with in a variety of settings,
including child and family services, mental health, residential, education,
and corrections. The social and human costs of antisocial behavior are
enormous, because of the damage done not only to the individuals concerned, but also to the larger web of community relations. Most antisocial
and violent behavior is not the result of "broken brains"; rather, family,
peer, school, and larger cultural arrangements shape and maintain this behavior (Mattaini, Twyman, Chin & Lee, 1996). Effective prevention and intervention therefore need to occur at those levels. Individual office therapy
for the children involved is almost guaranteed to fail, although it traditionally has been the most common social work response to these issues. On the
other hand, in the last 15 years, a great deal has been learned about effective work with antisocial repertoires, and we can now clearly elaborate the
current best practices for addressing them.

ANTISOCIAL BEHAVIOR

In discussing "antisocial behavior," we are referring to several overlapping
clusters of persistent behaviors that are damaging to the individual, to others, or both. The behaviors involved are those regarded as diagnostic of (1)
conduct disorder and, as youths move into adulthood (2) antisocial personality disorder in DSM-IV (American Psychiatric Association, 1994).
There are profound problems with both of these diagnostic formulations
(Mattaini & Kirk, 1991), but the behaviors involved are clearly important.
They include aggression toward people and animals, property damage, dishonesty, and rule violations. These problems, overall, have increased over

the past two decades as a result of changing social conditions. Fourteen children die each day as a result of gunshot wounds, and at least twice as many are wounded (Children's Defense Fund, 1998). (Increased availability of more lethal weapons is an important dimension of the problem [Canada, 1995].) The overall rate of victimization increased dramatically from 1987 until 1994 (Perkins, 1997). Since then arrests for violent crimes among youths have declined somewhat, but youths ages 12 to 17 are still three times more likely to be victimized than adults, usually by other young people (Children's Defense Fund, 1998). Most youths who will become involved in serious antisocial behavior in adolescence and adulthood can be identified by first grade (Embry, in press) and, unless the pattern is interrupted early, it tends to be highly chronic. Walker, Colvin & Ramsey (1995) report that an estimated 2 to 6 percent of children (mostly boys) could be diagnosed as conduct disordered; and that half will maintain the full pattern into adulthood, while many of the others will continue to have residual problems.

According to Walker and his colleagues (Walker, Colvin & Ramsey, 1995), the research indicates a variety of other related life problems associated with antisocial behavior. Their studies and those of Patterson and his colleagues (Patterson, DeBaryshe, & Ramsey, 1989) show that 62 percent of antisocial boys dropped out of school; most used alcohol, drugs or both, and their arrest rate was almost nine times that of a control group who could be considered "at risk" based on sociodemographic factors. Most have problems at home, and academic achievement is usually well below that of peers. About half of antisocial children become delinquent offenders, and more than half of those continue criminal trajectories into adulthood.

We now know a great deal about the developmental trajectories that children follow toward stable antisocial repertoires (Dodge, 1993; Kazdin, 1987; Patterson, Reid, & Dishion, 1992). Loeber, Wung, Keenan, Giroux, Stouthamer-Loeber, Van Kammen, & Maughan (1993) discovered three nonexclusive pathways to conduct disorder. One was characterized primarily by covert behavior problems (for example—stealing, lying, and substance use); a second path involved overt aggressive and coercive patterns; the final route involved primarily disobedience and oppositional behavior. Some children's developmental experience involves more than one of these pathways, and those children appear to be at the highest risk for chronic severe problems.

Patterson and his colleagues (Patterson, Reid, & Dishion, 1992) have conducted crucial longitudinal studies that suggest that the most common series of temporal processes involved is as follows:

1. Early in life, parenting is chaotic and coercive, often as a result of an accumulation of severe environmental and intrafamilial aversives (for ex-

ample, poverty, drug abuse, and family violence). In some cases, the child him- or herself may begin life with a challenging temperament. Antisocial models are common in these homes, as is extensive reliance on physical punishment (see discussion of spanking in chapter 7, and Gunnoe & Mariner, 1997; Straus, Sugarman, & Giles-Sims, 1997) and other forms of harsh, inconsistent discipline (Biglan, 1995). By early childhood, antisocial children learn that aggressive and other antisocial repertoires help them to escape aversives and obtain reinforcers in the family. Often they have no alternative repertoires available.

2. When the child begins school, he or she naturally brings those social repertoires with him or her, and is rapidly rejected by both prosocial peers and teachers.

3. Academic failure follows quickly, and bullying may develop as one way to obtain some level of social contact and control.

4. The child often finds that his or her only available peer group consists of other antisocial children, whose repertoires are familiar. As described by Walker, Colvin, and Ramsey (1995), by fourth or fifth grade, many anti-social children become members of deviant peer groups, which in turn encourage further antisocial behavior. Some, however, remain socially isolated and may engage primarily in covert antisocial behaviors. (Note that this extensive research clarifies that the either/or, family versus peer arguments about causation now being pursued in the popular literature are a false issue.)

In other words, by the time the at-risk child is about 10 years old, his or her experience includes a coercive, rejecting family; rejection by prosocial peers; rejection by teachers; academic failure; probably membership in a deviant antisocial peer group; and often early contact with the law. Such a child is on a trajectory toward failure in every significant life domain and may not have enough "attractive" repertoires for anyone to take a genuine, caring interest in him or her.

Although many discussions are couched in terms of a simple categor-ical framework in which a child either is, or is not, antisocial, the realities are far more complex. Every child acts in antisocial ways at times; early de-velopment ideally involves a process by which parents help to shape proso-cial alternatives and discourage antisocial behavior, but this is a matter of degree. Research consistently finds that practically every teenager does some things for which he or she could get in trouble with the law; "anti-social" youths, however, do far more. Some children are "early starters" (Walker, Colvin, & Ramsey, 1995, p. 21); their antisocial behavior typically begins near infancy in a context of family disorganization and coercion. Later starters have some stability in early life, but may be socialized into antisocial behavior in later childhood as a result of immersion in antisocial peer groups and other contextual factors; long term risks for this group are lower. And some children display considerable antisocial behavior in one context (for example, at home) while they may function adequately or very well in other contexts (at school). The severity and breadth of antisocial behavior, therefore, needs to be considered in planning intervention.

A great deal can be done both to prevent antisocial behavior in the first place and to ameliorate it in the long run. At the same time, given the chronicity of more severe forms of antisocial behavior, it may be necessary to think of more serious antisocial behavior as a persistent, handicapping condition for which prophylactic environments may be required for extended periods (Walker, Colvin, & Ramsey, 1995; Wolf, Braukmann, & Ramp, 1987).

CAN ANTISOCIAL BEHAVIOR BE REDUCED?

A decade ago, a review of behavioral, communications, and systems approaches for work with families of adolescents (Stern, 1989) was somewhat discouraging. It indicated that little had been clearly established about effective approaches for work with more severely distressed families, despite some promising hints. Since that time, much has been learned, and although this knowledge base will continue to evolve, it is now possible to identify best practices with some clarity. Traditionally, social work intervention in cases of antisocial behavior in schools consisted of primarily individual casework in the office, occasionally with adjunctive group work or family contact. Similarly, children referred to mental health programs for conduct disorders (the most common problem type among child referrals), often received primarily generic individual and occasionally family therapy. If these efforts failed, residential treatment was often the next step. We now know that a different array of services is usually required, including specific approaches for specific problem dimensions.

For example, most students in the United States (but not nearly as many in other countries, which tells us something important about our overall sociocultural milieu) report that they have been bullied at some point in school; bullying is a very common form of antisocial behavior. Solutions for bullying are now known; effective solutions need to be implemented on a school-wide basis and involve the entire staff and student body, and should include parents and the community as well (Walker, Colvin, & Ramsey, 1995). The basic principles of such intervention, which Walker and his colleagues draw from Olweus (1991), include the following:

It is important to create a school (and home) environment that is characterized by warmth, positive school interest, and involvement from adults *but that sets firm limits for unacceptable behavior.*
When violations of these limits occur, then nonhostile, nonphysical sanctions should be consistently applied.
Careful monitoring and surveillance of student activities should occur within and outside the school.
Adults should act as responsible authorities during all adult-child interactions, and especially when bullying occurs. (p. 191)

Many of the principles involved should sound familiar to readers of this book, including the emphasis on building positive exchange and noncoercive, but clear consequences for disrespectful and bullying behavior. Negative consequences for bullying will not work unless alternative payoffs for the child involved are also available. Olweus (1991) provides an extensive program at the organizational and community level for implementing this strategy. School social workers are ideally situated to work with the school community to develop such an arrangement, including work with teachers groups and parent circles; note how different this is from a traditional approach where a social worker might try to "counsel" a child who is bullying others.

Similarly, recall that the antisocial child is often rejected by teachers and peers very early in his or her school career. Specific programming at the classroom level can help to resolve this, as reported by Ervin, Miller, & Friman (1996). In their study, a very simple procedure of awarding points (later exchangeable for privileges) to classmates for making positive observations about the actions of the target student (and two others, to reduce potential resentment) was implemented. Comments needed to appear genuine to "count." As described by the authors, the student's preintervention pattern was typical of Patterson's coercive escalation: she was ignored, she acted in an aversive manner for attention, peers reciprocated the aversive contact, and she escalated further. With intervention, these patterns nearly disappeared, positive transactions increased dramatically, and peer sociometric ratings for the child also improved. Note that this procedure could easily be implemented in "recognition circles" scheduled on a regular basis in classrooms (as in the PEACE POWER! strategy, explained later in this chapter). This is a procedure that social workers could work at institutionalizing with students, parents, and school personnel.

The previous interventions all involve efforts to create cultures that shape and reinforce positive behaviors, and discourage or do not reinforce antisocial behaviors. They are largely preventive in nature and emphasize the construction of cultures that reinforce positive practices, and provide clear, inescapable, but not very severe penalties for infractions. Such practices can be institutionalized in schools, residential and recreation programs, families, and other cultural entities. For school settings in particular, Walker, Colvin and Ramsey's (1995) book, *Antisocial Behavior in School: Strategies and Best Practices*, provides a wealth of valuable information, much of which can also be transferred to other settings. The material that follows is divided into two sections: (1) data-based strategies for preventing violence and antisocial behavior at the community level, and (2) interventive strategies for intervening with children and youths who are already well advanced on an antisocial trajectory. Both are approaches to which family-centered social workers can contribute in important ways. Some may seem to go beyond a strictly "clinical" focus, but because family issues are deeply embedded in contextual webs, it is often necessary to rely on a broad generalist lens to provide adequate social work assistance.

PREVENTION OF ANTISOCIAL BEHAVIOR

Behavioral science has learned a tremendous amount about aggressive, violent, and antisocial behavior in children and youths in the past decade (for example, American Psychological Association, 1993; Embry & Flannery, in press; Mattaini, Twyman, Chin & Lee, 1996; Patterson, Reid, & Dishion, 1992). One of the crucial messages that has emerged from hundreds of millions of dollars in research is that we know enough about how to work with the cultures in which children are embedded to reduce violence and antisocial behavior by perhaps 50 percent, if we were to apply what we already know. Many current efforts address these issues; among others, a monograph supplement to Volume 12, Number 5 of the *American Journal of Preventive Medicine* provides introductions to 13 projects targeting the prevention of youth violence funded by the Centers for Disease Control and Prevention. The PeaceBuilders™ program for elementary-age children, based in Tucson, and the PEACE POWER! strategy for work with middle and high school age student are two programs particularly consistent with the available data and the current trend of working with children and families in their ecobehavioral context. Both programs emphasize broad-based approaches that include families, schools, and communities.

PeaceBuilders™

PeaceBuilders™ (Embry, Flannery, Vazsonyi, Powell, & Atha, 1996) is a mature school-based program that has developed a wide range of program materials for constructing a new community culture. It involves parent education and "marketing" of PeaceBuilders™ materials to families as integral components of the larger school and community program. The program draws on an enormous body of behavioral research, including biobehavioral research on the effects of environmental events on neurotransmitters and brain structure. The core strategy has particular roots in work done in the early 1980s in the Los Angeles County School system (Mayer, Butterworth, Nafpaktitis, & Sulzer-Azaroff, 1983) that demonstrated the practicality and power of interventions of this type. PeaceBuilders™ began in Tucson and has spread through much of Arizona and significant parts of southern California, as well as to the Chicago area. The nine central interventive strategies used in PeaceBuilders™ are:

> (1) common language for "community norms," (2) story and live models for positive behavior, (3) environmental cues to signal desired behavior, (4) role plays to increase range of responses, (5) rehearsals of positive solutions after negative events ("new way replays") and response cost as "punishment" for negative behavior, (6) group and individual rewards to strengthen positive behavior, (7) threat reduction to reduce reactivity, (8) self- and peer-monitoring for positive behavior, and (9) generalization promotion to increase maintenance of change across time, places, and people. (Embry et al., 1996, p. 92)

The program offers many structured activities and tools for institutionalizing positive reinforcement, including Peace Notes (written recognition of positive actions and attributes of others), Peace Boards (for public posting of Peace Notes), and Peace Circles in which students and teachers provide positive recognition in a group setting. The central PeaceBuilders™ practices are:

- Praise People (reinforcement)
- Give Up Put-Downs (to reduce threat)
- Notice Hurts (building empathy)
- Right Wrongs (taking action to resolve problems one has caused)
- Seek Wise People (teaching children to turn to older, wiser advisors when needed).

Families are encouraged to incorporate all of these practices in the home in a number of ways, including through media outlets and specially designed modules providing "'recipes' for reducing TV watching, sibling fighting, and angry outbursts, and strategies to increase homework completion" (Embry et al., 1996, p. 92), as well as by participating in community level PeaceBuilders™ activities.

Evaluations of the PeaceBuilders™ program indicate that it is effective in reaching its target audiences and reducing disciplinary problems and fights, and that it is highly acceptable to parents, children, and school personnel (for example, Heartsprings, Inc., 1996; http://www.peacebuilders.com).

Peace Power!

PEACE POWER! is a violence and antisocial behavior prevention strategy for middle- and high-school-age youths, their families, and their communities (Mattaini, Lowery, Herrera, & DiNoia, 1998; http://www.bfsr.org/PEACEPOWER.html). It is rooted in the research that has also shaped PeaceBuilders™, but emphasizes somewhat different repertoires for children and youths who are more developmentally advanced. Many violence prevention programs emphasize reducing behaviors (particularly antisocial and aggressive behaviors), rather than constructing alternatives. As has been discussed throughout this book, however, a primary emphasis on shaping and reinforcing positive alternatives leads to more powerful and resilient outcomes. Violent and other antisocial acts are *behavior*, and therefore are selected by their consequences. Antisocial behavior is functional: it produces outcomes. The challenge is to help young people and those with whom they associate find and develop new kinds of power that do not rely on coercion. The PEACE POWER! strategy relies primarily on constructing networks of positive practices that interlock in empowerment cultures (Lowery & Mattaini, in press). The program is grounded in both contemporary behavioral research and Native American culture; important confluences between the two can result in powerful synergy (Mattaini & Lowery, 1998).

The four core cultural practices involved in the PEACE POWER! strategy are shown in the wheel in Figure 8-1. While each stands on its own as an empirically and experientially supported practice associated with the reduction of antisocial behavior, there are also significant interlocks among them, as will become clear in the descriptions that follow. The wheel, and the language associated with it, can become omnipresent in a cultural network, which in turn can provide constant prompts for the associated actions.

Recognize Contributions and Successes

There is substantial research evidence as well as theoretical support for the utility of increasing levels of positive reinforcement in people's, including

Figure 8-1

Core practices of a PEACE POWER! culture.

youths', lives as a means to decrease undesirable behavior (see chapter 1; Mayer, Butterworth, Nafpaktitis, & Sulzer-Azaroff, 1983; Sidman, 1989). In fact, there is even a mathematical function (the matching law, Embry & Flannery, in press; Mattaini, 1991; McDowell, 1988) that predicts its occurrence. In an environment that provides rich reinforcement for alternative behavior, the level of antisocial behavior will be low, while in a deprived environment, even the poor quality reinforcers associated with antisocial behavior will have a high valence, and the level of antisocial behavior will be high (see Figure 8-2). In a PEACE POWER! culture, there is a high rate of recognition for personal successes, but also, explicitly, for contributions to the collective good. Recognition (social reinforcement) is the primary and driving force behind the entire program. High levels of recognition are the underlying "power" in PEACE POWER! It is enormously helpful to incorporate such recognition into family, organizational, and community cultures, since the same kind of reinforcer erosion that can happen in couples occurs in those networks as well (see chapter 6). For this reason, the use of structuring tools such as Recognition Notes, Recognition Boards, planners for scheduling Recognition Circles and other PEACE POWER! events, as well as home

Figure 8-2

The relationship between levels of antisocial behavior and other reinforcers available in a contextual situation.

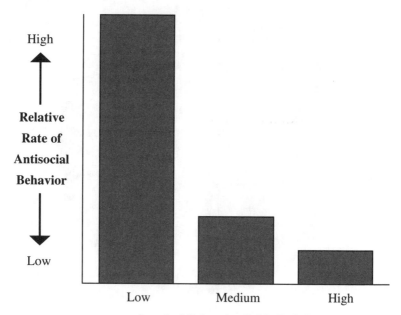

Level of Other Available Reinforcers

modules to increase the extent of recognition exchanged at home, is important. The business community, law enforcement, government, and other networks can also sponsor community level recognition activities, including regular media features, giveaways, and events to ensure high visibility.

Act with Respect

High levels of reinforcement are crucial, but so are low levels of aversives and threats. In the PeaceBuilders program described earlier, the primary strategy for reducing aversives is encouraging everyone involved to "Give Up Put-Downs." PEACE POWER! materials include giving up criticism, aggressive teasing, and threats (including those associated with weapons) as one aspect of acting with respect. They also seek to construct alternative repertoires (in particular respect for self, others, and the Earth). The language of "respect" and "disrespect" is used explicitly because it is so common among youths. Acting with respect involves learning assertive behavior, providing recognition (note the connection with the first core practice), giving up put-downs, developing empathy, and shifts in equivalence relations including those involving respecting diversity. Tools to shape acting with respect include group discussions modeling social reinforcement for respectful self-talk, talk, and action, role plays to rehearse respectful alternatives, questionnaires to be completed by youths and parents (or other caretakers) at home and returned to establish eligibility for prizes, and constant reference to respect in everyday interactions (which may be most likely to happen if staff, teachers, parents and youth leaders self-monitor such references). Sportsmanship curricula can be a particularly useful adjunct (Sharp, Brown, & Crider, 1995). These tactics are consistent with the extensive literature on social learning and social skills training (Hayes, Kohlenberg, & Melancon, 1989).

Share Power to Build Community

The third core practice is the sharing of power for the collective good. In a culture of shared power, everyone (youths, family members, staff, educators, and members of the larger community) has a strong voice in planning programs and community action; everyone is expected to contribute from their strengths, gifts, and power, and everyone shares responsibility for collective outcomes. In sharing power, youths come to discover and create their own power, giving them alternatives to coercive action, including the power of recognition, assertive behavior, and action grounded in the strengths of each. Sharing power is consistent with the youth empowerment literature (Gibson, 1993; Parsons, 1989). Sharing power to shape positive collective outcomes is also consistent with emerging data from the service-learning literature (Waterman, 1997). As Finn and Checkoway (1998) ask, "What would happen if society viewed young people as competent community builders?" (p. 335). (Again, notice the interlocks between shared power, recognition, and acting with respect).

Make Peace

Conflict resolution is a common strategy for reducing aggressive and other antisocial behaviors including conflicts, theft, and bullying (for example, Aber et al., 1996; Bosworth et al., 1996; Kruk, 1997). Anger management is often a part of such strategies (Prothrow-Stith, 1987), although it is, by itself, a weak intervention. Mediation, including family (Gold, 1997; Umbreit & Kruk, 1997) and peer mediation (Kaplan, 1997), is an increasingly popular strategy as well. While valuable, conflict resolution programs, by themselves, are not an overall solution. Their utility, however, is potentiated in the context of the other PEACE POWER! practices.

Native American and Canadian First Nations' wisdom suggests that simply finding an immediate solution to a conflict is not the core of making peace, however. The real issue in conflict is that relationships have been disrupted, and the disruption may affect relationships up to several steps removed from the initial participants (Ross, 1996). The core strategic requirement is to find ways to rebuild and strengthen all of the affected relationships. Making peace, therefore, requires contributions to the collective, recognition of those contributions, and increases in respectful action—all of the other core practices discussed thus far. Making peace involves moving toward constructive action, and actively giving up coercive punishment and threats.

Offenses against another person or the community call for justice, but indigenous peoples teach the importance of restorative, rather than retributive, justice. Restorative justice may involve restitution in a direct sense, but also involves restoration of relationship, restoration of the network of interlocking positive transactions that defines community. Considerable empirical evidence demonstrates that making peace in this broader sense can be a powerful intervention, even in very serious disruptions (Ross, 1996). In fact, peace making holds an important place even in cases of criminal and deeply abusive situations. These applications are discussed in a later section of this chapter as among the best practices not only for prevention, but also for intervention.

Embedding PEACE POWER! Practices in Cultural Networks

PEACE POWER! is a strategy rather than a tightly defined program. Community-level interventions, and in fact any practice that social workers hope to embed in natural cultural systems like families, need (according to Fawcett and his colleagues [Fawcett, Mathews, & Fletcher, 1980]) to be flexible, compatible with local conditions, and sustainable with local resources. Only in this way can a sense of ownership develop, which is required if the new practices are to be naturally maintained. The PEACE POWER! strategy, therefore, involves training regarding what is known from behavioral science, offering an extensive and flexible menu of tools and activities which can be combined and adapted to elaborate a locally designed project, and providing program materials (for example, basic posters, self-monitoring and planning tools, modules, patches, contest and media ideas, and other prompts). In an effective project, many locally developed materials will also be required; posters designed by local youths, for example, are much more powerful than commercially designed posters. The overall thrust of PEACE

POWER! is to provide information, support, and tools to construct and institutionalize new practices in existing cultural arrangements, while avoiding the colonial relationships present in inflexible, standardized programs (Fawcett, 1991). The core ecobehavioral principles involved in the strategy are very resilient and can be effective in a wide variety of permutations.

Prevention is crucial in dealing with antisocial behavior because this is one area where preventive measures are clearly less costly (socially and financially) than is intervention after the problems have become deeply rooted. The data actually suggest that strategies like those described save money (Mayer, Butterworth, Nafpaktitis, & Sulzer-Azaroff, 1983). Nonetheless, clinical social workers will often find themselves working with families where antisocial behavior is already well established. We now have considerable information about directions to pursue to intervene in those patterns.

INTERVENTION IN ANTISOCIAL BEHAVIOR

While many children and youths are involved in antisocial behavior across contexts and life domains, not all are. For example, the young people included in the Serna, Schumaker, Sherman and Sheldon (1991) study discussed in chapter 5 apparently experienced problems primarily in the home. For these issues, the family conference approach may be sufficient. In other situations, particularly when problems occur in multiple life sectors, more intensive approaches may be required. Functional family therapy, multisystemic treatment, and approaches grounded in indigenous cultures from several sources including New Zealand's Family Group Conferences and Canadian First Nations' Community Holistic Circle Healing Program, are the current state of the art. Each of these approaches is consistent with the ecobehavioral approach presented throughout this volume.

The Family Conference

In two of the three families with which Serna and her colleagues (1991) worked, long term communication issues within the family had been exacerbated among the adolescents to the point of threats of suicide, serious defiance, and physical abuse among the children. In the third family, similar problems were associated with the creation of a blended family. Standard interventions to improve communication, including individual and group skills training and rehearsal in the home, did not prove effective. The skills training provided for parents and children using the ASSET program

(Hazel, Schumaker, Sherman, & Sheldon-Wildgren, 1981) was quite extensive, and included training and guided practice in the following repertoires:

- giving positive feedback
- giving negative feedback
- accepting positive feedback
- accepting negative feedback
- negotiating
- problem solving
- resisting peer pressure (for youths)
- following instructions (for youths)
- giving rationales (for parents)
- giving instructions (for parents)
- teaching interactions (for parents).

Only when this training was combined with the introduction of a highly structured family conference format to examine issues, an approach that emphasized shared power and giving voice to every family member, did real, lasting change occur.

The process included the preparation of family conference cards that indicated, among other items, the identified issues, the family members involved, the communication skills required to address the issue, and results of the conference. These cards were used within a 7-step structure (see Chapter 5 for details of the family conference format.) The structure was only gradually faded after the family had been able to use it to solve problems. In the beginning, the family educator chaired the family conferences, provided *in vivo* coaching, and scheduled the next conference. These roles were shifted to the parent once the process was established, and the structure was maintained until the family was using it reliably. At this point, the level of structure was reduced; the family stopped using conference cards, and no moderator was formally named.

In each family, this approach resolved situations that years of intrafamily effort and months of professional training and consultation had failed to significantly change. The Serna model has substantial potential for practice with families where the level of antisocial exchanges present is quite high. The amount of resources required is modest—certainly as compared with out-of-home placement. Professional time is the major requirement, and the time required is comparable to that required for standard family treatment, which is unlikely to be nearly as effective. While more research is needed, the family-conference format currently should be regarded as among best practices for families in which intrafamily antisocial behavior has reached a serious level.

Functional Family Therapy

Many children and youths are involved in antisocial behavior both within the family and often with other systems, including schools and the courts. One approach that has repeatedly demonstrated its value is *functional family therapy* (FFT), as developed by James Alexander, Cole Barton, and their colleagues (Barton & Alexander, 1991). The approach appears to be particularly effective with moderately disrupted families in which youths may be involved in status offenses, or may be at risk of out-of-home placement (for example, as a person in need of supervision [PINS]). It repeatedly has achieved solidly positive outcomes. For example, Lantz (1985) found that the approach diverted 18 out of 22 youths who were recommended for out-of-home placement by the juvenile court. FFT also was associated with a reduction in placement rates from 48 percent to 11 percent in another study with a similar population (Barton, Alexander, Waldron, Turner, & Warburton, 1985). (While it may be of some value with more serious offenders, a review by Stern, 1989, suggests that FFT may not have as strong an impact with such severe cases, and other approaches described later in this chapter may be needed for that population.)

FFT is generally consistent with the material in earlier chapters of this book, but has particular areas of emphasis that may be important for cases of moderately disrupted families in which some antisocial behavior is present. The developers of FFT indicate that behavior does not have meaning in itself; rather the meaning of behavior derives from its relational context, particularly its context in the family. The same behavior may "mean" very different things in different families, or at different times. What is important is the *function* of the behavior—the outcomes (consequences) it relatively reliably produces. For example, angry outbursts may produce either attention or distancing in different families, and it is important to clarify the meaning in each case. FFT (and the ecobehavioral model) assumes that all behavior is adaptive, although it may also be costly. People often are not aware of the functions of their own or others' behavior, and may label it incorrectly. Particularly common in U.S. society is an attributional error in which the behavior of other people (but not oneself) is attributed to their internal intentions, without recognizing the ecobehavioral transactions that may shape and maintain it (Gueron, 1994). Shifting understandings to relational terms is one of the first objectives in FFT.

Alexander (1973) found that family processes were predictably different among the families of delinquents as contrasted with nondistressed families. In the latter, there was a more equal distribution of talk time among family members, and higher levels of supportive talk. In the delinquent families, verbal participation was less evenly distributed, and significantly more defensive. One goal of FFT, therefore, is to help distressed families to shift their processes toward those shown by nondistressed families. Given the variability among families, helping family members to achieve the outcomes they find reinforcing in ways that are less damaging to relationships is even more important. Assessment in FFT, therefore, places heavy emphasis on identifying repeated sequences in family process, identifying possible functions of those sequences, and constructing new repertoires consistent with those functions.

FFT theorists indicate that developing more positive reframing and reattributions of these sequences is the most important aspect. Somewhat troubling, however, is their assertion that, "The therapy process in the functional family model is admittedly very manipulative, and does not reflect 'reality' or 'truth'" (Barton & Alexander, 1991, p. 423). Within a shared power framework, "manipulation" is never appropriate. An ecobehavioral FFT practitioner, therefore, would try—with the family—to develop realistic relational hypotheses to explain the functions of behavioral patterns. And acknowledging that they are only hypotheses, he or she would always look for explanations of interlocking behavioral contingencies that were as reasonable and accurate as possible.

In its classic implementation, FFT includes two phases: the "therapy" phase and the "education" phase. The first includes the processes of identifying repeated patterns in family process, developing relational explanations of them, and working with the family toward accepting these formulations. In ecobehavioral terms, this involves identifying with the family the interlocking antecedents and consequences that shape and maintain common aversive exchanges. Both FFT and the ecobehavioral approach indicate that identifying the functions of the behaviors involved is critical.

The education phase of FFT uses essentially all of the common ecobehavioral interventions discussed in chapters 4 and 5, with particular emphasis on communication skills training in conjunction with contracting with older youths and contingency management with younger children. For example, if problem behavior seems to function to obtain parental attention, contracting might involve more positive alternative ways to get that attention. If problem behavior appears to be a way to get tangible reinforcers, assertive and request-making skills may be taught. If a parent appears to be using critical or angry talk to gain some distance—and therefore some peace and quiet—for himself, the FFT practitioner might help the family develop a plan to close a door, or even to put a small red flag on a table to signal, "This is not a good time."

These are only a few examples of the many possibilities which need to be adaptively and creatively tailored for each family. The original literature on FFT is quite rich, and the social worker interested in pursuing the model should certainly refer to that material. FFT tends to emphasize intrafamilial process, although some attention may be paid to issues outside the family system as well. In more serious cases of antisocial behavior, however, problems are often present in all, or nearly all, important life spheres, including families, peer groups, schools, the legal system, and other community-level entities. Two other approaches—multisystemic treatment and family group conferences—are the best-supported strategies thus far developed to deal with those cases.

Multisystemic Treatment

Multisystemic treatment (MST) is an approach that has evolved over the last 20 years and now enjoys very solid empirical support for work with children and youths manifesting antisocial behavior (Fraser, Nelson, & Rivard, 1997; Henggeler, Schoenwald, Bordun, Rowland, & Cunningham, 1998). The approach is based on causal modeling studies that indicate that:

- Association with deviant peers is virtually always a powerful direct predictor of antisocial behavior.
- Family relations predict antisocial behavior either directly (contributing unique variance) or indirectly by predicting association with deviant peers.
- School difficulties predict association with deviant peers.
- Neighborhood and community support characteristics add small portions of unique variance and indirectly predict antisocial behavior by, for example, affecting family, peer, or school behavior. (Henggeler et al., 1998, p. 8)

In other words, serious antisocial behavior and substance abuse are multideterminod and, in many cases, overdetermined; a number of interlocking antecedents and consequences that support problem behavior are commonly present in the cultural entities within which the young person is embedded and by which his or her behavior is shaped over time. MST is a broad-spectrum approach for dealing concurrently with such multiple factors, but does so in carefully targeted ways that are likely to directly influence the salient contingencies.

A significant number of studies support the utility of MST for reducing delinquency among inner city youths, out-of-home placements in child welfare, drug use, juvenile sex offender recidivism, rearrest among chronic delinquent offenders, and recidivism among chronic and violent youth offenders (Henggeler et al., 1998). The studies have been conducted by mul-

Table 8–1

MST Treatment Principles

Principle 1: The primary purpose of assessment is to understand the fit between the identified problems and their broader systemic context.
Principle 2: Therapeutic contacts emphasize the positive and use systemic strengths as levers for change.
Principle 3: Interventions are designed to promote responsible behavior and decrease irresponsible behavior among family members.
Principle 4: Interventions are present focused and action oriented, targeting specific and well defined problems.
Principle 5: Interventions target sequences of behavior within and between multiple systems that maintain the identified problems.
Principle 6: Interventions are developmentally appropriate and fit the developmental needs of the youth.
Principle 7: Interventions are designed to require daily or weekly effort by family members.
Principle 8: Intervention effectiveness is evaluated continuously from multiple perspectives with providers assuming accountability for overcoming barriers to successful outcomes.
Principle 9: Interventions are designed to promote treatment generalization and long term maintenance of therapeutic change by empowering caregivers to address family members' needs across multiple systemic contexts.

Reprinted from Henggeler et al., 1998; used with permission.

tiple investigators in multiple settings, and MST must be regarded as well established at this point.

MST is grounded in nine treatment principles, as listed in Table 8-1. Training and supervision are based on these principles as well. Each will be briefly discussed here. However, practitioners considering MST application with appropriate client groups should at a minimum become very familiar with written materials prepared by the developers. The practitioners may also want to consider participating in formal training in the approach since a high level of treatment integrity appears to be important to effectiveness. The core MST principles may at first glance appear fairly general, but as implemented they provide relatively specific interventive guidance. They are also highly congruent with ecobehavioral principles.

Principle 1: The primary purpose of assessment is to understand the fit between the identified problems and their broader systemic context.

MST assessment, consistent with the principle of behavioral specificity, concentrates on identified antisocial behaviors of concern, and aims to "'make sense' of behavioral problems in light of their systemic context" (Henggeler et al., 1998, p. 24). The emphasis is on identifying factors in any and all of the systems within which the client and family are embedded that increase or decrease the rate of the problem behavior. Specifically, the goal is to identify antecedents and consequences of those behaviors that may become targets of change, using an experimental, hypothesis-testing process.

Principle 2: Therapeutic contacts emphasize the positive and use systemic strengths as levers for change.

Consistent with shared power, MST begins from the position that family members have something positive to bring to the process; MST seeks to elaborate and clarify those strengths and gifts. Positive contributions are used in a constructional way to build and support positive repertoires, "focusing on how desired changes can happen as opposed to why problems are so bad" (Henggeler et al., 1998, p. 29). This requires, for example, the exclusive use of nonpejorative language, eschewing such terms as "resistant," and an emphasis on the worker's finding something to reinforce in the client's actions and efforts. This positive constructional approach builds hope. Given its multisystemic, wide-angled focus, MST practitioners look specifically for strengths that can be used in all of the systems within which the child and family are embedded, not just in the family.

Principle 3: Interventions are designed to promote responsible behavior and decrease irresponsible behavior among family members.

MST promotes shared responsibility, a crucial dimension of shared power, and thereby delivers a clear message that family members and others in the overall configuration are competent to contribute to change. Within this approach, collaboratively developed rules and consequences are clearly spelled out and are consistently applied (as discussed in several previous sections of this book). Specific guidance on appropriate consequences is also integrated in the model; this includes ensuring that negative consequences really are negative but do not last so long that the youth has nothing to gain by beginning to cooperate.

Principle 4: Interventions are present focused and action oriented, targeting specific and well defined problems.

Pinpointing specific behaviors and their antecedents and consequences is a core practice in MST. The emphasis on the present is particularly important since the past cannot be changed, and emphasis on the past—which can be demoralizing—also often does not lead to active, constructional work. Many social workers have been trained to attend intensively to the past, however, so this approach often represents a major shift.

Principle 5: Interventions target sequences of behavior within and between multiple systems that maintain the identified problems.

Recall that, in FFT, the emphasis was on sequences of behavior that occurred within the family and on the functions of behavior within those sequences. In MST, while a similar process is viewed as important, a wider field is examined, including transactions with peers, institutions, neighbor-

hoods, and other networks that may support undesirable or desirable behavior patterns. Chapter 3 in this volume provides guidance for work with
such extrafamilial systems, which often interact and interlock with family
transactions in families characterized by antisocial behavior. If substance
abuse is modeled and ignored by adult family members, prompted and supported by peers, and results in suspension from school (which is more desirable than aversive for many antisocial youths) for example, all of those
factors may need to become targets of collaborative interventive planning
with the family.

Principle 6: Interventions are developmentally appropriate and fit the
developmental needs of the youth.

While not the invariant process often described in the literature, child,
youth, and adult development involve the gradual learning of a variety of
repertoires required to survive and thrive in the natural environment.
Developmental processes vary by culture (since successful functioning in
each requires different skills). In many indigenous and Asian cultures, mat-
uration involves gradually learning ways to act for the benefit of the group.
In contrast, European American culture primarily shapes skills for au-
tonomously caring for oneself (although the critical support of the collective must be recognized). Parents of young adolescents in that culture may
need to learn to establish the clear expectations that teach how to follow
rules, while the parents of older youths may need to learn how to provide
more opportunities for autonomous action. Young children have often not
learned to regulate their own impulsive behavior very well, and interventions may need to help structure external controls rather than expecting
children to defer gratification and follow abstract rules, both of which are
developmental cusps that require considerable and gradual learning to
achieve.

Principle 7: Interventions are designed to require daily or weekly effort
by family members.

The requirement of regular effort, which can be monitored, is a particularly effective way of ensuring that interventions are specifically spelled out
and actually occur. Self-monitoring, which can gradually be learned in this
process, is also a potentially valuable repertoire for use with the future challenges that may arise. The same sort of specificity should be asked of social
workers: "What can each of us do this week that will help?"

Principle 8: Intervention effectiveness is evaluated continuously from
multiple perspectives with providers assuming accountability for overcoming barriers to successful outcomes.

This principle actually includes two important dimensions. First is the
requirement for regular monitoring, as discussed in some detail in chapter
2; note that monitoring with antisocial behavior should involve the use of

"[m]ultiple informants and multiple methods" (Henggeler et al., 1998, p. 40), because multiple stakeholders often have interests in the outcome of a case, including family members, court systems, schools, and other agencies and organizations. Second, the primary responsibility for determining when there is a need to change the approach used falls to the worker in MST. Expertise in identifying obstacles to an adequate outcome and in initiating the planning to address them is seen as the worker's responsibility—there is no room here for blaming "resistant" clients. We cannot help everyone, but it is our responsibility to be knowledgeable and resourceful enough to work with families toward successful outcome in most cases, since the available data indicate that such outcomes are usually possible.

Principle 9: Interventions are designed to promote treatment generalization and long term maintenance of therapeutic change by empowering caregivers to address family members' needs across multiple systemic contexts.

In addition to again validating the importance of sharing power with family members in working toward adequate outcomes, this principle suggests the importance of helping family members to learn the skills necessary to deal with systemic challenges themselves to the extent possible, thus giving the family members more control of their lives and reducing reliance on the social worker. If the family learns these repertoires, then maintenance of positive change is far more likely.

The MST literature indicates that it is difficult for practitioners to apply these principles on a consistent basis, and that supervision (or peer consultation) needs to specifically address the way these practices are actually being operationalized in each case. For example, supervisors need to ask:

- What are the specific problems you have agreed to work on with this family? What new configuration are you trying to construct?
- What strengths in the family and the larger ecological field are you working with?
- What actions did each of you agree to take this week?
- How are you working to empower family members to address their needs on their own?

MST is a powerful approach for work with quite serious family situations when the professional resources to use it are present. In other situations, the major available resources may be primarily nonprofessional natural networks. Reliance on such networks may be as effective as—or more effective than—the approaches discussed thus far, and may also support both maintenance of specific positive changes and enhancement of a collective sense of community, in which the good of "all of us" becomes a valued reinforcer.

Family Group Conferences and Related Indigenous Approaches

Community-level interventions with families where youths are involved in antisocial behavior, not surprisingly, have emerged primarily from indigenous cultures in which the recognition of the essential connections among people and other parts of the contextual field within which they live has always been strong. There are important points of confluence between Native American thought and the science of behavior (Mattaini & Lowery, 1998), as well as other emerging scientific perspectives on "autopoietic networks" (self-organizing, deeply interconnected living systems, Capra, 1996). The power of indigenous approaches like the *Family Group Conference* that originated with the Maoris of New Zealand is easy to understand from both scientific and indigenous philosophic perspectives.

No book, much less a small section of a chapter, can capture the richness of these approaches, but some introduction is clearly needed to direct social work attention to these emerging models. The Family Group Conference process is now used in New Zealand for all but the most severe criminal offenses for 14- to 16-year-old youths (MacElrea, 1994). Criminal acts, viewed from this perspective, are breaches of community harmony. The central purposes of the process, therefore, are to understand the roots of the offense and to take action to prevent further offenses and rebuild the damaged community relationships. The offender, his family, and other supporters are brought together with the victim and his or her family and supporters, to design a sentencing plan that fits the offense and moves toward community healing. In most cases, perhaps surprisingly to European American expectations, a consensus is reached. Most importantly, the use of the Family Group Conference approach has cut the number of youths entering juvenile facilities by nearly two-thirds, along with dramatically reducing the level of recidivism (Ross, 1996).

A similar process is involved in the Navajo Peacemaker Court, where the people involved in the dispute make the decisions, but the "Navajo Justice and Peace Ceremony" (Bluehouse & Zion, 1993) is guided by a *naat'aanii*, a wise elder functioning as a peace maker. The role is much richer than that of a Western mediator, involving teaching about traditional values and the need to reach an agreement that should "reflect traditional understandings about proper relationships" (Ross, 1996, p. 26). Similarly, the Ojibway Community Holistic Circle Healing Program at Hollow Water, Manitoba, uses healing circle processes in conjunction with the court system to resolve cases of sexual abuse in ways that move beyond punishment, toward restoring harmony in the extensive web of relationships affected by abuse (Ross, 1996).

All of these approaches are based on similar underlying understandings: that offenders require either teaching or the healing of damage that has affected them, that *victims* need to be involved in their own healing processes, and that offenses damage the community in multiple ways. This recognition of deep interconnections and of the way coercive processes tend to spiral out of control are characteristic of the ecobehavioral approach as well: behavior is shaped in multiple ways by the interpersonal and physical context, and in turn affects that context. An accurate definition of behavior includes both how something is done, and what is done (Lee, 1987)—the effects on the environment are an indissoluble part of what the behavior is. All of those involved in interlocking ecobehavioral networks are affected both by the offense and by the healing.

The Family Group Conference, which is well developed, can be directly replicated in other settings, but the ecobehavioral social worker may also be able to apply the core principles in other situations. The construction of a web of antecedents and consequences that do not support antisocial behavior and do not allow it to pay off, but that does support and help the construction of alternatives, is required. The alternatives so constructed should expand the web of interlocking reinforcers for building behaviors and cultural practices consistent with improving the overall ecobehavioral situation of the collective. The experiences of the indigenous programs discussed also provide considerable guidance about what will not work (Ross, 1996). Arrangements that are coercive, or are dishonest and manipulative (and therefore involve exploitation), or that do not genuinely involve the sharing of power lead to poor outcomes. Because they are not truly constructional, and do not offer genuine long term reinforcers, such adversarial or dishonest processes ultimately produce damage rather than positive contribution. Every action, including every social work intervention, either increases the aggregate level of positive exchange (contributions to the collective), or does damage through coercion or failure to reinforce the positive. This is a choice that family members, and social workers, make afresh at every moment.

REFERENCES

Aber, J. L., Brown, J. L., Chaudry, N., Jones, S. M., & Samples, F. (1996). The evaluation of the Resolving Conflict Creatively Program: An overview. *American Journal of Preventive Medicine, 12* (Supplement to Number 5), 82–90.

Alexander, J. F. (1973). Defensive and supportive communication in normal and deviant families. *Journal of Consulting and Clinical Psychology, 40,* 223–231.

American Psychiatric Association. (1994). *Diagnostic and statistical manual of mental disorders* (4th ed.). Washington, DC: Author.

American Psychological Association. (1993). *Violence and youth: Psychology's response.* Washington, DC: American Psychological Association.

Barton, C., & Alexander, J. F. (1991). Functional family therapy. In A. S. Gurman & D. P. Kniskern (Eds.), *Handbook of family therapy: Volume 1* (pp. 403–443). New York: Brunner/Mazel.

Barton, C., Alexander, J. F., Waldron, H., Turner, C. W., & Warburton, J. W. (1985). Generalizing treatment effects of functional family therapy: Three replications. *The American Journal of Family Therapy, 13*(3), 16–26.

Biglan, A. (1995). *Changing cultural practices: A contextualist framework for intervention research.* Reno, NV: Context Press.

Bluehouse, P., & Zion, J. (1993). Hozhooji Naat'aanii: The Navajo Justice and Harmony Ceremony. *Mediation Quarterly, 10,* 327–337.

Bosworth, K., Espelage, D., DuBay, T., Dahlberg, L. L., & Daytner, G. (1996). Using multimedia to teach conflict-resolution skills to young adolescents. *American Journal of Preventive Medicine, 12* (Supplement to Number 5), 65–74.

Canada, G. (1995). *Fist, stick, knife, gun.* Boston: Beacon Press.

Capra, F. (1996). *The web of life.* New York: Anchor.

Children's Defense Fund (1998, June 18). *Facts on youth, violence, and crime.* Washington, DC: Author. Retrieved September 26, 1998 from the World Wide Web: http://www.childrensdefense.org/safestart_facts.html

Dodge, K. (1993). The future of research on conduct disorder. *Development and Psychopathology, 5*(1/2), 311–320.

Embry, D. D. (in press). Reasons for hope: Creating a climate for change and resiliency. In W. L. Reed (Ed.), *Violence and childhood trauma: Understanding and responding to the effects of violence on young children.*

Embry, D. D., & Flannery, D. J. (in press). Two sides of the coin: Multi-level prevention and intervention to reduce youth violent behavior. In D.J. Flannery and C. Ronald Huff (Eds.), *Youth Violence: Prevention, Intervention and Social Policy.* Washington, DC: American Psychiatric Press.

Embry, D. D., Flannery, D. J., Vazsonyi, A. T., Powell, K. E., & Atha, H. (1996). PeaceBuilders: A theoretically driven, school-based model for early violence prevention. *American Journal of Preventive Medicine, 12*(Supplement to Number 5), 91–100.

Ervin, R. A., Miller, P. M., & Friman, P. C. (1996). Feed the hungry bee: Using positive peer reports to improve the social interactions and acceptance of a socially rejected girl in residential care. *Journal of Applied Behavior Analysis, 29,* 251–253.

Fawcett, S. B. (1991). Some values guiding community research and action. *Journal of Applied Behavior Analysis, 24,* 621–636.

Fawcett, S. B., Mathews, R. M., & Fletcher, R. K. (1980). Some promising dimensions for behavioral community technology. *Journal of Applied Behavior Analysis, 13,* 505–518.

Finn, J. L., & Checkoway, B. (1998). Young people as competent community builders: A challenge to social work. *Social Work, 43,* 335–345.

Fraser, M. W., Nelson, K. E., & Rivard, J. C. (1997). Effectiveness of family preservation services. *Social Work Research, 21,* 138–153.

Gibson, C. M. (1993). Empowerment theory and practice with adolescents of color in the child welfare system. *Families in Society, 74,* 387–396.

Gold, L. (1997). Marriage and family: Mediation of couple and family disputes. In E. Kruk (Ed.), *Mediation and conflict resolution in social work and the human services* (pp. 19–35). Chicago: Nelson-Hall.

Gueron, B. (1994). *Analyzing social behavior: Behavior analysis and the social sciences.* Reno, NV: Context Press.

Gunnoe, M. L., & Mariner, C. L., (1997). Toward a Developmental-Contextual Model of the Effects of Parental Spanking on Children's Aggression. *Archives of Pediatrics and Adolescent Medicine, 151,* 768–775.

Hayes, S. C., Kohlenberg, B. S., & Melancon, S. M. (1989). Avoiding and altering rule-control as a strategy of clinical intervention. In S. C. Hayes (Ed.), *Rule-governed behavior: Cognitions, contingencies, and instructional control* (pp. 359–385). New York: Plenum.

Hazel, J. S., Schumaker, J. B., Sherman, J. A., & Sheldon-Wildgren, J. (1981). *ASSET: A social skills program for adolescents* (leader's guide). Champaign, IL: Research Press.

Heartsprings, Inc. (1996). *Results from Alisal School District, Salinas, California.* Unpublished evaluation report; summary available on the Worldwide Web at http://www.peacebuilders.com.

Henggeler, S. W., Schoenwald, S. K., Borduin, C. M., Rowland, M. D., & Cunningham, P. B. (1998). *Multisystemic treatment of antisocial behavior in children and adolescents.* New York: Guilford Press.

Kaplan, N. M. (1997). Education: Mediation in the school system: Facilitating the development of peer mediation programs. In E. Kruk (Ed.), *Mediation and conflict resolution in social work and the human services* (pp. 247–262). Chicago: Nelson-Hall.

Kazdin, A. (1987). *Conduct disorders in childhood and adolescence.* London: Sage.

Kruk, E. (Ed.) (1997). *Mediation and conflict resolution in social work and the human services.* Chicago: Nelson-Hall.

Lantz, B. K. (1985). Keeping troubled teens at home. *Children Today, May–June,* 9–12.

Lee, V. (1987). The structure of conduct. *Behaviorism, 15,* 141–148.

Loeber, R., Wung, P., Keenan, K., Giroux, B., Stouthamer-Loeber, M. Van Kammen, W., & Maughan, B. (1993). Developmental pathways in disruptive child behavior. *Development and Psychopathology, 5*(1/2), 103–134.

Lowery, C. T., & Mattaini, M. A. (in press). The co-construction of empowerment cultures in social work. In W. Shera & L. Wells (Eds.), *International Perspectives on Empowerment Practice.* New York: Columbia University Press.

MacElrea, F. W. M. (1994). Restorative justice: The New Zealand Youth Court—A model for development in other courts? *Journal of Judicial Administration, 4,* 36–53.

Mattaini, M. A. (1991). Choosing weapons for the war on "crack": An operant analysis. *Research on Social Work Practice, 1,* 188–213.

Mattaini, M. A., & Kirk, S. A. (1991). Assessing assessment in social work. *Social Work, 36,* 260–266.

Mattaini, M. A., Lowery, C. T., Herrera, K., & DiNoia, J. (1998). *PEACE POWER!: The science of violence prevention.* Manuscript submitted for publication.

Mattaini, M. A., & Lowery, C. T. (1998). *The science of sharing power: Native American thought and behavior analysis.* Manuscript submitted for publication.

Mattaini, M. A., Twyman, J. S., Chin, W., & Lee, K. N. (1996). Youth Violence. In M. A. Mattaini & B. A. Thyer (Eds.), *Finding solutions to social problems: Behavioral strategies for change* (pp. 75–111). Washington, DC: American Psychological Association.

Mayer, G. R., Butterworth, T., Nafpaktitis, M., & Sulzer-Azaroff, B. (1983). Preventing school vandalism and improving discipline: A three-year study. *Journal of Applied Behavior Analysis, 16,* 355–369.

McDowell, J. J. (1988). Matching theory in natural human environments. *The Behavior Analyst, 11,* 95–109.

Olweus, D. (1991). Bully/victim problems among school children: Basic facts and effects of a school-based intervention program. In D. Pepler & K. Rubin (Eds.), *The development and treatment of childhood aggression* (pp. 411–446). London: Lawrence Erlbaum.

Parsons, R. (1989). Empowerment for role alternatives for low income minority girls: A group work approach. *Social Work with Groups, 11*(4), 27–45.

Patterson, G. R., DeBaryshe, B. D., & Ramsey, E. (1989). A developmental perspective on antisocial behavior. *American Psychologist, 44,* 329–335.

Patterson, G. R., Reid, J. B., & Dishion, T. J. (1992). *Antisocial boys: Vol. 4. A social interactional approach.* Eugene, OR: Castalia.

Perkins, C. A. (1997). *Age patterns of victims of serious violent crime.* Washington, DC: Bureau of Justice Statistics, NCJ-162031.

Prothrow-Stith, D. (1987). *Violence prevention curriculum for adolescents.* Newton, MA: Educational Development Center.

Ross, R. (1996). *Returning to the teachings: Exploring aboriginal justice.* Toronto: Penguin.

Serna, L. A., Schumaker, J. B., Sherman, J. A., & Sheldon, J. B. (1991). In-home generalization of social interactions in families of adolescents with behavior problems. *Journal of Applied Behavior Analysis, 24,* 733–746.

Sharp, T., Brown, M., & Crider, K. (1995). The effects of a sportsmanship curriculum intervention on generalized positive social behavior of urban elementary school students. *Journal of Applied Behavior Analysis, 28,* 401–416.

Sidman, M. (1989). *Coercion and its fallout.* Boston: Authors Cooperative.

Stern, S. B. (1989). Behavioral family therapy for families of adolescents. In B. A. Thyer (Ed.), *Behavioral family therapy* (pp. 103–130). Springfield, IL: Charles C. Thomas.

Straus, M. A., Sugarman, D. B., & Giles-Sims, J. (1997). Spanking by parents and subsequent antisocial behavior of children. *Archives of Pediatrics and Adolescent Medicine, 151,* 761–767.

Umbreit, M. S., & Kruk, E. (1997). Parents and children: Parent-child mediation. In E. Kruk (Ed.), *Mediation and conflict resolution in social work and the human services* (pp. 97–115). Chicago: Nelson-Hall.

Walker, H. M., Colvin, G., & Ramsey, E. (1995). *Antisocial behavior in school: Strategies and Best Practices.* Pacific Grove, CA: Brooks/Cole.

Waterman, A. S. (Ed.) (1997). *Service-learning: Applications from the research.* Mahwah, NJ: Lawrence Erlbaum.

Wolf, M. M., Braukmann, C. J., & Ramp, K. A. (1987). Serious delinquent behavior as part of a significantly handicapping condition: Cures and supportive environments. *Journal of Applied Behavior Analysis, 20,* 347–359.

CHAPTER NINE

Intervening in Child Maltreatment

Over 1 million children are confirmed as victims of child maltreatment each year, an increase of nearly 50 percent between 1988 and 1997 (Wang & Daro, 1998). About three children die of child maltreatment each day, and more than 40 percent of them have previously been known to child protective services. The youngest children are at highest risk for fatalities, since infants and small children are so deeply dependent on adult caretakers for the basic requirements of life and are more physically vulnerable than are older children. An infant can easily be killed by simply shaking him or her. Despite increased public awareness in recent years, many cases of child maltreatment, probably several times as many as are reported, are never identified. There currently is no reliable way of estimating the number of such cases.

But social welfare professionals do have contact with about 500 children who will die from either abuse or neglect each year, as well as with more than a million other cases where children are at serious risk of harm, or are damaged physically and emotionally, often severely and in ways that may persist through life. About 54 percent of confirmed cases involve primarily child neglect (often particularly difficult cases, as detailed later in this chapter), 22 percent physical abuse, 8 percent sexual abuse (a substantial decrease in recent years), 4 percent emotional maltreatment, and 12 percent "other" (a mix of factors like abandonment, lack of supervision, and medical neglect—reflecting differences in state reporting systems; Wang & Daro, 1998). Every state mandates reporting of child maltreatment, and investigation of the cases that are reported. In some states, however, there is no mandate for intervention, and in many cases no intervention occurs. When it does occur, intervention is often minimal or misdirected. This chapter considers what is known about helping those children and their families.

About half of the children who receive services are placed in foster or other alternative care for at least some period. Whether the child remains in the home or is placed in foster care, social workers are in a position to contribute to positive outcomes through work with the family, the extended family, the foster family, and other parts of the child's social network. Foster care is not necessarily damaging (NRC, 1993) but is also not a panacea, because of the further disruption and separation experiences involved. Some children are also further abused and neglected in foster care, although not as many as is commonly believed (Wang & Daro, 1998). Some foster care systems are well managed; others add societal abuse to that already experienced in the home (Nohl, 1998). Since children in foster care typically return home or reconnect with family at some point (even in seemingly horrific cases), in nearly all cases there is reason to consider some form of family intervention.

This chapter focuses on strategies known to be effective for work with families when it has been determined that the child can safely remain in the home, or when they are working toward the child's return to the home after an out-of-home placement. There is no magic; change comes slowly, and child maltreatment cases are among the most challenging and draining in all of social work practice. Often, child maltreatment is complicated by other issues such as substance abuse and family violence (a majority of men who batter their female partners also abuse the children if present, and simply observing battering is clearly abusive in itself.) Nevertheless, we have learned a great deal about helping in these cases over the past two decades. The material that follows summarizes this information in ways useful for practice.

One additional point: Child-welfare cases are commonly viewed as involving binary decisions—for example, to keep the child in the home or place him or her in foster care, or to award custody to a mother with her own problems or to her mother, the child's grandmother. The adversarial legal system often relies on such dichotomous decisions, but they may not produce the best options for children. Social workers can and should work with entire natural networks, foster and natural parents, and community members to develop custom-designed plans for a child. For example, a social worker was working with a family in which the mildly cognitively delayed 18-year-old mother of an infant was in a pitched custody battle with her own mother and sister over the infant. At least four attorneys were involved. The "right" solution clearly was not for anyone to win the case as it was structured; the child was well bonded to his mother, but also currently needed—and would at many later points continue to need—the support of the extended family, all of whom cared about the child. An adequate arrangement, therefore, had a place for each. Child welfare is a crucial venue for shared power. Foster parents can often offer a great deal to biological parents, for instance, but an atmosphere of mutual respect and contribution needs to be constructed if this is to occur.

THE DYNAMICS OF CHILD MALTREATMENT

"Child maltreatment" is not a single phenomenon. Most studies have combined child abuse and child neglect, but while there is some overlap among types of child maltreatment, there are also critical distinctions. *Child abuse*, at base, involves behavioral excesses, levels of physical and emotional action that are excessively punitive, damaging or threatening. *Child neglect*, by contrast, involves behavioral deficits: inadequate physical caretaking, inadequate emotional affection and nurturing, and inadequate monitoring of developmentally important considerations like education and health care. *Child sexual abuse* is a special case of child abuse, in which the behavioral dynamics are quite different from other forms of abuse. The three classes of child maltreatment, therefore, are best understood separately. The material that follows summarizes a more detailed analysis published elsewhere (Mattaini, McGowan, & Williams, 1996).

Child Abuse

Child abuse is somewhat better understood than is neglect or sexual abuse. The natural history of the development of child abuse has been documented to some extent, and a good deal is known about factors that may be exacerbative or protective (Wolfe, 1987, 1991). Child abuse is, in general, functional behavior—it is in some sense purposive, although the perpetrator need not be aware of the function. Just as in battering, child abuse patterns are generally functional, establishing power and control, and perhaps reducing emotional arousal. Some child abuse may occur as a result of high levels of aversives from other sources; an animal that experiences repeated and unpredictable aversives is likely to strike out at any available target (Sidman, 1989), and frustrated adult caretakers may strike out at a child. In general, however, the primary function commonly involves establishing control—discipline gone awry. A parent who is under great stress from other sources is more likely to become abusive, but abuse generally occurs when a child is acting in a way that the abuser finds aversive.

The general pattern is shown in the contingency diagram shown in Figure 9-1. The motivating condition (the situation that will be changed by acting) involves some mix of unsatisfactory child behavior and physiological arousal on the part of the parent. When the parent strikes out (physically or emotionally), both may change. This immediately suggests that if the function of the behavior can be achieved in a different way, there will be no need for the abuse, and there is evidence that this is true. As discussed in a later section of this chapter, learning parenting skills and anger manage-

Figure 9-1

Factors involved in acts of child abuse. Source: Reprinted from Mattaini, McGowan, & Williams, 1996, p. 235.

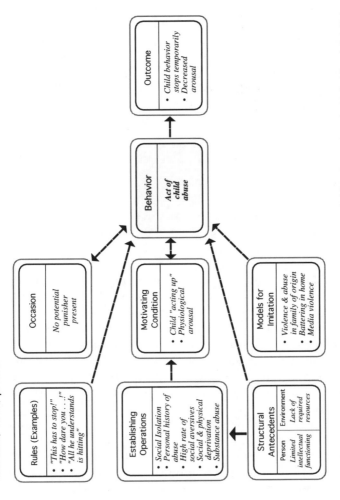

Mattaini, M.A., McGowan, B.G., & Williams, G. (1996). Child maltreatment. In M.A. Mattaini & B.A. Thyer (eds.), Finding solutions to social problems: Behavioral strategies for change (pp. 223–266). Washington, DC: American Psychological Association. Copyright © 1996 by the American Psychological Association. Reprinted with permission.

ment training both can play a part in reducing abuse. This is a primary strategy in preventing further abuse—helping the parent learn more acceptable ways to manage the child and him- or herself.

At the same time, a number of other antecedents that play a role in abuse can, and often must, also be targeted in intervention. Rules often play a key part in abuse: they may range from, "Spare the rod and spoil the child," to "Treating me like this is intolerable," to "All she understands is punishment." Alternative rules, including understanding the kinds of behavior that are developmentally normal for the child's age and developmental status, can be helpful in reducing the aversiveness of child behavior. Models are also important; persons who were themselves abused or who have observed abuse are more likely to use the same strategies themselves (Widom, 1989). Isolated parents are at particular risk for a number of reasons, including the lack of effective models and instructors for alternative ways of handling parenting challenges, as well as the lack of observers. When others are present who could act to prevent overly severe punishment, or who might help the parent manage feelings, abuse may be less likely than when such persons are not available.

Structural and motivating antecedents are often crucial, as well. Child maltreatment may be particularly high among persons with limited cognitive capacity, who may have more restricted problem-solving repertoires, as discussed in some of the cases presented later in this chapter. The parent in a family that lacks basic resources is always under stress; as the welfare rolls in Idaho dropped by 77 percent, for example, the rate of child maltreatment increased to a level three times the national average (Egan, 1998). Social isolation, social and physical deprivation, a history of personal abuse, high rates of current social aversives, and substance abuse may all function as motivating antecedents, producing a constant state of arousal (motivating condition) that may be temporarily attenuated (consequence) by an act of abuse (behavior).

All of these factors are traced in Figure 9-1, which, looked at analytically, suggests multiple possible interventive strategies. Teaching new ways to manage child behavior and parental emotions, reducing social isolation and aversives, providing new sources of social reinforcement, new models, new rules, and assistance in reducing substance abuse and battering, among other strategies, are all components of current state-of-the-art interventions, and the diagram clarifies why they are valuable. Although each case is different, and a unique mix of factors may need to be addressed by the parent/social worker team in each, the general patterns are clear.

Child Neglect

Child neglect, paradoxically, may be more difficult to resolve than abuse, although it involves the direct construction and stabilization of new repertoires without the complication of needing to reduce undesirable patterns. Parental figures in child neglect do not act to meet the child's needs, emotionally, physically, educationally, or otherwise. While the information we have is somewhat tentative, there appear to be a number of reasons why constructing and ensuring maintenance of such behaviors can be challenging. Somewhat separate analyses of acts of physical caretaking and acts of affection can be useful (as illustrated in Mattaini, McGowan, and Williams, 1996), but for reasons of space, we will concentrate on acts of physical caretaking in this section (both are addressed by the interventive strategies outlines under "Best Practices" later in this chapter).

The core of Figure 9-2 is the progression from motivating condition, to behavior, to consequence. The motivating condition is usually somewhat aversive (often resulting from deprivation). The behavior relieves that condition; for example, eating (the behavior) relieves hunger (the motivating condition). In the case of acts of caretaking, a "child in need" ideally functions as a motivating condition, and the act of caretaking relieves that condition so that the child is no longer in need. These connections have not been constructed in cases of child neglect. The parent may not know how to tell that the child is in need, or how to provide what the child needs—the parent has not learned the necessary repertoires. The repertoires required are sometimes complex, for example knowing how to plan and prepare nutritionally adequate and good-tasting meals, or how to recognize illness and what to do about it. Particularly where there is limited intellectual functioning, or where there have been no adequate models of parenting, skills training may be a critical intervention (see, for example, the first case in Greene, Norman, Searle, Daniels, & Lubeck, 1995, discussed below). These are in some sense the easy cases, because the child's need is motivating; the parent simply does not know what to do about it.

Effective parenting also requires "self-discipline"—well established rule-governed repertoires that bring behavior under the control of long term rather than immediate consequences. Unfortunately, life experiences sometimes do not teach these lessons to parents; they may have every intention of taking their children in for immunizations, for example, but may not get around to it. Working with clients to learn these repertoires is likely to require relatively long term involvement, during which reliance on more immediate prompts from the social worker, or ideally members of

Figure 9-2

Contingencies associated with acts of physical caretaking. Source: Reprinted from Mattaini, McGowan, & Williams, 1996, p. 243.

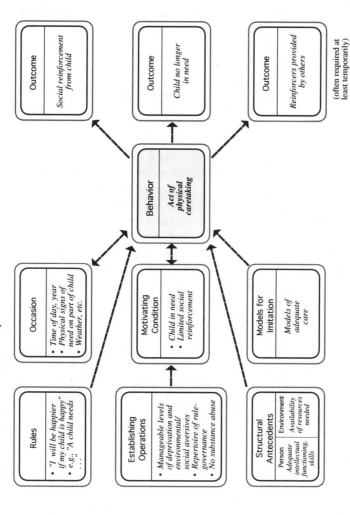

Rules
- "I will be happier if my child is happy"
- e.g., "A child needs . . ."

Occasion
- Time of day, year
- Physical signs of need on part of child
- Weather, etc.

Outcome
Social reinforcement from child

Establishing Operations
- Manageable levels of deprivation and environmental/social aversives
- Repertoire of rule-governance
- No substance abuse

Motivating Condition
- Child in need
- Limited social reinforcement

Behavior
Act of physical caretaking

Outcome
Child no longer in need

Structural Antecedents

Person	Environment
Adequate intellectual functioning, skills	Availability of resources needed

Models for Imitation
Models of adequate care

Outcome
Reinforcers provided by others

(often required at least temporarily)

Mattaini, M.A., McGowan, B.G., & Williams, G. (1996). Child maltreatment. In M.A. Mattaini & B.A. Thyer (eds.), Finding solutions to social problems: Behavioral strategies for change (pp. 223–266). Washington, DC: American Psychological Association. Copyright © 1996 by the American Psychological Association. Reprinted with permission.

the natural network, are gradually faded. (Of course, the necessary resources—structural antecedents—like transportation also need to be present).

Perhaps the most challenging cases, and those that experienced child welfare workers often find the most personally difficult, are cases of neglect in which the child's needs are not motivating, or in which the child's well-being and happiness do not seem to be valued. Such cases of neglect appear to involve a long-term pattern of nonresponsiveness to the child (Bousha & Twentyman, 1984). However frustrating it can be for the social worker, this pattern is not the result of an active choice on the part of the parent. Severely deprived parents who experience high levels of aversives may be deeply depressed due to extinction and punishment. In such depression, often nothing is experienced as effectively motivating or reinforcing (Dougher & Hackbert, 1994). Severe poverty, battering, lack of personal nurturing as a child and currently, and many other forms of deprivation, isolation, and threat can contribute to such depression, and to hopelessness. Social isolation and insularity reduce the effectiveness of parent education as well (see chapter 7). Many neglecting parents may have significant social skills deficits which contribute to their social isolation (Polansky, Gaudin, Ammons, & Davis, 1985), which in turn may foster depression. Substance abuse is another complicating factor which can interfere in several ways. The immediate deprivation associated with withdrawal and craving, and the immediate relief associated with substance use, literally compete with the reinforcement of meeting the child's needs which may be experienced as less urgent (the matching law explains mathematically how this can happen; Mattaini, 1991). Substance-abusing lifestyles may result in the parent's spending less time with the child and may involve contact with other models of poor parenting. At the same time, substance abuse also commonly produces both hopelessness and self-punishment (resulting from guilt), which can further generate depression. It is easy, from this perspective, to see why some cases of neglect can be very difficult to address.

Many parents find the child's learning and happiness reinforcing; this is not automatic for everyone, however. When it is not the case, theory suggests several possibilities for intervention. The social worker can act as a bridge, by prompting and reinforcing the parent to pay attention to the child's behavior. In many cases, once this happens, the parent begins to enjoy the child more, and the child, and the child's happiness, become potentiated as reinforcers. In the few cases where this is not sufficient, the child needs to be paired with other sources of reinforcement that are already valued, for example, attention from a respected family member, social worker, or parent educator, so that the child becomes a conditioned reinforcer. This may sound coldly clinical, but is actually the way we all gradually learn to value others. Even in such cases, the social worker should operate from a shared power stance, in which everything is handled honestly, and the parent has a strong voice in determining whether, and how, to proceed. The safety, development and happiness of their children are valued by most parents, even those who are neglecting; skills and experiences required to provide adequate care, however, are often lacking.

Child Sexual Abuse

Child sexual abuse is a specialized field. The treatment of perpetrators of sexual abuse, victims and survivors of sexual abuse, and members of the wider family and community affected by the abuse requires both specialized knowledge and the support of multiple community systems including child protection, the courts, and treatment resources (Maletzky, 1991, 1998; Ross, 1996; Salter, 1988). Although the sexual abuse of a child is often horrifying and seems inexplicable, and many questions remain about how such patterns develop, the basic behavioral dynamics involved are becoming clearer (Maletsky, 1998). Early conditioning may well be involved, and models and experience of being abused oneself are common, although many perpetrators have not themselves been sexually abused. Summarizing recent work, Maletsky (1998) indicates that, "[L]ack of parental care, physical punishment, and frequent or aggressive sexual activity within the family may all predispose children to begin sexual offending," supporting social learning models for the development of the pattern.

The major issue in sexual abuse is that sexual behavior (which is naturally reinforcing) occurs on inappropriate occasions—with a person who is developmentally unprepared and therefore likely to be damaged by the experience, and who is also not able to give genuine consent. Some perpetrators find more-appropriate partners too threatening and anxiety provoking. In some cases, there is a strong sexual attraction to inappropriate partners, and in other cases, there is probably an element of coercive power and control present (as in battering and rape). In other words, in some cases there is a substantial sexual component, whereas in others the primary function of the behavior may be coercive aggression. Experience suggests that the risk of relapse in sexual abuse is substantial, which is not surprising given that the acts involved generally remain reinforcing for the perpetrator.

Because the behavioral dynamics involved in sexual abuse are quite different from those in other forms of abuse and neglect, best practices for intervention look quite different from those for other forms of child maltreatment. They will be discussed in a final section of this chapter.

KNOWN ELEMENTS OF EFFECTIVE INTERVENTION

In a review of the effectiveness of family preservation services, Fraser, Nelson, and Rivard (1997) identified a number of critical factors that are relevant to family-centered work with child maltreatment, particularly physical abuse and neglect: "[A] set of core service elements appears to characterize innovative family-based services in child welfare, juvenile justice, and mental health . . . these appear to be the essential and cross-cutting elements of family preservation programs with promising findings." (p. 144) General practices important to potentially promising outcomes identified in that review included:

- an *in vivo*, action-oriented focus, delivered in home and community
- sharing of power with the family in setting service goals and in case planning
- 24-hour crisis availability
- an emphasis on skills building
- availability of services to de-escalate family conflict
- provision of "collateral" and "concrete" services.

Fraser and his colleagues also found that it is generally very difficult to provide innovative services with integrity in larger systems, because "Child welfare systems have enormous inertia and appear capable of absorbing much innovation without substantive change" (Fraser, Nelson, & Rivard, 1997, p. 148). The general findings of the study also suggested that family-based services may be less effective for families with younger children (where parent behavior is typically the primary focus) than for families where older children's behavior is a primary concern. Those authors and many others suggest that work with families in which the major issue is neglect may be tougher. The evidence is generally impressionistic because most outcome studies do not differentiate abuse cases from those where neglect is the main issue, but the impression is widely accepted. As discussed earlier in this chapter, many of the dynamics of the two patterns are different.

The core elements of effective intervention listed by Fraser, Nelson and Rivard (1997) are consistent with the ecobehavioral model of practice with families. The need for working with collaterals and for dealing with concrete issues is consistent with the principles elaborated in chapter 3 and throughout this book. It is a mistake to view this work as separate from (and it is certainly not less professional than) work with the clients themselves. (Recall that working with the family to improve its members' reality is the core purpose of ecobehavioral practice.) The Fraser review's emphasis on skill building (chapters 5 and 7) and work in the family's natural environment (and in their natural time) is also consistent with discussions in earlier chapters.

The sharing of power (which produces empowerment) consistently emerges as central to effective services in child welfare and is consistent with the "Family Support Principles" of the National Association of Social Workers as cited in Zlotnick (1997), as well as other empirically grounded literature (Mattaini & Lowery, under review). To share power, however, social workers must accept that doing so is important, must know how to do so, and must have support from their agencies (Lowery & Mattaini, in press). Each of these is a challenge.

Social workers must begin by valuing natural parents, foster parents, other members of the natural and formed networks, and the child enough to respect their voices and believe that they have something to contribute. Being human, social workers may find it hard to accept the fact that even abusive parents have often done the best they can, given their available repertoires and resources. A single mother lost in substance abuse and depression who neglects her child is not a sympathetic figure; understanding that neither substance abuse nor depression is a condition she has freely chosen is a step toward respecting the person while working with her to address the problems. Some people have been biologically and experientially lucky enough to have a great deal of control over the factors that shape their behavior, but others have not. Only if each individual involved in the case is respected, and only if the strong voices of others are not threatening to the social worker's sense of self, can he or she embrace the sharing of power.

If genuinely willing to share power, the social worker can enact and encourage a number of practices consistent with this process (Lowery & Mattaini, in press; Mattaini & Lowery, under review), including:

- *Recognizing talents and gifts.* Behavioral social workers have discovered that there is always something to recognize—to reinforce—in people's actions, and that recognition is a process that tends toward reciprocation and further positive action.
- *Authentic dialogue and receptive listening.* Honest dialogue among all actors in the case, consistent with the principles discussed in chapter 2 for empathic, respectful communication, is more likely to identify contingencies important to achieving a positive outcome in the case.
- *Relationship.* Engaging the client in a respectful and reinforcing relationship is core to all ecobehavioral practice (see chapter 2), but this can be particularly difficult in cases involving child welfare where the client's behavior may challenge the worker's own values.

- **Knowing the community.** Familiarity with the resources and obstacles present in the community is clearly important to help client families to enhance overall environmental exchanges (chapter 3) and requires an active effort on the part of the worker.
- **Room for expanding roles.** It is common for the social worker to find the "expert" role reinforcing, and to hold onto the apparent power that tight control of information, for example, offers. In genuinely sharing power, however, the social worker lets go of that dominance hierarchy and operates from a stance in which every actor participates in the same equivalence relation—essential participant ≈ valuable observer of contingencies ≈ contributor to outcome—rather than a we/they dichotomy. As a result, the roles of foster parents, children, biological parents, paraprofessionals, volunteers, and others in a case may expand depending on the contributions that they are prepared to make.
- **Evaluation methods emphasizing inclusion.** In cases characterized by shared power, evaluation is not seen as exclusively a professional product, but is instead viewed as a shared process, to which everyone contributes from his or her own perspective. Clients, for example, should have opportunities to read and comment on the materials prepared by the social worker, and to contribute their own materials to reports for outside systems like the courts.
- **Shared information.** One of the easiest ways to determine the level of shared power in an organization is to look at the extent to which information is shared. Do social workers and clients have access to budget information, for example? Does each important stakeholder in a case have access to the case record? Or is information tightly and competitively held to preserve each actor's own relative position of advantage or privilege?

While individual social workers can to some extent act independently from a shared power stance, the sharing of power can really be thoroughly operationalized only within an organizational culture of empowerment, which can only be the co-creation of multiple actors (Lowery & Mattaini, in press). Constructing an empowerment culture requires, first, identifying important classes of scenes that operationalize the sharing of power. Such scenes might include ones in which (1) social worker, foster parent, and biological parent dialogue about ways to best meet the developmental needs of a child or (2) groups of foster parents meet both to teach each other and to identify together the multiple ways that foster parents can contribute to positive case outcomes. Once such desirable scenes are identified, groups of organizational actors need to identify and construct the networks of practices required at many levels and among many clusters of actors (for example, professionals, foster parents, maintenance staff, and administrators) that will support the desired scenes.

The co-construction of such empowerment cultures may sound overly idealistic, particularly in systems like child welfare and substance abuse treatment, which are often rooted in the inertia mentioned earlier. Where to begin? As it turns out, there is a body of literature that can guide this process (Axelrod, 1984; Nowak, May & Sigmund, 1995). The literature indicates that a small cell of participants who authentically reinforce each other's efforts, and those of others that are at least partially consistent with shared power, can be resilient and begin a "contagious" process that reverberates through a larger field. The organizational change literature can also be helpful in spelling out steps involved in the gradual construction of change from the bottom up (Frey, 1990; Hanson, 1998). Note that only strategies that are consistent with the honesty involved in shared power, however, are likely to contribute to the construction of empowerment cultures; a culture of shared power cannot emerge from coercive or covert processes.

BEST PRACTICES

Social workers have learned a good deal about approaches for intervening in child maltreatment. In a review a decade ago, Howing, Wodarski, Gaudin, & Kurtz (1989) indicated that behavioral group interventions for parent and child were valuable in all forms of maltreatment and emphasized the need for attention to other support services (homemakers, respite care, etc.). The research at that point indicated that extended services, lasting for 6- to 18-month periods, were often required. Recent evidence indicates that while brief intensive services may be adequate for work with families with older children (particularly when child behavior is a primary focus), short term family preservation services (which often last only a few weeks) in cases where parenting of young children is the issue may not be adequate (Fraser, Nelson, & Rivard, 1997).

These findings are not particularly surprising if one refers back to the analyses of the dynamics of abuse presented earlier. Addressing many of the environmental issues involved may require substantial commitment, and some of the behavioral deficits present require learning and stabilizing quite complex repertoires. There is often no fast and easy way to deal with such challenges. There are, however, a number of interventive strategies that can be of use if carefully tailored to the case, including parent education, reductions in insularity, multisystemic interventions, and carefully individualized behavioral interventions (as in Project 12-Ways, discussed later in this chapter). All need to be implemented within a context of shared power and empowerment. Researchers and theoreticians from many perspectives—including scientific research, traditional Native American philosophies, and practice wisdom—consistently identify the sharing of power as essential to adequate outcomes (see, for example, Fraser, Nelson, & Rivard, 1997; Lowery and Mattaini, in press; Minuchin, 1995; Webster-Stratton, 1997; Zlotnick, 1997).

Less data are available regarding the treatment of child victims/survivors themselves. Generally, children are treated as part of the family system when it remains intact. Other treatments that seem to be useful include behavior therapy for specific problems, specialized day care, and groups of many kinds (Howing, Wodarski, Gaudin, & Kurtz, 1989). Children who remain at home, or are placed in foster care sometimes receive supportive treatment of various kinds to help them deal with trauma and separation. Groups may be particularly helpful in normalizing the experiences of children and youth. It may be easier for them to discuss some of these issues with peer support, and there is probably value in hearing others sort out their experiences. Child and adolescent victims of sexual abuse require special interventive strategies. Only limited data are available to guide those interventions, but some tentative recommendations are included in the final section of this chapter.

Parent Education

Parent education is a potentially powerful interventive strategy, and also one that can be misused. In some places, parents in every confirmed case of abuse and neglect are referred to generic parenting classes, regardless of case specifics or the particular repertoires at issue in the family. Although such classes, if well done, can without a doubt be useful to many parents, more is commonly needed. In the case of child abuse, learning alternative ways to deal with challenging child behaviors is often central, and parent education potentially can help in such cases. Either individual (Mattaini, McGowan, & Williams, 1996) or group parent education (Cohn & Daro, 1987) may be of value. There is substantial evidence however that, to be effective, parent education in cases of child abuse requires specific in-home coaching to transfer skills learned in parent education to naturally occurring situations in the home (Goldstein, Keller, & Erné, 1985). For example, four transfer-enhancing strategies proved necessary in Goldstein et al.'s parenting groups:

1. Overlearning (the parent practices until achieving "fluency"—a level of almost automatic mastery)
2. Situational variability (the parent practices applying the skills in the group with multiple partners and in various types of behavioral episodes)

3. Identical elements (skills learned in group are practiced at home with coaches in exactly the same way they were practiced in the group), and
4. Programmed reinforcement (parenting coaches who went into the home recognized the performance of parents when they use the new skills, rather than simply expecting this).

Parent education conducted in the home, of course, avoids the need for such strategies, but does not offer the mutual support that group parent education can. There clearly are advantages to each.

The parent education provided needs to target changes that will be meaningful for the particular case. Some children are more challenging than others as a result of temperament (Thomas & Chess, 1977) or developmental problems like autism or mental retardation (see, for example, Maurice, 1993). One common goal of parent education is to work with parents to improve the child's behavior so that the behavior becomes less challenging to deal with. If the child learns more acceptable ways of accessing reinforcers he or she values, the child is more likely to function as a reinforcer, and less likely as an aversive, for the parent (see discussion and single-case study in Mattaini, McGowan, & Williams, 1996).

In many cases of child abuse, central repertoires to emphasize include using reinforcement, ignoring, and time-out as alternatives to the current ways of handling child behavior. When environmental factors are contributing to the problems, other repertoires including assertiveness (Rakos, 1991) and the learning of new ways to access resources can be important, and families report that participation in parent training groups can help by providing both models and concrete information about community services and resources (Brunk, Henggeler, & Whelan, 1987). Parenting groups of many kinds, of course, can also affect the level of social isolation parents experience; this dimension is discussed later in this chapter.

As is clear from Figures 9-1 and 9-2, simple parenting skills, however, are not the only repertoires that may need to be a focus of parent education. Wolfe's work (1991) is some of the most important here. Not only are skills for behavior management and communication critical; in many cases skills involving increasing parental sensitivity, responsiveness, and prosocial involvement are required (particularly in some cases of neglect). These repertoires are discussed in chapter 7; the reader is also referred to Wolfe's (1991) excellent book for further detail. Other skills that may be useful include anger management (Mattaini, 1997; Wolfe, 1991), and advocacy skills (chapter 7). The most crucial point is that the parent education provided be responsive to the specific needs of the case. If the case involves a very challenging child and a parent with few child management skills, for example, education in child management skills (often along with work with the child) may be the primary requirement. In contrast, if the case involves a parent who is generally unresponsive and inattentive to the child, sensitivity and involvement repertoires need to receive more attention.

Simply teaching parenting skills, even quite subtle ones, is sometimes not enough, however. In cases of poor, insular parents who lack social support, the likelihood of success through parent education alone is very low (Dumas & Wahler, 1983; Webster-Stratton, 1997). Assistance in obtaining tangible resources, when this is possible, is certainly a social worker's responsibility. There are also ways to expand social supports, and doing so is often a crucial part of state-of-the-art practice.

Reducing Insularity and Building Social Support

A lack of social support, and the resulting insularity, are consistently identified as important antecedents of both neglect and abuse. As discussed in chapter 7, child rearing is not a one-person job; rather it requires a community effort. Involvement with family support programs (see chapters 3 and 7) can be preventive of child maltreatment, and involvement in parenting groups can clearly be a source of such support (Brunk, Henggeler, & Whelan, 1987), particularly when the goals of the group specifically include building such support. For example, the most recent versions of Webster-Stratton's (1997) parenting program incorporate training in social and communication skills, and in reaching out for support. That model also emphasizes training in natural social settings where support developed during the group sessions can be maintained. A good deal is known about building social and communication skills (see chapter 5 and Mattaini, 1997), which can be critical to increasing social connections. Individuals in especially trying circumstances probably need to have particularly strong skills to make and keep friends in the midst of the other challenges they face.

A number of specific strategies for providing social support are also included in Wolfe's (1991) program. Group activities for families are offered twice a week; the focus of these activities is not educational or treatment oriented, but rather is on friendship and recreation. These gatherings include discussion and activities for parents (primarily single mothers), as well as nursery services for children. A further support that can be crucial to a good outcome is the availability of adequate respite services. In Wolfe's program, respite is not only used as a safety valve for times when the parent is becoming frustrated and may be at risk for abuse; rather it is structured to be accessible so that the parent can pursue other positive and social activities while providing responsible child care. Staff of the respite program are trained to observe and help with parenting, as well, thus providing another resource for the isolated parent.

Another potentially useful approach to building social support may be multifamily group therapy (MFGT), where parents and children from multiple families are brought together to construct more effective family repertoires. Meezan & O'Keefe (1998) describe an MFGT program in Los Angeles County that targeted increasing social support, increasing parent-to-child nurturing behaviors, improving child behavior, and enhancing children's social competence. The program also included a significant focus on case management. The outcomes were better than those of traditional office-based family therapy. The changes achieved were modest, however. Looking closely at the program, this is not surprising, for several reasons:

- The services provided were not as intensive as those that appear optimal.
- There is a clear and problematic distinction between "treatment" and "case management" (which was probably underemphasized).
- Neither the experimental nor the family therapy intervention was home based.
- The "themes" around which the program was organized did not address some of the core variables identified above.

At the same time, the data do indicate that multifamily groups are helpful in building social support and could therefore at least be a useful component of a larger program. If their design were enhanced to be consistent with the criteria discussed above, they may prove to be an effective primary modality.

Despite their power, groups are not always available when a social worker is working with an insular parent. In those cases, the worker and client may need to work together to develop a realistic, individualized plan for building positive connections with others in the community (see "Parenting and the Community" in chapter 7). This requires the development of an extensive menu of possible activities that permit the parent to be among, and—to a greater or lesser extent—involved with other adults who can provide some measure of positive social exchange. While some of the alternatives identified should be independent of the child (child care obstacles may also require creative problem solving), some can simply put the parent in the company of other parents with the children. The first cluster of activities could include work, volunteer activities, church involvement, and recreation programs sponsored by local governments or school districts. For one client where this was not problematic, going to a bar with cousins proved useful. Possibilities of the second type range from simply going to a playground at about the same time regularly (increasing the probability of being in contact with the same people more often), to arranging reduced fees (or fees spread over time) for mother-child exercise programs. In some areas, getting a dog increases opportunities for contact while out walking the dog. There is enormous room for creativity, and much is often required; it is common that at first, few if any simple possibilities for increasing reinforcing social contact seem obvious.

Multisystemic Interventions

Multisystemic treatment (MST) is the state of the art for work with families of antisocial children and youth, as discussed in chapter 8. There is evidence that similar approaches may be useful in reducing child maltreatment as well. Brunk, Henggeler & Whelan (1987) found that both behavioral parent training and MST were effective in several ways with parents at risk for child maltreatment, but found that the MST condition produced more desired change in parent-child interaction. Large-scale extensions and replications of this approach are currently underway (Henggeler, Schoenwald, Borduin, Rowland, & Cunningham, 1998), including one testing the combination of the community reinforcement approach, the state of the art in substance abuse treatment described in the next chapter, with MST for families characterized by both child maltreatment and substance abuse. Given the strong empirical support for each component of that package and its consistency with the analyses presented earlier in this chapter, this approach should clearly be regarded as promising.

Intensive family preservation-type services, as discussed earlier, have shown mixed results (Fraser, Nelson, & Rivard, 1997). There is apparently considerable utility for such approaches with families where children are being reunited with the family after an out-of-home placement (Fraser, Walton, Lewis, Pecora, & Walton, 1996). In other cases, two factors may contribute to the uncertain results. In the larger studies, there appeared to be serious problems in implementing the intervention with integrity. This should not be seen as a research artifact; rather, it suggests that making major shifts in large child welfare systems is very difficult. This argues for smaller programs, in which adequate supervision and programmatic fidelity can be ensured. Secondly, given the analyses presented earlier, while families facing a short term crisis probably benefit from brief periods of intervention of a few weeks (typical of intensive family preservation services), many clearly require longer-term involvement to address the myriad of antecedent-consequence matrices and skills deficits from which child maltreatment emerges. This is particularly true in many cases of child neglect. Theoretical analysis suggests that multisystemic interventions that incorporate both the key components of MST (chapter 8, Figure 8-3) and the core service elements identified by Fraser, Nelson, & Rivard (see above, "Known Elements of Effective Intervention"), and that are provided over an adequate period of time, have substantial potential. In fact, Project 12-Ways, an intensive program based at Southern Illinois University at Carbondale, has been operating a demonstrably effective program that meets many of those criteria for the past 20 years.

Project 12-Ways

Project 12-Ways is a child abuse and neglect intervention project with a 20-year history of success; it has been successfully replicated and is extensively documented. It clearly needs to be viewed as the current state of the art. Developed originally by John Lutzker and his colleagues, and maintained and extended by Brandon Greene and colleagues, the approach is designed to have high ecological validity—the term "ecobehavioral" originated with this program. As Lutzker (1997) indicates: "treatment strategies need to be developed that produce naturally maintaining contingencies from the environment (Stokes & Baer, 1977). The very behaviors that are taught need to be practical for the individual and the society, or there are not likely to be natural maintaining contingencies . . . to produce lasting behavior change, we must apply procedures that are easy to use and that set the occasion for adaptive behavior, thus preventing challenging behaviors" (p. 243).

Project 12-Ways uses direct teaching approaches to construct a rich array of needed repertoires. For example, if a child is removed from the home due to inadequate nutrition, the mother is taught to plan, shop for, and prepare adequate meals. If the mother is illiterate, this can be done by using color-coded cards on which food is pictured: planning a nutritious meal involves putting the right number of food cards, color-coded for the four food groups, into envelopes on a planning board; a shopping "list" may consist of a looseleaf binder showing pictures of the same foods. If the physical environment in the home is an issue, an audiotape can be used to help a parent move about the house identifying and correcting hazardous conditions. Caring for the health of the child is often a repertoire of concern; the program therefore worked with physicians to identify 13 core healthcare skills for parents, and has developed modeling and role-play procedures to teach those skills. A procedure called *planned activities training* or PAT has been developed in which at-risk parents learn to structure activities (for example at the grocery store) in ways that keep the child occupied and learning, an arrangement that simultaneously precludes many possible problem behaviors. All Project 12-Ways procedures are carefully spelled out; clear records are kept, and substantial attention is paid to constructing behaviors that will produce naturally reinforcing consequences. For example, demonstrating enhanced skills often produces more time with the child when the child is in foster care, a procedure that is effective in many (but not all) cases.

Greene, Norman, Searle, Daniels, and Lubeck (1995) describe two cases that provide realistic examples of the utility and limitations of the Project 12-Ways approach. In the first case, the 22-year old mother—whose IQ was just above the cutoff for a diagnosis of retardation, and whose history included having been abused, extended placement in foster care, and special education—lost her newborn son to foster care due to his "failure to thrive." Assessment indicated that she lacked many of the necessary skills to adequately care for the child. A list of skill deficits (including diapering, stimulation, bathing, temperature taking, feeding, eliminating home hazards, illness recognition, responsive play, planned ignoring for negative behavior, and a number of others) was developed, and those skills were systematically taught to her over the course of nearly two years, near the end of which period the child was returned to her full time. Primary active consequences included program staff approval and additional time with her child. The results were consistently positive, with booster sessions required for only a small number of areas (in which they were consistently effective). Monitoring indicated no further need for intervention or supervision over several years of follow-up. This case is telling for several reasons. In part, it was successful due to precision in identifying and teaching the skills that were needed. The mother also had a good deal of social support, including strong relationships with her own long-term foster parents and others, so that she had places to turn for help. The importance of networks of parenting resources, rather than single isolated individuals, cannot be overstated (see chapter 7 and Lowery, 1998).

The second Project 12-Ways case reported in Greene, Norman, Searle, Daniels, and Lubeck (1995) did not have as positive an outcome, which is not surprising given the case specifics. The family involved included a violent male partner of the mother, and was very insular. The children had already become entrenched in foster care. The mother also experienced severe depression. Many of the antecedent factors identified as increasing risk were present in this case. The presence of the children also did not appear to be as reinforcing for the mother and her partner as in the previous case, which complicated the work substantially. While its description suggests a number of other possible avenues for intervention, the case was closed due to lack of progress and threats of further violence. There clearly must be a limit to such efforts, since the lack of a permanent home situation for children over a long period can be very damaging.

Intervention in Sexual Abuse

A great deal has been learned about the dynamics of child sexual abuse in recent years, and some data on intervention are also available. This material can only be summarized here; the treatment of families where sexual abuse is present requires extensive familiarity with the available information, and the social worker specializing in work with such cases has the responsibility to become well grounded in the data. The emphasis in this chapter is on intrafamilial sexual abuse, in which the family itself is usually severely damaged. At one time, traditional family therapy was commonly used in cases of incest and sexual abuse: this is no longer generally seen as appropriate in most cases, since it may not convey a strong enough message of protection to the child, nor a strong enough message of responsibility to the perpetrator. The most common arrangement at this point is to begin with separate individual or group treatment for perpetrators and victims/survivors, and in some cases for the nonoffending spouse or partner (usually the mother). Subsequently dyadic work with the survivor and the mother, and with the couple if they are staying together, may be useful. Finally, in cases where families decide to stay together, joint work with all parties is usually indicated.

Intervention with Victims/Survivors

Surprisingly little research has been conducted to guide intervention with the child victim of sexual abuse. General treatment for trauma and its emotional sequelae is usually recommended—specific emphasis is given to perceptions of safety, the expression of feelings, increasing a sense of personal empowerment, education about sexual offenses, sex education, assertiveness and communication skills, and dealing with issues of guilt, trust and ambivalence associated with the events in the family (Salter, 1988). Many victims receive mixed or critical messages from family and other significant figures (particularly if the perpetrator is jailed or the abuse becomes publicly known) and may themselves feel enormous responsibility for the events that have occurred, and for their effects on all members of the family.

The first and most important consideration in work with victims is to ensure their safety, which ordinarily requires court involvement to remove the offender from the home until safety can be ensured. Group work is often recommended to help the child move along the journey from victim to survivor, particularly for older children and adolescents (Howing, Wodarski, Gaudin, & Kurtz, 1989; Salter, 1988): it may help the victim to feel less alone with the her struggles, and it may be easier to share feelings with peers than with adults. If the perpetrator is eventually to return to the home, the victim needs to feel certain of her safety through family work. At some point, it is possible to move to family healing (Ross, 1996), but only when the perpetrator has accepted full responsibility, and safety has been ensured.

Intervention with the Nonoffending Parent

It was once believed that the nonoffending partner (I will use the term, "spouse" here for simplicity) universally "colluded" in or even orchestrated sexual abuse. It is now clear that this is seldom the case, and that mothers usually believe their children and move to protect them when sexual abuse is exposed (Birns & Meyer, 1993; Corcoran, 1998; Faller, 1988; Lovett, 1995; Sirles, 1989). Sexual abuse and its sequelae for the family can create enormous emotional strain, however, and support and education about sexual abuse can be quite helpful for the spouse. Many mothers are interested in ways that they can contribute to healing for the victim; and in cases where the family will eventually reunite, the spouse has a critical role to play in ensuring safety, reinforcing the responsibility of the perpetrator, and ultimately in healing. Group support is often suggested for spouses; while there is little specific data here, this strategy is consistent with other situations in which support groups have proven empowering, as with battered women (Tutty, Bidgood, & Rothery, 1993).

Intevention with the Offender

Recent years have seen considerable advances in the treatment of offenders (Maletsky, 1998; Reid, 1997). While it is too early to suggest that optimal approaches have yet been developed, "a consensus has arisen that cognitive-behavioral therapies form the standard against which other approaches must be judged" (Maletsky, 1998, p. 483). Such treatment usually includes some form of respondent conditioning; the techniques used have evolved considerably from reliance on physical aversives like electric shock to covert sensitization arrangements which begin with relaxation and imagery that moves from deviant sexual arousal, to an aversive consequence, to a scene of escape by actively turning away from the deviant situation. Several variations of this approach are used with different types of cases, including the use of videotaped scenarios that may be useful in building empathy for the victim or disgust for the behavior.

Responses to these aversive procedures are often sluggish, and it is clear that various positive strategies need to be used in addition to, or in some cases in lieu of, aversives. These include the use of coping imagery, relapse prevention techniques (identifying and preparing coping strategies for high-risk situations), self-reinforcement for progress, and various forms of social skills training. One clearly crucial area is shifting attributions and self-talk, so cognitive strategies are essential. According to Maletsky (1998), among common themes that need to be examined are misattributions of blame, minimizing or denying sexual intent, debasing the victim, minimizing consequences, deflecting censure, and justifications. Group work may be particularly useful in modeling changes in self-talk in these areas. Empathy training, relying on role playing and videotapes, or actual contact with victims, also appears to be useful.

If the perpetrator will be returning to the family, couples work will clearly be critical (see chapter 6). Finally, work needs to occur in which the offender faces the victim, listens to her experiences, expresses his remorse, and commits to her safety. The entire family has been affected, and therefore is in need of healing. As some cultural traditions clearly recognize, the web of damage, and the need for healing, can also extend far beyond the family.

Family and Community Healing

As noted at several points in the preceding discussions, child maltreatment has effects that resonate through the family, the extended family, and potentially far into the community network. If a child is taken from his mother, or a man is arrested for sexually abusing his teenage stepdaughter, the event affects every member of the family, their friends, those who work with them, and others who simply hear about it. A child in school misses her classmate; a grandson is arrested. Sexual abuse can be particularly damaging in this way. Healing may be needed throughout this extended web of relationships because the events that occurred are deeply aversive and are accompanied by all of the side-effects of aversives: reductions in trust, efforts to escape, counteraggression, depression (Sidman, 1989). "Healing" might be viewed ecobehaviorally as the construction of stable (reliable, trustworthy, predictable) social networks that (1) shape and maintain positive practices including respect, recognition, caring, and empathy; (2) potentiate the well-being of others as a deeply valued reinforcer; and (3) minimize reliance on punishment, instead focusing on acting to take responsibility for and to repair the damage one has done.

Perhaps the most promising emerging approaches for moving in those directions are those being developed by Canadian First Nations peoples

(Ross, 1996). This is not surprising, of course, since many indigenous cultures have traditionally valued the good of the collective to a substantially higher degree than do European American cultures and have therefore learned how to nurture and heal human networks. The central dynamic is the use of healing circles, in which others who have both been victims and perpetrators of abuse speak honestly ("from the heart") to perpetrators and victims, and where all participating recognize that punishment is not needed as much as teaching and healing. That healing often includes a strong element of making things right, of restitution, to repair damage done to the collective web and contribute to its strengthening. Early results of these strategies appear promising. The approaches and data are consistent with the solid empirical results found in using similar strategies in situations of juvenile crime (see chapter 8). Social work is not primarily about work with individuals; even work with families cannot be amputated from the larger community. And so, it is likely that "best practices" for work with child maltreatment in the future will increasingly emphasize family and community healing. The power of the group is bound to play a major part in this work.

REFERENCES

Axelrod, R. (1984). *The evolution of cooperation*. New York: Basic Books.
Birns, G., & Meyer, S-L. (1993). Mothers' role in incest: Dysfunctional women or dysfunctional theories? *Journal of Child Sexual Abuse, 2,* 127–135.
Bousha, D. M., & Twentyman, C. T. (1984). Mother-child interactional style in abuse, neglect, and control groups: Naturalistic observations in the home. *Journal of Abnormal Psychology, 93,* 106–114.
Brunk, M., Henggeler, S. W., & Whelan, J. P. (1987). Comparison of multisystemic therapy and parent training in the brief treatment of child abuse and neglect. *Journal of Consulting and Clinical Psychology, 55,* 171–178.
Cohn, A. H., & Daro, D. (1987). Is treatment too late? What ten years of evaluative research tell us. *Child Abuse and Neglect, 11,* 433–442.
Corcoran, J. (1998). In defense of mothers of sexual abuse victims. *Families in Society, 79,* 358–369.
Dougher, M. J., & Hackbert, L. (1994). A behavior-analytic account of depression and a case report using acceptance-based procedures. *The Behavior Analyst, 17,* 321–334.
Dumas, J. E., & Wahler, R. G. (1983). Predictors of treatment outcome in parent training: Mother insularity and socioeconomic disadvantage. *Behavioral Assessment, 5,* 301–313.
Egan, T. (1998, April 16). In Idaho, the poor fear they will go the way of state's

Democrats. *The New York Times.* Retrieved April 16, 1998 from the World Wide Web: http://www.nytimes.com

Faller, K. C. (1988). The myth of the "collusive mother": Variability in the functioning of mothers of victims of intrafamilial sexual abuse. *Journal of Interpersonal Violence, 3,* 190–196.

Fraser, M. W., Nelson, K. E., & Rivard, J. C. (1997). Effectiveness of family preservation services. *Social Work Research, 21,* 138–153.

Frey, G. A. (1990). A framework for promoting organizational change. *Families in Society, 71,* 142–147.

Goldstein, A. P., Keller, H., & Erné, D. (1985). *Changing the abusive parent.* Champaign, IL: Research Press.

Greene, B. F., Norman, K. R., Searle, M. S., Daniels, M., & Lubeck, R. C. (1995). Child abuse and neglect by parents with disabilities: A tale of two families. *Journal of Applied Behavior Analysis, 28,* 417–434.

Hanson, M. (1998). Practice in organizations. In M. A. Mattaini, C. T. Lowery, & C. H. Meyer (Eds.), *The foundations of social work practice: A graduate text* (2nd ed.) (pp. 240–264). Washington, DC: NASW Press.

Henggeler, S. W., Schoenwald, S. K., Borduin, C. M., Rowland, M. D., & Cunningham, P. B. (1998). *Multisystemic treatment of antisocial behavior in children and adolescents.* New York: Guilford Press.

Howing, P. T., Wodarski, J. S., Gaudin, J. M., Jr., & Kurtz, P. D. (1989). Effective interventions to ameliorate the incidence of child maltreatment: The empirical base. *Social Work, 34,* 330–338.

Lovett, B. B. (1995). Child sexual abuse: The female victim's relationship with her nonoffending mother. *Child Abuse and Neglect, 19,* 729–738.

Lowery, C. T. (1998). Social work with families. In M. A. Mattaini, C. T. Lowery, & C. H. Meyer (Eds.), *The foundations of social work practice: A graduate text* (2nd ed.) (pp. 165–187). Washington, DC: NASW Press.

Lowery, C. T. & Mattaini, M. A. (in press). The co-construction of empowerment cultures in child welfare. In W. Shera and L. Wells (Eds.), *International perspectives on empowerment practice.* New York: Columbia University Press.

Lutzker, J. R. (1997). Ecobehavioral approaches in child abuse and developmental disabilities mirroring life. In D. M Baer & E. M. Pinkston (Eds.), *Environment and behavior* (pp. 243–257). Boulder: Westview Press.

Maletsky, B. M. (1991). *Treating the sexual offender.* Newbury Park, CA: Sage.

Maletsky, B. M. (1998). The paraphilias: Research and treatment. In P. E. Nathan & J. M. Gorman (Eds.), *A guide to treatments that work* (pp. 472–500). New York: Oxford.

Mattaini, M. A. (1991). Choosing weapons for the war on "crack": An operant analysis. *Research on Social Work Practice, 1,* 188–213.

Mattaini, M. A. (1997). *Clinical practice with individuals.* Washington, DC: NASW Press.

Mattaini, M. A., McGowan, B. G., & Williams, G. (1996). Child maltreatment. In M. A. Mattaini & B. A. Thyer (Eds.), *Finding solutions to social problems: Behavioral strate-*

gies for change (pp. 223–266). Washington, DC: American Psychological Association.

Mattaini, M. A., & Lowery, C. T. (under review). *The science of sharing power: Native American thought and behavior analysis.*

Maurice, C. (1993). *Let me hear your voice: A family's triumph over autism.* New York: Fawcett Columbine.

Meezan, W., & O'Keefe, M. (1998). Multifamily group therapy: Impact on family functioning and child behavior. *Families in Society, 79,* 32–44.

Minuchin, P. (1995). Foster and natural families: Forming a cooperative network. In L. Combrinck-Graham (Ed.), *Children in families at risk: Maintaining the connections,* (pp. 251–274). New York: Guilford Press.

National Research Council (1993). *Understanding child abuse and neglect* [Report of the Panel on Research on Child Abuse and Neglect]. Washington, DC: National Academy Press.

Nohl, M. Van de K. (1998, September). Great expectations. *Milwaukee Magazine,* 74–85.

Nowak, M. A., May, R. M., & Sigmund, K. (1995). The arithmetics of mutual help. *Scientific American, 272*(6), 76–83.

Polansky, N. A., Gaudin, J. M., Jr., Ammons, P. W., & Davis, K. B. (1985). The psychological ecology of the neglectful mother. *Child Abuse and Neglect, 9,* 265–275.

Rakos, R. F. (1991). *Assertive behavior: Theory, research, and training.* New York: Routledge.

Reid, W. H. (1997). Sexual and Gender Identity Disorders. In W. H. Reid, G. U. Balis, & B. J. Sutton, *The treatment of psychiatric disorders* (3rd ed.) (pp. 293–317). Bristol, PA: Brunner/Mazel.

Ross, R. (1996). *Returning to the teachings: Exploring aboriginal justice.* Toronto: Penguin.

Salter, A. C. (1988). *Treating child sex offenders and victims.* Newbury Park, CA: Sage.

Sidman, M. (1989). *Coercion and its fallout.* Boston: Authors Cooperative.

Sirles, E. A., & Franke, P. J. (1989). Factors influencing mothers' reactions to intrafamily sexual abuse. *Child Abuse and Neglect, 13,* 131–139.

Stokes, T., & Baer, D. M. (1977). An implicit technology of generalization. *Journal of Applied Behavior Analysis, 10,* 349–367.

Thomas, A., & Chess, S. (1977). *Temperament and development.* New York: Brunner/Mazel.

Tutty, L. M., Bidgood, B. A., & Rothery, M. A. (1993). Support groups for battered women: Research on their efficacy. *Journal of Family Violence, 8,* 325–343.

Wang, C-T., & Daro, D. (1998). *Current trends in child abuse reporting and fatalities: The Results of the 1997 Annual Fifty State Survey* [Working paper Number 808]. Chicago, IL: National Committee to Prevent Child Abuse. Retrieved October 4, 1998 from the World Wide Web: http://www.childabuse.org/50data97.html.

Webster-Stratton, C. (1997). From parent training to community building. *Families in Society, 78,* 156–171.

Widom, C. S. (1989). Child abuse, neglect, and adult behavior: Research design and findings on criminality, violence, and child abuse. *American Journal of Orthopsychiatry, 59,* 355–367.

Wolfe, D. A. (1987). *Child abuse: Implications for child development and psychopathology.* Newbury Park, CA: Sage.

Wolfe, D. A. (1991). *Preventing physical and emotional abuse of children.* New York: Guilford Press.

Zlotnick, J. L. (1997). *Preparing the workforce for family-centered practice: Social work education and public human services partnerships.* Alexandria, VA: Council on Social Work Education.

CHAPTER TEN

Substance Abuse and Serious Mental Illness

In addition to the normative challenges that affect most families, like maintaining a positive couple relationship and parenting, some families find themselves facing especially difficult behavioral issues and conditions. For example, a child diagnosed with childhood autism or a teenager who is wasting away from anorexia raises the stakes dramatically for parents; the emergence of psychosis in late adolescence, or substance abuse at any point similarly ratchets up stress for everyone in the family. Interestingly, many of these conditions were once (and occasionally still are) blamed primarily on family processes. For example, autism was seen as the result of very inadequate mothering, anorexia as emerging primarily from dysfunctional family communication and marital struggles, psychosis as shaped by schizophrenogenic mothers, and substance abuse as at least supported—if not caused—by needy codependent spouses or family members. In each of these cases, we now know much more about causation, which seldom lies in the family, and paradoxically, the family turns out to be a—and often the— primary resource for improvement.

Childhood autism clearly is not the result of parenting, but rather is based in neurological dysfunction. We have recently learned that about half of autistic children, if identified early enough, can return to the mainstream early in grade school, and that most of the others can improve substantially if the family and professionals provide intensive services and support of very specific kinds (Lovaas, 1987). Family members, usually parents, are typically the only ones able to provide the advocacy and consistency over years and programs needed to achieve those outcomes (for example, Maurice, 1993).

The family also is often the major resource in work with anorexic patients. Most cases of anorexia probably begin with cognitive distortions usually shaped by the larger society (though family may contribute), but the central problem very quickly shifts to one of physiological imbalance, which then feeds on itself (Pierce & Epling, 1994). The general pattern appears to be as follows: Decreased food intake stimulates physical activity (the result of genetic adaptations that increased survival in hunting and gathering days). Physical activity in turn stimulates the production of beta-endorphin, which further depresses appetite, and also produces a sort of endogenous addiction to which tolerance develops, which spurs even higher activity levels and lower food intake. The family has a central role to play in helping to prompt and support behavior changes for the patient (which are difficult, due to the physiological processes involved). Being able to return and stay at home is often the major reinforcer used in effective programs.

This pattern is repeated over and over again; the family, far from being the cause of the most severe behavioral and psychiatric issues, is usually the major resource on which the client and professionals must rely. No empirical evidence supports the notion that women who are paired with alcoholic men are "codependent" and encourage their partners to continue to drink to meet their own needs, although that explanation is common in the popular literature (Anderson, 1994). Schizophrenia and manic-depressive illness are biologically based, although environmental stresses can certainly exacerbate symptoms under some circumstances. Family members sometimes present as quite emotionally distressed, but it has become clear that rather than family members' emotional problems causing psychosis, the typical pattern is the other way around. The burden associated with watching powerlessly as your loved one slips away despite your best efforts is, of course, deeply affecting.

In this chapter, we will focus on practice with families facing two of the most common issues that social workers in general practice are likely to see: substance abuse and severe mental illness. The purpose of the chapter is not to provide full models for treating substance abuse or psychosis; each of those is a specialized area. Rather, the purpose is to provide tools for use when these cases are identified in general practice settings. For example, given that roughly a quarter of adult Americans have some level of alcohol problem at any time (Sobell & Sobell, 1993), and that this number does not include other drugs, in every practice setting some cases will include drug and alcohol issues.

The material here provides strategies for assisting substance abusers to discover the motivation to change and to take initial steps toward change. In addition, this chapter will summarize strategies for assisting concerned others (COs) to act in ways that maximize the probability that the abuser will seek and make the best use of treatment. When the clinical social worker sees a family struggling with substance abuse, he or she can then pull this book off the shelf to review what we now know may be helpful, and can adapt these strategies to the setting.

Similarly, social workers in almost any setting may work with clients in whose family major mental illness is present. These conditions often place enormous burdens on the family; recent research informs us of approaches for attenuating that burden at least somewhat, while concurrently decreasing the probability of relapse. In mental health settings, social workers need to know how to initiate and maintain such programs. Many other social workers, however, will have occasion to be involved with such families. These professionals should be able to assist families in the short run to cope with current crises, as well as assisting them to connect over the longer run with programs that are consistent with the state of the art. Doing so requires knowing something about current best practices.

This chapter then is meant primarily as a resource for the family-practice social worker who will occasionally work with these issues. It also provides a starting point for those who work in those specialized fields; they will also need to read further and participate in ongoing training to stay current. In every case, as will be seen, the overall approach remains ecobehavioral and emphasizes the sharing of power with client and with family.

SUBSTANCE ABUSE

Every social worker deals with families in which substance abuse is an issue, although the problem is commonly overlooked. Even in cases where the primary intervention is with one family member (the substance abuser or a concerned other), both the problem and the intervention strategy used resonate throughout the family system and often larger networks as well. Substance abuse, therefore, is not only an individual issue.

Motivational Interviewing

As with all of the other issues discussed in this book, intervention in substance abuse involves a collaborative process of shared power; while a substance abuser may experience coercive pressures from outside to take action, the final decision to do so must lie with the person, and the social worker's primary role is support in making that decision as healthy a one as possible. Until the client authentically acknowledges that he or she has concerns about substance use, a healing process cannot begin. The state of the art for assisting a client to consider the options is a strategy called *motivational interviewing*, developed by William R. Miller and his colleagues (Miller & Rollnick, 1991). Research suggests that traditional confrontational approaches are likely to elicit denial—in fact, some of the denial that has often been seen as integral to substance abuse may be iatrogenic, the result of coercive intervention attempts. (Coercion in this area, as in others, is inconsistent with shared power. This is *not*, however, to say that others in the client's social networks should not allow the abuser to experience the consequences of his or her actions, including interpersonal ones like separation and divorce. There are crucial distinctions here that are discussed later in this chapter.)

Motivational interviewing involves a collaborative examination of the client's use of substances, the outcomes, and any concerns that those outcomes may elicit. This strategy, which is consistent with European practice, appears to be quite valuable for helping substance abusers find the motivation to take active steps to address their problems. Motivational interviewing is increasingly used in specialized substance abuse treatment settings, but its greatest potential is probably in general practice settings, including the family service, health, and mental health settings in which many social workers practice. Rollnick and Bell (1991) have developed a set of clinical guidelines for motivational interviewing by nonspecialists in general settings that are outlined below. Before looking at those guidelines, however, it may be helpful to examine the possible place of family, in particular the spouse or primary concerned other (CO), in this process.

Zweben's (1991) research indicates that substance abusers will more likely remain involved in treatment if their primary CO is also engaged in some way. He indicates that the CO can be helpful in two ways: (1) by providing ongoing support for sobriety, and (2) offering an additional perspective on the costs and benefits of substance use in the life of the client. Depending on the quality of the relationship, the CO may play a major part in motivational interviewing sessions (if the relationship is strong and the CO committed to being helpful in sobriety), or a simple "witness" role if those conditions are not present. (It is increasingly common for the clinician to begin by working with the CO to help move the client toward treatment; this strategy is discussed in detail later in this chapter.) Except when the CO is likely to be a serious obstacle, inclusion produces clinical advantages, including better information and powerful support for change in the natural environment.

Motivational interviewing in general practice settings usually occurs in the context of general assessment, where the social worker asks about general areas of concern and gathers data about those areas. If substance abuse is even a possibility, which it certainly can be in many social work cases, in the natural course of the interview the social worker should ask open-ended questions like, "How is your use of alcohol (or drugs) connected here? Can you tell me a bit about that?" Questions like this are not asked to "trick" the client; they are honest inquiries about possible connections that may be important for the client to explore.

Several motivational interviewing approaches are recommended by Rollnick and Bell (1991) for general practice settings. The worker would not ordinarily use all of these with one client or in one interview; rather those that are appropriate to the agency and the client can be creatively adapted. Rollnick and Bell suggest that the social worker:

- In the course of an assessment interview, explore the use of substances in a detailed way, primarily relying on open-ended questions (rather than simply asking whether or not one uses, or has a problem with substances—or, worse yet, not asking at all). Useful questions may include, "Tell me about your use of . . ." or "How does alcohol affect you?" In many settings, this should be a standard section of the intake interview.
- Ask about typical episodes in detail (for example, "So you went to the bar right after work, and had . . . six? . . . drinks. How did it feel to have the first one?").
- Discuss aversive conditions and events the client deals with, and how he or she copes with these. Substance abuse may come up, and can be asked about in such discussions.
- Ask about substance abuse in the context of general questions about health and health-related behavior, and draw out connections.
- Ask about both what is satisfying about substance use (the reinforcers it offers—often called "good things" about use in motivational interviewing) and what is aversive ("less good things"). It is important, as in many other areas, to acknowledge that a behavior may produce multiple consequences, both positive and negative. Discussion of aversive consequences can lead to discussion of concerns.
- Ask about changes in substance use over time.
- Offer information and then ask about its application to the client. For example, the worker might provide basic information about increasing tolerance in a factual way and then ask, "I wonder if that applies to you?"
- Ask about the client's concerns. This is the central strategy toward which all of the others can move discussion. Once the client acknowledges use and some problems related to it, asking, "What concerns do you have about this?" can move the conversation a step closer to commitment to change.

The last strategy (eliciting concerns) is the key in motivational interviewing; the others may be useful for moving in that direction. Once concerns have surfaced, the social worker should ask about next steps: "So, you're concerned about the health risks. . . . What steps would you consider taking next?" This is a challenging moment for both client and social worker; it should not be handled as a confrontation, but rather as a movement toward problem solving. As in all problem solving, typically multiple behavioral options are available, each of which may be associated with multiple positive and negative, short and long term consequences. The "Choices and Consequences" strategy (Mattaini, 1997) for analyzing the multiple short and long term, positive and negative consequences associated with each possible choice may be particularly helpful in elaborating the possibilities. Entering treatment of one kind or another, "sobriety sampling" (a short period during which the substance is not used; Meyers, Dominguez, & Smith, 1996), collecting more information through self-monitoring or by reading, talking about the issue with family or friends, or any number of other possibilities may be considered at this stage.

A comprehensive substance use assessment may be useful if the setting where the client is being seen offers treatment services itself, or if the social worker and client need more information to determine which of the possibilities may be the best match for this client. Further information about conducting such an assessment can be found in Mattaini (1997). One simple tool for screening for alcohol (and probably other drug) problems is the *CAGE* (Mayfield, McLeod, & Hall, 1974), a series of four simple questions: (1) have you ever tried to Cut down on your drinking? (2) have you ever become Angry when someone complained about your drinking? (3) have you ever felt Guilty about your drinking? and (4) have you ever had an Eye-opener—a drink first thing in the morning? (A recent revision [U.S. Pharmaceuticals Group of Pfizer, 1996] substitutes the question "was there ever a day in which you had five or more drinks?" for the last.)

The research suggests that these four simple questions identify most drinking problems (except in cases where the client has reason not to be honest); if one question is answered positively, the possibility of a problem should be explored further, and if more than one question is answered with "yes," a problem of some kind is likely (Mayfield, McLeod, & Hall).

Work with Clients Involved in "Problem Drinking"

One finding from a screening assessment may be that the client is not severely dependent on alcohol, but might be classified as a "problem drinker." The Institute of Medicine (1990) suggests that there are about four times as many problem drinkers, who may constitute about 20 percent of the adult population in the United States, as persons with clear addictions. In recent years, more attention has turned to this group, who can often be treated effectively in nonintensive outpatient programs. In some cases, substance abuse can be caught early, before more serious problems develop (note, however, that the traditional belief that alcohol problems are invariably progressive has not stood up to empirical scrutiny). Much personal and family pain and problems in other life spheres can be prevented if effective intervention with problem drinkers is available.

The *guided self-change approach* is the current state of the art for this work. A comprehensive manual outlining the approach is available (Sobell & Sobell, 1993; Mattaini, 1997, includes a brief summary as well). Since this is an individual approach, it is not considered in detail in this book, but knowing that help in such cases may be available can be extremely valuable information for both the problem drinker and COs. In less severe cases, this approach may be one of the choices suggested during motivational interviewing, and may also be one possibility that emerges from work directly with COs.

Work with Concerned Others

Family members are inevitably involved in the matrix of events in which substance abuse is embedded. Traditional wisdom among some in the field suggests that the person with an addiction needs to be ready before change is possible and that the only realistic option for COs is "loving detachment." The data are now clear, however: COs can often make a difference in the process of moving the abuser toward entering, and participating in, substance abuse treatment. One alternative is some form of "intervention" (Johnson, 1986) in which family members actively confront the abuser and work toward engagement in treatment. These interventions, however, are sometimes not conducted in a way that reserves to the substance abuser a voice in planning or opportunities to contribute to the process. Also many families that receive the training in conducting such interventions do not carry them out; the overall success rate for the procedure in terms of moving the abuser into treatment was 24 percent in one study (Liepman, Nirenberg, & Begin, 1989). Although these results are somewhat disappointing, at least three other active forms of intervention have demonstrated better outcomes. Two of those are summarized, and the third outlined in detail, later in this chapter. Before examining those approaches, however, two clarifications need to be made.

First, the fact that COs can often influence the abuser in a positive fashion in no way suggests that the COs are to blame for the current behavior. Many COs do "enable" addictive behaviors, but the data do not support the notion that this is the result of a disorder called *codependence*. This label is often used to place responsibility for other's problems on women (Anderson,

1994). Enabling behaviors often emerge as means of coping with addictive behaviors and are not reflections of a unique mental disorder. (Addictions, and responses to them, are also deeply rooted in larger sociocultural forces.) Better coping strategies, however, can often be developed, as described below. Contingencies provided by family members can make an enormous difference in people's lives, whether children with diabetes, persons with developmental delays, or those struggling with addictions, but that does not mean that the family is responsible for any of those conditions.

Second, only under certain circumstances do COs have enough control of the relevant contingencies to have an immediate influence on the substance abuser, and only by experimentation can we learn whether this will be true at a particular time, for a particular case. The strategies discussed below can maximize the possibilities, but when they prove inadequate, the client can and probably should be referred to an Alanon group to learn loving detachment and acceptance. Over time, these shifts also change the relationship with the abuser, and when the CO participates in Alanon, it is not uncommon for the abuser to subsequently enter treatment (Dittrich & Trapold, 1984, cited in Meyers, Dominguez, & Smith, 1996).

Three effective programs in which significant others can contribute toward moving the drinker toward treatment demonstrate several points on the continuum from adversarial to shared power, and from the use of coercion to the use of reinforcement. One program, *pressures to change*, is designed to move through several graduated levels of action on the part of the nondrinking partner, at each of which the "pressure" is increased (Barber & Gilbertson, 1996, 1997). While not all of the levels employ adversarial strategies, the very name of the program suggests coercive underpinnings, and in fact the developers experienced substantial resistance from families to the most coercive level of confrontation. There are five levels in this program. The first level involves education about the change process and introduction to the interventive program. The second level involves increasing the rate of activities incompatible with drinking. The third level involves changes in the way the CO responds to drinking episodes. At the fourth level, the focus shifts to examination of direct interactions with the drinker about drinking behavior, through a contracting process. Originally, the fifth level, which most COs failed to implement, was called "confrontation"; in the current program, however, the fifth level of pressure is called "involving others" in which the CO engages help from others in the social network.

In *unilateral family therapy* (Thomas, Santa, Bronson, & Oyserman, 1987; Thomas & Yoshioka, 1989), the CO is also trained in a number of skill areas, culminating in either a "programmed confrontation" in which specific negative consequences of refusing to engage in treatment are clarified, or a "programmed request" in which the significant other and the social worker plan for the way to make a potentially effective request for entering treatment. Interventive activities before that point include enriching the CO's own life, monitoring the abuser's intake, providing increased levels of reinforcers when drinking is not occurring, and discontinuing both punishment and enabling. One limitation is that the strategy has not been tested with cases where violence is seen as a possibility; the final option, *community reinforcement training* (Sisson & Azrin, 1986; Meyer, Dominguez, & Smith, 1996) also addresses this issue directly. Given its wide applicability, this approach will be discussed here in particular detail.

Community Reinforcement Training

Community reinforcement training is further along the shared power continuum than either of the other two approaches for work with COs discussed so far. In this approach, a CO (usually the spouse) learns skills for (1) reducing the risk of physical abuse to herself, (2) encouraging sobriety, (3) encouraging engagement in treatment, and (4) assisting in treatment once the drinking partner enters. In addition, clients learn strategies for minimizing the distress they themselves and other family members experience as a result of the addictive behaviors. COs are offered a range of skills (providing options), and are assisted in developing their own individualized approach. They learn, not how to "confront" their partners, but when and how to effectively suggest treatment while supporting sobriety, in simple, honest and authentic ways. A detailed treatment manual has been developed for this program (Meyer, Dominguez, & Smith, 1996); the material that follows provides a brief outline of this important strategy.

The major goals of community reinforcement training, according to Meyer, Dominguez, & Smith (1996), are:

- To help diminish the CO's pain and anguish associated with his or her relationship to the drinker
- To help the CO learn new strategies to reduce the drinking behavior of the loved one, and ultimately to coax him or her into treatment
- To reduce the risk of violence
- To help heal the relationship between the CO and the loved one through [Community Reinforcement Approach] couples therapy. (p. 263)

Community reinforcement training is offered to COs who wish to continue in the relationship and who want to take an active part in efforts to change the family situation. It is not, therefore, recommended for every case. Some

COs are ready to leave a relationship that they feel is irrevocably broken, and others may feel that they have already done enough to try to resolve the situation. These decisions should absolutely be respected.

Social workers planning to implement this program should examine the original, detailed sources (for example, Meyers, Dominguez, & Smith, 1996; Meyers & Smith, 1995; Sisson & Azrin, 1986) because community reinforcement training and the larger community reinforcement approach to addictions treatment, of which it is one component, are nuanced, highly developed packages. A brief summary of strategies used to reach each of the four goals listed above, however, may provide useful guidance for beginning work with clients who are appropriate for community reinforcement training. While many elements of the strategy may sound familiar, the systematic application of each component relevant to the case is essential to adequate outcomes. Poor treatment integrity, in which only a vague approximation of the most useful approaches may be present, is likely to lead to very weak effectiveness. To ensure interventive integrity, the social worker who is going to implement this approach with a CO should, in concert with the client, develop a written plan for addressing each goal area. For some clients, only a few sessions may be necessary; but the process can be wrenching, and some COs may require several months of contact to support them as they gradually change their interactions with the substance abuser.

Goal #1: Diminishing the Pain and Improving the Personal Experiences of the CO

Several strategies are useful here. First, providing accurate information about addiction, the overall community reinforcement strategy (see below), and the possibility of change can build hope and commitment. Many COs have struggled with the problem largely on their own for a long time; assistance in seeking out social support of both formal and informal kinds can help the CO to access new sources of strength. COs also need to plan, and permit themselves, to self-reinforce for the actions they take as part of this work, since it may be some time before any noticeable change occurs in the abuser's behavior. One common strategy is for the CO to list a number of possible reinforcers that she or he could give her or himself for taking active steps, including buying oneself a small gift, or participating in a valued activity to "give oneself a break." Many people do not think that they need such small tokens of self-recognition, but in experimenting discover that they can be very helpful.

A second major thrust for achieving the first goal is to work toward enriching the personal life and increasing the independence of the CO. The primary consideration is increasing the CO's access to reinforcers that do not depend on the behavior of the abuser. This process begins with developing lists of recreational and social activities that might be reinforcing: those that the CO currently enjoys and could do more of, those that the CO used to enjoy and could re-engage in, those that the CO has always wanted to try but has not yet, and those that even *might* be reinforcing if tried in an experimental way. Meyers, Dominguez, and Smith (1996) suggest that the clinician keep a list of ideas developed by clients to be shared with later clients—offering a rich menu of ideas and opportunities to contribute to positive outcomes for others as well. In addition, many COs have financial and occupational concerns, and working with those individuals to develop job-search plans is often a major contribution to the welfare of the family, which should be seen as an essential aspect of clinical work in these cases. The development of resumes, practicing interview skills, and developing job leads and overall search strategies are major components of this work (see Azrin, Flores, & Kaplan, 1975, and Meyers & Smith, 1996, for more information about job counseling within a community reinforcement paradigm).

Goal #2: Developing New Strategies to Reduce Substance-Using Behavior of the Loved One, and Encourage Treatment

As they examine their exchanges with the substance abuser, most COs find that they rely heavily on the use of unsystematic punishment, provide very few reinforcers for sober behavior, engage more with the abuser when he or she is using than at other times, and protect the abuser from negative consequences of use (often out of concern for the abuser, and sometimes to simplify life for oneself or other family members in the short run). It is easy, from an outside perspective, to see how each of these patterns can evolve, and yet to see that in fact each tends to increase the likelihood of substance abuse. A major focus of community reinforcement training, therefore, is on constructing alternatives to these patterns.

First, it is crucial to give up the use of unsystematic punishment (yelling, tears, the silent treatment) and other "home remedies" like hiding or pouring out liquor that tend to further poison the relationship for everyone without reducing substance use (in fact, such interactions are sometimes used as excuses to use more). Punitive coercion is an ineffective mechanism for encouraging change in relationships. Giving up such efforts, however, requires, first, a clear understanding of one's current actions, and secondly, a clear plan for the way common home situations can be handled differently. Making such plans is often the core of the work done between the CO and the social worker. Some challenges and obstacles require individualized and creative problem solving; this work is not easy, but is possible.

While punishment is generally ineffective, withdrawing reinforcers when the abuser is drinking can be powerful. Two general classes of consequation need to be considered here. The first is planned nonreinforcement, in which positive reinforcers like attention, concern, time together, sexual contact, and so forth are withdrawn when the abuser is using. One spouse discussed by Meyer, Dominguez, and Smith (1996), for example, would go to a movie when his wife came home drunk. The first step in shifting these patterns is a careful examination of the kind of reinforcers the CO may currently be offering the abuser; the second step is deciding on realistic ways to withdraw those. Negative repercussions for such withdrawal are often likely so that realistic plans need to be made in advance, and possible scenarios role-played and problem-solved before the CO may be ready to attempt these shifts at home.

A second class of consequences to examine is negative reinforcers. If the CO deals with problems, including those caused by the abuser, when the abuser is using so the abuser does not have to, substance use may be being maintained partly by negative reinforcement—escape from responsibility, for example. In many cases, the CO actively "enables" the substance use by cleaning up after the abuser, literally (cleaning up vomit) or figuratively (calling to make excuses at work). *The substance abuser is much more likely to stop if he or she is allowed to experience the natural consequences of the behavior.* COs often believe that they are acting to protect the people they love, but in doing so are blocking this natural process. This material needs to be handled very sensitively with the CO, however, and with a clear understanding that the patterns have developed out of concern rather than pathology.

Another major area of emphasis in community reinforcement training is increasing reinforcement for sobriety. It is important, again, to handle this area sensitively. The CO may experience considerable anger and may therefore be uncertain of the interest he or she has in providing reinforcers until the abuser changes. The social worker needs to be sensitive to this, but clarify the "change first" principle (see chapter 6), and emphasize that one is not rewarding the drinker, but rather is recognizing and supporting sober behavior. There is a country song entitled, "You ain't much fun since I stopped drinking." In the song, the newly sober husband finds himself with many chores to do, and few reinforcers when he is not drinking. Sober behavior is unlikely to increase or be maintained unless it pays off somehow.

Reinforcers that can be offered when the abuser is sober may include pleasant company, small favors, sexual involvement, favorite meals and activities, and other forms of positive attention. Like the other steps discussed here, these changes should be planned systematically. Lists of possible positive reinforcers should be developed, and each option should be examined to determine whether it is something the CO is willing and able to provide at this time. Meyers, Dominguez, and Smith (1996) also indicate that it is important to carefully plan and rehearse ways to verbally express the linkage between sobriety and the reinforcers (for example, "I really love being with you physically when you are sober"), to make the connection clear to the abuser.

Many substance abusers also do not use substances when involved in certain activities, and it is often possible for the CO, the abuser, and the family to plan to do more of those things. If the abuser does not drink when visiting with relatives, or does not use drugs when skiing, the couple or family may want to engage in those activities more, and the CO will again want to draw out verbally his or her appreciation of this time with the abuser when he or she is not using. As in every case above, a clear, specific, systematic plan is required to make this work.

Finally, the CO and the social worker, together, can think through and practice ways to suggest treatment to the substance abuser at times when this is most likely to be effective, for example when a crisis has occurred, or when the abuser is expressing regret for his actions. The request should be made respectfully and calmly, remembering that this is not the one and only time that the request can be made. As Meyers, Dominguez & Smith (1996) indicate, consistent with a shared power framework, "COs have the right to suggest treatment, and drinkers have the right to refuse it" (p. 292). (If the CO is at a point where he or she is unwilling to stay with the abuser any longer unless a change happens, Thomas's unilateral approach—see references above, or Mattaini, 1997—may be useful in helping the CO to script a clear request and clarify consequences.) By the time the CO is ready to make these requests, the social worker should have made connections with one or more treatment programs that are willing to see the abuser very quickly for intake—motivation for treatment is a shifting, dynamic process, and it is important that treatment be available when motivation is highest.

Goal #3: Reducing the Risk of Violence

Violence of moderate or severe proportions is common in families in which substance abuse is an issue. Substance abuse does not cause violence (see chapter 4), but substance abuse increases risk, and efforts on the part of the CO to influence substance use may also increase risk, so this is an area that needs to be taken seriously in work with COs. The general strategy for reducing the risk of violence in community reinforcement training begins with completing a thorough assessment of current and past levels of violence. The potential for escalating violence if the CO refuses to call the abuser's employer to make an excuse for him, or otherwise takes the actions consistent with the areas discussed above should be given careful consideration with the CO (who is an expert on her own family). If she (or occasionally he) determines that it is very dangerous to remain in the home, the social worker and the CO may shift to an emphasis on finding other safe accommodations, accessing a safe house or shelter, or initiating legal interventions including calling the police, obtaining restraining orders, and other possibilities as discussed in chapter 4.

If the CO decides to remain in the home, attention should turn to development of a safety plan, recognition of possible signs of escalating danger and possible steps to take if they occur, expanding connections with family and friends who may offer shelter and move the violence and substance abuse out of the realm of secrecy (thus increasing accountability), and building connections with formal resources or support groups. Once such a plan is in place, the CO may choose to turn to strategies for influencing substance use directly. Refer to chapter 4 for further information about work with battering; all of the material in that section is applicable as part of community reinforcement training.

Goal #4: Healing the Relationship

It is unlikely that the relationship between the CO and the substance abuser will improve in a stable way until the abuser has taken action to change his or her pattern of substance abuse. Once this begins to occur, however, the CO is often in an excellent position to support involvement in treatment, and to participate actively in certain areas as a partner in the work. The community reinforcement approach to substance abuse treatment involves a number of interlocking components that are summarized in the next section of this chapter. Two of those components offer particular opportunities for involvement by the CO, and the research suggests that these components are among the most powerful.

First, the CO can participate in the *Antabuse assurance* procedure (Azrin, Sisson, Meyers, & Godley, 1982; Meyers and Smith, 1996). Antabuse (disulfiram) is a medication administered daily; it makes a person taking it very sick (the reaction can, in fact, be life threatening under some circumstances) if the person uses alcohol. The medication is by no means a magic bullet, but it has proven very useful in helping alcohol-abusing patients establish an initial period of sobriety (Antabuse is specific to alcohol and is most helpful in the first 30 to 90 days of treatment). People who are not motivated to stop drinking are unlikely to agree to use it, of course, but for those whose motivation is high, it can be particularly useful because they only need to make a decision once a day to take the medication (and therefore not to drink). Not every client will be willing to take the medication (and a few cannot take it for physical reasons), but it is important to offer it with a clear message about its potential value, and to ask those who refuse it to consider taking it if they continue to struggle, perhaps after 30 days. The medication can be prescribed by the family physician, who in this way can become part of the "team" working together toward family healing.

In Antabuse assurance, *the drinker asks* the CO to observe him or her taking the medication each day. When the drinker takes it, the CO expresses his or her genuine appreciation. If the drinker does not take the medication, both drinker and CO agree that they each should contact the counselor (but not punish). Notice that the CO is not placed in a coercive role here. Rather, she or he is responding to a request from the abuser and providing reinforcement. Research suggests that the Antabuse assurance procedure alone can have a major impact on use of alcohol among employed patients who are in stable primary relationships (Azrin, Sisson, Meyers, & Godley, 1982).

The second major community reinforcement procedure involving the CO is reciprocity couple counseling (Azrin, Naster, & Jones, 1973; Meyers & Smith, 1996). This approach, while incorporating many of the communication skills training and problem-solving skills discussed in early chapters of this book, places a particularly strong emphasis on constructing a reciprocally more reinforcing relationship. Reciprocity counseling should often begin very early in the treatment process, concurrently with other components listed below. The process begins by asking each partner to independently complete the Marital (or Relationship) Happiness Scale (Azrin, Naster, & Jones, 1973), where they rate 11 dimensions on a 10-point scale, based on how happy the respondent is with his or her partner *today* (the instrument, therefore, can reflect changes very quickly; Meyers & Smith, 1996). The usual dimensions rated are listed below (there are several somewhat varied versions of the scale):

- household responsibilities
- raising the children
- social activities
- money management
- communication
- sex
- job or school
- affection
- partner's independence

- personal independence
- general happiness.

The partners next complete instruments or interviews in which they specify how they would ideally like their partner to act in each area. The couple and social worker then discuss ways to construct a relationship closer to the ideal, usually beginning by negotiating for increased positive exchange in areas in which there is already a relatively strong positive base, then moving toward the more challenging areas. In the version of reciprocity counseling described by Meyers and Smith, a daily reminder form is also used, on which each person notes whether he or she has accomplished each of seven positive things toward his or her partner that day, including expressing appreciation and giving compliments ("Daily Reminder to Be Nice!"). In general, the overall strategy involved in reciprocity counseling clearly is gradually to construct a relationship characterized by high levels of positive exchange, which may be particularly helpful in maintaining sobriety, and healing a relationship that has often been severely battered by years of substance abuse-related struggles. In the context of the full community reinforcement approach to substance abuse, a strong primary relationship can be a major force for recovery.

Summary of Other Components of the Community Reinforcement Approach

The overall strategy in the community reinforcement approach is to expose the person wishing to end substance abuse to a completely new network of social and community contacts, a network that provides rich reinforcers for sobriety and associated positive actions, but withdraws all of those supports if the client begins to use substances. Although each component by itself may be useful, the real power lies in their combination. For example, a stable job can be very important but by itself is unlikely to be adequate. This approach, of course, is highly congruent with the ecobehavioral perspective taken in this book. The community reinforcement approach has produced dramatically positive effectiveness data, and clearly must be regarded as state of the art in substance abuse treatment today. Because the focus of this volume is on work with families, the preceding materials have emphasized the aspects of the approach that relate directly to work with families. Detailed information about other components of the approach, which go beyond our purpose here, is readily available (see, for example, http://www.nida.nih.gov/TXManuals/CRA/CRA1.html; Meyers & Smith, 1996). For the sake of completeness, however, the overall package, briefly, includes an individualized mix of the following:

- **Sobriety Sampling.** Asking a client to give up alcohol or drugs forever, although many may need to do so, can be overwhelming. At the same time, a reasonably extended period of sobriety produces opportunities to experiment in many other areas and is associated with positive outcomes. The sobriety sampling technique begins by suggesting a period of 90 days without any substance use (but may be negotiated down to as little as one day as a beginning). The Community Reinforcement materials provide techniques for encouraging and planning for such periods.
- **Antabuse Assurance.** This technique, discussed above, can be particularly helpful in supporting sobriety sampling.
- **Job Counseling.** One area crucial to maintaining a sober, drug-free lifestyle is a stable and rewarding job, or other major life pursuit, often one that involves considerable contact with the public and is therefore inconsistent with concurrent substance use. Working with clients to locate and keep such positions is a major component of the community reinforcement approach. The originators of the approach also developed "job-finding clubs," now used in many other settings as a component of their job counseling efforts.
- **Reciprocity Counseling.** Work with the spouse or significant other, as discussed above. Such work is a particularly powerful component of the overall strategy; in cases where a significant other is not involved, much more emphasis is needed in other areas.
- **Social and Recreational Counseling.** For many persons with addiction problems, their only significant social contacts occur among persons using substances. Others have few such contacts of any kind. In either case, social and recreational counseling can help the client to access other reinforcers that may reduce the deprivation experienced when one stops using substances. Larger programs often include sober "social clubs" and activities as well.
- **Communication and Problem-Solving Skills Training.** Family communication and problem-solving skills are discussed in depth in chapter 5. Many persons with substance abuse problems also have other social skills deficits, for example in assertive or conversational skills. Skills training is important in such cases (see Mattaini, 1997, chapter 8).
- **Drink Refusal Training.** This is actually a subset of assertive skills. Many clients benefit from practice at how to say no when offered a drink, even in situations where the person offering is very insistent.

• **Relapse Prevention.** Relapse prevention is a major programmatic thrust in contemporary substance abuse treatment. Components of relapse prevention include, among others, (1) examining the behavioral chain that commonly leads to substance use and identifying ways to interrupt it early, (2) identifying high-risk situations and developing new coping strategies to deal with them, (3) developing an "early warning" system to move the client toward help at the first sign of trouble, and (4) cognitive coping strategies to deal with craving and other high-risk events.

The overall community reinforcement program has demonstrated tremendous power, even with hard to reach populations like street addicts (with special modifications). Every social worker, therefore, will want to gain some familiarity with the model.

Other approaches with some empirical support also indicate the need for social reinforcement for sobriety, and lack of reinforcement for drinking. For example, the Project MATCH Twelve Step Facilitation treatment (Longabaugh, Wirtz, Zweben, & Stout, 1998) found relatively poorer outcomes for clients who had low involvement in Alcoholics Anonymous, and high social support for drinking. Self-help groups like AA can provide substantial community reinforcement for sobriety either by themselves or as components of a larger plan that also involves family work. The family clearly can contribute in very significant ways to recovery from substance abuse. Family members mediate many of the most important contingencies for each other; this is true in happy families, as well as in those who face any of many types of critical struggles. Not surprisingly, although the specifics are different, many of the core strategies for work with families facing addictive behaviors also are valuable for families that are living with severe mental illness.

SEVERE MENTAL DISORDERS

Practice in community settings with families that include persons with mental illness is increasingly common for social workers. The requirements of such practice typically include a mix of case management, psychoeducation, and personal and family consultation. This practice should be seen as an integrated whole, in which the worker and family are involved in the co-construction of an overall configuration that works for the family, rather than as a series of narrow functions.

Every social worker working with families needs to know something about the lives of such families, although only some will specialize in this work. The purpose of this chapter is to provide overall familiarity with ecobehavioral practice with the families of those with mental illness, and to suggest places to look for more in-depth information if the reader begins to do intensive work in this field of practice. The discussion focuses on clients coping with psychoses (including schizophrenia, schizoaffective disorder, and mood disorders of psychotic dimensions). It does not deal in depth with clients who carry diagnoses of "personality disorders" (for coverage of those cases, please refer to Mattaini, 1997).

While there is much yet to learn about psychoses, we know much more than we did a generation ago. Schizophrenia affects about 1 percent of the population and usually first emerges (at least in full form) in late adolescence or early adulthood. It is not, in general, the result of poor parenting or emotional trauma, although life events can probably trigger psychotic disorders in persons who have an underlying susceptibility. Current data indicate that most psychotic disorders are rooted primarily in biological factors, but the course of the illnesses can be dramatically affected by environmental conditions and events, and cultural factors and meanings may profoundly affect the course of the condition (Castillo, 1997). The role of social workers in such cases is not to "cure," but rather to help client, family, and community construct an adequately reinforcing reality despite the illness and to minimize symptoms and disability. Reducing the "burden" experienced by caregivers (especially family members) is an important facet of this role.

The social worker in these cases should join with client, family, and social networks in a collaborative effort to determine target outcomes, and develop interventive plans consistent with these goals. The power for change emerges from interlocking, noncoercive, reinforcing exchanges among all of those with a stake in the outcome. It is common in practice with severe mental disorders (as with substance abuse) to slip into a coercive emphasis on "compliance" rather than on co-construction of reinforcing realities. Clients with mental illness, however strange and sometimes frightening their symptoms may be, are human, and are coping (often extremely well) with very challenging biological and social realities. While others, including social workers, may find it reassuring to associate themselves with equivalence classes distinct from those with which they associate mentally ill clients, this is inconsistent with ethical practice.

One of the clearest findings in the research is that stresses related to environmental conditions and events are associated with the severity and probably the frequency of relapse in most psychotic disorders. In part as a result of the deinstitutionalization movement and the development of antipsychotic drugs over the past half century, most people living with severe and persistent mental illness now live in the community. Almost half live with family members, often aging parents, and most of the others are in regular contact with their relatives. The family, therefore, is in a critical position to buffer, or to exacerbate, such stresses. Much attention has focused on a process called *expressed emotion* (EE) (Halford, 1991). EE is an atheoretical construct that emerged from research with the families of mentally ill individuals, and is generally measured by clinician ratings on three dimensional scales following a structured interview with the family. The dimensions rated are: (1) criticisms of the client by family members, (2) "emotional overinvolvement" (the extent to which family members are upset by events in the client's life and tend to be overly involved in trying to manage those events), and (3) the presence of hostility. Most of the research suggests that the risk of relapse is greater for patients living in families characterized by high EE. (It is reasonable to assume that high-EE–like characteristics in other living arrangements may have a similar relationship with symptoms; most professionals believe this to be the case.)

The EE literature presents a number of complexities and anomalies, however, and behaviorists have recently suggested that the data are most consistent with viewing the underlying dynamic as the escalation of coercive exchanges in the family (Halford, 1991). (Note the commonalities between this explanation and the dynamics of other families discussed throughout this volume.) Although coercive cultures are present in some families before the illness strikes, this is often not the case. Coercive coping is commonly a result of the enormous strains the illness places on both client and family. Reducing expressed emotion, or even coercive escalation, by itself is not, of course, constructional. The literature on effective family work in mental health settings, therefore, emphasizes not only reductions in coercive exchanges, but also the construction of new repertoires for both patient and family.

Both "negative symptoms" and "positive symptoms" of psychotic disorders can be very challenging for families. Negative symptoms include apathy, social withdrawal, lack of interest in daily activities, and lack of active involvement with the family; they are often viewed by family members as signs of "laziness" rather than as symptomatic of the illness. In part, this perspective is a matter of inaccurate equivalence relations that may be modified by psychoeducation; in part, it may be a natural pattern of denying the dramatic losses for client and family associated with psychoses.

Positive symptoms, particularly those involving conflict and aggression in the home, and hallucinatory and delusional experiences, are also major struggles for many family members to deal with, and are among the primary areas addressed in both education and problem solving in the state-of-the-art models for intervention discussed below. Because of the possibility of relapse if the level of stress escalates too far, family work in these cases often

must proceed gently and relatively slowly to avoid increasing the level of coercive exchange present and overwhelming the client's capacities.

The discussion that follows is organized into three sections. In the first
section, the essential social work function of helping the client and family
to meet their basic needs is briefly elaborated; if needs for safety, shelter,
food, often medication, and other life supports are not met, interventions
of other kinds will be unsuccessful. The next area considered is work with
families that include mentally ill members with particular focus on psychoeducation, managing symptoms, multifamily groups, and behavioral
family intervention in the home. The chapter concludes with a brief discussion of other treatment components that are often required in work with
clients with mental illness.

Meeting Basic Needs

While active delusions or severe family conflict may be the most manifest
needs in the case, there is little or no hope of an adequate outcome if the
clients' most basic survival needs are not first met. For all its limitations,
Maslow's (1971) hierarchy has an important message for social work: people need to be safe, fed, and reasonably comfortable before they can attend
to work on other areas. Up to one-third of homeless people experience psychosis or very severe mood disorders (Jencks, 1994; Rossi, 1989). It should
be no surprise that many of those people struggle to take their medications
regularly or otherwise manage their symptoms, given the chaos and danger
of their lives.

There is no justification for dividing client needs artificially into the
"concrete" and the "clinical"—the social worker is responsible for working
with the whole configuration, and it is all clinical work. The clinical social
worker's function is to work with client, family, and involved others in a relationship of shared power to construct a life configuration that provides
adequate reinforcers and minimizes aversives. This clearly includes food,
clothing, shelter, and reinforcing human contact. A social worker's best
clinical skills may be required to convince others (family members, agency
staff, landlords) to act to help meet the client's needs. As with any other
client, a person with mental illness needs to be seen by the social worker as
the center of a living ecomap, a dynamic web of exchanges; and the social
worker must be ready to work at whatever points on that web are most important for meeting the needs of the case. *Assertive community treatment*
(Stein & Santos, 1998; Stein & Test, 1980) is a strategy for doing so that involves "assertive engagement, *in vivo* delivery of services, a multidisciplinary
team approach, staff continuity over time, low staff-to-client ratios, and fre-

quent client contacts" (Farmer, Walsh, & Bentley, 1998, p. 260). All of these components, according to a recent review (Farmer, Walsh, & Bentley, 1998), are generally required for an adequate outcome, as is family involvement. Monitoring of medication is commonly also needed.

Among the basic needs of many psychotic clients is adequate and appropriate psychotropic medication (Bentley & Walsh, 1996). Taking such medications regularly as one dimension of a comprehensive program minimizes symptoms and can reduce full-scale relapses (Bentley, 1998; Hogarty, 1991). Prescribing medication is outside the social work function, but the social worker nonetheless carries several responsibilities in this area. Many severely mentally ill clients who come to the attention of social agencies do not have access to medical assistance, and the social worker often needs to facilitate those connections. Remembering to take medication regularly in the midst of an often disrupted and chaotic world (and one that may appear even more so subjectively), is difficult, and many clients find their medications at least somewhat unpleasant to take as well. In fact, most people who are *not* psychotic do a relatively poor job of taking prescribed medications according to instructions.

The social worker can help with self-monitoring and self-management techniques, and can provide ongoing support for taking medication. He or she may also need to repeatedly go over the reasons for taking the medication, listen empathically to the client's experiences, monitor for side effects (Bentley, 1998), and advocate with the client for changes if such side effects become intolerable. Assistance in managing symptoms in other ways (see below) can also help to minimize the amount of medication required. For example, some clients can learn to discriminate events that are real from those that are hallucinatory; then they may not need to take as much medication as would be required to completely suppress the cognitive symptoms. Be aware that many psychotropic medications suppress pleasant experiences as well, so an optimum balance may be difficult to achieve.

Family Interventions

In their examination of intensive, family-based services, Fraser, Nelson, and Rivard (1997) note that services that "educate family members about the etiology of mental illnesses (often emphasizing the biological bases of disorders), the structure of the mental health system, and the use of medications" as well as "problem-solving and communications-skills training . . . appear to have moderate to large effects on relapse, hospitalization, and symptoms" (p. 144). The reported effects are much larger than those found in intensive family preservation in child welfare, for example. Several mod-

els for such work with families have been developed and tested over the past
two decades.

Psychoeducation

The term *psychoeducation* originated with programs aimed at teaching people with severe mental illness and their families facts about the disorders
and skills to live with those disorders as well as possible. Both patients and
family members commonly hold misconceptions that can interfere with taking effective action. Parents often overtly or covertly blame themselves for
the illness, and may blame the patient for symptoms. Patients typically do
not know that they are struggling with a neurochemical imbalance, rather
than with a mysterious force. Education about causes and symptoms of mental illness, medication, and strategies for coping and living with the conditions, therefore, can be enormously valuable, and sometimes freeing. The
research consistently indicates that family psychoeducation, in combination
with medication, reduces symptoms and relapses (Anderson, Reiss, &
Hogarty, 1986; Farmer, Walsh, & Bentley, 1998).

Although not all benefit from it equally, psychoeducation can also be
enormously helpful to clients with mental illness themselves. Accepting the
diagnosis can be very painful for many, in part because of the enormous
stigma involved (Link, 1987). Many persons, clients, families, and professionals alike, have learned equivalence relations like

$$\text{mental illness} \approx \text{"crazy"} \approx \text{social rejection} \approx \text{hopeless}$$

and therefore experience associating themselves with mental illness diagnoses as very aversive. Mental illness usually involves significant losses of actual or potential reinforcers (social, vocational, and other) for both patient
and family. The social worker needs to be able to empathize with those
losses, and still help the client and family to build hope that a fulfilling life
can be constructed. Accepting that proposition involves learning new, incompatible equivalence relations like

$$\text{mental illness} \approx \text{treatable}$$
$$\text{and}$$
$$\text{my life} \approx \text{potentially rich.}$$

Even for those who cannot accept the formal diagnosis, psychoeducation
regarding medication, family relations, or other specific areas may still be
helpful.

Symptoms Management

Positive symptoms of psychosis, like bizarre speech and behavior, can in part be shaped by environmental contingencies (Wong, 1996). While the origin of symptoms does not lie primarily in the environment, most severely mentally ill people have few repertoires available that naturally produce social or other rewards. The repertoires they do have available therefore tend to be emitted at high rates, including those that produce attention from others. Family members are among the crucial actors in managing these symptoms. (Individualized functional analysis is important to understand such behaviors, since bizarre speech for one person may produce attention, while another may use topographically similar actions to escape from anxiety-producing social contacts.) The frequency of delusional speech increases if those around the person reinforce it, especially if there is a high level of overall social deprivation. Over time, however, others tend to withdraw from the contact because they find it aversive. The natural response from the client then is to further escalate bizarre behavior in an extinction burst. Simply ignoring delusional talk or other bizarre behavior, therefore, is not enough. It is important to help the client learn new ways to obtain the reinforcers he or she values (through social skills training, for example), and for the family to systematically work on reinforcing approximations to healthy behavior. A general intention to do so is unlikely to be adequate; a clear, collaboratively developed, written plan in which the patient has also been involved if possible, is essential.

Families, social workers, and others in the client's world can also help the client to deal with the emotional experiences associated with symptoms. Clients who hear voices (auditory hallucinations) or experience periods of depersonalization (feeling out of touch with one's self), for example, are naturally deeply disturbed. Sensitive responses require walking a fine line between (1) reinforcing behavior that may produce costly social consequences in the long run (for example, extended discussions of the details of hallucinations) and (2) helping the client to deal with the genuinely troubling symptoms. One helpful approach is to empathize with, and discuss, the *emotions* that accompany and follow such experiences (for example, "It could be terrifying to have that experience; what was it like for you?"). A second approach is to help the client to re-examine for him- or herself the realities through a process that Wong (1996) refers to as "tactful suggestions and leading questions" (p. 323). Empathizing with how hard it is to tell the difference ("Sometimes it's hard to tell what's real from what only seems real, isn't it?"), gently asking about evidence ("What makes you think it's real?"), and suggesting that some experiences may not be objectively real ("Sometimes what really seems real to us is just the mind playing tricks on us due to chemical imbalances . . .") are among the useful approaches in the context of an engaged relationship. Many clients learn to distinguish psychotic symptoms from reality ("It seems real, but I know it's not"), and this can be very helpful in working with the client to avoid psychotic talk when this will result in social punishment.

Intervention in the home

Clinic-based services that include psychoeducation, medication management, and family work are without a doubt often effective (Farmer, Walsh, & Bentley, 1998). However, there are particular advantages for work with this population, like with many others, in the home. Falloon (1991), a pioneer in effective home interventions in schizophrenia, indicates that "Despite the added cost of having the therapist journey to the family home, there are several benefits, including (1) increased efficiency in applying skills learned in treatment sessions, (2) improved attendance of "resistant" family members, (3) enhanced assessment of household stressors, and (4) more relaxed participation by anxious family members" (p. 79). In the approach used by Falloon and his colleagues, not only are medication monitoring and general psychoeducation provided, but so is assistance with working toward specific goals important to the family.

Typically, such goals involve resolving problems that are of importance to individual family members, as well as constructing an overall family reality that is as positive as possible at times when problems are not occurring (Falloon, 1988; 1991). In assessing problem behaviors (for example, aggressive behaviors), the questions of particular interest for planning include:

1. How does this specific problem handicap this person (and/or the family) in everyday life?
2. What would happen if the problem were reduced in frequency?
3. What would this person (and his or her family) gain if the problem were resolved?
4. Who (or what) reinforces the problem with attention, sympathy, and support?
5. Under what circumstances is the specific problem reduced in intensity?
6. Under what circumstances is the specific problem increased in intensity?
7. What do family members currently do to cope with the problem?
8. What are the assets and deficits of the family as a problem-solving unit? (Falloon, 1991, p. 76)

These questions are related to the functional analysis of the problem behavior, as well as to examining motivation for acting to make changes. The professional challenge is to understand the problem behavior in context, and to construct alternatives, primarily by working to change the context so that it offers higher levels of reinforcement for positive alternatives.

Falloon's model for work with families in the home has strong empirical support, and social workers who will be doing this kind of work should carefully study the details of the approach. The general strategies included are by now familiar, although professionals have not always recognized their applicability to serious mental illness: education, communication training, problem-solving training, contingency contracting, and "operant conditioning strategies" (Falloon, 1991). The last category particularly emphasizes shaping, in which precision reinforcement is provided for pinpointed behaviors.

Families struggling to cope with severe mental illness commonly carry a heavy burden, often with enormous commitment and courage (Lefley, 1989; National Institute of Mental Health, 1991). All of the services discussed thus far can be helpful in managing that burden, but not surprisingly other families experiencing similar challenges can offer types of support that no one else can. The value of multifamily groups for this population is therefore increasingly recognized.

Multifamily Psychoeducation Groups

The use of multifamily groups with the families of severely mentally ill people has emerged as a particularly valuable approach in recent years. Multifamily psychoeducational groups have proven effective in preventing relapse—more effective than psychoeducation conducted with individual families, or multifamily groups that do not include psychoeducation (McFarlane, 1994; McFarlane et al, 1995). Such groups may be particularly useful in cases where expressed negative emotion in the family is high. McFarlane (1991) discussed the development of the multifamily group approach that began in the 1970s when parents and patients came together to discuss problems in mental hospital wards and problems associated with the transfer of heavy responsibility to families with deinstitutionalization. At the time, families were still often viewed by professionals as being causal factors in the illnesses. Contact with other families, however, could and did "neutralize" (McFarlane, 1991, p. 365) the effects of this blaming.

The general model for multifamily psychoeducation groups involves meetings (which on some occasions do, and on others do not, include the person with the mental illness). They provide education about mental illness, medication, and the treatment system, along with discussions of ways to cope with problem behaviors as well as ways to maintain one's own and the family's life as normally as possible. Not surprisingly, the need for advocacy often surfaces in such gatherings of parents, and families of mentally ill individuals have in recent years become powerful advocates for improved services and research for mentally ill people, a group that is often systematically neglected and oppressed (see http://www.nami.org).

Other Treatment Considerations

In addition to work with families, several other types of intervention are demonstrably important in work with severely mentally ill clients; these protocols will be mentioned here for the sake of completeness. For more detail, refer to Wong (1996), and Mattaini (1997). *Skills training*, in particular, is useful in both preventing rehospitalizations and improving the life of the client. Training in functional skills (including work, social, and recreational) can produce dramatic drops in bizarre or repetitive behaviors and provides access to higher quality reinforcers. Social skills are particularly useful, because they can reduce the isolation and rejection so often experienced by persons with mental illness, and simultaneously open the door to meaningful relationships. Self-care, prevocational and vocational, independent living, and many other areas of skills training can also contribute to the client's quality of life.

Lifestyle enrichment is a critical consideration in work with seriously mentally ill people (Mattaini, 1997). Service systems often do an adequate (and sometimes an excellent) job of ensuring that the physical and safety needs of such clients are met; but even clients in model programs often report limited satisfaction in other areas of life, including social integration, spiritual and religious dimensions, and access to a rich range of reinforcing alternatives. Creativity and individualization are required here from the social worker, and family members have a part to play as well, given their knowledge of the client. Some clients may have clear ideas of how they would like to enrich their lives, while others may require a good deal of support and encouragement to experiment. There are many possibilities, including the following general categories:

- recreational activities, including spectator activities such as music, movies, or watching sports; involvement with computerized electronic communities; and participation in clubs
- outdoor activities, which provide a different class of reinforcers than urban activities for many of us, whether done alone or with others
- involvement in self-help groups, which have demonstrated an extraordinary capacity to empower many clients with severe mental disorders, pro-

viding social connections, prompts, and reinforcement for taking steps to manage their lives
- vocational activities at whatever level the client can manage, whether in a regular job, in assisted employment, or in a sheltered workshop setting
- volunteer work, which can provide a sense of belonging and of making a contribution
- involvement with religious groups, which are sometimes particularly tolerant of atypical behavior
- ethnic-cultural associations. (Mattaini, 1997, p. 177)

As with all social work clients, the primary goal is to participate with the client in achieving a more reinforcing and less aversive life situation.

REFERENCES

Anderson, C. M., Reiss, D. J., & Hogarty, G. (1986). *Schizophrenia and the family*. New York: Guilford Press.

Anderson, S. C. (1994). A critical analysis of the concept of codependency. *Social Work, 39*, 677–685.

Azrin, N. H., Flores, T., & Kaplan, S. J. (1975). Job-finding club: A group-assisted program for obtaining employment. *Behaviour Research and Therapy, 13*, 17–27.

Azrin, N. H., Naster, B. J., & Jones, R. (1973). Reciprocity counseling: A rapid learning-based procedure for marital counseling. *Behaviour Research & Therapy, 11*, 365–382.

Azrin, N. H., Sisson, R. W., Meyers, R., & Godley, M. (1982). Alcoholism treatment by disulfiram and community reinforcement therapy. *Journal of Behavior Therapy and Experimental Psychiatry, 13*, 105–112.

Barber, J. G., & Gilbertson, R. (1996). An experimental investigation of a brief unilateral intervention for the partners of heavy drinkers. *Research on Social Work Practice, 6*, 325–336.

Barber, J. G., & Gilbertson, R. (1997). Unilateral interventions for women living with heavy drinking. *Social Work, 42*, 69–78.

Bentley, K. J. (1998). Psychopharmacological treatment of schizophrenia: What social workers need to know. *Research on Social Work Practice, 8*, 384–405.

Bentley, K. J., & Walsh, J. (1996). *The social worker and psychotropic medication: Toward effective collaboration with mental health clients, families, and providers*. Pacific Grove, CA: Brooks/Cole.

Castillo, R. J. (1997). *Culture and mental illness: a client-centered approach*. Pacific Grove, CA: Brooks/Cole.

Dittrich, J. E., & Trapold, M. A. (1984). A treatment program for the wives of alcoholics: An evaluation. *Bulletin of the Society of Psychologists in Addictive Behaviours, 3*, 91–102. Cited in R. J. Meyers, T. P. Dominguez, & J. E. Smith (1996), Community reinforcement training with concerned others, In V. B. Van Hasselt & M. Hersen (Eds.), *Sourcebook of psychological treatment manuals for adult disorders* (pp. 257–294), New York: Plenum Press.

Falloon, I. R. H. (1988). *Handbook of behavioral family therapy.* New York: Guilford Press.

Falloon, I. R. H. (1991). Behavioral family therapy. In A. S. Gurman & D. P. Kniskern (Eds.), *Handbook of family therapy, Volume II* (pp. 65–95). New York: Brunner/Mazel.

Farmer, R. L., Walsh, J., & Bentley, K. J. (1998). Schizophrenia. In B. A. Thyer & J. S. Wodarski (Eds.), *Handbook of empirical social work practice* (pp. 245–270). New York: John Wiley & Sons.

Fraser, M. W., Nelson, K. E., & Rivard, J. C. (1997). Effectiveness of family preservation services. *Social Work Research, 21,* 138–153.

Halford, W. K. (1991). Beyond expressed emotion: Behavioral assessment of family interaction associated with the course of schizophrenia. *Behavioral Assessment, 13,* 99–123.

Hogarty, G. E. (1991). Social work practice research on severe mental illness: Charting a future. *Research on Social Work Practice, 1,* 5–31.

Institute of Medicine (1990). *Broadening the base of treatment for alcohol problems.* Washington, DC: National Academy Press.

Jencks, C. (1994). *The homeless.* Cambridge, MA: Harvard University Press.

Johnson, V. E. (1986). *Intervention: How to help those who don't want help.* Minneapolis: Johnson Institute.

Lefley, H. P. (1989). Family burden and family stigma in major mental illness. *American Psychologist, 44,* 556–560.

Liepman, M. R., Nirenberg, T. D., & Begin, A. M. (1989). Evaluation of a program designed to help family and significant others to motivate resistant alcoholics into recovery. *American Journal of Drug and Alcohol Abuse, 15,* 209–221.

Link, B. (1987). Understanding labeling effects in mental disorders: An assessment of expectations of rejection. *American Sociological Review, 52,* 96–112.

Longabaugh, R., Wirtz, P. W., Zweben, A., & Stout, R. L. (1998). Network support for drinking, Alcoholics Anonymous and long-term matching effects. *Addiction, 93,* 1313–1333.

Lovaas, O. I. (1987). Behavioral treatment and normal educational and intellectual functioning in young autistic children. *Journal of Consulting and Clinical Psychology, 55,* 3–9.

Maslow, A. H. (1971). *The farther reaches of human nature.* New York: Viking Press.

Mattaini, M. A. (1997). *Clinical practice with individuals.* Washington, DC: NASW Press.

Maurice, C. (1993). *Let me hear your voice: A family's triumph over autism.* New York: Fawcett Columbine.

Mayfield, D., McLeod, G., & Hall, P. (1974). The CAGE questionnaire: Validation of a new alcoholism screening instrument. *American Journal of Psychiatry, 131,* 1121–1123.

McFarlane, W. R. (1991). Family psychoeducational treatment. In A. S. Gurman & D. P. Kniskern (Eds.), *Handbook of family therapy, Volume II* (pp. 363–395). New York: Brunner/Mazel.

McFarlane, W. R. (1994). Multiple-family groups and psychoeducation in the treatment of schizophrenia. *New Directions in Mental Health Services, 62,* 13–22.

McFarlane, W. R., Link, B., Dushay, R., & Marchal, J. (1995). Psychoeducational multiple family groups: Four-year relapse outcome in schizophrenia. *Family Process, 34,* 127–144.

Meyers, R. J., Dominguez, T. P., & Smith, J. E. (1996). Community reinforcement training with concerned others. In V. B. Van Hasselt & M. Hersen (Eds.), *Sourcebook of psychological treatment manuals for adult disorders* (pp. 257–294). New York: Plenum Press.

Meyers, R. L., & Smith, J. E. (1996). *Clinical guide to alcohol treatment: The community reinforcement approach.* New York: Guilford Press.

Miller, W. R., & Rollnick, S. (Eds.), (1991). *Motivational interviewing: Preparing people to change addictive behavior.* New York: Guilford Press.

National Institute of Mental Health (1991). *Caring for people with severe mental disorders: A national plan of research to improve services.* Washington, DC: Supt. of Documents, U. S. Government Printing Office. DHHS Publication Number (ADM)91–1762.

Pierce, W. D., & Epling, W. F. (1994). Activity anorexia: An interplay between basic and applied behavior analysis. *The Behavior Analyst, 17,* 7–23.

Rossi, P. H. (1989). *Down and out in America: The origins of homelessness.* Chicago: University of Chicago Press.

Rollnick, S., & Bell, A. (1991). Brief motivational interviewing for use by the non-specialist. In W. R. Miller & S. Rollnick (Eds.), *Motivational interviewing: Preparing people to change addictive behavior* (pp. 203–213). New York: Guilford Press.

Sisson, R. W., & Azrin, N. H. (1986). Family member involvement to initiate and promote treatment of problem drinkers. *Journal of Behavior Therapy and Experimental Psychiatry, 17,* 15–21.

Sobell, M. B., & Sobell, L. C. (1993). *Problem drinkers: Guided self-change treatment.* New York: Guilford Press.

Stein, L. I., & Santos, A. B. (1998). *Assertive community treatment of persons with severe mental illness.* New York: W. W. Norton.

Stein, L. I., & Test, M. A. (1980). Alternative mental hospital treatment: I. Conceptual model, treatment program, and clinical evaluation. *Archives of General Psychiatry, 37,* 392–397.

Thomas, E. J., & Yoshioka, M. R. (1989). Spouse interventive confrontations in unilateral family therapy for alcohol abuse. *Social Casework, 70,* 340–347.

Thomas, E. J., Santa, C., Bronson, D., & Oyserman, D. (1987). Unilateral family therapy with the spouses of alcoholics. *Journal of Social Service Research, 10*(2/3/4), 145–162.

U.S. Pharmaceuticals Group of Pfizer, Inc. (1996). *PRIME-MD™.* New York: Author.

Wong, S. E. (1996). Psychosis. In M. A. Mattaini & B. A. Thyer (Eds.), *Finding solutions to social problems: Behavioral strategies for change* (pp. 319–343). Washington, DC: APA Books.

Zweben, A. (1991). Motivational counseling with alcoholic couples. In W. R. Miller & S. Rollnick (Eds.), *Motivational interviewing: Preparing people to change addictive behavior* (pp. 225–235). New York: Guilford Press.

Conclusion

BEST PRACTICES FOR SOCIAL WORK WITH FAMILIES

Ultimately . . . there are no parts at all. What we call a part is merely a pattern in an inseparable web of relationships. (Capra, 1996, p. 37)

In recent decades, molecular biology and genetics have advanced knowledge and practice in medicine through a process of examining phenomena at ever-smaller levels. Paradoxically, one primary limit to this work has been the discovery that the vast majority of genetic material is used for integrative processes, requiring an expanded perspective, and in fact that understanding of living organisms requires understanding entire ecosystems (Capra, 1996). Similarly, behavioral science and professional practice have learned an enormous amount about individual behavior over the past several decades, but in the process have also realized that such behavior cannot be understood except in its environmental context (Baer & Pinkston, 1997; Germain, 1979). This understanding is both scientific and spiritual; as Einstein (n.d.) noted, the two, if rightly understood, may ultimately be one and the same.

Ecosystems science and biology, as well as behavioral science, have recently experienced an epistemic shift (a shift in how we know, and how we question), recognizing that the key to understanding biological and social phenomena lies in their organization as transactional networks. The transactions, rather than the entities that are members of the networks, are primary. What makes a family a family, for example, are the transactional patterns of exchange among the members. Networks, in turn, are nested in other, higher-order networks. Families are networks of human beings, and communities are networks of families. Human beings are also often members of multiple overlapping transactional networks (families, organizations, work networks, friendship networks, and ethnic cultures). Some branches of social work have neglected the environment, focusing instead on individual behavior, emotions, and experience (Kemp, Whittaker, & Tracy, 1997). But even the distinction between "individual" and "environment" can be seen as an epistemic oversimplification, which is why Kemp and her colleagues refer to their approach as "person-environment" practice.

Individuals are organic parts of the overall transactional field, rather than just in contact with it. An individual can be understood only within his or her environmental matrix (of which the family is usually a central network). Effective social work intervention must therefore always be ecological, and any division between work with the person and work with the environment is artificial.

BEST PRACTICES

Several general principles for practice with families, consistent with the best current knowledge, can be extracted from the foregoing chapters:

1. Professional practice with families involves four recursive and iterative processes, all of which are essential, and in each of which both family members and the social worker have crucial roles. These include (a) engaging the family in a genuine relationship of shared power, (b) envisioning a goal-state toward which intervention aims, (c) assessing the contextual situation to determine the kinds of intervention that may be useful, and (d) completing interventive tasks that emerge from that assessment. Other practice processes occur concurrently (monitoring the progress of the case in particular, and an orderly process for terminating the social worker's involvement and planning for maintenance of change).

2. A key component of assessment is functional analysis. Most behavior occurs for reasons. Most behavior is functional—people do what they do because it is the best means they currently have available to achieve functions important to them. Simply asking a person to stop doing something that is functional (though it may also be costly) is much less likely to work than helping the individual to construct new repertoires through which to obtain what he or she values in better ways.

3. Constructional practice (practice that aims to construct new repertoires) is much more likely to have lasting effects than is practice that attempts primarily to reduce or eliminate behavior (Schwartz & Goldiamond, 1975). Behavior problems are best resolved, ordinarily, by constructing alternatives. Constructional practice (and satisfying family relationships) rely on extensive use of positive reinforcement. Coercive techniques are often only temporarily effective (if at all) and risk serious damage to relationships.

4. Cultural variations in terms of what is valued, what is reinforcing, and how the world is understood are enormously important in practice. The social worker has an obligation to learn as much as possible, to directly address cultural factors with client families who are the only experts in terms of what they value and why, and to maintain a sense of humility about how well any professional can truly understand the realities of others.

5. Environmental interventions should often be privileged over intrapersonal interventions. Maintenance of change usually requires that the environment support and encourage healthy and healing behavior. Changing behavior is easy; maintaining change, however, requires networks of reinforcement.

6. Effective family practice can occur only in a relationship of shared power. Every participant must have a strong voice, and the contributions of each must be encouraged and valued. It is ultimately damaging to have practice within a dominance hierarchy in which the social worker is viewed as powerful and the client is not. Although the social worker, family members, and others who may be involved in a case each have different powers, talents, and repertoires to bring to the case, each of these contributions is crucial; one is not more important than another. The social worker is not responsible for "curing" a pathological, damaged client or family; rather, the social worker and family share responsibility for contributing to an improved life configuration, and healing the collective transactional web of which all are part. This is a spiritual process to which science can contribute.

7. Science and social justice are not incompatible. Intervention with families can be scientific and based on data, while acknowledging and working to change oppressive structures and violations of basic human rights. Behavioral science can help elaborate the mechanisms of social problems and find possibilities for addressing them.

For all families seen by social workers, whether they are struggling with poverty, internal conflict, substance abuse, or lack of positive connection, an ecobehavioral approach within a process of shared power has the same final goal. This is simply the co-construction of a life configuration that offers all members of the family access to high-quality reinforcers; minimizes exposure to excessive aversives, including those associated with systematic oppression; and allows the family to participate in and contribute more deeply to the larger collective of which we all (the social worker included) are part. This is social work.

REFERENCES

Baer, D. M., & Pinkston, E. M. (Eds.). (1997). *Environment and Behavior.* Boulder, CO: Westview Press.

Capra, F. (1996). *The web of life.* New York: Anchor Books.

Einstein, A. (no date). *The world as I see it* (abridged ed.). Secaucus, NJ: Citadel Press.

Germain, C. B. (Ed.). (1979). *Social work practice: People and environments: An ecological perspective.* New York: Columbia University Press.

Kemp, S. P., Whittaker, J. K., & Tracy, E. M. (1997). *Person-environment practice: The social ecology of interpersonal helping.* New York: Aldine de Gruyter.

Schwartz, A., & Goldiamond, I. (1975). *Social casework: A behavioral approach.* New York: Columbia University Press.

INDEX

Alphabetization is letter by letter (e.g., Children precedes Child welfare). The letters f and t following page numbers indicate figures and tables, respectively.

A

AA (Alcoholics Anonymous), 281
Abuse in family. *See* Child maltreatment;
    Domestic violence
Abuse of substances. *See* Substance abuse
Academic achievement. *See also* Schools
    antisocial behavior and, 212–13
    parenting practices and, 190
Acceptance, 114, 134–38
    assessment of in family, 38
    aversive exchanges and, 101–03
    communication and, 137
    couple interventions, 157–60
    domains of, 135–36, 136t
    family interventions, 134–35, 138
    importance of addressing, 135, 158
Acceptance and commitment therapy
    (ACT), 102, 136–37
Active listening, 121, 124
Addiction. *See* Substance abuse
Adolescents. *See* Children and adolescents
Adoption, and genograms, 43
Advocacy, 52, 55, 81
    child maltreatment and, 251–52
    collective advocacy, 207–08
    parenting practices and, 183, 206–08
    psychotropic medications and, 285
Affairs. *See* Infidelity
African Americans
    extended kinship networks among, 16, 65
    religious communities among, 70
Aggression, 42, 198. *See also* Antisocial
    behavior; Violence
Aging. *See* Elderly
Alanon, 271
Alcohol abuse. *See* Substance abuse
Alcoholics Anonymous (AA), 281
Alliances within family, and flexibility, 39–40

Anger management. *See also* Conflict
    management
    antisocial behavior and, 221
    child maltreatment and, 241, 251–52
Anorexia, 264–65
Anorgasmia, 173
Antabuse, 277–78, 280
Antecedents of behavior, 10–13
    assessment of environmental exchanges,
        33–36
    child maltreatment and, 239–44, 240f,
        243f
    occasions. *See* Occasions (as antecedents
        to behavior)
Antipsychotic drugs, 282, 285
Antisocial behavior, 211–33
    behavioral elements of, 211–12
    bullying and, 214–15
    corporal punishment and, 199
    developmental trajectories, 212–14
    early starters, 213
    family conferences and, 223–24
    Family Group Conferences, 223, 232–33
    functional family therapy (FFT), 223,
        225–27
    identification of, 211–12
    importance of addressing, 211
    indigenous approaches, 232–33
    interventive strategies, 214–16, 223–33
    late starters, 213–14
    life problems related to, 212
    multisystemic treatment (MST), 60, 223,
        227–31
    parental monitoring and, 205–06
    PEACE POWER! programs and, 218–23
    PeaceBuilders™ programs and, 216–18
    peer groups and, 66, 213, 215, 227
    prevention, 215–23

residential treatment, 214
schools and, 212–16, 227
Antisocial personality disorder, 211
Arrests. *See also* Legal system
antisocial behavior and, 212
violent crimes by youths, 212
Asian culture
group versus individual, valuing of, 16
Japanese Americans, interracial marriages
among, 3
shame, perspective on, 21
Assertive community treatment for psychotic
clients, 284–85
Assertiveness, ethnic and cultural
differences in valuing of, 16
Assessment
ecobehavioral. *See* Ecobehavioral
assessment
functional family therapy (FFT), 226
motivational interviewing and, 267–69
multisystemic treatment (MST), 228–29
Assessment instruments, 43. *See also specific
instruments*
Assumptions. *See* Equivalence relations;
Rules
Autism, 13, 264
parental advocacy and, 207
record keeping and, 186
reinforcement and, 196
Autonomy versus intimacy, 137–38
Autopoietic networks, 232
Aversive exchanges, 8–10, 13–14, 42. *See also
specific exchange (e.g., Punishment)*
acceptance of differences and, 101–03
assessment of exchanges within family, 37
conduct disorder and, 95
conflict resolution and, 99–101
couple exchanges, 145–47, 146f
decreasing in intrafamily exchanges,
95–103
environmental exchanges, 17, 18f, 64, 96
functional analysis of, 98–99
ineffectiveness of, 95–96
intrafamily exchanges, 13–14, 86, 95–103
mapping, 35
self-awareness of, increasing, 97–98,
117–18
transactional ecomap of, 9–10, 9f
Avocational activities. *See* Recreational
activities

B

Back to School Pledge Campaign, 182–83
BARS (behaviorally anchored rating scale),
53–54, 53f
Battered women. *See* Domestic violence
BE (behavior exchange) procedures, 92–93,
154, 156
Bedtime, and reinforcement, 195–96
Bedtime Game, 189
Behavior exchange (BE) procedures, 92–93,
154, 156
Behavioral repertoires, 13–19. *See also specific
behavior (e.g., Antisocial behavior)*
antecedents. *See* Antecedents of behavior
consequences. *See* Consequences of
behavior
contingencies, 13
definition of behavior, 6–8
development of, 6
discrimination of appropriate occasions
for behavior, 49–50
ethnic and cultural influences on, 16
flexibility and, 38–40, 39f
functional analysis. *See* Functional
analysis
ignoring problem behavior, 201–03, 251
monitoring. *See* Monitoring
motor behavior, 6, 7f
observational behavior, 6, 7f
pinpointing problem behaviors, 185–86,
229
profile of abusive mother, 7f
record keeping. *See* Record keeping of
child's behavior
sexual problems and, 171–72
verbal behavior. *See* Verbal behavior
visceral behavior, 6, 7f
Behavioral theory, 5
Behaviorally anchored rating scale (BARS),
53–54, 53f
Beliefs. *See* Equivalence relations; Rules; Self-
talk
cultural. *See* Ethnic and cultural influences
religious. *See* Religion and spirituality
Best practices, 296–97
Bi-culturalism, 16
Black Americans. *See* African Americans
Blended families, 3, 9–10, 9f
Boundaries of clinical intervention, 17
Bullying, 214–15

C

CAGE screening, 269
Canadian First Nations
  Community Holistic Circle Healing
    Program, 223, 259–60
  PEACE POWER! programs and, 222
"Caring days" tasks, 91, 154–56
Centers for Disease Control and Prevention,
    youth violence prevention projects, 216
"Change first" approach, 89, 101, 153–54,
    275
Chaotic families, 40, 212–13
Child maltreatment, 237–60. *See also*
    Domestic violence
  advocacy and, 251–52
  anger management and, 241, 251–52
  antecedents of behavior, 239–44, 240f,
    243f
  behavioral profile of abusive mother, 7f
  conflict management and, 246
  core elements of effective intervention,
    246–49
  depression and, 244, 247
  domestic violence and, 106, 238
  dynamics of, 239–45
  economic influences, 241, 244
  emotional abuse, 239–41, 240f
  employment and, 253
  family support programs and, 76, 252
  foster care and, 237–38
  group interventions, 249–50
  healing of family and community, 259–60
  in vivo training and, 246–47, 250–51
  incidence of, 103, 237
  interventive strategies, 237–38, 246–60
  legal system and, 237–38, 245
  modeling and, 240f, 241–42, 243f
  multifamily groups and, 79–80, 253
  multisystemic treatment (MST), 249,
    254–55
  neglect, 239, 242–45, 243f
  parent education and, 179, 241, 244,
    249–52
  physical abuse, 239–41, 240f
  Project 12-Ways, 255–57
  respite services, 252–53
  reunification of family, 254
  sexual abuse, 239, 245, 257–59
  skills training and, 246, 251–52, 255–56
  social isolation and, 76, 241, 244

  social support and, 249, 252–54
  substance abuse and, 238, 241, 244, 247
Children and adolescents. *See also* Parenting;
    *specific behaviors or issues (e.g.,
    Delinquency)*
  discipline. *See* Discipline of children
  family support programs and, 76
  infidelity of parents, effect of, 169
  peer groups and, 66
  volunteer activities, 73
Child welfare services. *See* Child
    maltreatment; Legal system
Chinese, valuing of assertiveness, 16
Choices and Consequences strategy, 269
Client-centered therapy, 115
Co-mediation, 130
Codependency, 5, 41, 265, 270–71
Coercive discipline, 96, 98, 197–99
Coercive families, 8–9, 42, 98, 100. *See also*
    Domestic violence
  antisocial behavior and, 212–13
  modeling by, 12
  psychoses and, 283
  reciprocal exchanges within, 86
Coercive interventions, 26–27, 266–67
  lack of effectiveness of, 296
Cognitive-behavioral theory, 5
Cognitive-behavioral therapy, of child sexual
    abuse offenders, 258–59
Cognitive factors. *See* Equivalence relations;
    Rules; Self-talk
Collaborative contracts, 26, 28, 89, 91
Collaborative empiricism, 151
Collaborative process of assessment, 54–55
Communication, 114–35. *See also* Verbal
    behavior
  acceptance and, 137
  assessment of, 37–38, 119–20
  barriers to, 119–21
  channels of, 116–18
  content of, 118–19
  contingency contracting, 130–31, 193
  core skills, 121–32
  dimensions of, 115–19
  ethnic and cultural influences on, 117
  expressive skills. *See* Expressive skills
  family conferences. *See* Family conferences
  functional communication, 118
  importance of addressing, 114–15,
    118–19

interventive strategies, 132–35. *See also*
Communication training
listening skills. *See* Listening skills
mediation services. *See* Mediation
nonverbal communication, 116–18
paraverbal communication, 116–18, 123
parenting and, 85–86, 120
problem-solving skills, 115–16, 127–32
punishment and, 120
school and home, between, 68
sexual problems, 170
Communication training
antisocial behavior and, 223–24
community reinforcement approach to
substance abuse, 280
couple interventions, 160–64
enactment, 133
functional communication training, 50
functional family therapy and, 226
home assignments, 134
in vivo training, 133
multifamily groups, 134
parent education, 115, 184–85
problem solving and, 128
psychotic symptoms management and,
288
red/green prompting card, 97–98, 117–18
skills training, 49, 54, 121–22, 133
tools and prompts, 134
Communities of interest, enhancing
exchanges with, 74–75
Community groups. *See* Neighborhood and
community groups
Community reinforcement training, 272–81
diminishing pain and improving personal
experiences, 273–74
healing relationships, 277–79
reducing risk of violence, 276–77
reducing substance use and encouraging
treatment, 274–76
summary of other components of
approach, 279–81
Conduct disorder
antisocial behavior and, 211–12, 214
aversive exchanges and, 95
parenting practices and, 183–84
Conferences, family. *See* Family conferences
Conflict management, 99–101
antisocial behavior and, 221–22
child maltreatment and, 246

couple interventions, 164–66
skills training, 49
Conjoint family therapy, 114
Conjoint interviews, 28
Consequences of behavior, 8–11
Choices and Consequences strategy, 269
contingency contracting, 130–31, 193, 288
contingent and noncontingent
consequences in parent-child
exchanges, 52, 89, 90f
flexibility and, 38–40, 39f
functional analysis and, 50–51
parenting practices and, 192–93
Constructional life-sculpting, 28
Constructional process, 26
lasting effects of, 296
Contextual analysis of focal issues, 32, 31t,
46, 49–52, 153
type of intervention based on, 296
Contingencies, 13, 89, 90f
Contingency contracting, 130–31, 193, 288
Contracts
collaborative contracts, 26, 28, 89–91
contingency contracting, 130–31, 193, 288
functional family therapy and, 226
Corporal punishment. *See* Coercive
discipline; Spanking
Couple exchanges, 143–74
assessment of, 147–49
coercive demands in, 98, 162
conflict styles, 145–47, 146f
ethnic and cultural influences, 152
family cultures, confluence of, 144, 144f,
148–49
importance of couple relationship, 143
infidelity, 148, 162–63, 166–69
Marital Happiness Scale, 43, 46, 47f,
278–79
microculture of, 144–49
open relationships, 167
parenting and, 180–81
rates of positive and aversive exchanges,
145–48, 146f
reciprocal exchanges, 85–86
rules in, 150–51, 158
self-talk and, 149–51, 158
sexual problems. *See* Sexual problems
unilateral reinforcers and, 93
Couple interventions, 19, 144, 151–74
acceptance and commitment therapy
(ACT), 102, 137

accepting skills, 157–60
batterers, with, 107, 110
behavior exchange (BE) procedures,
  92–93, 154, 156
"caring days" tasks, 91, 154–56
collaborative empiricism, 151
communication skills training, 160–64
community reinforcement approach to
  substance abuse, 278–80
conflict management, 164–66
depersonalizing of issues, 159
disputing of irrational beliefs, 151
empathic joining, 137, 158–59
essential skills, sharing with couple,
  151–52, 152t
expressive skills, 161–62
focal issues, 149, 153
giving skills, 153–56
individual work within, 148
integrative couple therapy (ICT),
  157–59
listening skills, 160
positive exchanges, increasing, 88–89,
  153–60
problem solving, 163–64
reciprocity counseling, 278–80
recognizing skills, 156–57, 157f
requesting rather than demanding,
  162–63
self-care enhancement, 159
sexual abuse of child, 257, 259
skills training, generally, 152–53
tolerance-building, 159
truth telling, 166
Courts. See Legal system
Credibility of social worker, 27
Criminal behavior. See also Arrests;
  Delinquency; Legal system
  antisocial behavior and, 212
Crisis intervention practice, 115
Cross-cultural issues, 27. See also Ethnic and
  cultural influences
Cross-cultural marriages, 3
Cultural-analytic theory, 5
Cultural assimilation, 16
Cultural entities, 4. See also Environmental
  influences; *specific entity (e.g.,* Schools)
  interlocking practices, 8
  transactions with. See Environmental
    exchanges

Cultural influences. *See* Ethnic and cultural
  influences
Culture of family. *See* Family cultures and
  practices

D
Death. *See* Fatalities
Deception, and couple exchanges, 166–68
Deinstitutionalization movement, 282
Delinquency
  antisocial behavior and, 212
  environmental exchanges and, 61
  family processes and, 225–26
  multisystemic treatment (MST) and, 227
Delusions, 283, 287
Depersonalization, in psychosis, 287
Depersonalizing of issues, in couple
  interventions, 159
Depression
  child maltreatment and, 244, 247
  environmental exchanges and, 61
  functional analysis of, 51
  manic-depressive illness, 265
  multidimensional intervention with, 51
  oppressive relationships and, 87
  parenting and, 180–81
Developmental appropriateness
  multisystemic treatment (MST) and, 230
  parent education, 179–80
Developmental disabilities, and parental
  advocacy, 207
Disability. *See* Physical illness or disability
Discipline of children, 9. *See also* Parent
  education; Parenting
  antisocial behavior and, 213
  coercive discipline, 96, 98, 197–99
  ethnic and cultural influences on, 16
  time-out, 203–05, 251
Discrimination of appropriate occasions for
  behavior, 49–50
Disputing of irrational beliefs, 151
Divorce, 143
  incidence of, 3
  interventive strategies, 168–69
Domestic violence, 5, 85, 103–10, 149. *See
  also* Child maltreatment
  batterers, interventive strategies, 107–10
  consequences of, 104
  functional analysis of, 104–05
  incidence of, 103

interventive strategies, 104–10
safety planning, 105–06
self-help and support groups for victims,
73–74, 105–07, 110
social isolation and, 66
societal issues and, 104
substance abuse and, 276–77
victims and survivors, interventive
strategies, 105–07
Dropping out of school, and antisocial
behavior, 212
Drug abuse. See Substance abuse
"Dry pants" training, 195
Duluth Model for work with batterers,
107–08, 108f, 109f

E
Eating disorders, 264–65
Ecobehavioral assessment, 29–57
collaborative process of, 54–55
contextual analysis of focal issues, 32, 31t,
46, 49–52, 153
core functions, 30, 30f
couple exchanges, 147–49, 153
identification of focal issues, 31, 30t–31t,
44–46
identification of interventive tasks, 32, 31t,
52–56
scan. See Ecobehavioral scan
Ecobehavioral perspective, 3–21. See also
Family cultures and practices
behavioral dynamics, 13–19. See also
Behavioral repertoires
concepts, 6–13
definitions, 6–13
elements, 3–5
functional family therapy and, 225–26
Ecobehavioral practice, 24–57. See also
Interventive strategies
assessment. See Ecobehavioral assessment
engagement, 24–27, 56
envisioning, 28, 29t, 56
key principles, 24, 25f, 56–57
shared power paradigm. See Shared power
paradigm
Ecobehavioral scan, 32–44, 30t
collecting data for, 41–44
environmental exchanges, 33–36
family repertoires, 36–40
individual factors, 40–41

observation of family dynamics, 41–42
outcomes of, 44
Ecomaps. See Transactional ecomaps
Economic influences, 3
child maltreatment and, 241, 244
divorce and, 143
domestic violence and, 104
multideficit families and, 44
parenting and, 181, 190
recreational activities and, 72
Ecosystemic approach, 5
Education. See also Schools; Skills training
higher education entities, enhancing
exchanges with, 69–70
parenting. See Parent education
psychoeducation. See Psychoeducation
sexual problems, 170–71
vocational education entities, enhancing
exchanges with, 69–70
Elderly
friends and, 66
maltreatment, 103. See also Domestic
violence
Emotional abuse of child, 239–41. See also
Child maltreatment
factors involved in, 240f
incidence of, 237
Emotional abuse of partner. See Domestic
violence
Empathic joining, 137, 158–59
Empathic listening, 137–38
Empathy
acceptance and, 138
PEACE POWER! programs and, 221
PeaceBuilders™ programs and, 217
psychotic symptoms management and,
287–88
social worker's empathy toward family, 25,
27
Employment
child maltreatment and, 253
community reinforcement approach to
substance abuse, 274, 280
enhancing exchanges with work settings,
69–70
job-finding clubs, 77–78
psychotic clients, 291
Empowerment cultures
child maltreatment interventions and,
248–49

core practice principles and, 80
family support programs and, 76
job-finding clubs and, 78
multifamily groups and, 79–80
multisystemic treatment (MST) and, 231
neighborhood and community groups
    and, 74
PEACE POWER! programs and, 221
Enabling, 49–50, 270–71, 275
Enactment, in communication training, 133
Engagement (in ecobehavioral practice),
    24–27, 56
Environmental exchanges, 17, 60–81. *See also*
    specific environment (e.g., Schools)
advocacy and, 81
assessment of, 33–36
aversive exchanges, 17, 18f, 64, 96
constructing new support networks, 75–80
core practice principles, 80–81
delinquency and, 61
depression and, 61
differential family exposure clusters,
    61–64, 63f, 86
ecobehavioral scan, 33–36
enhancing exchanges with existing
    systems, 65–75
importance of addressing, 60–61, 295–96
multisystemic treatment (MST) and,
    229–30
positive exchanges, 17, 18f, 64
shared power paradigm and, 80–81
transactional ecomaps, 17, 18f, 64–65, 80
Environmental influences, 4. *See also specific*
    influences (e.g., Economic influences)
structural antecedents, as, 13
Envisioning, 28, 29t, 56
Equality Wheel, 109f
Equivalence relations, 11–12
couple exchanges and, 149–50
ethnic and cultural influences on, 16
mental illness and, 286
parenting practices and, 185
shared meanings, 88
Ethnic and cultural communities,
    enhancing exchanges with, 71–72, 291
Ethnic and cultural influences, 4, 15–17, 21.
    See also specific ethnicity, race, or culture
communication and, 117
couple exchanges, 152
credibility of social worker and, 27

flexibility and, 40
importance in practice, 296
mental illness, perspective on, 71
multisystemic treatment (MST) and, 230
parenting practices, 177
European Americans
assertiveness, valuing of, 16
shame, perspective on, 21
teasing among couples, 152
Exchanges. *See specific type of exchange (e.g.,*
    Environmental exchanges)
Expectations of family members, 11, 102
Expressed emotion (EE) process, 283
Expressive skills, 37, 115–16, 124–27
acceptance and, 138
couple interventions, 161–62
Extended family and kinship networks
African Americans, among, 16, 65
enhancing exchanges with, 65–66
Native Americans, among, 65
Extinction burst, 202, 202f
Extramarital affairs. *See* Infidelity
Extremely isolated families, 44

F
Family. *See also* Parenting; *specific types (e.g.*
    Blended families)
changes in, 3–4
cultures. *See* Family cultures and
    practices
definition of, 4
exchanges within. *See* Intrafamily
    exchanges
violence in. *See* Domestic violence
Family conferences, 100, 131–32
antisocial behavior and, 223–24
sibling exchanges and, 200
Family cultures and practices, 4–8, 11–15. *See*
    also Behavioral repertoires; *specific*
    influences (e.g., Ethnic and cultural
    influences)
couple exchanges and, 144, 144f, 148–49
definition, 4
development of, 6
equivalence relations and, 12
interlocking practices, 8, 11, 14
roles of family members and, 14
social workers as member of family
    culture, 25–26
transactions with environment.

See Environmental exchanges
transactions within family. *See* Intrafamily
exchanges
transmission, 8, 38
Family Group Conferences, and antisocial
behavior, 223, 232–33
Family mediation. *See* Mediation
Family myth, 19
Family practices. *See* Family cultures and
practices
Family rituals, 40, 88
Family structure, 8, 19
Family Support Principles, 247
Family support programs, 183
child maltreatment and, 76, 252
constructing new programs, 75–77
Family to Family Program, 79–80
Family violence. *See* Domestic violence
Fatalities
child maltreatment and, 237
firearms and, 212
FFT (functional family therapy). *See*
Functional family therapy (FFT)
Filipinos, communication styles among,
117
Firearms causing children's injury and
death, 212
Flexibility, assessment of in family, 38–40,
39f
Focal issues
contextual analysis, 32, 31t, 46, 49–52, 153
couple interventions, 149, 153
environmental exchanges and, 61
identification, 32, 30t–31t, 44–46
monitoring, 46, 47f, 48f
Foster care. *See* Residential care and
treatment
Friends and peers
antisocial behavior and, 66, 213, 215,
227
enhancing exchanges with, 66, 67t
modeling by, 12
Functional analysis, 50–51
aversive exchanges, 98–99
domestic violence, 104–05
key in social worker's assessment, 296
psychotic symptoms, 287, 289
Functional communication training, 50
Functional family therapy (FFT), 14, 50
antisocial behavior and, 223, 225–27

G
Genograms, 43
Giving skills
couple interventions, 153–56
intrafamily exchanges, 87–88, 91–93
Goal Attainment Scaling, 54
Goals. *See* Focal issues
Grandma's Law, 196
Group interventions. *See also* Multifamily
groups
batterers, with, 107–10
child maltreatment, 249–50
parent education, 178–80
sexual abuse of child, 257–58
Guided self-change approach for "problem
drinking," 270
Guns causing children's injury and death,
212

H
Hallucinations, 283, 287
Health care. *See* Medical treatment
Healthy families, 3–4, 36–37
Higher education, enhancing exchanges
with, 69–70
Home assignments
acceptance and, 138
communication training, 134
I-statements, 161–62
sensate focus, 171–72
Home-based interventions, 41–42, 89. *See
also In vivo* training
conflict resolution training, 100
family support programs and, 76
parent education, 178
psychotic symptoms management, 288–89
Homelessness, and mental illness, 284
Homosexuality, 4, 71
Hypersexuality, 173

I
I-statements, 125–26, 161–62
ICT (integrative couple therapy), 157–59
Identification of focal issues, 32, 30t–31t,
44–46
Identification of interventive tasks, 32, 31t,
52–56
Ignoring problem behavior, 201–03, 251
Illness. *See* Mental illness; Physical illness or
disability

Imitation, 12. *See also* Modeling
Immigration, effect on family functioning, 19, 20f
Impotence, 170, 173
In vivo training. *See also* Home-based interventions
child maltreatment and, 246–47, 250–51
communication training, 133
family conferences and, 224
Index of Family Relations, 43
Individual factors, ecobehavioral scan, 40–41
Individual interventions
antisocial behavior and, 211, 214
child maltreatment and, 249
couple interventions and, 148
parent education and, 178
sexual abuse of child, 257
Infants, and reinforcement, 195
Infidelity, 148, 162–63, 166–69
incidence of, 167
interventive strategies, 168–69
Insularity. *See* Social isolation and loneliness
Integrative couple therapy (ICT), 157–59
Interest communities, enhancing exchanges with, 74–75
Intermittent reinforcement, 96, 202
Interracial marriages, 3
Interventive strategies, 57. *See also* Ecobehavioral practice; *specific strategies*
acceptance, 134–38, 157–60
antisocial behavior, 214–16, 223–33
best practices, 296
boundaries of clinical intervention, 17
child maltreatment, 237–38, 246–60
coercive interventions, 26–27, 266–67
communication, 132–35. *See also* Communication training
couples. *See* Couple interventions
crisis intervention, 115
divorce, 168–69
domestic violence, 104–10
environmental exchanges, for, 60–81. *See also* Environmental exchanges
identification of tasks, 30, 32t, 52–56
infidelity, 168–69
intrafamily exchanges, 85–110. *See also* Intrafamily exchanges
multisystemic treatment (MST), 229–31
sexual abuse of child, 257–59
shared power paradigm. *See* Shared power paradigm

substance abuse, 266–81
Interview guides
assessment, 32, 30t–31t, 51
envisioning questions, 29t
Intimacy versus autonomy, 137–38
Intrafamily exchanges. *See also* Couple exchanges; Family cultures and practices
acceptance and, 134–35, 138
assessment of, 36–40
aversive exchanges, decreasing, 95–103
behavior exchange (BE) procedures, 92–93
differential family exposure clusters, 61–64, 63f, 86
ecomaps, 14–15
importance of addressing, 85–86
mutual reinforcement, increasing, 86–95
mutually enjoyable activities, planning, 91–92
observation of, 41–42
rates of positive and aversive exchanges, 13–14, 86
self-monitoring of, 42–43, 52–53
transactions over time, 19, 20f
Isolation. *See* Social isolation and loneliness

J
Japanese Americans, interracial marriages among, 3
Jesse Jackson's PUSH/Rainbow Coalition, 68, 182–83
Jewish
interracial marriages among, 16–17
Orthodox communities, 71
Job counseling, and community reinforcement approach to substance abuse, 274, 280
Job-finding clubs, 77–78
Job-readiness skills training, 78
"Joining" the family, 26–27

K
Korean Americans, religious communities among, 70

L
Learning disabilities, and assessment of family, 44

Legal system. *See also* Arrests
  child maltreatment and, 237–38, 245
  domestic violence interventive strategies
    and, 108–10
  sexual abuse of child and, 257
Lifestyle enrichment, for psychotic
    disorders, 290–91
Listening skills, 37, 115–16, 121–24
  active listening, 121, 124
  couple interventions, 160
  empathic listening, 137–38
  furthering responses, 122–23
  nonverbal skills, 122
  reflecting feelings, 123–24
Literacy, 68, 189
Loneliness. *See* Social isolation and
    loneliness

M
Mainstreaming, of autistic child, 13, 264
Maltreatment. *See* Child maltreatment;
    Domestic violence
Manic-depressive illness, 265
Marital Happiness Scale, 43, 46, 47f, 278–79
Mediation, 100–01, 129–30
  antisocial behavior and, 221
  Navajo Peacemaker Court, 232
Medical treatment
  Antabuse, 277–78, 280
  child maltreatment and, 255
  psychoses, 282, 285
  sexual problems, 173
Mental illness, 264–66. *See also* Psychoses;
    specific illness (e.g., Depression)
  assessments and, 41, 44
  ethnic diversity in perspective on, 71
  parenting and, 180–81, 207
Mental Research Institute (MRI), 114–15
Microculture of couple, 144–49
Microculture of family. *See* Family cultures
    and practices
"Mirroring" family patterns, 26
Modeling, 12
  acceptance and, 138
  child maltreatment and, 240f, 241–42,
    243f
  listening skills, 124
  PEACE POWER! programs and, 221
  social worker, by, 25, 49
Monitoring, 52–56
  behaviorally anchored rating scale

  (BARS), 53–54, 53f
  classroom behavior, 69
  focal issues, 46, 47f, 48f
  multisystemic treatment (MST) and, 230
  record keeping of child's behavior. *See*
    Record keeping of child's behavior
  self-monitoring. *See* Self-monitoring
Mood disorders. *See* Depression
  psychotic dimensions. *See* Psychoses
Motivating antecedents, 10–11
  child maltreatment and, 239–44, 240f,
    243f
Motivational interviewing, 266–69
Motor behavior, 6, 7f
MRI (Mental Research Institute), 114–15
MST (multisystemic treatment). *See*
    Multisystemic treatment (MST)
Multideficit families, 44
Multifamily groups
  child maltreatment and, 79–80, 253
  communication training in, 134
  constructing new groups, 79–80
  parent education and, 181–82
  psychoeducation groups, 79, 289–90
Multisystemic treatment (MST)
  antisocial behavior, 60, 223, 227–31
  child maltreatment, 249, 254–55
  principles, 228–31, 228t
Mutual aid groups. *See* Self-help and support
    groups

N
National Alliance for the Mentally Ill, 79
Native Americans
  antisocial behavior intervention and
    Native American thought, 232–33
  communication styles among, 117
  cultural expectations of, 16
  extended kinship networks among, 65
  interracial marriages among, 3
  PEACE POWER! programs and, 218, 222
  shame, perspective on, 21
  teasing among couples, 152
Natural reinforcers, 51–52, 195–96
Navajo Peacemaker Court, 232
Negative exchanges. *See* Aversive exchanges
Negative reinforcement, 8–9
Neglect of child, 239, 242–45. *See also* Child
    maltreatment
  contingencies associated with, 243f

incidence of, 237
Neighborhood and community groups
   enhancing exchanges with, 74
   PEACE POWER! programs and, 218–23
   PeaceBuilders™ programs and, 217
Networks
   extended family. *See* Extended family and
      kinship networks
   nesting within networks, 295
   Social Network Map, 61, 62f
   social support. *See specific support networks*
      (e.g., Friends and peers)
New Zealand's Family Group Conferences,
   223, 232
Noncontingent consequences, 52, 87, 89,
   90f
Nonverbal communication, 116–18
Nonverbal listening skills, 122

O
Observational behavior, 6, 7f
Occasions (as antecedents to behavior), 10
   assessment of environmental exchanges,
      33–36
   child maltreatment and, 239–44, 240f,
      243f
   flexibility and, 38–40, 39f
Ojibway Community Holistic Circle Healing
   Program, 223, 232
Open relationships, 167
Operant conditioning, and psychotic
   symptoms management, 288
Oppositional behavior, 98–99
Oppositional defiant disorder, 95
Oppressive families, and noncontingent
   reinforcers, 87
Out-of-home placements. *See* Residential
   care and treatment

P
Pacific societies, teasing among couples, 152
Paraprofessionals, and job-finding clubs, 78
Paraverbal communication, 116–18, 123
Parent education, 49, 183–208. *See also*
   Parenting
   advocacy, 183, 206–08
   child development education, 179–80
   child maltreatment and, 179, 241, 244,
      249–52
   coercive discipline, 197–99

communication, 115, 184–85
   components of, 177–78
   consequences of child's behavior, 192–93
   family support programs and, 76
   father groups, 178, 180
   grandparent groups, 180
   group education, 178–80
   home-based interventions, 178
   ignoring problem behavior, 201–03, 251
   importance of, 183–84
   individualized education, 178
   instructions to children, 191–92
   multifamily groups and, 181–82
   parental monitoring of antisocial
      behavior, 205–06
   participants, 178, 180
   PeaceBuilders™ programs and, 217
   pinpointing behaviors, 185–86
   positive exchanges, 93–94
   prevention and redirection, 199–201,
      201f
   prosocial involvement, 189–91
   recognition and praise, 194, 196
   record keeping. *See* Record keeping of
      child's behavior
   reinforcement, 88, 193–97
   schools and, 182–83, 206–08
   self-talk and, 179–80
   spanking, 96, 198–99
   time-out, 203–05, 251
   videotapes and, 179
Parenting, 177–208. *See also* Discipline of
   children; Parent education
   academic achievement and, 190
   communication and, 85–86, 120
   conduct disorder and, 183–84
   contingency contracting, 130–31, 193
   contingent and noncontingent
      consequences, 89, 90f
   couple exchanges and, 180–81
   depression and, 180–81
   economic influences on, 181, 190
   equivalence relations and, 185
   ethnic and cultural influences on, 177
   flexibility and, 39
   mediation services, 100–01, 129–30
   mental illness and, 180–81, 207
   reciprocal exchanges, 86
   requests, 125–26
   self-monitoring of, 42–43, 94

social support and, 181–83
Parenting communities, 178, 182–83
Parent resource programs, 75–77
Parent support groups, 74
PAT (planned activities training), 255–56
PEACE POWER!, 218–23
    acting with respect, 220–21
    core cultural practices, 218, 219f
    embedding practices in cultural networks,
        222–23
    making peace, 221–22
    recognition of contributions and
        successes, 218–20, 220f
    sharing power for collective good, 221
PeaceBuilders™, 216–18
Peers. *See* Friends and peers
Personality disorders, 185, 211, 282
Physical abuse of child, 239–41. *See also*
    Child maltreatment
    factors involved in, 240f
    incidence of, 237
Physical abuse of partner. *See* Domestic
    violence
Physical illness or disability
    assessments and, 41, 44
    developmental disabilities, parental
        advocacy, 207
    divorce and, 143
Pinpointing behaviors
    multisystemic treatment (MST) and, 229
    parenting practices, 185–86
Planned activities training (PAT), 255–56
Planned nonreinforcement, and community
    reinforcement approach to substance
    abuse, 275
Political activism, 74, 207–08
Positive exchanges, 42, 86–95. *See also*
    Reinforcement; *specific exchange (e.g.,*
    Recognition and praise)
    assessment of exchanges within family,
        36–37
    classroom management skills for
        increasing, 69
    collaborative agreements for increasing,
        89, 91
    couple exchanges, 88–89, 145–47, 146f,
        153–60
    deficits in, reasons for, 87–89
    environmental exchanges, 17, 18f, 64
    healthy families, 36–37

importance of, 88
intrafamily exchanges, 13–14, 36–37,
    89–95
    mapping, 35
    parent education, 93–94
    predictability of, 88
    unilateral exchanges, 93–94
Power and Control Wheel, 107–08, 108f
Practice. *See* Ecobehavioral practice;
    Interventive strategies
Practices of family. *See* Family cultures and
    practices
Praise. *See* Recognition and praise
Premack Principle, 196
Premature ejaculation, 173
Prevention
    antisocial behavior, 215–23
    parent education and, 199–201, 201f
    youth violence, 216–23
Privileges as reinforcers, 51–52, 193–97
Problem-solving skills, 38
    activities planning, 91
    communication and, 115–16, 127–32
    community reinforcement approach to
        substance abuse and, 280
    couple interventions, 163–64
    family conferences and, 100, 131–32
    PeaceBuilders™ programs and, 217
    psychotic symptoms management and,
        288
    social isolation and, 66, 67f
Project 12-Ways, 255–57
Project MATCH Twelve Step Facilitation
    treatment, 281
Prosocial involvement, in parent education,
    189–91
Psychoeducation, 79, 286, 289–90
Psychoses, 264, 281–91. *See also* Mental
    illness; Schizophrenia
    assertive community treatment, 284–85
    basic needs interventions, 284–85
    causes, 282
    expressed emotion (EE) process, 283
    family interventions, 285–90
    home-based interventions, 288–89
    interventive strategies, 282, 284–91
    lifestyle enrichment, 290–91
    medication needs, 285
    multifamily psychoeducation groups, 79,
        289–90

negative symptoms, 283
positive symptoms, 283–84, 287
psychoeducation, 79, 286, 289–90
relapse, 282
skills training, 290
symptoms management, 287–88
Punishment, 9, 95–96, 98. *See also* Aversive
exchanges; Discipline of children
communication styles and, 120
community reinforcement approach to
substance abuse and, 274–75
reciprocal exchanges of, 86
PUSH/Rainbow Coalition, 68, 182–83

R
Racial influences. *See* Ethnic and cultural
influences
Rapid assessment instruments, 43
Reattribution, in functional family therapy,
226
Reciprocal exchanges, 35, 85–86
Reciprocity couple counseling, 278–80
"Reclaim our Youth" project, 183
Recognition and praise
couple interventions, 156–57, 157f
intrafamily exchanges, 52, 87–89, 90f, 94
parenting practices, 89, 90f, 194, 196
PEACE POWER! programs, 218–20, 220f
Record keeping of child's behavior, 186–89,
187f, 188f, 194–95
preventive strategies, 200–01, 201f
time-out and, 204–05
Recreational activities, 72
child maltreatment and, 252–54
community reinforcement approach to
substance abuse and, 274, 280
psychotic clients, 290
Referrals, 81
domestic violence victims, 107
sexual problems, 169–70, 172–73
Reframing, in functional family therapy, 226
Reinforcement, 8–10, 51–52. *See also* Positive
exchanges
autism and, 196
bedtime and, 195–96
child maltreatment and, 251
community reinforcement approach to
substance abuse, 272–81
healthy families, 36–37
infants and, 195

intermittent, 96, 202
intrafamily exchanges, 86–95
natural reinforcers, 51–52, 195–96
negative reinforcement, 8–9
parenting practices and, 88, 193–97
PEACE POWER! programs, 218–20, 220f
PeaceBuilders™ programs, 217
psychotic symptoms management and,
287
social reinforcers, 52, 196
social worker, by, 25–26
substance abuse interventions, 93, 275–76,
281. *See also* Community reinforcement
training
tangible reinforcers, 196–97
time-out and, 203–05
toilet training and, 194–95
unilateral reinforcers, 93–94
verbal behavior as, 94
Reinforcer erosion, 87, 91
antisocial behavior prevention and, 219
couple exchanges and, 147, 153
Reinforcer exchange tasks, 91–95
Reinforcer menus, 72
Reinforcer sampling, 10, 81
Reinforcers. *See* Positive exchanges;
Reinforcement
Religion and spirituality, 70–71. *See also*
specific religious groups (e.g., Jewish)
child maltreatment and, 253
psychotic clients, 291
Remarriage, incidence of, 3
Residential care and treatment
antisocial behavior and, 214
child maltreatment victims, 237–38
functional family therapy as alternative to,
225
multisystemic treatment (MST) and, 227
Resistance, 26–27
multisystemic treatment (MST) and, 229,
231
Respite services, and child maltreatment,
252–53
Restorative justice, and PEACE POWER!
programs, 222
Restructuring of family, 8
Rituals of family, 40, 88
Role playing
acceptance and, 138
listening skills, 122, 124

PEACE POWER! programs and, 221
toilet training and, 194
tolerance-building, in couple
    interventions, 159
Roles of family members, 14
Rules
    child maltreatment and, 240f, 241–42,
        243f
    couples' rules, 150–51, 158
    ethnic and cultural influences on, 16
    families' rules, 11–12
    shared rules, 88

S
Scan. *See* Ecobehavioral scan
Schizoaffective disorder. *See* Psychoses
Schizophrenia, 41, 265, 282. *See also*
    Psychoses
Schools. *See also* Academic achievement
    antisocial behavior and, 212–16, 227
    community groups and, 74
    enhancing exchanges with, 68–69
    family life education classes, 178
    parent education and, 182–83
    parental monitoring and advocacy,
        206–08
    PeaceBuilders™ programs, 216–18
    unstructured time in, 200
Scientific approach to family intervention,
    296
Self-awareness of aversive exchanges, 97–98,
    117–18
Self-care enhancement, in couple
    interventions, 159
Self-determination. *See also* Empowerment
    cultures
    domestic violence victims and, 105
Self-help and support groups
    child maltreatment and, 76
    constructing new groups, 77
    domestic violence victims, 73–74, 105–07,
        110
    enhancing exchanges with, 73–74
    psychotic clients, 290–91
    substance abuse, 281
Self-injurious behavior (SIB), 50
Self-management, 52–53
    psychotropic medications and, 285
    unilateral reinforcers and, 93–94
Self-monitoring, 42–43, 52–53

classroom behavior, 69
multisystemic treatment (MST) and,
    230–31
parenting and, 42–43, 94
psychotropic medications and, 285
recognizing skills, in couple interventions,
    156–57, 157f
sibling exchanges, 200
unilateral reinforcers and, 93–94
Self-talk
    acceptance and, 136–37
    awareness of aversive exchanges and, 97
    couple exchanges and, 149–51, 158
    functional family therapy and, 50
    parent education and, 179–80
    PEACE POWER! programs and, 221
Sensate focus, 171–72
Sequential ecomaps, 19, 20f, 46, 48f
Serenity prayer, 135
Serna model of family conferences, 223–24
Sex therapy, 172–73
Sexual abuse of child, 239, 245, 257–59. *See
    also* Child maltreatment
    incidence of, 237
    nonoffending parents, interventive
        strategies, 258
    offenders, interventive strategies, 258–59
    victims, interventive strategies, 257–58
Sexual addictions, 173
Sexual problems, 166–67, 169–74
    behavioral changes, 171–72
    education, 170–71
    incidence of, 169
    interventive strategies, 170–74
    permission to communicate, 170
    referrals, 169–70, 172–73
    severe disorders, 172–73
Shame
    domestic violence victims and, 105
    ethnical and cultural perspectives on, 21
Shared power paradigm, 18, 25
    best practices for family intervention,
        296–97
    child maltreatment and, 246–50
    environmental exchanges and, 80–81
    envisioning and, 28
    family conferences. *See* Family conferences
    family support programs and, 76–77
    functional family therapy and, 226
    identification of interventive tasks and, 54

intrafamily exchanges and, 100–01
multifamily groups and, 79
multisystemic treatment (MST) and, 229,
    231
PEACE POWER! programs and, 221
reinforcer exchange tasks and, 94–95
self-management and, 52
substance abuse and, 266–67
SIB (self-injurious behavior), 50
Sibling exchanges, 199–200
Sibling violence, 103. *See also* Domestic
    violence
Single-parent families
    parent education, 178
    self-help and support groups, 77
Skills training, 49, 52. *See also specific skills
    (e.g.,* Communication training)
    antisocial behavior and, 223–24
    child maltreatment and, 246, 251–52,
        255–56
    couple interventions, 152–53
    psychoses and, 290
    social isolation and, 66, 67f
Sobriety sampling, 269, 280
Social isolation and loneliness, 61, 66, 67t
    child maltreatment and, 76, 241, 244
    extremely isolated families, 44
    parenting and, 181–82
Social Network Map, 61, 62f
Social skills training
    PEACE POWER! programs and, 221
    psychotic clients, 290
Social support, 61–62. *See also specific support
    networks (e.g.,* Friends and peers)
    child maltreatment and, 249, 252–54
    community reinforcement approach to
        substance abuse and, 273–74, 280
    parenting and, 181–83
Spanking, 96, 98, 198–99
Spectatoring, 171
Spirituality. *See* Religion and spirituality
Stepfamilies. *See* Blended families
Strategies of clinical intervention. *See*
    Interventive strategies
Stress management, 41
Structural antecedents, 12–13
    child maltreatment and, 239–44, 240f,
        243f
Substance abuse, 5, 41, 264–81
    Antabuse, 277–78, 280

antisocial behavior and, 212
assessments and, 44
child maltreatment and, 238, 241, 244,
    247
codependency and, 5, 41, 265, 270–71
coercive interventions, 266–67
community reinforcement approach,
    272–81. *See also* Community
    reinforcement training
concerned others, involvement in
    interventions, 267, 270–81
domestic violence and, 276–77
enabling, 49–50, 270–71, 275
genograms and, 43
interventions (confrontations), 270
interventive strategies, 266–81
motivational interviewing, 266–69
multisystemic treatment (MST) and, 227
pressures to change strategy, 271
"problem drinking" interventions, 269–70
Project MATCH Twelve Step Facilitation
    treatment, 281
recreation counseling and, 72
reinforcement of positive behavior and,
    93, 275–76, 281
sobriety sampling, 269, 280
12-step groups, 73, 77
unilateral family therapy, 271–72
violence and, 276–77
Support groups. *See* Self-help and support
    groups

T
Tantrums, 202, 202f
Task-centered model of practice, 128–29
Teachers. *See* Schools
Teens. *See* Children and adolescents
Time-out, 203–05, 251
Toilet training
    record keeping and, 186, 187f, 188f
    reinforcement and, 194–95
Tolerance-building, in couple interventions,
    159
Tracking. *See* Monitoring
Training. *See* Education; Skills training
Transactional ecomaps, 5–6, 5f
    assessment phase, during, 34–35, 34f, 35f
    aversive exchanges, 9–10, 9f
    environmental exchanges, 17, 18f, 64–65,
        80

intrafamily, 14–15, 15f
Quick Scan forms, 35, 35f
sequential, 19, 20f, 46, 48f
symbols, 35
Transactions. *See specific type of exchange (e.g.,*
Environmental exchanges)
Truth telling, in couple interventions, 166
12-step groups, 73, 77, 281, 291

U
Unidirectional exchanges
increasing positive exchanges and, 93–94
mapping, 35
Unilateral family therapy, and substance
abuse, 271–72
Universal Declaration of Human Rights, 104

V
Vaginismus, 173
Verbal behavior, 6, 7f, 10–12. *See also*
Communication
consequences of behavior, as, 11
equivalence relations and, 11–12
motivating antecedents, as, 10–11
reinforcers, as, 94

Violence. *See also* Child maltreatment;
Domestic violence
modeling of, 12
multisystemic treatment (MST) and,
227
PEACE POWER! programs, 218–23
PeaceBuilders™ programs, 216–18
prevention of youth violence, 216–23
youth arrest rates for violent crimes,
212
Visceral behavior, 6, 7f
Vocational education, 69–70
Volunteering, 73
child maltreatment and, 253
psychotic clients, 291

W
Welfare reform, 3
Work settings, enhancing exchanges with,
69–70

Y
Youths. *See* Children and adolescents

About the Author

Mark A. Mattaini, DSW, ACSW, is associate professor and director of the doctoral program, Jane Addams College of Social Work, University of Illinois at Chicago. His writing and research focus on prevention of and intervention with issues that carry significant social justice implications, including violence, homelessness, and substance abuse; the visualization of practice theory and events; and ecological and behavioral analysis of human networks. With experience in child and family services, mental health, and substance abuse settings, he continues to do part-time clinical and community practice and is chair of Behaviorists for Social Responsibility.

ESSENTIAL CLINICAL SOCIAL WORK RESOURCES FROM NASW PRESS

Clinical Intervention with Families, *by Mark A. Mattaini. (Companion Volume to* Clinical Practice with Individuals). Written for social workers in family practice as well as for instructors and advanced-level students, this book is a state-of-the-art treatment guide for family practice. It is an essential volume for those seeking to understand the extrinsic family factors affecting the theory and practice of family social work!

ISBN: 0-87101-308-8. 1999. Item #3088. NASW Members $26.35, Nonmembers $32.95.

Clinical Practice with Individuals, *by Mark A. Mattaini.* Practitioners and educators alike will find this guidebook invaluable. Mattaini presents practice guidelines that are firmly rooted in contemporary knowledge and that are both accessible and immediately applicable to practice.

ISBN: 0-87101-270-7. 1996. Item #2707. NASW Members $23.15, Nonmembers $28.95.

Outcomes Measurement in the Human Services: Cross-Cutting Issues and Methods, *Edward J. Mullen and Jennifer L. Magnabosco, Editors.* This is the first-ever handbook to cover outcomes measurement for the human services profession. You'll benefit from a wide range of expert thinking on outcomes measurement in mental and behavioral health and child and family services. It is essential reading for practitioners dealing with managed care requirements and an important text for preparing new practitioners.

ISBN: 0-87101-275-8. 1997. Item #2758. NASW Members $29.55, Nonmembers $36.95.

Current Controversies in Social Work Ethics: Case Examples, *by NASW Code of Ethics Revision Committee, Frederic G. Reamer, Chair.* Presents a cross-section of real examples of ethics dilemmas faced by social workers in contemporary practice situations. A companion work to the NASW *Code of Ethics,* this practical and thought-provoking handbook offers commentaries of related considerations and implications that help the reader untangle the controversies and assess the competing values associated with ethical decision making.

6" x 9" pamphlet. Item #3002. 1998. 100 pages. NASW Members $6.80, Nonmembers $8.50.

Humane Managed Care?, *Gerald Schamess and Anita Lightburn, Editors.* This state-of-the-art volume looks at one of today's most complex challenges for social workers in managed care. With *Humane Managed Care?,* you'll get an excellent grounding in major facts and issues and gain practical knowledge of real-life situations—everything you need to work critically and proactively in the new environment.

ISBN: 0-87101-294-4. 1998. Item #2944. NASW Members $23.95, Nonmembers $29.95.

Prudent Practice: A Guide for Managing Malpractice Risk, *by Mary Kay Houston-Vega and Elane M. Nuehring with Elisabeth R. Daguio.* Social workers and other human service professionals face a heightened risk of malpractice suits in today's litigious society. NASW Press offers practitioners a complete practice guide to increasing competence and managing the risk of malpractice. Included in the book and on disk are 25 sample forms and 5 sample fact sheets to distribute to clients.

ISBN: 0-87101-267-7. 1997. Item #2677: book with Word for Windows disk; item #2677A: book with Macintosh disk. NASW Members $34.35, Nonmembers $42.95.

(Order form on reverse side)

ORDER FORM

Title	Item #	NASW Member Price	Non-member Price	Total
__ Clinical Intervention with Families	3088	$26.35	$32.95	_____
__ Clinical Practice with Individuals	2707	$23.15	$28.95	_____
__ Outcomes Measurement in the Human Services	2758	$29.55	$36.95	_____
__ Current Controversies in SW Ethics	3002	$6.80	$8.50	_____
__ Humane Managed Care?	2944	$23.95	$29.95	_____
Prudent Practice				
__ Book with Word for Windows disk	2677	$34.35	$42.95	_____
__ Book with Macintosh disk	2677A	$34.35	$42.95	_____
			Subtotal	_____
		+ 10% postage and handling		_____
			Total	_____

❏ I've enclosed my check or money order for $ _____.

❏ Please charge my   ❏ NASW VISA*   ❏ Other VISA   ❏ MasterCard

_____   _____

Credit Card Number   Expiration Date

Signature _____

Use of this card generates funds in support of the social work profession.

Name_____

Address _____

City _____ State/Province _____

Country _____ZIP _____

Phone _____ E-mail _____

NASW Member # (if applicable) _____

(Please make checks payable to NASW Press. Prices are subject to change.)

NASW PRESS
P. O. Box 431
Annapolis JCT, MD 20701
USA

**Credit card orders call
1-800-227-3590**
(In the Metro Wash., DC, area, call 301-317-8688)
**Or fax your order to 301-206-7989
Or order online at http://www.naswpress.org**

CIFbin